PHYSICAL

EDUCATION

IN CANADA

This publication is sponsored and approved by

THE CANADIAN ASSOCIATION

FOR

HEALTH, PHYSICAL EDUCATION AND RECREATION

Physical Education

in Canada

Edited by

M. L. VAN VLIET

Scarborough, Ontario
PRENTICE-HALL OF CANADA, LTD.,

© 1965 by Prentice-Hall of Canada, Ltd.,
Scarborough, Ontario

613.709
V26p

57822
May 1967

Library of Congress Catalog Card No. 65-26306

PRINTED IN CANADA

For some years there has been serious concern among Canadian physical educators about the lack of published information which might provide an insight into the development and progress of physical education in the schools and communities throughout the country. This concern has been a topic of discussion for many years at biennial meetings of the Canadian Association for Health, Physical Education and Recreation and in correspondence and discussions among individual members between national convention dates. In 1962 the editor agreed to accept the responsibility of co-ordinating the efforts of various contributors toward a publication which might be expected to reflect a realistic, if somewhat sparse, over-view of physical education in Canada as it has slowly expanded and developed over the years. It is hoped that this initial effort will be a mere forerunner to subsequent editions which will improve in accuracy and content to the point of properly reflecting a chronicle of the Canadian scene in physical education, athletics, and recreation.

Only recently have there been enough senior people in Canada in the field of physical education to consider co-operative efforts toward a compilation of information which might provide valuable recorded observations both for Canadian students of the field and for colleagues in other countries seeking to interpret Canadian philosophies and policies. An effort has been made to allow for views which are representative of both sexes and of all parts of the country. The views expressed are individual observations and convictions, and no claim is made that these represent the correct, final, or complete interpretation of physical education as it exists today in Canada.

The contributors to this publication have been selected because of their wide experience and major contributions to the profession throughout the country. Each chapter has been submitted as a gratuitous contribution to the field. The Canadian Association of Health, Physical Education and Recreation takes pride in the fact that these very busy people were willing to take the time from their regular duties to offer their services for such a professional publication.

It is intended and hoped that this book may be used as the basic text for introductory and orientation courses for first-year students in all Canadian universities and colleges offering a major, minor, or a degree course in physical education. There is reason to believe that this book should be considered a valuable reference in university libraries around the world, particularly in those institutions offering undergraduate courses in the field of physical education.

A tentative selection of topics was originally submitted to a panel of seven senior professional people in the field of physical education. The first list contained thirty-three proposals. These were reduced to twenty-one topics, including a chapter on recreation. It was finally decided that this topic could better be dealt with in a special recreation supplement. This left the twenty topics shown as chapter headings. The task of finding suitable and available authors was then begun. The final result incorporates the insights of those who have been closely involved in the history of the profession, and those of the younger generation whose efforts have been recognized as outstanding in their respective positions and fields.

The major evolution in Canadian physical education is currently unfolding. More teachers from other parts of the world are being added to school and university staffs. The number of students enrolled in undergraduate programs has tripled in the last three years and continues to increase each year. The number of personnel with graduate degrees has doubled each year for several years; as of 1964-65 there are approximately 260 engaged in graduate programs in Canada and other parts of the world. These factors, coupled with greater depth of inquiry, study, and research, should make the next decade the most significant one in the history of Canadian physical education. The most productive scholarship is yet to come. Perhaps this book will, in some small measure, motivate the bright young minds in the profession to provide written evidence of the cultural and scientific advancements as well as a proper historical assessment in the areas of physical education, athletics, and recreation.

M. L. VAN VLIET

CONTENTS

Appendices

Iveagh Munro

Director, Department of Athletics
Physical Education, and Recreation for Women
McGill University, Montreal

EARLY CANADA

Organized physical education is a by-product of urbanization, the real demand for it coming about as a direct result of the loss of natural opportunity for outdoor physical activity in rural areas. It is not surprising that Canada's early history would include games and dances brought over from France and England with the addition of certain native activities such as lacrosse. In fact there was little else. These were hard times during which the people felt little need for physical education in the modern sense.

Because Canada is a young country, just emerging from the rigors of pioneer life, any phase of physical education other than the most casual and informal of approaches is a product of the twentieth century. Documentation referring to physical education before this period is extremely limited. Information that sheds light on the "early history" of physical education in Canada is mainly available through club minutes, reported speeches, and newspaper accounts.

The earliest signs of organized endeavor centered in clubs formed for the purpose of developing opportunities in specific sports by local interest groups: clubs such as the Halifax Curling Club (1824) and the Halifax Yacht Club (1837), later known as the Royal Halifax Yacht Club, were typical examples of a recognized need for recreation and friendly competition. Later clubs such as the Wanderers Athletic Club (1861) of Halifax expanded their sponsorship of sports to lacrosse, soccer, rugby, cricket, lawn bowling, and track and field.

Other clubs prominent in this period included the Montreal Cricket Club and a Snow-Shoe Club, both formed in 1840. These were followed by a Lacrosse Club, a Gymnastic Club, a Lawn Bowling Club, and, in 1878, a Bicycle Club. Three of the clubs (Lacrosse, Snow-Shoe, and Gymnastics) affiliated to form the Montreal Amateur Athletic Association and in 1881 obtained a charter from the Government of Quebec. Within the year, the Bowling and Bicycle Clubs joined the Association, followed by the Toboggan Club and the Hockey Club in 1884, the Football Club in 1885, and the Tennis Club in 1894. This Association has continued to play an important role in the life of Montreal citizens down through the years.

Typical of most communities in the years of Canada's early development was the formation of such groups as the Antigonish Highland Society founded in 1861 for the purpose of " . . . preserving the martial spirit, language, dress, music and antiquities of the Caledonian. . . ." This particular organization adopted a resolution in 1862 which stated: "Resolved that in the opinion of this meeting it would conduce materially to carry out the objects of this Society that prizes be offered for competition in Highland Games and that such prizes be offered during the course of the ensuing year. . . ." In one form or another, sports and physical recreation were developed and encouraged through such community groups.

Few regular physical education programs existed before 1900. However, in the Y.M.C.A.'s and Y.W.C.A.'s and universities, independent programs were beginning to emerge.

The first official plea for a physical education program in the school was made by Egerton Ryerson in 1846. This was followed by a short but complete course of exercises published in 1852. Ten years later, the first normal school was equipped with a gymnasium so that teachers could be trained to give leadership in this area of the curriculum. About the same time, cadet training began and from the outset was closely affiliated with schools. In 1865, the government made a grant of fifty dollars to every school conducting "Drill and Gymnastics," and in 1892 a regulation made physical education and gymnastics compulsory in the schools.

In "A Brief History of Physical Education in Nova Scotia," Hugh Noble mentions an attempt made to establish physical education in the public schools of Nova Scotia in 1888. A military gymnastic instructor was appointed, who drew up a curriculum known as "Physical Drill for Public Schools." Nothing is recorded of its success; however, in the mid-nineties there were no traces of "physical drill" in the curriculum of the schools.

In a Province of Manitoba report the following appears:

When W. Cyprian Pinkham, Superintendent of Education for the Protestant Schools of Manitoba, in 1882, returned from a trip to Eastern Canada [he] wrote that he was "pleased to find considerable attention given, both in Toronto and Montreal, to singing and calisthenic exercises."[1]

1900–1914

In the period between 1900 and the First World War, greater awareness of the need for physical education became evident and programs developed in various institutions. The earliest programs were definitely influenced by Per Henrik Ling's Swedish System of Gymnastics, by the German Turnverein societies, and by Dr. Dio Lewis, founder of the Normal Institute of Physical Education in Boston. Around the turn of the century there was further influence felt from teachers of the Boston area, such as Dr. Dudley Sargent of Harvard, Dr. William Skarstrom of Wellesley, and Dr. Luther Gulick. Later there was considerable change in the physical education programs due to the influx of ideas from various European teachers: the Medeau system from Germany, the Sokol movement from Czechoslovakia, and the Dalcroze eurythmic movement.

In most localities the only physical education programs carried out at the secondary school level during this period were the games played by the representative school teams. For the most part, these games were confined to the "selected few" top athletes in the school. However, various sports and "physical culture" classes were carried on in both boys' and girls' private schools throughout the country, as well as in some of the universities.

At McGill University, the calendar for the session 1900–1901 contains a very lengthy announcement under the heading "The Royal Victoria College." Included in the description of the building is a brief write-up of the gymnasium —"The gymnasium fully equipped in accordance with the regulations of the Swedish system is in the basement. In connection with the gymnasium there are bath rooms and dressing rooms."[2]

Under the general heading "Gymnasium" the work for both men and women is outlined.

> The gymnasium for women is in charge of Miss Holmstrom, graduate of the Posse Gymnasium, Boston and Harvard Summer School, who teaches on Swedish principles. Special attention is devoted to the application of exercises in cases of physical weakness, Miss Holmstrom having had considerable experience in the medical branch of her work. All students

---

[1] *Report of the Superintendent of Education.*
[2] Slack, *Development of Physical Education*, p. 11.

undergo a physical examination on entering upon the gymnastic course under the superintendence of Dr. R. Tait McKenzie, B.A., M.D., assistant lecturer in Anatomy at the University. Teams of basketball are formed and when weather permits this and other exercises are practiced on the lawn, at the back of the college building. This ground is also provided with tennis courts.[3]

In 1906, Miss Ethel Mary Cartwright became the first Physical Education Director for Women in Canada. Following her appointment at Mc-Gill University, there was an increased interest in physical education, especially for women, and during the college year 1908–9 a two-year compulsory physical education program for women was approved. Twenty-five students took gymnastic classes, the work including free and corrective exercises, club swinging, skipping, running, and apparatus work.

The calendar for 1910–11 for the first time included a large section under the title "Physical Education." This included work for both men and women. The announcement for women was as follows: "The Department is in charge of the Medical Director of Physical Education of McGill and a graduate of a physical education college. The physical education offered to undergraduate students includes educational, remedial and recreational gymnastics."

This same pattern was paralleled at the University of Toronto. In the various colleges—University College, Victoria College, and St. Hilda's—mention is made of fencing, ground hockey, and basketball having been played just around the turn of the century.

> In 1906–7, a "Miss Wreyford," a graduate of the Sargent School, was appointed as instructor in University College and it would appear that she was also engaged by Victoria College as in 1907–8 the account states that "fancy steps and marching" has been added to the classes and that Miss Wreyford was preparing both University College and Victoria classes for an exhibition, to "include folk dances etc."
>
> From the beginning of organized athletics in the University, there was an increasing concern for the physical fitness of the students involved and also of those who did not participate in athletics. The Constitution of the Women's Athletic Association, as drawn up in 1920-21, required every athlete participating in competition to pass a prior medical examination. Then on March 8, 1922, the Directorate passed a motion recommending to the University authorities that two periods of "Physical Training" a week should be required of first year women students. This regulation, originally approved by the Senate for University College students, has since been extended to cover all first year women in the University of Toronto.[4]

---

3 Slack, *Development of Physical Education*, p. 11.

4 Parkes, *Development of Women's Athletics*, pp. 2, 14.

Strathcona Trust Fund—Lord Strathcona

In 1908 the Province of Nova Scotia entered into an agreement with the Department of Militia in regard to physical education and military drill in public schools. This included the formation of cadet corps, the practice of rifle shooting, and the training of teachers for certification of competency in instructing in these fields. In return, the Department of Militia agreed to provide competent instructors to enable teachers to qualify in physical training and military drill, to pay a bonus to qualified teachers who instructed cadet corps, to provide supplies and drill books, and to conduct examinations.

Lord Strathcona was so impressed by this plan that on April 17, 1909, he entered into an agreement with the Government of Canada in the establishment of the Strathcona Trust Fund. Through this fund $500,000 was set aside to be administered by the National Department of Militia. It was to provide annual grants to the participating provinces. Recipients of this Strathcona Fund were to incorporate physical training as an integral part of the curriculum in all schools above the primary grades, to form cadet corps, and to provide teacher training in physical education. The instructors were to be supplied and paid by the Army, provided the provincial Department of Education would allocate time at the Normal College for "physical training instruction," and encourage the teachers, once they left the Normal College, to include "physical drill" as part of the school program. Canada had few professionally trained physical educators, so most provinces availed themselves of the funds established by this trust, and entered into agreement with the federal government. As a result, the work was carried on by Army sergeants. Their teaching was supplemented in the normal schools by the use of the British Syllabus of Physical Exercises for Public Elementary Schools, printed in 1904. This was based on the Ling system of gymnastics. Later, in the 1933 revision of the syllabus, the British interest in games became very evident.

With the increase in the number of teachers graduating from Canadian universities in the field of physical education, the influence of the Strathcona Trust Fund has diminished. Nevertheless, this Trust Fund has played a very important role in the field of physical education in Canada.

United States-Canadian Relationship

Physical education in Canada has, of course, been directly affected by physical education in the United States. The United States, because of its large population, had professional schools of physical education and professional organizations many years before Canada. This has meant that Canadians interested in this field went to the United States to gain more knowledge through courses or from professional meetings. They also called on well-known American physical educators to bring to Canada information and inspiration.

It is interesting to note that,

> in February, 1912, the American Physical Education Association held its nineteenth convention in Montreal. At this time, Dr. R. Tait McKenzie was its president [see Appendix B]. Many of the sessions were held in the Royal Victoria College; lectures were given by members of the staff of McGill and the women students gave a demonstration of gymnastics in the High School.[5]

1949–29

During the First World War physical education was retarded in some districts and made forward strides in others. In general the period immediately following the war was marked by increased interest in fitness influenced by military programs. Y.M.C.A.'s were at the height of their influence and were providing needed leadership in the larger centers.

DEPRESSION YEARS

The stock market crash of 1929 and the years of unemployment and depression that followed had definite effects on physical education.

Some boards of education considered physical education a frill and had it dropped from the school curriculum. Very few new schools were built, and most of those that were built did not have gymnasiums. Many people had enforced leisure time and so the need for recreation was apparent.

During these years the Provincial Recreation Movement, commonly referred to as the Pro-Rec, developed in British Columbia to provide for unemployed youth. Similar measures, although perhaps not so extensive, were undertaken in many Canadian communities.

It was at this time that the forward-thinking leaders of this field realized that physical education could do much for the situation. The various communities of the Dominion were faced with similar problems and they realized that concerted effort was necessary to strengthen and expand worth-while programs which could contribute to enriched living.

As a result of untiring planning the Canadian Physical Education

---

[5] Slack, *Development of Physical Education*, p. 11.

Association was formed. The first meeting was held in Toronto on April 19, 1933. A full history of its inception and progress is outlined by C.R. Blackstock in Chapter XX.

DOMINION-PROVINCIAL YOUTH TRAINING PROGRAM

The severe economic depression and unemployment created many social problems. In an attempt to alleviate this condition the Dominion government passed a Youth Training Act on May 19, 1939.

This act provided for the training of young people to fit them for gainful employment. It provided for the expenditure of $4,500,000 with payments to be made to each province upon an agreement's being entered into by the Minister of Labour and the government of the province. The grant was not to exceed the amount paid by the province.

One province that might be cited as having gained greatly from this act was Manitoba, which had established youth training centers a year before on its own initiative under the able directorship of Mr. Robert Jarman. However, with the passing of the Federal Youth Training Act an enlarged program was undertaken in 1939–40: the site chosen for this purpose was Gimli.

> That among those students who attended the first Gimli Leadership Training Camp were seventy-six teachers is a fair indication of the influence that this project was to have on physical education in the schools in Manitoba. Many other young and able leaders were also in attendance. As a result of this influence, many recreation centres were organized throughout Manitoba and literature and supervision was made available to all leaders. They also received remuneration for their part-time services. The plan operated successfully with more than 100 centres in operation until communities were depleted of young people by the requirements for service in World War II. The Gimli Leadership Camp continued under the authority of the Minister of Education, and has since that time helped thousands of young teachers develop skills in the planning and teaching of programs of physical education.[6]

This act also influenced and helped other provinces in furthering their programs.

SECOND WORLD WAR

The War with its demands on personnel, equipment, and funds had a

---

[6] Manitoba, *Program* of *Studies*, P. 5.

decided effect on the physical education programs throughout the country.

There was an increasing shortage of teachers at all levels of education; to counteract this shortage on the elementary and secondary levels, school boards had to lower the standards of qualification. The Army had priority in regard to equipment, so even in school systems where funds had not been curtailed it was not always possible to purchase the required athletic supplies.

The physical education programs changed in character, with the stress on formal calisthenics, obstacle courses, and endurance activities and other programs requiring no equipment.

Cadet training, which for some years had been abolished in many of Canada's secondary schools, was revived. Each of the armed forces had cadet corps in operation. While some schools conducted an army, navy, or air force cadet corps, others instituted defense training programs combining the main features of the basic training of all three services. The high schools of Ontario are examples of the latter, and those of British Columbia, of the former method. In most provinces girls as well as boys had compulsory defense training.

Because of the National Selective Service mobilization regulations, the only male students over eighteen and a half years attending university were those who were "pursuing a course essential to the national interest." These students had to be doing satisfactory academic work and complying with the requirements of military training. To satisfy this compulsory training, which was under the Department of National Defence, a student had to have active membership in either the Canadian Officers' Training Corps, the University Air Training Corps, or the University Naval Training Division. In most universities women students as well as men had war service training. This varied in time involvement and type of program. The time required was at least three hours a week.

Physical education formed the basis of all war service programs for women, with particular emphasis on health. In addition most universities required the study of first aid and home nursing. However, many other courses were offered, sometimes on a voluntary basis. These included such subjects as air-raid precautions, fire fighting, motor mechanics, etc. In some universities, units of the Red Cross Corps were organized: these would form the basic training for the women's service corps.

1943: THE NATIONAL PHYSICAL FITNESS ACT

Medical examinations at the beginning of and throughout World War

II revealed that many men and women were unfit for military service. This fact and the Government's concern for the physical fitness of the youth of the country resulted in the passing, on October 1, 1943, of Canada's National Physical Fitness Act. This was followed on February 15,1944, by the appointment of a National Council on Physical Fitness, consisting of a director and nine other persons, each to represent one of the provinces of Canada participating in the National Physical Fitness Plan.

The National Physical Fitness Act established a fund of $250,000 to be provided to provincial governments on a matching basis with a per capita quota for each province. The object of the act was to promote the physical fitness of the people of Canada through the extension of physical education in schools, universities, and other establishments; to train teachers and lecturers in the principles of physical education; to organize activities designed to promote a greater measure of physical fitness; to provide facilities; and to co-operate in an attempt to better those physical defects amenable to improvement through physical exercise. Its broader purposes were the development of a desire for the well-being associated with physical fitness in persons of all ages, the strengthening of morale through a nation-wide program, and the enlistment of support by interested volunteers and organized physical fitness agencies.The provision of scholarships for graduate study stimulated the development of better professional training.

Eight of the ten provinces in Canada were encouraged by the passing of the Fitness Act to initiate or expand their programs of physical education and/or recreation. It is interesting to note that the western provinces concentrated most of their attention on the development of recreation programs for post-school youths and adults. On the other hand, some provinces concentrated on developing school physical education programs.

In British Columbia, it helped to subsidize the Pro-Rec movement which was already established. In Manitoba,

> during the period covered by the Physical Fitness Administration, two revisions were made in the elementary school program (1946-51), one in the junior high school program (1947) and one in the senior high school program (1948). This series of revisions represented the first attempt to establish a complete and consistent program of physical education throughout the grades of Manitoba schools. The growing emphasis on free movement and rhythmics was reflected in these new outlines.[7]

At the same time, Nova Scotia initiated and established a successful program of physical education administered under the Physical Fitness

---

[7] Manitoba, *Physical Education and Recreation*, p. 58.

Branch of the Department of Public Health for the province (since 1950 under the Department of Education).

In New Brunswick, a provincial physical education program under the Department of Education was initiated in 1947, and the Division of Physical Education and Recreation was established, through which New Brunswick participated under the act until its repeal in 1954.

In Saskatchewan a Division of Physical Fitness and Recreation was formed, initially under the Department of Public Health and later under the Department of Education. This division continued after the Fitness Act was repealed and has been very effective in setting up the organizational structure of school athletics, giving support to recreation, and providing leadership training at the community and provincial levels.

ORGANIZED PHYSICAL EDUCATION

The first official programs specifically designed for developing physical education teachers were established at the Margaret Eaton School of Literature and Expression (later known as the Margaret Eaton School of Physical Education) in Toronto and at the McGill University School of Physical Education in Montreal. Both of these programs were for women only and go back as far as 1910 and 1912 respectively.

The years since the Second World War have seen great strides in the physical education profession. The "population explosion" meant a shortage of qualified teachers and lack of school facilities. To meet this difficult situation there has been an unprecedented building program. Most of these schools have included one or even two gymnasia, and some have built swimming pools. The number of courses for prospective teachers of physical education has also increased.

The major change took place when male teachers of physical education were greatly in demand during and after World War II. To meet this acute shortage of physical education personnel and to provide for the training of men as well as women, a number of universities established degree courses. These were developed in the following order: University of Toronto, 1942; McGill University, 1943; University of British Columbia, 1946; Queen's University, 1946. University of Western Ontario, 1947; University of Alberta, 1949; University of Ottawa, 1949; University of Montreal, 1955; University of New Brunswick, 1957; University of Saskatchewan, 1958; Laval University, 1954; McMaster University, 1959; Memorial University, 1960; University of Manitoba, 1964; Waterloo University, 1964.

RECENT DEVELOPMENTS

The most significant event of importance to physical education in recent years has been the enactment, on September 29, 1961, of Bill C-131, "An Act to Encourage Fitness and Amateur Sport" (see Appendix A).

Seeking to fulfill changing environmental demands, Canada's progress in physical education has been conservative but steady. Halfway between the British view of physical education for pleasure, fitness, and character development and the American emphasis on competitive sport, Canada's philosophy of physical education is now being influenced by increased immigration from many European countries. There is reason to believe that the stage is set for a unique and valuable contribution to modern physical education programs.

Federal interest and support through research, scholarships, surveys, special projects, training centers, national games, etc., should greatly expand the contributions possible in the field of physical education. Improved provincial school curricula and recreational programs will allow for recognition of the natural provisions of Canada's climate and topography. Botany, sailing, skiing, skating, swimming, hunting, hiking, camping, fishing, and the like have all been prominent in Canada's past and must not be overlooked in the physical education of the future.

BIBLIOGRAPHY

1. Canada, *The National Physical Fitness Act*. Ottawa: The King's Printer, 1944.
2. Downie, David Alexander, "A History of Physical Education in the Public Schools of Manitoba." Unpublished Master's thesis, University of Toronto, 1961.
3. Innis, Mary, *Unfold the Years*. Toronto: McClelland and Stewart, 1950. A history of the Y.W.C.A. in Canada.
4. Manitoba, "Physical Education and Recreation in Manitoba." Winnipeg, 1958.
5. ———, *Program of Studies*. Winnipeg: Department of Education, 1909.
6. ———, *Report of the Superintendent of Education for the Protestant Schools of Manitoba for the Year Ending 31st January, 1882*. Winnipeg: The Queen's Printer, 1882.
7. Parkes, A. E. Marie, "The Development of Women's Athletics at the University of Toronto." Toronto: The Women's Athletic Association, University of Toronto, 1961.
8. Slack, Zerada, "Development of Physical Education for Women at McGill University." Thesis for the Higher Diploma, McGill University, 1934.
9. Canada, The House of Commons of Canada, Bill C-131, *An Act to Encourage Fitness and Amateur Sport*. Ottawa: The Queen's Printer, 1961.

Stanley T. Spicer

Director, Adult Education and Fitness Branch
Department of Education, Fredericton

CONTRIBUTING AGENCIES

An over-all survey of certain developments in the field shows that at the present time all provinces and territories have government agencies with either direct or indirect responsibilities for physical education programs. These vary widely in scope, responsibility, budget, and staff, but it is important to note that consistently across the country governments increasingly recognize the need for properly supervised programs.

For many years teachers' colleges in Canada have included physical education as part of their curriculum. However, in recent years the trend has been toward increased time allotments and the appointment of staff members with the necessary qualifications and experience to teach a program scientifically planned and designed to adequately prepare young teachers in this field.

The number of universities offering degree programs in physical education has increased steadily in the past few years. Now more than fourteen institutions offer such degrees, while many also offer opportunities for some specialization within other degree offerings, such as, arts, science, and education. The fact that the universities of British Columbia, Alberta, Saskatchewan, and Western Ontario are now offering postgraduate degrees in physical education is yet another sign of its coming of age.

On the public school level, carefully planned programs, utilizing the best information available from research and designed to meet the needs of children in particular school situations, have been devised. Most provinces now have permanent or semi-permanent committees continually working on the revision and improvement of their physical education programs.

An increasing public interest in fitness has had definite implications for physical education. National, regional, and local television and radio programs on various aspects of fitness are being produced with increasing frequency. Syndicated newspaper articles as well as articles in leading popular magazines have contributed to this public interest. Two of the most popular publications printed by the Queen's Printer in Ottawa are the R.C.A.F. exercise booklets, 5BX and XBX. Canadian books by Canadian authors on health, physical education, sports, and fitness are appearing more frequently and are being well received by Canadians.

In the last few years the Canadian Medical Association has become actively interested in problems relating to physical education and fitness. In a subject so closely allied to health and medical status, the prestige given by the interest of the C.M.A. will have positive benefits to physical education in the future.

One of the most important developments has been the passage of Bill C-131 (see Appendix A). Besides the tangible support the federal government can now render, the act will also serve as a cohesive force in dealing with fitness problems in Canada as a country.

The activities and problems of Canadian sports-governing agencies also influence physical education programs throughout the country. In recent years the Royal Canadian Legion has emerged as an important force in sports and fitness. The Canadian Legion's Sports Training Plan has led to the appointment of one of the foremost track and field authorities in the world as Canada's first full-time track and field coach on the national level. Travelling across Canada under Legion auspices, this appointee may be expected to do much to improve the quality of the sport in Canada.

Canada's consistently poor showing in international athletic competitions and the need for improved facilities and coaches have led many of the national sports-governing agencies to give serious study to these and other problems. This internal concern, the activities of the Canadian Amateur Sports Federation, and the assistance of the federal government can all be expected to result in greater emphasis and more soundly based planning for amateur sports in Canada.

These, then, reflect some of the developments and activities across Canada at the present time. All have an effect on physical education and, at least to some extent, indicate current activities in each of the provinces.

Since the British North America Act leaves the administration of education to each province there are, in effect, ten provincial systems of education. The close alliance of physical education with the school system means that physical education programs vary from province to province. At the same time there is a somewhat consistent pattern across the nation of certain conditions and developments. All provinces continue to have a number of rural schools with extremely limited facilities and poorly trained teachers in physical education. Running tracks continue to be considered a luxury and hence are only to be found in large cities and urban areas.

On the credit side, thousands of gymnasia, some tracks, and a few swimming pools have become part of school equipment in the last few years. Hundreds of additional pools have been installed by local communities. Consolidation of scattered small schools in districts or divisions has greatly improved opportunities for rural youth as reflected in facilities and teacher capabilities.

In order to understand the national picture of physical education it is necessary to look at each of the provinces. Within each, several common subject areas may be considered.

NEWFOUNDLAND

Canada's newest province does not yet have a government department or branch specifically entrusted with physical education programming. However, this is now under careful study by the provincial government, owing particularly to the stimulation of the Fitness and Amateur Sport Act. A full-time qualified adviser has been appointed to assist the government with the Fitness and Amateur Sports Program and to provide a curriculum guide in physical education.

Although physical education is not a required subject in Newfoundland schools, there are at present in the province ten full-time teachers and supervisors of physical education and another twenty-five teachers involved in physical education programs along with other school subjects. This number is expected to increase rapidly as government policy is enacted and a provincial physical education program becomes established.

The most significant new development has been the establishment of a four-year degree program at Memorial University of Newfoundland. The first graduates convocated in 1964 and the program has been expressly designed for the Newfoundland situation.

Professionally, a St. John's Branch of the Canadian Association for Health and Physical Education and Recreation was established in 1957.

At present there is no provincial agency controlling interscholastic sports. In St. John's the St. John's School Athletic Federation controls programs in soccer, basketball, and hockey for boys while the Girls' High School Athletic League administers a girls' basketball schedule in the City.

As in all provinces first embarking on organized programs in physical education, Newfoundland faces a problem of providing adequate activity opportunities for all rather than only highly competitive programs for the few. Gradually public interest is growing and the construction of consolidated high schools throughout the province is providing proper facilities. As facilities improve, as qualified teachers become available through the provincial university program, and as the provincial government takes expected steps in implementing a province-wide program, Newfoundland will be the scene of rapid development in future years.

PRINCE EDWARD ISLAND

The present physical education program in Prince Edward Island is administered by the Division of Alcohol Studies and Physical Education under the Department of Education. Established in 1960, the division includes a director, a supervisor of girls' physical education programs, and additional summer staff.

The primary responsibilities of the division include teacher training, curriculum development, provision of informational materials and teaching aids, and the supervision of physical education programs in the schools. The division also administers grants to teachers for summer school study and for certain approved facilities such as rinks and playgrounds.

Physical education is a required subject at all grade levels with recommended minimum time allotments of three forty-minute periods per week. Curriculum guides have been approved for the various grade levels and are now being used in the schools.

In 1964 there were nearly twenty-five physical education teachers in the province either working full-time in the field or else responsible for a full physical education program. Six of these teachers were members of the Atlantic Provinces Physical Education and Recreation Association, the regional branch of C.A.H.P.E.R.

There is no degree program in physical education in Prince Edward Island. Teacher training candidates at Prince of Wales College and St. Dunstan's University receive instruction in elementary and intermediate physical education programs which is supplemented by in-service teacher training programs. However, teachers interested in specialized training usually attend the University of New Brunswick or the Nova Scotia Summer School.

In 1961 a provincial Interscholastic Athletic Association was established to promote and supervise interscholastic athletic programs for junior and senior high schools. Approximately thirty schools are members.

NOVA SCOTIA

Nova Scotia was among the first provinces to establish a government agency to develop physical education programs. The Physical Fitness Branch of the Department of Education was established in 1944 and operates under the authority of the provincial Education Act. By 1964 the staff consisted of a director and four supervisors, each responsible for a particular segment of the province's physical education and recreation program.

The primary responsibilities of the Physical Fitness Branch include leadership training, curriculum development, provision of informational materials and teaching aids, assisting other agencies and organizations active in fitness programs, and various consultative functions.

Physical education is a required subject from Grades I through IX in Nova Scotia schools; ten per cent of the school time is allotted for the combined health and physical education program. Between 1962 and 1964 the curriculum in physical education was completely revised and new teaching guides were made available for all grades.

Personnel in 1964 included approximately seventy-five full-time teachers and supervisors of physical education and more than sixty additional teachers responsible for a full program in physical education while teaching other subjects. Many of these teachers have been members of the Halifax and District Physical Education and Recreation Association and/or the Atlantic Provinces Physical Education and Recreation Association.

Since 1954 the Nova Scotia Summer School has included a special program for teachers wishing to specialize in physical education. This is a four-summer course following graduation from Grade XII and Teachers' College. Many students from Nova Scotia interested in physical education as a career have enrolled at the University of New Brunswick in the past few years and these, plus graduates from other Canadian and American universities, form the majority of the specialist teachers in this field. In addition the Physical Fitness Branch conducts regular in-service teachers' institutes and clinics for teachers and coaches.

The provincial interscholastic athletic program is supervised by the

Nova Scotia Headmasters' Association. This Association is composed of principals and teachers, with the Director of Physical Fitness for the province as its permanent secretary. Eighty schools are members of the Association, which conducts programs in over a dozen interscholastic activities.

NEW BRUNSWICK

New Brunswick was among those provinces which undertook a province-wide physical education and recreation program under the stimulation of the old National Physical Fitness Act. A division of Physical Education and Recreation was established under the Department of Education in 1947. In 1960 the organizational plan of this branch was changed to include non-vocational adult education programs, and its name became the Adult Education and Fitness Branch. Currently the branch is staffed with a director, two supervisors in physical education, an Adult Education Supervisor, and a Music Education Supervisor.

In 1961 the provincial government established a Department of Youth and Welfare with certain responsibilities in the field of sports and recreation. Under this department financial assistance is available to students interested in undertaking university studies in physical education, and various sports clinics are offered for teachers, coaches, and students.

The Adult Education and Fitness Branch has responsibilities in physical education similar to those of corresponding bodies in the other Maritime Provinces: leadership training, selection of curriculum, teaching aids, and materials, work with agencies and organizations active in fitness, and various advisory duties.

Since 1962 the complete provincial program of studies has been revised and physical education has been designated as a required subject. A committee consisting of school superintendents, principals, and physical education personnel has brought in new programs for the elementary and junior high school level and is now working on a new high school program. The recommended minimum time allotment for elementary grades is twenty minutes per day and for the junior high school level it is three periods per week.

New Brunswick employs about sixty full-time specialist teachers and supervisors and more than fifty others responsible for physical education programs while teaching other subjects. Many of these teachers belong to the Atlantic Provinces Physical Education and Recreation Association; those in the Fredericton-Oromocto area also belong to the Fredericton District Physical Education and Recreation Council. Some thirty-five of these teachers and administrators possess university degrees.

In 1962 the provincial Teachers' College expanded its program from one year to two. It is possible for teachers interested in physical education, particularly at the elementary school level, to specialize in physical education over and above the basic course required for all student teachers.

The University of New Brunswick established a four-year degree program in 1957. The success of this program may be noted in the fact that during the 1962-63 academic year nearly 180 students were enrolled. While this program attracts students from the four Atlantic provinces, Quebec, and Ontario, it has done much toward alleviating the serious shortage of qualified teachers of physical education in New Brunswick. The university also conducts an extensive summer school program in physical education courses which may be applied toward degree credits or for purposes of higher teacher certification. In addition to Teachers' College and U.N.B. programs, the Adult Education and Fitness Branch conducts in-service teacher training projects and clinics in various sports and fitness activities.

The interscholastic athletic program is administered by the New Brunswick Interscholastic Athletic Association. Composed of teachers and principals, the N.B.I.A.A. has approximately seventy member schools and conducts programs in over a dozen interscholastic activities.

The New Brunswick Command of the Royal Canadian Legion has been one of the most active provincial commands in Canada. For the past five years it has sponsored a physical fitness and sports efficiency program which annually involves some ten thousand school children. This is a motivational program designed to complement school physical education programs through three progressive test batteries and regular participation in some sport or recreational activity. Two years ago the Legion began sponsoring the Legion Athletic Leadership Training Camp for high school students selected according to academic ability, sports participation, and leadership potential. Over 100 students from New Brunswick and Nova Scotia attended the camp in 1962.

QUEBEC

Education in Quebec has recently been reorganized with a provincial supervisor of physical education being appointed in 1964. Before these developments, those programs and policies which had been developed, with a few exceptions, evolved from the local level.

The Strathcona Trust Fund had a profound effect on Quebec schools. The physical training syllabus issued by the Strathcona Trust is, according to one report, still used in many schools. Other than this syllabus or more recent programs developed at the local level, there has been no provincial program of studies at either the elementary or the secondary school level. However, this entire situation has been carefully reviewed and will no doubt be restricted by the new government Department of Education.

Teacher training programs are conducted at normal schools, classical colleges, and three universities in Quebec. At the normal schools there is a thirty-hour course in physical education. The classical colleges are affiliated with different universities and offer programs leading to the Bachelor of Arts degree. Physical education is now included as a subject within their curriculum and studies are now under way toward improving the quality and integration of this subject. Among the universities, Laval now offers a four-year program leading to the B.Ed. degree in physical education and a two-year diploma program.

In Quebec, interscholastic athletics are planned and governed by a number of regional associations. The largest of these is the Greater Montreal Interscholastic Athletic Association formed in 1946 by an amalgamation of the English and Catholic secondary school athletic bodies. The G.M.I.A.A. is composed of the principal of each member school with various advisory committees involving professional personnel. Approximately forty schools in the Montreal area belong to the G.M.I.A.A. The Association sponsors programs in over a dozen interscholastic athletic activities.

Education in Quebec has been recently studied by a royal commission. It is anticipated that the recommendations of this study, when fully implemented, will stimulate plans for a comprehensive system of teacher training and programming in physical education. The Minister of Youth has also appointed a special committee to consider extracurricular physical education and sports programs and to recommend methods whereby such programs can be effectively organized and conducted in Quebec. In addition committees are now at work on the preparation of new programs at both the elementary and secondary school levels.

These activities reflect a new interest in physical education and fitness in Quebec and it can be reasonably assumed that, as in the rest of Canada, new and dynamic events will take place in the coming years.

ONTARIO

Until recently, the physical education program in Ontario was under the direct administration of the Physical Education Branch of the Department of Education. This branch was established in 1944 primarily because of public pressure and recommendations of the Ontario Education Association. The branch operated under the authority of the Department of Education Act and consisted of the director, four secondary school inspectors, and three elementary school inspectors.

The main responsibilities of the branch included school supervision, curriculum development, teacher training, operation of the Ontario Leadership Camp and of a camp for training camp counsellors, and various advisory services. Although it did not grant funds itself, the branch did provide advisory services for grants to non-profit camps as well as various awards, bursaries, and scholarships.

Physical education is a required subject from Grades I to XII in Ontario schools and is optional in Grade XIII. The required time allotment is at least three activity periods per week and one period in health. Two of the texts produced for Ontario elementary schools, *Physical Education for Primary Grades* and *Junior Division—Physical Education,* have been adopted by a number of other Canadian provinces. Some 1,400 men and women are full-time teachers, supervisors, or administrators of physical education programs in the province. Many of them belong to such Ontario professional organizations as the Ontario Education Association, the Ontario Supervisors' Association, and the provincial Physical Education Council.

Undergraduate training in physical education is offered through degree programs at the Universities of Toronto, Western Ontario, Ottawa, Queen's, McMaster, and Waterloo. The Ontario College of Education conducts a full year's program for teachers holding an approved bachelor's degree. Physical education courses at both the elementary and the secondary school levels are available through the annual Department of Education Summer School, and the branch conducts regular refresher courses for heads of departments in Ontario schools.

Interscholastic athletics come under the direct jurisdiction of the Ontario Federation of School Athletic Associations. Composed of twelve federated high school athletic associations, the O.F.S.A.A. has a legislative council of thirty-seven members and a board of directors of sixteen members. The Department of Education, Headmasters' Association, and the High School Athletic Associations are represented on both the board of directors and the legislative council. The O.F.S.A.A. was formed in 1948 and in 1963 had a membership of 410 schools. The Department of Education provides an annual grant, office space, and advisory services.

MANITOBA

Manitoba established a Physical Fitness and Recreation Branch of its

Department of Health and Welfare under the old National Physical Fitness Act. When this act was repealed in 1954 the branch was dissolved and its services discontinued. In 1957 a supervisor of physical education was appointed under the Department of Education. Upon the resignation of this supervisor in 1961, his responsibilities were turned over to the Director of Special Services in the Department of Education.

It is of related interest that the Government of Manitoba established in 1962 a Fitness and Amateur Sport Branch under the Department of Welfare. This new branch has been charged with the responsibility of leadership training, assistance to agencies and organizations active in fitness and amateur sports programs, general promotion of fitness and sports, and provision of various advisory services.

Physical education is a required subject in Manitoba from Grades I to XI inclusive. Minimum time allotments range from twenty minutes per day at the elementary school level to ten per cent of the school time for health and physical education at the junior high school level and six per cent of school time for health, physical education, and guidance in senior high schools. While authorized texts are not now available in physical education, a committee of professional physical educators is revising the high school program. The teacher training institutions provide recommendations regarding suitable materials and texts for all grade levels.

Student teachers at the Manitoba Teachers' College and those in the Faculty of Education at the University of Manitoba each receive about sixty hours' instruction in physical education. In addition courses in this field are available through the summer school programs of both institutions. The first students were admitted to the new degree course in physical education at the University of Manitoba in 1964.

Interscholastic athletics are controlled and promoted by the Manitoba Secondary Schools Athletic Association. Established in 1962, the Association is comprised of representatives of ten provincial zones, who elect an executive. Commissioners are appointed to supervise the ten major sports conducted by the M.S.S.A.A. At present, 292 public and private high schools are members.

There are a number of problems currently affecting the physical education program in Manitoba. These include the fact that teachers wishing to specialize at the university level in physical education will not graduate until 1968 under the new degree program. There is also a need for full-time professional leadership in physical education at the provincial level. However, the school building program is making provision for physical education facilities in most new schools and the number of qualified teachers being appointed is gradually increasing.

SASKATCHEWAN

Saskatchewan, like many of the other provinces, initiated a provincial program under the National Fitness Act of 1943. The agency directly responsible has been the Fitness and Recreation Division of the Department of Education.

This division has maintained its original concern with community recreation programs; however, it has added a new concern, the school physical education programs, although there is presently no official in the division with full-time administrative responsibilities in this field. The division's interest in community recreation and sports programs led to the creation of a number of field offices located throughout the province.

In 1963 the division was amalgamated into a new branch of the Department of Education, the Department of Adult and Continuing Education.

The University of Saskatchewan offers both the bachelor's and the master's degree in physical education as well as a major in the Faculty of Education.

Interscholastic athletics have developed rapidly in the province. Saskatchewan, along with Nova Scotia, New Brunswick, and Ontario, is affiliated with the National Federation of State High School Athletic Associations and in 1962 became the first Canadian province to host the Annual Conference of the Federation.

Facilities for physical education programs in the schools have improved tremendously in recent years owing to the school building program and a policy of school consolidation. There is, however, a continuing shortage of indoor facilities in many elementary schools and in such specialized facilities as tracks.

ALBERTA

The Province of Alberta does not as yet have a government branch with direct jurisdiction in the promotion and supervision of physical education. However, the Recreation and Cultural Development Branch of the Department of the Provincial Secretary does have responsibilities which relate to provincial physical education programs.

This branch was established in 1945 and has divisions active in music, libraries, drama, and arts and crafts, as well as in community programs and athletics and outdoor education. The primary responsibilities of the branch are to assist communities with the organization and operation of recreation and cultural programs and in training leaders in these fields through regional and provincial courses. The branch also provides grants to encourage communities to appoint qualified recreation leaders, for the construction of approved recreation facilities, and for provincial athletic winners attending Canadian championships leading to Olympic, Commonwealth, and Pan-American Games.

There are no normal schools or teachers' colleges in Alberta. These have been assimilated into the Faculty of Education at the University of Alberta. All specialist certificates have been abandoned and students interested in teaching physical education at the secondary school level are encouraged to take their Bachelor of Physical Education degree. A full five-course major is provided for Bachelor of Education students preparing for an elementary school teaching career. The degree program in physical education at the University of Alberta was established in 1950. The Faculty of Physical Education now offers the undergraduate B.P.E. degree, a B.A. degree with a major in recreation, and Master of Science and Master of Arts degrees in physical education. There are over 250 students enrolled in these degree programs.

Approved physical education programs are available for all grade levels. These were all revised within the last ten years and currently are being revised again. The time allotment for physical education ranges from two to five periods per week.

Interscholastic athletics in Alberta are sponsored and supervised by local school systems. However, a provincial Interscholastic Athletic Association has been formed and is gaining momentum. In Edmonton, for instance, the Edmonton Public High Schools Athletic Board conducts interscholastic athletic programs for all public schools in the city. It is composed of principals and physical education personnel concerned and is headed by a president, vice-president, and a secretary. Approximately twelve activities for boys and girls are sponsored annually.

At present there is no firm assurance that the province will establish a provincial office for the administration of physical education. However, the Minister of Education has signified his approval in principle of the appointment of a provincial supervisor of physical education.

BRITISH COLUMBIA

British Columbia does not have a government branch directly responsible for physical education. However, the Community Programs Branch of the Department of Education does have several direct relationships. This branch was established in 1953 following a reorganization of the old provincial Pro-Rec program. It is concerned with all forms of recreation and only recently appointed an assistant director in charge of physical recreation.

In British Columbia, physical education is a required subject for all grade levels with minimum time allotments for health and physical education ranging from 140 minutes per week for elementary grades to 160 minutes per week for the junior and senior high schools. Curriculum guides have been prepared by committees of professional teachers for use in the schools.

Student teachers in the teacher training institutions are required to take basic courses in health and physical education. The University of British Columbia instituted a degree program in 1946. There are now approximately 200 students involved in programs leading to a bachelor's and/or a master's degree in physical education.

In addition summer courses in physical education are offered by the university and many workshops and short courses in allied areas such as coaching and officiating are conducted annually by the Community Programs Branch.

The British Columbia High School Boys' Basketball Association formed in 1948, has just over 120 member schools. It consists of a board of directors, eight zone representatives, and a tournament committee of twelve. All interscholastic school activities are governed by school authorities.

Full-time specialist teachers of physical education tend to be appointed in the larger urban areas while in rural areas the physical education teacher also teaches academic subjects. Specialist teachers may belong to the British Columbia Physical Education Teacher's Association and the national parent body, the Canadian Association for Health, Physical Education and Recreation.

Northwest Territories

Education in the Northwest Territories is the direct responsibility of the Education Division, Northern Administration Branch of the Federal Department of Northern Affairs and National Resources. This department assumed responsibility for the education of the Eskimos in the Northwest Territories in 1949 and the territorial government participated in a physical fitness program under the old National Physical Fitness Act of 1943.

At present work is under way in preparing curriculum guides in physical education for all grade levels. An interim guide in Health and Physical Education for Grades I to III has been completed and a similar program for Grades IV to VI should be available soon. In the meantime the territories follow the curricula of three provinces as follows:

Mackenzie District—Alberta
Keewatin Region—Manitoba
Baffin Island Region—Ontario

Physical education is a required subject at all grade levels and time allotments follow these respective provincial programs. While there are no full-time specialist teachers now working in the Northwest Territories there are at least six teachers conducting full programs of physical education and the number will increase as the educational program is further implemented.

The Department of Northern Affairs and National Resources provides annual grants of $500 for playground equipment for new classrooms and $50 per classroom for recreational equipment. In addition, it is interesting to note that $5,600 has been allocated for a physical recreation program in forty-six communities. Basic equipment for physical recreation includes swings, teeters, slides, jungle gym, giant stride, horizontal ladder, three-way climber, and sports equipment for indoor use.

While there is no territorial interscholastic athletic association or program, there are hostels in some communities to board children attending school, and inter-hostel athletic competitions are developing.

The Northwest Territories are also experiencing a school building boom. In spite of the tremendous cost of constructing schools, all large schools are provided with good gymnasium facilities while others utilize activity rooms and community halls. Although children in the north are accustomed to playing outdoor games at 30° below, there will always be obvious shortages in such facilities as tracks and playing fields.

A physical education specialist is currently conducting a study of the territories and this report plus a growing interest in physical education has positive implications for the future.

YUKON

Education in the Yukon comes under the responsibility of the Commission of Yukon Territory which, in turn, is responsible to the federal Department of Northern Affairs and National Resources. To date no agency or individual has been specifically entrusted with the development of a physical education program.

Of the twenty-three schools in the territory, all except three are operated by the territorial government and any provision for physical education facilities or program is the direct responsibility of this government.

Yukon schools use the programs of the British Columbia Department of Education. Physical education is a required subject for Grades I to XI, and time allotments are the same as for British Columbia. While there are no full-time specialist teachers working in the Yukon, two teachers conduct full programs and the number is expected to increase in coming years.

There is no territorial interscholastic athletic association. However, inter-school competitions in volleyball and basketball are regular events in the city of Whitehorse. The Skagway-Whitehorse basketball tournament is another regular event.

The Yukon, like the Northwest Territories, is faced with the problem of long periods of extreme cold weather. Thus while gymnasium facilities are increasing there is a real lack of outdoor facilities. A planning grant has been received from the federal government and consideration is now under way toward participating under the terms of the Fitness and Amateur Sports Act. This, it is anticipated, would do much to alleviate present problems arising out of the lack of facilities and leadership.

BIBLIOGRAPHY

1. Alberta, *Report of the Royal Commission on Education in Alberta*. Edmonton: The Queen's Printer, 1959.
2. Althouse, J. C., *Structure and Aims of Canadian Education*. Toronto: W. J. Gage & Company, 1950.
3. American Association for Health, Physical Education and Recreation, *International Congress on the Essentials of Physical Education for Youth*. Washington, D.C.: A.A.H.P.E.R., 1955.
4. British Columbia, *Report of the Royal Commission on Education in British Columbia*. Victoria: Queen's Printer, 1960.
5. Bucher, Charles A., *Foundation of Physical Education*. St. Louis: The C. V. Mosby Company, 1962.
6. Canadian Association for Health, Physical Education and Recreation (Greater Montreal Branch), "Physical Education Brief to the Royal Commission of Inquiry on Education of the Province of Quebec." Montreal: The Association, May 1962.
7. Hope, J. A., *Report of the Royal Commission on Education in Ontario*. Toronto: King's Printer, 1950.
8. Larson, Leonard A., *The Foundations for Physical Education*. Marison: University of Wisconsin Publications Committee, 1962.
9. MacFarlane, R. O., *Report of the Manitoba Royal Commission on Education*. Winnipeg: Queen's Printer, 1959.

3

W. F. R. Kennedy

W. F. R. Kennedy, Head
School of Physical Education
University of Manitoba, Winnipeg

HISTORICAL FOUNDATIONS

The view that one of the first responsibilities of a state is the education of its citizens found general acceptance in Canada, as indicated by the willingness of its citizens to support public education. Cultural influences brought by the early settlers found official scope for development within the framework of the British North America Act of 1867, which, in the distribution of authority between the provinces and the federal government, assigned the responsibility for education to the individual provinces. The various provinces authorized systems of education, and although their philosophies, purposes, and needs were modified by various forces, the unique aggregation of provincial systems of education is generally characterized by uniformity rather than by difference.

The struggle for a livelihood during the early pioneer days did not encourage the inclusion of physical education in the school curriculum. Education was held in high esteem but it was felt that children had little need for physical exercise beyond their normal home duties. Moreover the concept of education in the early days of Canadian settlement excluded physical education.

Although it was not too long before some recognition was given to the need for organized play, it was not until Egerton Ryerson's early design for public education that physical education was formally adopted into the curriculum. It was natural that military drill, calisthenics, and gymnastics were included in early curricula. Public education was possible

27

only through considerable effort and sacrifice, and was considered a serious endeavor. The curriculum was comprised of only that subject matter which contributed to the *proper* upbringing of the child. Physical education was included by virtue of its contribution to discipline, obedience, and the development of health through correct positions of posture and carriage. Military drill was held in high regard, not only because it fostered the development of discipline, but also because it contributed to national defense.

Sports activities, naturally evoking the interest of youth, found scope for development in colleges and universities, where enthusiasts soon arranged matches on an intercollegiate basis. The popularity of games and sports did not immediately affect the prescribed curriculum of physical education, but teachers who had participated in athletics in their undergraduate days were encouraged to organize and coach sports for their students on an informal basis.

The growing recognition of the benefits to be derived from physical exercise and the increased popularity and participation in games and sports gave new prominence to physical education. Social movements and professionally educated leaders both at home and abroad made their influence felt.

The Hamilton School of Physical Culture, the International Y.M.C.A. Training School at Springfield, James Naismith, Tait McKenzie, Ethel Mary Cartwright, and Dr. Arthur Lamb at McGill, and Mary Hamilton at Toronto provided distinguished leadership and left an indelible mark in a broadened philosophy of physical education meeting increasing acceptance in the general scheme of public education.

Another influence, the interest and desire of Lord Strathcona to give a strong and vigorous impetus through practical method to the physical education movement, has already been delineated.

A BROADENING PHILOSOPHY

The first half-century found physical education established within the framework of the philosophy held for general education by virtue of its formal contribution to remedial and disciplinary needs of pupils. But during the second half-century a meaningful change in emphasis took place. A new concept of education gradually replaced that of training. Insight into growth and development superseded early European theories. The modern philosophy considered education more of a process concerned with every aspect of the individual's development. As the philosophy of education broadened, new thinking about the role of physical education as a means of realizing the maximum potential of youth

evolved. Social and emotional as well as physical objectives gave direction
to curricula and teaching. Physical education now came to accept the
same aim as other subjects—the use of activities as means in the total
educational process.

Provincial and institutional philosophies of education, found in the
literature and in curricula themselves, have recognized the unified nature
of individuals and list intellectual development, the acquisition of basic
skills, the ability to think effectively, the accumulation of knowledge, and
the development of physical fitness as worthy aims.

Philosophies of physical education, on the other hand, are seldom discussed in the limited literature; indeed it is impossible to discover a
Canadian philosophy, if one exists. (This is not incongruous, however,
when one considers the difficulty of describing Canadian culture.) Philosophies of physical education are reflected in aims and objectives which
are listed in courses of study and in directions emanating from centralized authorities. These may contain some unique features due to social or
economic forces or to prominent professional leadership in particular
spheres. By and large, though, a consensus of these aims represents the
current concept of physical education.

A Modern Concept

Physical education is meant to include all the experiences the individual may gain through the instructional, intramural, and interscholastic
programs which are planned with a unity of purpose. This purpose, one
held also by the entire educational system, is to contribute significantly to
the development of the total individual.

The individual, even in Canadian society, is to some extent deprived
of the natural opportunity for vigorous physical activity which is a biological necessity for optimum growth. The development of strength and
endurance, the mastery of body mechanics, and the acquisition of a wide
variety of motor skills are fundamental human needs. To this primary
aim of physical efficiency educators have added objectives of social, emotional, and moral competence to be realized best through activity.

Regardless of the merits of the objectives which are held for physical
education in the scheme of general education, they are effective only so
far as basic principles can be brought to bear on actual practice. In this it
would appear that the many "unique" contributions expected of physical
education have obscured the primary objective of physical competence.
Physical education has become a catch-all. The ability to work hard is
being lost in a world of too many softening influences.

The examination of what is being done rather than what is being said is revealing. It is stated that physical education is for all—yet unequal time and effort is devoted to the gifted. It is known that activity is essential for growth and development—but comparatively scant attention is paid to the locomotor needs of the elementary school child. Claim is made to promote learning through doing—while valuable time allotted for physical activity is lost through over-verbalization.

It is said that of all areas of education, physical education is probably the least understood. This may be because beliefs need to be more clearly expressed and activities thoughtfully selected and consciously taught if educational objectives are to be more nearly realized.

Despite all previous efforts, it must be admitted that at present physical education does not play a very important role in Canada's culture. But society does not exist by itself; society can be redirected. In times of crisis man turns to education and evaluates its achievements and practices so that improvements may be effected. Educational institutions must now accept their traditional responsibility to become a forceful means for improving the level of total fitness in society. Physical education, utilizing activity to develop the individual's potential, can foster and enrich those capacities necessary for survival, growth, and progress in society.

Canada is a young nation, and the majority of her professional physical educators are also young. National development and an increased number of graduates are factors that will make for progress toward a realistic and applicable philosophy of Canadian physical education.

BIBLIOGRAPHY

1. Alberta, *Report of the Royal Commission on Education in Alberta*. Edmonton: The Queen's Printer, 1959.
2. Althouse, J. C., *Structure and Aims of Canadian Education*. Toronto: W. J. Gage Limited, 1950.
3. American Association for Health, Physical Education and Recreation, *International Congress on the Essentials of Physical Education for Youth*. Washington, D.C.: A.A.H.P.E.R., 1955.
4. British Columbia, *Report of the Royal Commission on Education in British Columbia*. Victoria: The Queen's Printer, 1960.
5. Bucher, Charles A., *Foundations of Physical Education*. St. Louis: The C. V. Mosby Company, 1962.
6. Canadian Association for Health, Physical Education and Recreation (Greater Montreal Branch), "Physical Education Brief to the Royal Commission of Inquiry on Education of the Province of Quebec." Montreal: C.A.H.P.E.R., May 1962.

7. Larson, Leonard A., *The Foundations for Physical Education*. Madison: University of Wisconsin Publications Committee, 1962.
8. Manitoba, *Report of the Manitoba Royal Commission on Education*. Winnipeg: The Queen's Printer, 1959.
9. Ontario, *Report of the Royal Commission on Education in Ontario*. Toronto: The King's Printer, 1950.

4

Robert F. Osborne

Professor and Director
School of Physical Education and Recreation
University of British Columbia, Vancouver

"A noble aim Faithfully kept, is a noble deed." *William Wordsworth*

Any profession worthy of the term has to have goals which are nobler than self-interest, which go beyond personal aggrandizement and strive for the betterment of mankind.

This should be, and can be, true of physical education if it is to mature as a profession. It would appear to be self-evident that an essential characteristic of a profession would be a complete and unanimous understanding of the meaning of its own name or title. Furthermore, it would seem that the term should be universal, or should possess such a high degree of universality that a definition of meaning and function would be redundant.

THE MEANING OF PHYSICAL EDUCATION

Yet this not true of physical education, and so it would be wise for us to examine the meaning of the term itself before proceeding to a study of the goals which it customarily sets for itself and the principles on which its function is based. So much literature, especially from the United States of America, has been available to Canadians since World War II that the difficulty of interpretation has perhaps been compounded rather than simplified. The difficulty is quite clearly illustrated in the following excerpts from *Physical Education* by Oberteuffer and Ulrich, one of the most recent and most comprehensive texts dealing with the principles of physical education:

> . . . . The more he [man] moves about, the further his education pro- gresses. Call this, if you will, his physical education. In Cassidy's words, ". . . physical education is the sum of the changes in the individual caused by experiences centering in basic movement patterns." [Rosalind Cassidy, *Curriculum Development in Physical Education,* (New York: Harper & Row, Publishers, 1954), p. 133].
>
> . . . The primitive man taught his young how to shoot an arrow or stalk an animal. The pioneer taught youth how to ride and how to fell a tree. In the ceremonial dances of the Indians, the young were taught the symbolism of certain movements and postures. It is in this group of planned and purposeful movements that the modern program of school physical education finds its origins. It seeks to advance and enrich man's culture, foster his best interests, and contribute significantly to his own personal growth through participation in activities which are purposefully selected and carefully taught to provide the desired outcomes.[1]

To add to the confusion, the authors, in an introduction to the mean- ing of physical education, begin by stating that "the term physical educa- tion is unfortunate." Some aspects of the problem immediately become obvious. If every movement made by a person is to be classified as being physical education, or related to it, then physical education cannot be considered as existing only in a school situation. Physical education is in danger of becoming "all things to all persons." Texts on the one hand refer frequently to the importance of evaluating activities for the good they do the *whole child.* On the other hand they refer to the importance of physical education for university students. Or, as Williams maintains: "Physical education should be prepared to support and to participate in adult education."[2]

In general, the literature published in the United States rejects such terms as "physical training," "physical culture," and "calisthenics," on the grounds that they describe inadequately the function of physical education and savor at best of anti-democratic processes. Yet these terms are still used in many countries as synonyms for physical education.

For purposes of review a few typical definitions of physical education are listed here:

> *Hetherington* (1922): Physical education is that phase of education which is concerned, first, with the organization and the leadership of children in big-muscle activities, to gain the development and the adjust- ment inherent in the activities according to social standards; and second,

---

[1] Oberteuffer and Ulrich, *Physical Education,* p. 2.
[2] Williams, *Principles of Physical Education,* p. 141.

with the control of health or growth conditions naturally associated with the leadership of the activities so that the educational process may go on without growth handicap.[3]

Nash (1931) : Briefly, physical education is the administrative or teaching division of education that is concerned with the vigorous total body activities as distinct from the manual, musical, or scientific activities and from the tool subjects.[4]

Williams, Brownell, Vernier (1958): Physical education is the sum of man's physical activities, selected as to kind, and conducted as to outcomes. Since physical education is to be considered as a means of education *through* physical activities rather than an education *of* the physical, the phrases "selected as to kind" and "conducted as to outcomes" assume considerable importance.[5]

The emphasis on the educative possibilities involved in physical activities is not a new concept even when the element of compulsion exists. Plato in *The Republic* stated: "Bodily exercise, when compulsory does no harm to the body."[6] He felt that gymnastics should begin in childhood and continue in adolescence on a more systematic basis for military demands. He stressed the point, however, that the principal aim should be the improvement of the soul—or, in other words, the educative process. In spite of differing cultures and ideologies many countries, both oriental and occidental, have recognized this significance in recent years with the result that the disparity of purpose and conduct is not nearly so great as we are sometimes led to believe. For example, Antonio Leal d'Oliveira of Portugal, President of the Fédération Internationale D'Éducation Physique, states:

> We call "physical education" the aspect of Education which specifically uses bodily exercises and physical natural agents, having in view above all the harmonious improvement of the system and its adaptation to the more general exigencies of a psycho-motor nature in social life.[7]

THE RELATIONSHIP BETWEEN PHYSICAL EDUCATION AND SPORT

During the past decade or so in many countries a close relationship seems to have developed between physical education and sport. Without doubt very significant factors in this respect have been the expansion of the Olympic Games and the extension of the Olympic ideal through

---

3 Hetherington, *School Programs*, p. 45.

4 Nash, *Interpretations*, p. 3.

5 Williams *et al.*, *Administration of Health Education*, p. 10.

6 Plato, *Republic*, VII, 536.

7 d'Oliveira, *General Concepts*, p. 75.

international conferences relating to all aspects of sports competition and preparation. Inevitably, physical education has become more and more involved in this whole process. For example, an article in the Bulletin D'Information of the Bulgarian Olympic Committee reporting on the Congress of the Bulgarian Union for Physical Culture and Sport held in May 1962 included the following references:

> . . . pointed out that observations and data collected at the "A. Atanasov" factory in Rousse have shown that systematic physical exercise has considerably reduced sick leave. She fully seconded a motion to bring 80 per cent of our industrial workers under a regular physical education schedule, during the morning gymnastics recess.
>
> G. Ganev, deputy-minister of education and culture, made valuable proposals regarding physical education in the schools and future working program of the Central Council of the Bulgarian Union for Physical Culture and Sport.[8]

In Canada physical education has been influenced particularly by the United States and Great Britain, especially as far as the English-speaking population is concerned; a great debt is owed to both of them, but especially to the United States of America, in the field of professional preparation. Both of these countries, like Canada, have decentralized systems of education, and so Canadians have tended to overlook other systems and practices and perhaps even to assume that other systems cannot possibly have anything to offer. This attitude represents a grievous oversight, particularly with respect to the French-speaking population of Canada. The fact that Quebec's 1961 Program of Studies for Secondary Schools does not make any direct reference to physical education indicates the variation which exists in Canada. On the other hand the Program of Studies for the Elementary Grades (1959) contains a section headed "Physical Training" in the English edition and "Culture Physique" in the French edition. Both editions include statements which refer to the recognition of the importance of adequate programs. The relationship to hygiene is stressed in such statements as:

> Training, practiced in this manner and in accordance with hygienic rules, constitutes what is known as "Physical Education."[9]
>
> . . . C'est par la culture physique que l'on peut améliorer la santé et le maintien de nos enfants, stimuler leur croissance, développer harmonieusement leur physique et leur donner des habitudes de récréations saines et hygiéniques qu'ils conserveront tout leur vie.[10]

---

8 Chervenoushev, *Optimistic Congress*, p. 21.
9 Quebec, *Course of Studies*, p. 126.
10 Québec, *Programme . . . elementaires*, p. 578.

In contrast with Canada, England, and the United States of America, all of the "Popular Republics" are organized more or less similarly to the U.S.S.R. with a high degree of state (federal) control or influence. There are significant differences, but these are not really pertinent to the present discussion, which is merely aimed at illustrating the connection of physical education and sport at the official level. Examples of this principle include the following: The Council of Physical Education and Sports (Hungary), The Union of Physical Culture and Sports (Rumania), Supreme Committee of Physical Cultural (Poland), German Union of Gymnastic and Sports (East Germany), and the Czechoslovakian Association of Physical Culture (Czechoslovakia). Two other examples will suffice. France provides an interesting organization which guarantees the general direction of physical education and sport through the office of the Ministry for Youth and Sports but which leaves non-school sport to the guidance and control of federations which are independent of the state. In Italy, physical education and sport are placed under the jurisdiction of the Central Committee for Physical and Sportive Education, which is attached to the Ministry of Public Instructions. The Italian National Olympic Committee, however, deals with all aspects of sport not related to the schools.

Finally, the development of new organizations at the international level reveals an interesting trend. The International Olympic Committee, founded in 1896, has in a very real sense led the way for dozens of sports federations which have spread their operations to all parts of the globe. These have had a definite effect on physical education, but the ones which have been established in the last decade represent a new kind of international interest in physical education and sport, particularly from the educational point of view and the possible contributions to better human relations. Such examples include the International Council for Sports and Physical Education, founded in 1960, the International Association of Feminine Physical Education and Sports, founded in 1949, the International Council of Health, Physical Education, and Recreation, founded in 1959 by the World Confederation of Organizations of the Teaching Profession, and the International Association of the Higher Schools of Physical Education, founded in 1962. UNESCO as long ago as 1954 adopted in General Conference a resolution authorizing the Director General to undertake studies which in 1956 resulted in a very interesting and informative report on the role of sport in modern culture. This interest on the part of UNESCO continued, with the result that encouragement was given to the formation of the International Council for Sports and Physical Education, referred to previously. Finally, with the initiative of UNESCO an International Conference was organized in Asia in 1963 for the purpose of developing better understanding of the significance of exercise as an educational medium around the theme: "The Cultural Values of Sport in the East and the West." In discussing this topic Ernst Jokl sums up an attitude which is gradually being appreciated by more and more individuals who have analyzed seriously the basic relations between physical education and sport and the principal reasons for their claim to recognition and support, both public and private.

> . . . But I shall try to show that the final goals of sport and physical education are humanistic. . . .
>
> The modern sports and physical education movement is a child of the industrial revolution. It has grown pari passu with the technological transformation of our globe. Sport and physical education represent the reassertion of an irrepressible instinct of man vis-à-vis the automatization of production, the bureaucratization of society and the mechanization of life. But the sport and physical education movement also promises to become a moral force by virtue of the fact that it is the means of establishing a new kind of intimate connection between the masses. Sport conveys a universally understood social meaning, making millions aware of an otherwise unknowable quality of identity of human values and human hopes. . . .
>
> . . . In sport and physical education the genius of man reveals its desire and ability to steer the ship of fate towards better shores.[11]

The main purpose of citing these various examples is to show that in spite of differing terminologies and differing practices there is a basic similarity, a kinship which suggests that the philosopher of physical education has to consider physical education in a much broader sense than hitherto. If physical education is accepted as being the "sum total" of physical activity experiences, the concept of "cradle to the grave" responsibility takes on new meaning. The role of adult education in relation to recreation and to sport becomes more evident. It also becomes clear that physical education cannot be exclusively the function of "formal schooling." Community institutions need to be assessed from the point of view of their potential contributions to the school-age group as well as to the pre-school and post-school population.

PROFESSIONAL NOMENCLATURE

With the scope of physical education understood, it can be defined, on a basis which is almost universal, as an aspect of education which uses bodily activities, in both individual and group situations, as the means

---

[11] Jokl, *Sport and Physical Education*, pp. 187-92.

for reaching toward the educational ideal. The definition of this ideal may be stated in many ways, but there is always a general understanding of its nature in a particular country or community, and this in turn is more specifically spelled out in official publications of the Department of Education or its equivalent ministry. For example, the province of Manitoba commences its 1960-61 Program of Studies with the statement: "The two major objectives of education in a democracy are:

1. The development of broad literacy, and
2. The promotion of democratic citizenship."

The province of Saskatchewan, on the other hand, includes in its Program of Studies for the High School (as reprinted in 1958) a longer preamble entitled "Basic Concepts in the Education of Youth," which contains along with others the following headings:

1. General Purposes:
   (a) The fullest realization of the personal potentialities of every boy and girl.
   (b) The preservation and improvement of our democratic social order.
   (c) The understanding, utilization, and improvement of our physical environment.

2. Functional Objectives:
   (a) Personal development—[with health and physical fitness listed first].
   (b) Growth toward competence in citizenship.
   (c) Growth in family living.
   (d) Occupational preparation.

The significance of the education of youth is well stated in Alexander Pope's succinct lines

> 'Tis education forms the common mind,
> just as the twig is bent the tree's inclined.[12]

Physical education, if properly conducted, can play a vital role in advancing several of these basic concepts.

It is important for a student of physical education to have a clear understanding of what he hopes to achieve in his educational program and of how he plans to realize this achievement. Many terms are used, often in a rather confused way, to illustrate what may be called aims, goals, purposes, objectives, etc. In an attempt to simplify the terminology for the balance of this chapter the words *goal* and *object* will be considered as most important and as being synonymous.

The *goal* in a figurative sense is the object of effort or ambition, or in other words, the terminal point of a race.

---

12 "Moral Essays: Epistle I," ll. 149-50.

The *object* can be described as "that to which action, thought or feeling is directed; the thing aimed at; purpose, end."

Aim can then be defined as the "act of aiming or the course or direction."

This leaves the term *objective* as the most frequently used expression to indicate some facet "pertaining to the object or end as the cause of action." In the military sense this may be considered as the objective point or intermediate strategic site which must be occupied in order to ensure the success of the larger operation.

There is an old proverb which says, "One cannot take true aim at things too high." This saying perhaps was less open to criticism in the days before space capsules, but it still represents a good cautionary piece of advice to teachers of physical education. One must aim high and yet there must be a reasonable chance of hitting the target or at least one of the secondary targets. On this basis the aim can be adjusted as new goals are established. A number of objectives may be fairly precisely defined with respect to an operational goal which may under ideal conditions be attained. This may be considered as an intermediate goal or a kind of second stage of power release by means of which an attempt may be made to reach more remote goals and finally an ultimate goal. In an analogy of this type the "ultimate" must be considered as the philosophical ideal which will always be evanescent in nature, kindling our desires and our hopes toward the "perfect life."

CANADIAN GOALS AND OBJECTIVES

Almost all of the written statements of the purposes of physical education programs are to be found in publications of Departments of Education or in textbooks designed for the professional preparation of students. A list of some of the goals and objectives most frequently referred to in the programs of studies or official bulletins of the provincial Departments of Education follows. Slightly different approaches are to be found in the Elementary Programs as compared with the Secondary Programs, but the avowed purposes are basically the same. Complete statements have been omitted, but quotations from various provinces attempt to give a composite impression.

ONTARIO (Elementary)

1. Provide for vigorous and happy self-expression, *not* suppression. Activities should be at once joyous and disciplined. The play spirit should be emphasized.
2. To develop good health habits.

MANITOBA (Elementary)

1. To develop skills and co-ordination.
2. To develop an enjoyment of physical activities.
3. To apply the principles of good hygiene.
4. To develop emotional control.

ALBERTA (Elementary)

A. General Objectives

Attitudes

Self-respect:	self-control, self-direction, confidence, poise.
Creativeness:	through rhythmics, dances, and action stories.
Objectivity:	focus on activity rather than personal feelings.
Co-operation:	willingness to participate in group activities and team games.
Responsibility:	willingness to carry out activities with a minimum of supervision.
Social Concern:	desire to forego some personal advantages in order to help others.

Understandings

Through engaging in physical education activities the children should gain an understanding that:

1. Physical well-being depends partly on good body mechanics.
2. Sports and recreational activities are necessary in a well-balanced scheme of living.
3. Group activities enhance the opportunities for satisfying physical needs.
4. Sports and recreational activities play an important part in community life.

Habits, Skills and Abilities

1. Efficient habits of posture and movement.
2. The practice of good health habits in physical activities.
3. Neuro-muscular skills necessary for increased enjoyment in games and other predominantly physical activities.
4. Skills and abilities which will protect the child from harm and be useful in times of emergency.
5. Skills in rhythmic activities which will increase the child's ability to express himself.

B. Specific Objectives

1. Walking
2. Running
3. Jumping
4. Throwing
5. Hanging
6. Climbing
7. Catching—throwing Games
8. Chasing—fleeing Games
9. Jumping—hopping Games
10. Rhythms Activities (including folk, square, social and modern dance)

[Note: For each of the above items specific details are given such as in 4. Throwing

(a) Throwing an object given distances accurately.
(b) Developing the shoulder girdle muscles.]

NEW BRUNSWICK (Elementary)

1. The development of a high level of organic fitness with emphasis on general body development, strength, agility, and flexibility and co-ordination.
2. The development of motor skills in the areas of sports, aquatics, gymnastics, rhythmics and recreational activities and interests.
3. The development of sound social and personal behavior characteristics—responsibility, co-operation, self-control, enthusiasm, respect for authority.

These three objectives are directly related to the first three specific objectives of elementary education. Physical education does assist, as well, in the development of the child's natural creative tendencies through the use of creative and dramatic activities of the general body development, skill or group participation type.

QUEBEC (Protestant Schools) (Elementary)

A. General Objectives

1. To develop organic fitness which will protect and improve the health and physical stamina of the pupils.
2. To provide opportunities for controlled participation in physical activities.
3. To develop skills, habits, and attributes in activities which will contribute to:
   a. wholesome living including leisure time pursuits.
   b. the development of a mature adult.
4. To inculcate the highest standards of ethical behavior.

B. Specific Objectives

Note: [Specific objectives are listed for different grades with the statement that the pupil should be able to participate in the following activities as indicated. Specific achievements, such as 'Perform six dances or more" or "Pass Junior Red Cross or Y.M.C.A. swimming test" are described under each appropriate heading. The Grade VI headings from which the two foregoing examples are taken are listed below.]

GRADE VI

A. Marching
B. Calisthenics
C. Rhythmical Activities—Dancing
D. Apparatus work
E. Games
F. Swimming

SASKATCHEWAN (Elementary)

1. Develop and maintain a desirable level of physical fitness thus laying a foundation for full and efficient living.

2. Develop fundamental physical skills including running, jumping, throwing, catching, climbing and lifting, thus helping to establish some proficiency in a variety of activities contributory to living safely and successfully.
3. Build socially acceptable character traits which will help him live in socially useful and personally satisfying ways.
4. Acquire a number of physical recreational skills and interests which may serve as a basis for participation in wholesome leisure-time activities in school and adult years, thus contributing to improved physical, mental and emotional health.

Fundamental Exercises

Physical fitness is the primary objective of physical education. As the ability to read is basic to an understanding and appreciation of literature, so physical fitness is basic to the skill, social and recreational objectives of physical education.

BRITISH COLUMBIA (Secondary)

The aim of physical and health education is to assist the normal growth and development of the individual through health instruction and participation in planned physical activities.

Specific Objectives

1. The development of physical fitness.
2. The development of desirable health habits.
3. The development of fundamental skills in, and knowledge of, prescribed activities.
4. The development of good sportsmanship.
5. The development of interest and enjoyment in, and desire for, participating in leisure-time physical activities.

ONTARIO (Secondary)

The Aim of Physical Education

Physical education contributes to the realization of the general objective of all education—the well-rounded development of all children and youth as responsible citizens.

The Objectives of Physical Education

1. To promote the healthy development and physical fitness of all pupils through participation in vigorous physical activity.
2. To develop the fundamental physical skills; good posture; and the derived skills peculiar to games, athletics, and dance.
3. To promote an interest in physical activity which will carry over into leisure time.
4. To develop good mental health—e.g. self-confidence, courage, initiative, cheerfulness, and to encourage desirable attitudes and behaviour towards others, e.g. sportsmanship, loyalty, co-operation, tolerance and sense of responsibility.
5. To develop leadership ability.

SUMMARY OF THE GOALS OF PHYSICAL EDUCATION

What simple, straightforward conclusions may be drawn from a consideration of the foregoing? First, that in Canada four conditions prevail:

1. there is general agreement that the principal goals of physical education are identical to those of education.
2. there is a strong similarity of interests and programs amongst the provinces.
3. there is agreement that physical education should stress physical activity without minimizing the other elements which contribute to total fitness.
4. in spite of the foregoing statement there is a lack of definite emphasis on physical fitness.

Second, that there is no common terminology with respect to aims, objectives, and goals. It might be appropriate, therefore, to refer back to the definitions used earlier in this chapter and restrict the word *aim* to the general course or direction, such as the aim of a physical education program, the term *objectives* to indicate precise factors specifically attainable at certain levels, and the term *goals* to general qualities which progress or advance from immediate to ultimate.

On this basis, physical education may always be considered as having four major goals in any one stage of an individual's development, all of which are related to his self-sufficiency. This concept would be compatible with the federal government's definition of "fitness" for purposes of interpreting Bill C-131, An Act to Encourage Fitness and Amateur Sport. In this context the word *fitness* means "the state in which a person is able to function at his physical and mental optimum." It can be seen, therefore, that the fitness of a grade VII girl would probably be quite different from the fitness of a Grade XI boy, and consequently the specific objectives of their physical education programs could be outlined on a different basis. The general goals might be the same but the emphasis on the different factors and the qualitative levels would be quite different.

There are various expressions used to describe these general factors which incidentally are often referred to as objectives but which in the

	Personal Self-Sufficiency Goals			
I *Growth*	Physical	Organic	Developmental	Biological (Maturative)
II *Skills*	Motor	Neuromuscular	Functional	Technical
III *Emotions*	Mental	Intellectual	Recreative	Psychological
IV *Human Relations*	Social	Sociological	Behavioral	Cultural

chart above are listed as goals of physical education leading to personal self-sufficiency. The chart is an attempt to summarize approximate equivalents using different nomenclature. The columns are all headed in the same direction with the items listed in an order which may be considered as going from concrete to general, or from the most easily measured to the least easily measured.

PRINCIPLES ON WHICH PHYSICAL EDUCATION IS BASED

By this time it is rather obvious that physical education, if it is to be successful and to achieve results in even a few of the areas in which it claims an interest, must be rooted strongly in certain clearly recognized disciplines. It must be based on fundamental sources yielding basic laws or truths which generally are considered to be immutable. These we call principles. In other words, a principle is "a fundamental truth or proposition on which many others depend." The scope of this chapter does not permit a thorough examination of the sources of principles of physical education, but perhaps it is sufficient to permit a brief discussion of a few of them by way of illustration.

HUMAN BIOLOGY A knowledge of the construction and function of the body is essential to the proper understanding of the role of physical education. The functional capacities of individuals may vary considerably, and so if an assessment of fitness is to have any real meaning it must be based upon recognized biological principles. Similarly, decisions regarding suitable activities for girls at various age levels have validity only if they are made on the basis of established knowledge of sex differences, female characteristics, and growth patterns.

EDUCATION AND THE LEARNING PROCESS Physical education may be reduced to meaningless or random activity at the elementary school level if the teacher does not take advantage of and put into practice principles which are based on the nature of learning. A proper understanding of the significance of play can make all the difference in the way in which a teacher guides the education of young children. Dame Olive Wheeler *et al.* illustrate this in the following excerpts:

> The impulse for free movement is particularly powerful in late infancy. To run, to jump, to skip, to climb, to exercise the different parts of the body and to extend the exploration of the environment by movement is natural in this period. . . . It is not only desirable for the healthy growth of young children that they should have lots of exercise. It is equally important that their activities be freely chosen, within the limits of safety and of consideration for the rights of others. . . .

. . . Play is the natural method employed by young children to gain control of their bodies, to learn the ways of adults through imitation, and gradually to make adjustments to the complex civilized society of which they are to become members. It has the great advantage over other methods that it does not deny, but indeed makes use of, the children's own dynamic impulses and individualites.[13]

The comment on the nursery school (children aged 3-5 years) in the same publication has special relevancy for physical education:

It stands out from the rest of the educational system in that it is explicitly designed for the harmonious many-sided growth of children, and does not neglect their emotional and social needs in ministering to their physical and intellectual development.[14]

PSYCHOLOGY In discussing "The Nature of Man—His Psychological Foundations," Williams stresses the principle of the unity of man and states: "It is not to be supposed that integration of the personality is inherent in all experiences or that divisive forces do not exist that tend to cause disintegration. The contrary is true."[15] Physical education must constantly be aware of the contributions of modern psychology because of the significance placed upon modifications of behavior. It must consequently seek out approved ways of effecting the desired integration.

The interrelationships of various disciplines as they affect physical education and contribute to it are becoming increasingly evident. Publications such as Johnson's *Science and Medicine of Exercise and Sports* and the University of Illinois' *Exercise and Fitness* exemplify this interdependence very well and provide specific examples in several fields, including psychology.

SOCIOLOGY AND PHILOSOPHY A great deal has been written about the importance of the role of physical education in the preparation for democratic living. Unless the teacher or the organizer thoroughly understands the nature of democracy and changing society, he is very likely to be like the trainer described by Cox and Mercer.

Trainers all too readily confuse ends and means. They are likely to value docility and obedience and faith somewhat more highly than honesty, judgment, and independence. All social leaders, especially teachers, who consider education as training, are prone to assume that acquiesence is synonymous with assent.[16]

---

[13] Wheeler *et al.*, *Mental Health*, pp. 85-88.

[14] Wheeler *et al.*, *Mental Health*, p. 82.

[15] Williams, *Principles of Physical Education*, p. 181.

[16] Cox and Mercer, *Education in Democracy*, pp. 10-11.

Later they say that in spite of lip service to democracy "many adults, even in the teaching profession, fear to permit children to make significant choices; to them the possibility of 'wrong' decisions seems fraught with danger. They do not grasp the meaning of self-education as the reconstruction of experience."[17]

It is necessary to plan the physical education program so that opportunities for the realization of goals are presented in the most favorable light. This means that programs have to exist at various levels both in school and non-school situations. According to Wheeler *et al.*,

> the basic curriculum [for adolescents] should therefore be socially relevant and founded on a sound philosophy of life. . . . First, there should be health education, involving not only the acquiring of skill in the management and exercise of the body, but also the understanding of the conditions of health and sex functions. . . . Fourthly, there will need to be social training, including not only social studies but opportunities for co-operation in work, as in games.[18]

The concept of co-operation in competitive situations is of vital importance to all who profess to be professionally competent in physical education. The whole problem of the social significance of games and competition is provocatively posed by Ashley Montagu in a chapter entitled "Play or Murder?"

> Because of our confusion between co-operative competition and competitive competition, and because of our failure to recognize and give co-operative competition a name, we have mostly attributed to competitive competition what properly belongs to co-operative competition. In addition to co-operative competition there is such a thing as competitive co-operation in which one vies with others to achieve for the benefit of all the advantages one seeks together. This form of competition also often goes unrecognized and is also often confused with competition pure and simple. . . .
> In the middle of the twentieth century we have to recognize that the competitively most valuable quality of human beings is co-operation, and that in a world which stands so much in need of co-operation we are teaching our children to become competitive competitors. We have to change our views and conduct as adults if, recognizing the desirability, we are to change those of our children and of our culture. And toward this end where games are concerned we can begin by attempting to understand the true meaning and significance of playing games for human beings.
> Being taught to play games, in addition to the fun they can provide, should constitute one of the most important of all educational devices for the training of character and personality.[19]

---

17 Cox and Mercer, *Education in Democracy*, p. 23.
18 Wheeler *et al.*, *Mental Health*, pp. 110-11.
19 Montagu, *Humanization of Man*, p. 294.

The Future of Physical Education

The goals of physical education will probably remain the same for many generations to come, even as society fluctuates. Suggestions to change the name of physical education to "kinesiology" or "educational gymnastics" or "movement art" may receive temporary support and prominence in some educational quarters, but the most significant development will probably take place in the non-school area, in the realm of adult education and recreation. Therefore, the principles in these spheres must be considered by physical educators. The following quotation gives some weight to this thesis.

> It must never be overlooked, moreover, that, even during school years, when growing physically and socially is the main business of living, the child is controlled by the community process far more than by the so-called "disciplines" of the scholastic institution that he attends physically for twenty-five or thirty hours a week for forty or fewer weeks a year. The child is seldom under school discipline as much as one-sixth of his waking hours.
>
> Much more important than the limited time under the influence of school disciplines is the relative emotional intensity of the out-of-school and in-school experiences.[20]

Finally, educators need to recognize priorities in programs. As Oberteuffer has stated it: "Primarily, the problem of the physical education teacher is that of teaching his students motor skills."[21] Perhaps more important, however, is raising our sights beyond the pupil level to consider the possibilities involved in society as a whole. This requires faith in the value of activity of all kinds including sports, and the placing in proper perspective of the commercial aspects involved. Only in this way is it possible to rise above the spiritual smog that threatens to engulf the lethargic and unwary.

---

[20] Cox and Mercer, *Education in Democracy*, p. 9.
[21] Oberteuffer and Ulrich, *Physical Education*, p. 235.

Bibliography

1. Alberta, *Bulletin 4: Elementary School Physical Education.* Edmonton: Department of Education, 1951.
2. ———, *Junior and Senior High School Physical Education.* Edmonton: Department of Education, 1957.

3. British Columbia, *Secondary School Physical and Health Education*. Victoria: Department of Education, 1961.
4. Bucher, Charles A., *Administration of School Health and Physical Education Programs*, (3rd. ed.). St. Louis, Mo.: The C. V. Mosby Company, 1963.
5. Chervenoushev, Lieuben, *An Optimistic Congress*. Bulletin d'Information, Bulgarian Olympic Committee, 1962.
6. Cox, Philip W. L., and Blaine E. Mercer, *Education in Democracy: The Social Foundations of Education*. New York: McGraw-Hill Book Company, 1961.
7. Havel, Richard C., and Emery W. Seymour, *Administration of Health, Physical Education and Recreation for Schools*. New York: The Ronald Press Company, 1961.
8. Hetherington, C. W., *School Programs in Physical Education*. Yonkers, New York: World Book Co., 1922.
9. Howard, Glenn W., and Edward Masonbrink, *Administration of Physical Education*. New York: Harper & Row, Publishers, Inc., 1963.
10. Johnson, Warren R., *Science and Medicine of Exercise and Sports*. New York: Harper & Row, Publishers, Inc., 1960.
11. Jokl, Ernst, *Sport and Physical Education in East and West: A Synoptic View*. Bulletin de la fédération internationale d'éducation physique, No. 3-4. Lisbon, 1962.
12. Manitoba, Physical Education Grades I-VI. Winnipeg: Department of Education, 1959.
13. ———, *Programme of Studies for the Schools of Manitoba: Senior High Schools*. Winnipeg: Department of Education, 1962.
14. Montagu, Ashley, *The Humanization of Man*. Cleveland: The World Publishing Company, 1962.
15. ———, *Physical Activities for the Primary Grades*. Montreal, 1956.
16. ———, *Physical Education for Elementary Schools*. Montreal, 1955.
17. Montreal Protestant School Board, *Dances and Rhythms for Elementary Schools*. Montreal, 1955.
18. Nash, Jay B., *Interpretations of Physical Education*, Vo.l I. New York: A. S. Barnes & Co., 1931.
19. Newfoundland, *Physical Education for Grades VII to XI, A Teaching Guide*. St. John's: Department of Education, 1962.
20. Nova Scotia, *Physical Activities for the Primary Grades*. Halifax: Department of Education, 1960.
21. ———, *Physical Education, Grades 4, 5, 6*. Halifax: Department of Education, 1961.
22. Oberteuffer, Delbert, and Celeste Ulrich, *Physical Education*. New York: Harper & Row, Publishers, Inc., 1962.
23. d'Oliveira, Antonio Leal, *General Concepts of Physical Education and Sport in the Occident*. Bulletin de la fédération internationale d'éducation physique, No. 3-4. Lisbon, 1962.
24. Ontario, *Intermediate Division Physical Education*. Toronto: Department of Education, 1952.
25. ———, *Senior Division Physical Education, Grades 11, 12, 13*. Toronto: Department of Education, 1959.
26. Plato, *The Republic*, Book VII. Trans. Benjamin Jowett. New York: Heritage Press, 1944.

27. Quebec, *Course of Studies for the Elementary Grades (I-VII)*, English Language Catholic Schools (rev. ed.). Quebec: Department of Education, 1959.
28. ———, Comité Catholique du Conseil de l'Instruction Publique, *Programme d'études des écoles secondaires*. Quebec, 1961.
29. ———,*Programme d'études des écoles élémentaires*. Quebec: Department of Education, 1959.
30. Saskatchewan, *Elementary School Curriculum Guide II for Health and Physical Education*. Regina: Department of Education, 1956.
31. ———, *Programme of Studies for the High School*. Regina: Department of Education, 1958.
32. University of Illinois College of Physical Education and The Athletic Institute, *Exercise and Fitness*. Chicago: The Athletic Institute, 1960.
33. Wheeler, Olive, William Phillips, and Joseph P. Spillane, *Mental Health and Education*. London: University of London Press, Ltd., 1961.
34. ———, Clifford Lee Brownell, and Elmon Louis Vernier, *The Administration of Health Education and Physical Education*. Philadelphia: W. B. Saunders Co., 1958.
35. Williams, Jesse Feiring, *The Principles of Physical Education*. Philadelphia: W. B. Saunders Co., 1959.

5

John H. Passmore   *Professor of Physical Education*
Ontario College of Education

HISTORICAL DEVELOPMENT

In reviewing the early history of physical education in Canada one fact is abundantly clear: that little real progress was made toward establishing a sound public educational system until a satisfactory teacher education program was introduced.

It is also interesting to note that, almost from the beginning, the courses of study of the first provincially-supported teacher training schools included some kind of physical education activities.

THE GOVERNMENT ASSUMES CONTROL Educational progress followed much the same pattern in all provinces. In the beginning private schools and church authorities provided limited education for a small number of children. Gradually the State began to assume more and more control over the issuing of certificates. The next step was the introduction of teacher training on a voluntary basis. Finally, compulsory normal school training was required of all candidates for teachers' certificates.

This last development did not come about easily; and, because it is the basis of the present-day teacher education program in Canada, it deserves special study.

The first government-controlled normal school established in Canada was opened in Montreal in 1863. Lacking support and encouragement, it had to close six years later.

Between 1847 and 1905 normal schools were established in all provinces for the training of elementary school teachers. New Brunswick and

Ontario opened the first training centers in 1847, with Nova Scotia, Quebec, and Prince Edward Island following about ten years later. The prairie provinces and British Columbia established their normal schools between 1882 and 1905.

Government control of education at a provincial level was established for all time by the British North America Act of 1867. Provincial autonomy in education has been vigorously defended ever since, with the State providing more and more direction, control, and financial support.

THE INFLUENCE OF EGERTON RYERSON The history of teacher training in Canada is closely linked with the career of Dr. Egerton Ryerson, who was appointed Chief Superintendent for Upper Canada in 1846. From the very beginning he recognized the importance of the teacher in any successful educational system. His concept of what a teacher should be was somewhat revolutionary for that period. He publicly announced that teachers should not only be persons of high character who were well qualified to teach, but that they should also be adequately paid. (These are surely criteria that every present-day teachers' organization would enthusiastically endorse.)

But Egerton Ryerson was also aware that, if this kind of teacher was to be discovered and trained, some kind of teacher education must be provided. In spite of bitter political opposition he continued to maintain that a normal school was absolutely necessary if teaching was to be established as a worth-while profession. The founding of such a school in Ontario became an objective which he pursued with relentless determination. The derivation of the term *normal school* is somewhat obscure. It is probably of European origin, since both Horace Mann and Egerton Ryerson who travelled widely in Europe used the expression *normal school* to describe model or demonstration schools where teachers were given training. At the founding of the Toronto Normal School in 1847, Ryerson described it as "a school in which the principles and practice of teaching according to the rule are taught and exemplified."

Many of Ryerson's ideas were embodied in the Common School Act of 1846. This act was, indeed, epoch-making, lifting the common schools from their confusing and chaotic condition and, for the first time, creating a planned system of education in Upper Canada.

Teacher training was, of course, an integral part of this system; and even more significant for the future of education in Canada was placing the normal school directly under the central authority.

Through this legislation Ryerson established the principle that the training and certification of teachers was a provincial, rather than a local, responsibility. In this respect, and for what he must have regarded as good and sufficient reason, he differed radically from the British tradition.

FOUNDING OF THE TORONTO NORMAL SCHOOL   The establishment of the Toronto Normal School in 1847 was preceded by two previous attempts to train teachers in Ontario. A monitorial school was started in Kingston and a central school at York, but both experiments ended rather abruptly. The establishment of township model schools had some initial success but the low standard of training provided could not survive in anything but a pioneer society.

Ryerson, a man of great educational vision who had read widely and travelled extensively, studied education in Europe during the year preceding the establishment of the Toronto Normal School. He was greatly influenced by the philosophy of Pestalozzi, who had revived Rousseau's thesis of a "natural education." It was Pestalozzi who wrote that: "The educator who wishes to bring the art of education to bear upon the development of human capacities should have a thorough knowledge of the human organism."

Ryerson was also greatly impressed with the work he observed in the Prussian normal schools. [The work of Jahn and Ling, which penetrated the educational systems of Europe and Scandinavia, probably stimulated this early interest in physical training.]

He found much to admire, and later to imitate, in the teacher training programs he found in Ireland, and he must have been aware of the interest awakened in physical training in Great Britain, largely through the efforts of Archibald McLaren.

BROAD CONCEPT OF TEACHING EDUCATION   Ryerson's ideas of what education should be brought him into constant conflict with the traditionalists. He believed that art and music, home economics, hygiene, and physical training were all part of a sound educational program.

Once the Toronto Normal School was well established and a gymnasium built, Major H. Goodwin was appointed to the staff as "Master of the Art of Gymnastics," a position he held from 1852 to 1877. His work largely involved instruction in drill and calisthenics, which, at that time, probably included a considerable amount of gymnastic and apparatus work.

Present-day physical education students will be surprised to learn that attending normal school in the middle of the nineteenth century was a full-time job. Classes in a great many different subjects began early each day. Lectures often continued from six in the morning until eight o'clock in the evening, and flowed over into Saturday morning. Sunday, also a full day, began with compulsory church services.

Some aspects of the early teacher training program have survived until the present day. For instance, a policy was established whereby future teachers were required, in addition to their professional and philosophical courses, to prepare themselves to teach a considerable number of academic subjects. This policy, although somewhat controversial, is characteristically Canadian.

The first session of the Toronto Normal School ran from November 1, 1847, to April 13, 1848. School authorities received a shock from which, fortunately, the educational system has never recovered, when the second session started on May 15: in addition to the ninety-six men who registered, twenty-two women applied for admission. This came as a great surprise, because co-education in any form was extremely rare and was viewed by some serious-minded educationists with a good deal of alarm— so much so that as late as 1859, one local superintendent of schools wrote in his official report: "Few females possess the mental ability and decision of character which are so essential to the successful teacher."

EARLY REFERENCES TO PHYSICAL TRAINING It is most interesting to discover that as early as 1852 educational authorities were concerned about professional improvement in physical training. A series of articles was published in the *Journal of Education,* under the personal supervision of Egerton Ryerson. These articles included tables of free gymnastic exercises and described movements for the horizontal bar and wooden horse.

Dr. Ryerson urged the general use of these exercises and equipment in the school program by all teachers. He also promised (and this is very significant) that the government would provide financial assistance in purchasing athletic equipment and apparatus.

It is not surprising to learn in this day and age, when the purposes of education are still being seriously debated, that the objectives of physical education were frequently misinterpreted in the early days. Toward the end of the nineteenth century one prominent school inspector reported that: ". . . some parents still have the idea that sufficient physical training is obtained from the buck-saw. Some teachers have the notion that if military drill is conducted, there is no need for gymnastic activities. There is often confusion between physical exercise and physical education."

EARLY REFERENCES TO HEALTH EDUCATION Health education was rather closely identified with physical training in the pioneer teaching training programs. In his official report prepared in 1868, Dr. Ryerson says in part, "I think that every child should know the nature of the food he eats, the beverage he drinks and the air he inhales—together with the organs of his body, the faculties of his mind, and the rules of his conduct."

A careful study of other reports of this period reveals that the term "hygiene" and the expression "the health of school children" were used interchangeably. "Physiology" and "temperance education" were also closely linked with teacher training programs of physical education.

All this suggests that in Canada, at least, the close relationship between health and physical education is traditional.

THE FIRST NORMAL SCHOOL GRADUATES   It was acknowledged earlier that there was a great deal of opposition to normal schools. It would probably be fair to say that, if it had not been for Ryerson's enlightened convictions and his dogged persistence, teacher training in Canada might have been delayed considerably.

In pioneer days education was almost entirely the prerogative and responsibility of local school boards, and any attempt on the part of a government to impinge on this autonomy was, quite naturally, strongly opposed. So there must have been some doubts, even in Ryerson's mind, as to how the first normal school graduates would be received. Would prejudice and local politics make it extremely difficult for these men and women to obtain teaching positions? Would this new teacher training plan, that was so desperately needed, flounder because of widespread opposition?

It must be reported that Toronto (York) with the largest school district in Ontario, refused to employ normal school graduates; and that this policy was not changed for quite a number of years.

Happily, however, there was a brisk demand for these newly-trained teachers elsewhere in the province. As a matter of recorded fact, there was so much competition for their services that salaries as high as £100 were offered. This was unprecedented as it was nearly four times the going rate for "unqualified" teachers.

The attitude that most school boards eventually assumed was reflected in the report of a local superintendent in 1848: "Wherever I have found these teachers (and we have about a dozen of them in this district) the parents tell me . . . they can scarcely hire their children to stay at home. . . . The value of the normal school is beyond all price."

THE IMPORTANT CONTRIBUTION OF McGILL   In any reference book dealing with the development of physical education in Canada and, in paricular, with teacher education in this field, the important contribution made by McGill University cannot be emphasized too strongly. Reference is made to this in Chapters I, VII, and VIII. A number of dedicated women had much to do with pioneer efforts to establish professional training courses, but in this author's opinion, the person who earned the well-deserved title of "Father of modern physical education in Canada" was Dr. A. S. Lamb of McGill (see Appendix B). For it was Dr. Lamb who led the way in providing teacher education in physical education for both men and women.

NORMAL SCHOOL INFLUENCE From the time of its introduction in 1910, the Strathcona Trust regulations strongly influenced the teacher education physical training programs in all provinces. While it is true that the activities taught were rather narrow in scope and that the military influence was evident, it did represent a good beginning.

Once a provincial government entered into an agreement with the Strathcona Trust Committee, normal school students were required to take a regular course in physical training.

Students qualifying for the third-class certificate received thirty hours of instruction, while a second-class certificate required sixty hours. The instruction consisted largely of exercises (calisthenics) prescribed for the Strathcona "B" certificate, in addition to folk dancing and school games.

To promote interest in Strathcona work, local committees frequently sponsored calisthenic competitions between schools and classes. This well-intended idea frequently hampered the work of physical education in the school because it gave the public an inaccurate picture of the program. The unjustified amount of time and effort required to prepare a class for a competitive level frequently left both teachers and pupils with an intense dislike for formal exercise.

As more trained teachers became available in all provinces, dissatisfaction became evident. A report of an educational conference held in Alberta in 1921 states: "These educators saw a need for teacher training in the area being conducted by professional educators, rather than the military."[2]

This was the beginning of an attitude among educators that gradually became evident in all provinces. The Strathcona instructors were gradually replaced by teachers with a broader educational background; and teacher training programs in physical education were altered to meet the present-day needs of the schools.

PRESENT-DAY TRENDS

After World War II, the National Strathcona Committee quite wisely, while continuing to operate within the original provisions of the trust, made a number of very important policy changes, undoubtedly influenced by the thinking of many physical educators serving on local and provincial committees. But they also recognized that the professional preparation of teachers in physical education had now been largely assumed by Canadian universities and teachers colleges.

While continuing to promote rifle shooting and cadet work in the

---

[2] "Downie, History of Physical Education."

schools, in one province at least, they supported "hunter safety training." A fairly large number of bursaries were provided for students attending teachers colleges, books and reference materials were made available, and films and filmstrips dealing with physical education were produced.

There is little doubt that Lord Strathcona's generous Trust Fund will continue to stimulate interest in physical education for many years to come. The profession will always owe Strathcona a debt of gratitude.

TEACHER CERTIFICATION   Under the broad provisions of the British North America Act (1867), and appropriate provincial statutes, authority for establishing teacher qualifications and controlling teacher certification has been given to the ten provincial governments.

Each provincial public school system is headed by a cabinet minister who is called (except in Quebec) the Minister of Education. This post is considered so important that on occasion it has been assumed personally by the Premier of the province.

While there are considerable differences in provincial certification standards, they may be classified in a general way as follows:

(1) a basic or regular certificate. Ordinarily this is valid for traditional academic subjects in an elementary or secondary school.

(2) A "special" certificate. The reference here is to the "non-tool" subjects such as art, music and physical education.

The term *teacher certification* as used in this chapter means the granting of permission by the Department of Education of a provincial government to teach in the public school system of that province.

COURSE CONTENT   Most educational authorities in Canada hold the view that general teacher preparation should precede specialist training; that a common base of academic and professional education should be given to all prospective teachers.

Most provinces require a high school graduation diploma as a prerequisite for a teacher training course at an elementary school level. Here professional preparation usually includes psychology and philosophy, sociology and administration, as well as considerable emphasis on methods, courses, and practice teaching. On the high school level, where teacher training courses are affiliated with university courses in arts and sciences, special subjects are correlated with professional training.

An alternative plan for securing a high school certificate normally available in all provinces, and definitely required in Ontario, involves first obtaining a liberal arts, or some other approved degree, and following this by a year of professional preparation which includes the basic courses common to practically all teacher training programs.

LEGISLATION AND CERTIFICATION   The following excerpts from the British Columbia Public School Act of 1958 illustrate the kind of legislation enacted by the provinces regarding certification:

> The council of Public Instruction may, by rule, or order, or both
> (b) Establish institutions for the training of teachers and others, regulate their conduct and management, and establish therefore appropriate scales of tuition fees.
> (e) Suspend or cancel for cause the certificates of qualifications of a teacher.
> (f) Determine the grades and classes of certificates of qualification to be issued to teachers or to other persons to whom this act applies, and govern the granting of certificates.

TEACHER EDUCATION IN PHYSICAL EDUCATION

There continues to be variation from province to province in specific programs and methods of certification. Two provinces require at least two years at a teachers college or university, the remainder only one for general certification. However, special qualification in physical education at the secondary level is normally regarded as calling for an undergraduate degree in that field or at the least a physical education major in a three- or four-year undergraduate degree program. This may be accompanied by professional teacher education courses, or an additional year may be taken in which education courses leading to certification are provided. The Ontario College of Education is designed to serve the latter purpose, while the Faculty of Education at Alberta and the College of Education at the University of British Columbia provide the composite systems as well as acting in the same capacity as O.C.E.

Elementary specialists in physical education have rarely been provided for in the past. Most of the teachers for this level have come from teachers colleges, normal schools, and/or special summer schools. The Universities of Alberta and British Columbia now offer strong majors in elementary school physical education through their respective Faculty and College of Education. Other universities are studying this development.

It now seems probable that special certificates and sub-standard certification in physical education will be replaced by major, minor, and degree qualification. This is particularly true in Alberta, British Columbia, Ontario, and New Brunswick.

Quebec has been slow to develop a pattern of certification specifically for qualified physical education teachers. The recent change to a centralized administrative unit of education in the government will no doubt lead to the rectification of this gap in the cross-Canada development of teacher education.

PRACTICE TEACHING IN TEACHER EDUCATION   Practically all surveys that have been made in this area strongly enforce the opinion that practice teaching is considered the most valuable part of teacher education.

Many different plans are followed in providing this experience. In most teachers colleges for both elementary and secondary schools it is arranged on a weekly basis, varying from four weeks to nine weeks.

In British Columbia an interesting plan has been devised to provide pre-teacher experience. "Future Teacher Clubs" have been organized at both public and secondary school levels. This permits pupils who have indicated an interest in teaching to spend about a year as a "teacher's aide."

This idea is particularly applicable, in this writer's opinion, in solving the serious shortage of women teachers in physical education in Canada.

The Role of the Critic Teacher No chapter on teacher education would be complete without some reference to the important role played by the physical education critic teacher.

It is customary in Canada to choose these experienced teachers quite carefully. Normally it is considered an honor to be chosen, although frequently older teachers find the additional responsibility rather onerous, especially since there is little, if any, compensation provided. Ontario is a notable exception to this rule. Small honoraria are occasionally paid by other provinces.

Through the years the role of the critic teacher has changed considerably. One early headmaster of the Toronto Normal School had this to say in this regard: "I was trained to believe that my supreme duty was to criticize destructively the teaching of normal students while they were practice teaching." This attitude was probably fairly typical in the early days of the normal schools—but fortunately a new philosophy began to emerge. The same headmaster went on to say:

"I have no sympathy with such a course now, and am glad I saw the great evil of this method of training."

A Valuable Experience for the Student Teacher Physical education critic teachers exert an enormous influence over student teachers. While the demonstrations of teaching methods and classroom procedures are very important, the experience is valuable to the student in many other ways:

> –Here is the opportunity to view at close proximity a normal teacher-pupil relationship.
> –Here is a practical demonstration of all the educational theories to which they have been exposed.
> –Here the student has an opportunity to evaluate different methods of class management.
> –Here, too, his own philosophy of teaching and education begins to take shape.

–Here he sees the educational process in action.

–Here he begins to develop his own innate teaching skills.

During his practice teaching experience a student majoring in one field finds out that the role of the physical education teacher is a very special one. He discovers:

–that, while Physical Education is different, it should not necessarily be a subject completely apart from the other subjects in the curriculum.

–that he is teaching students and not just subject matter.

–that, while his relationship with the pupil is different, their respect and his authority must be maintained.

–that the challenge to provide for every child, regardless of his interests and abilities, can be met by the skilful, knowledgeable teacher.

–that physical and health education have a very vital role to play in the total growth and development of the child.

Schools of physical education provide a broad practice teaching experience in many different ways. Most universities require students to participate in "mutual instruction" sessions as well as to assume various kinds of leadership roles ordinarily involved in teaching.

At the University of New Brunswick students are required to enroll in a program called "Floor Leadership" in their junior year. This involves observing high school physical education classes for not less than six half days and teaching four to six classes.

At the end of the junior year, each student is assigned to a high school for three full weeks of continuous practice teaching. During this period he is responsible for teaching full days and also assisting with intramural and interscholastic athletics. Most students do teach at least one academic subject as well during this period.

During their senior year at the University of New Brunswick, students with an unsatisfactory practice teaching record are required to teach for twelve half-days. Only six half-days is required of the others.

In Ontario a teacher education course is mandatory after an undergraduate degree is obtained. Since most university schools of physical education provide little, if any, practice teaching experience, Ontario considers this the function and responsibility of the Ontario College of Education. Of the nine full weeks of practice teaching, the physical education major spends at least three in his special field.

TRENDS IN TEACHER EDUCATION   One of the most important trends in nearly all provinces is that teacher education is becoming more closely associated with universities. While in Ontario, teachers colleges for elementary school teachers are still administered by the Department of Education, it is significant that the Ontario Men's Public School Teachers'

Assocation has recommended that they become affiliated with universities.

Another important development is that teacher education programs for elementary and secondary schools have been brought closer together. This has resulted in higher admission standards for elementary school teachers.

Closely associated with this trend is the recent decision of Canadian universities to grant degree credits for courses completed in Department of Education training colleges and normal schools. In a recent survey made of twenty-one universities, all but one indicated that this arrangement was acceptable.

The greater emphasis being placed on practice teaching is in accordance with student findings that this is the most valuable part of their training. The trend to provide longer and more continuous experiences instead of teaching individual lessons is also part of the picture.

Because of serious teacher shortages and the availability of special emergency courses, a considerable number of mature men and women are entering the teaching profession. This is particularly evident in Ontario where three times as many students are qualifying to teach in secondary schools during special summer sessions as during the regular winter course.

Forecasts of mounting enrollments indicate that there will likely be a continuing demand for more teachers. This means that public pressure will be brought to bear upon Departments of Education for permission to employ university graduates who have not yet completed their teacher education courses.

The freedom presently permitted teachers to move from one province to another is greater than previously. For example, Ontario and Saskatchewan no longer require summer school attendance of elementary school teachers from outside, if they hold adequate qualifications for regular certification.

It would also appear that fewer special certificates are being issued. For many years Ontario issued more than one hundred special certificates. At the moment this number has been reduced to approximately fifty, British Columbia and Alberta appear to be the only provinces where no special certificates are issued.

While the minimum qualifications required to enter the profession vary considerably from province to province, some attempt is being made at standardization. However, this is not accompanied by experimentation to determine valid methods of selecting promising teachers.

Present university enrollments indicate that the problem of a shortage in physical education teachers will continue for some years to come. It is particularly acute in Ontario where it is estimated that more than one half of all the women teaching are unqualified. A solution being considered by one province is to offer a special summer course to experienced normal school graduates. These young women would be permitted to teach at a high school level provided they continue to work toward their degree.

The establishment of so many university schools of physical education in Canada has been one of the most striking post-war developments in teacher education. This is significant because authorities responsible for higher education have thus acknowledged that physical education is an important subject area, essential in a well-rounded education.

The most recent development at the University of British Columbia may have long-term implications for the profession. In 1962 university authorities decided (for administrative purposes, at least) to place the School of Physical Education under the Faculty of Education. What the eventual outcome of this arrangement will be is still somewhat obscure; but it would seem to indicate that, in the opinion of university administrators, the chief function of the School of Physical Education is to train men and women for the teaching profession.

Few special subjects have brought as many teachers into the profession in recent years. And these men and women have a broad scholarly and professional background, which enables them to teach tool subjects successfully.

Another change that has taken place in the course requirements at the Ontario College of Education may be an indication of a new attitude. Students are now permitted to elect physical education on an equal basis with other optional subjects.

Physical education, art, music, etc. are no longer regarded as supplementary courses. Students who choose one of these subjects as an option are required to complete the course successfully to secure a basic High School Assistant's teaching certificate.

Egerton Ryerson certainly would have approved. As noted previously, he was the first prominent educator in Canada to promote this broad concept of a teacher education program, perhaps the most significant development in the field along with the introduction of degree courses. It should go a long way to alleviate the demand for teachers of physical education which continues to exceed the supply. Some large high schools already employ as many as six teachers with degrees in physical education.

The attitude of most administrators can be summed up in the words of one principal who said recently: "What happens in the physical education program largely determines the tone and morale of my school."

PROFESSIONAL PROMOTION For a long while teachers with specialized training in the subjects of the "outer" curriculum were rarely considered for promotion up the educational administrative ladder. However, a noticeable change has taken place. In the larger provinces many teachers with degrees in physical education have moved into important administrative positions, once they have demonstrated that they have a comparable educational background, as well as successful teaching experience and organizing ability.

STUDENT APPRAISAL OF TRAINING PROGRAMS A survey conducted in British Columbia is fairly typical of the student attitude toward teacher education programs across Canada. Students there rated them roughly as follows at both an elementary and secondary school level: "very good," 25 per cent; "satisfactory," 50 per cent; "poor," 25 per cent.

As indicated elsewhere in this chapter, an overwhelming number of students stated that the practice teaching program provided was of "much value"; and over 50 per cent recommended that more time be spent on this important aspect of the teacher education program.

Many student teachers stated that there was not enough intellectual challenge in their courses, and that much of the material presented in the lecture course was repetitious.

CONCLUSION

The objectives of education, the functions of a school, and the purposes of teacher education will continue to be debated for many years to come. The writer of this chapter has searched for authoritative references to support his own viewpoint. He has found it expressed with great clarity in a speech given by Dr. C. E. Phillips, distinguished Canadian educator and a past president of the Canadian Educational Association. Among many other important statements dealing with the current educational scene, Dr. Phillips had this to say:

> If the school attempts to perform a purely intellectual function, a great many students will become intellectually moribund. Young people are interested in life and will study with spontaneous zest only what is related to life.

> Motivation is the key to learning and the highest function of the teacher is to ensure motivation. To do this the teacher must, among other things, understand young people and the world in which they live.

> Professional education for the teacher, both pre-service and in-service, has been and is the greatest single factor in strengthening the efficacy of education. It is no less important than professional education for the doctor.

There is no better way of concluding any review of teacher education in Canada than by quoting the late Dr. J. C. Althouse, a man who will undoubtedly be remembered as one of the greatest of all Canadian educators. Some years ago, Dr. Althouse wrote:

> The road that the teacher has trodden [in Canada] since 1800 has been a rough one with many ups and downs. He entered upon it a creature of mean estate and small esteem. We leave him still en route, but a traveller now with some assurance of place and respect. This progress has been made possible by the ever-growing realization that education is the greatest public and national enterprise.

BIBLIOGRAPHY

1. Althouse, J. G., "The Ontario Teacher: An Historical Account of Progress." Unpublished Doctor's thesis, Ontario College of Education, 1929.
2. Anderson, L. F., *Pestalozzi*. New York: McGraw-Hill Book Co., 1931.
3. Downie, D. A., "A History of Physical Education in the Public Schools of Manitoba." Unpublished Master's thesis, University of Toronto, 1961.
4. Lazerte, M. E., *Teacher Education in Canada*. Toronto: W. J. Gage, Limited, 1950.
5. Lussier, Mgr. Irénée, *Roman Catholic Education and French Canada*. Toronto: W. J. Gage, Limited, 1960.

PROFESSIONAL PREPARATION

6

John W. Meagher

Professor and Head
Department of Physical Education
University of New Brunswick, Fredericton

INTRODUCTION

Although university education in Canada is as old as Canada itself, programs designed to prepare physical education and recreation personnel at the university level came into being only as recently as 1940. As a matter of fact, to illustrate further the infancy of such programs, it was not until 1957 that all four major areas of Canada—the Pacific Coast, the Prairies, Central, and Atlantic Canada—were served by professional schools of physical education and/or recreation operating as integral parts of Canadian universities.

The University of Toronto was the first in Canada and the British Commonwealth to establish a program which led to an undergraduate degree in these fields. Five years later, in 1945, the school of Physical Education at McGill University in Montreal opened its doors to candidates who would work towards a Bachelor of Science degree in physical education. Until very recently, professional programs have been established in thirteen English-speaking and in four French-speaking universities—and this number continues to grow at an average rate of one per year.

In many instances, these new programs have been developed by people who were directly or indirectly associated with the technical program which operated for many years on the McGill University campus in Montreal or at the Margaret Eaton School for Women in Toronto. The director or one or more senior staff members of nine of the professional schools in operation in 1964 were graduates of one of these institutions.

Any discussion of professional preparation programs for physical education and recreation in Canada must therefore begin with a brief summary of the origin and development of the Schools of Physical Education at McGill and Toronto.

THE BEGINNING—McGILL

The first attempt at the development of "professional preparation" programs for physical education and recreation personnel was made at McGill University in 1911 with the establishment of a four-week summer school course. It is interesting to note that this first program included courses which are still considered today as being the very foundations of an undergraduate professional curriculum—physiology, history, genetics, anatomy, hygiene, first aid, anthropometry, kinesiology, pedagogy, gymnastics, games, and aquatics. So successful was this first attempt that in September 1912 the program was increased in length to one full academic year in addition to the four-week summer session. Additional emphasis was placed on the study of massage and remedial gymnastics, primarily because of the need created by the onset of the First World War. It should be pointed out that this marked the beginning of a long and close association which was to exist for forty-one years between the McGill School of Physical Education and the McGill Faculty of Medicine.

In 1919 Dr. Arthur S. Lamb was appointed to the position of Director of Physical Education at McGill and was charged with the responsibility of directing all aspects of the athletic, physical education, and health services programs. He immediately brought about an increase in the length of the course to two full academic years and developed a large number of additional quasi-medical courses specifically designed for physical education and recreation personnel.

In 1933 McGill initiated a program open only to students with a degree in arts or science. This program was one year in length and led to the awarding of "a higher diploma." This event is significant in that it marked the first occasion in Canadian history when physical education teachers were required to be university graduates. Unfortunately, this program appealed to only a very small number of students. In 1934, in addition to the new higher diploma program, McGill operated its regular course but increased the length to three full academic years. On May 23, 1945, after twelve years of negotiation, the McGill University Senate was finally persuaded by Dr. Lamb and his staff. . . . to approve the establishment of a four-year course leading to the degree of Bachelor of Science in Physical Education. This program remained, for administrative purposes, under the Faculty of Medicine. Thus, thirty-four years after the first summer school was established and twenty-six years after Dr. Arthur S. Lamb was appointed to the staff of the Physical Education Department at McGill, the physical education program at McGill achieved the status which permitted it to be called "professional" rather than "technical."

THE BEGINNING—
THE MARGARET EATON SCHOOL
AND THE UNIVERSITY OF TORONTO

During most of these years, a second professional program was in operation in Canada, in Toronto,—a program which was to achieve degree-granting status five years earlier than that which was in operation at McGill. This school was known as the Margaret Eaton School of Literature and Expression and could be considered Canada's first truly national teacher preparation institution in physical education.

In 1901 the "School of Expression" was established in association with Victoria University, Toronto, by Emma Scott Raff with the following objectives in mind: the interpretation of literature, the problems of voice production, and the promotion of physical education.

This school was so successful that in 1905 it was necessary to secure larger and more comprehensive accommodation. In 1906, Timothy Eaton donated the land, building, and furnishings in honor of his wife, and the school was renamed "The Margaret Eaton School of Literature and Expression." The aims of the school were expanded to include both the provision of courses for personal culture and the provision of training for teachers of literature, dramatic art, and physical education.

By 1910, twenty-nine graduates had passed through the program and moved to positions of importance and leadership in all parts of Canada. It can truly be said that by that date, the school was established as a center for language, literature, dramatic art, and physical education.

The school calendar of 1915-16 included the following paragraph relative to its offerings in the field of physical education:

> A recognition of physical education as an essential in the curriculum of every school and college, has created a demand for thoroughly qualified teachers. Through the rapidly increasing interest in the establishment of playgrounds and recreation centers throughout the country, the demand for trained instructors and workers exceeds the supply. The aim of this department is to provide young women with a thorough training which will enable them to take advantage of these opportunities for service as teachers and supervisors of physical education in all its phases.

By 1920, the school had developed to the point where three specific departments were established: (1) the Department of Literature and Dramatic Art, (2) the Department of English and French, and (3) the Department of Physical Education.

High school graduates were accepted into three specific programs:

(1) a three-year course leading to the diploma "Literature and Expression";

(2) a two-year normal course in literature and dramatic art leading to a teacher's license;

(3) a two-year normal course in physical education leading to a teacher's diploma.

In September 1924, Mrs. Emma Scott Raff Nasmith resigned as principal of the School and Miss Mary G. Hamilton was appointed Director of the Department of Physical Education. From the date of her appointment to 1933, Miss Hamilton constantly endeavored to secure the future of physical education by co-ordinating the Margaret Eaton School with the resources of the University of Toronto.

In May 1934, Miss Florence Somers, formerly Associate Director of the Sargent's School in Boston, became director of the school. During her term of office, the program expanded in many directions and increased emphasis was placed on athletics, the organization of recreational activity clubs, the areas of modern and creative dances, and in-service training for Ontario teachers.

In 1940, through the efforts of Miss Somers, Mr. Warren Stevens, Director of Athletics for Men, and Dr. E. Stanley Ryerson, a new program was organized for both men and women and was called "a course in physical education."

In 1941, the Margaret Eaton School merged with this department to become a school within the University of Toronto—the School of Physical and Health Education.

It was at this point that the undergraduate training in physical education in Canada, and indeed, in the British Commonwealth, at last reached a level which would allow it to be called "professional."

One cannot emphasize too strongly the tremendous influence that the Margaret Eaton School and its staff had on the development of professional education in health and physical education in Canada. The combined influence of the McGill School of Physical Education, the Margaret Eaton School, and the University of Toronto was responsible to a very large degree for the successes which have been enjoyed since 1940 in the area of professional undergraduate education in all parts of Canada.

THE RAPID DEVELOPMENT OF NEW PROGRAMS

Encouraged by the successes enjoyed by programs at the University of Toronto and McGill University, and influenced, no doubt, by the tremendous interest shown in physical education and recreation by returning veterans of the Second World War, and further, anxious to meet the demand for professionally educated and technically trained personnel for the hundreds of new urban, regional, and rural high schools which began to spring up all across Canada, the administrators of other universities decided to investigate the feasibility and desirability of establishing an undergraduate professional physical education program at their university. In Table I are listed the universities which, in 1964, operated undergraduate and/or graduate programs in physical education and recreation, their locations, the type of degree(s) awarded, and the year in which the program was established.

It should be noted that although undergraduate professional education got its start at the University of Toronto, graduate programs in both physical education and recreation have been initiated, to date, only by the three westernmost universitites, Alberta, British Columbia, and Saskatchewan, and more recently by the University of Western Ontario.

VARIATIONS IN PROGRAM EMPHASIS

A close study of Table I would suggest that tremendous differences must exist in the type of undergraduate and graduate programs available in Canada, for the seventeen universities offer no less than nine different degrees ranging from Master of Science to Bachelor of Physical Education. These differences indicate, to some extent at least, variations in academic content, university acceptance, areas of emphasis, and the relationship between the undergraduate professional program and the university family of faculties and schools. The most common degree awarded is the Bachelor of Physical Education. It should further be noted that almost all the universities offer a professional degree as opposed to one that is academic in title. In those few instances where a Bachelor of Arts degree is awarded to successful students, it is qualified by the use of letters which indicated professional content.

Most of the professional schools attempt to offer students an opportunity to earn the Bachelor of Arts degree prior to, subsequent to, or simultaneously with the professional degree. Queen's University, for example, requires its students to earn the Bachelor of Arts degree first and then the professional degree in one additional year. The University of Toronto and the University of New Brunswick stress that students who

TABLE I

Universities Offering Degree Programs in Physical Education and Recreation—1965

Name	Location	Degree offered	Degree program started in
University of Toronto	Toronto, Ont.	Bachelor of Physical and Health Education	1940
McGill University	Montreal, Que.	Bachelor of Education (Physical Education)	1945
		* Diploma in Physical Education	
University of British Columbia	Vancouver, B.C.	Bachelor of Physical Education	1946
		Master of Physical Education	
Queen's University	Kingston, Ont.	Bachelor of Arts and Bachelor of Physical and Health Education (combined)	1946
University of Western Ontario	London, Ont.	Bachelor of Arts (Physical and Health Education)	1947
		Master of Arts	
Ottawa University	Ottawa, Ont.	Bachelor of Arts (Physical Education)	1949
University of Alberta	Edmonton, Alta.	Bachelor of Physical Education	1950
		Bachelor of Arts (Recreation)	
		Master of Arts, Master of Science	
University of Saskatchewan	Saskatoon, Sask.	Bachelor of Arts (Physical Education)	1954
		Master of Science	
Laval University	Quebec, P.Q.	Bachelor of Education (Physical Education)	1954
McMaster University	Hamilton, Ont.	Bachelor of Physical Education	1956
University of New Brunswick	Fredericton, N.B.	Bachelor of Physical Education	1957
University of Montreal	Montreal, P.Q.	Bachelor of Physical Education and Recreation	1961
Memorial University	St. John's, Nfld.	Bachelor of Physical Education	1962
University of Alberta	Calgary, Alta.	Bachelor of Physical Education	1964
University of Manitoba	Winnipeg, Man.	Bachelor of Physical Education	1964
Sherbrooke University	Sherbrooke, P.Q.	Bachelor of Education (Physical Education)	1964
University of Waterloo	Waterloo, Ont.	Bachelor of Physical Education	1964

* Curricula in physical education and in recreation.

complete the Physical Education degree may earn the Bachelor of Arts degree in one additional year. Graduates from the University of Alberta may take an additional year in the Faculty of Education for teacher-certification purposes, or may proceed directly to the graduate program at the Edmonton campus. Special mention should be made of the McMaster University professional program since it was the first of its kind in Canada. Students who wish to enter the course leading to the Bachelor of Physical Education degree must first have earned an undergraduate degree in Arts, Science, Commerce, or Nursing. It is interesting to note the similiarity between this approach and that which was used in the "higher diploma" program at McGill in 1933. Waterloo University and the University of Sherbrooke initiated programs in 1964 similar in content and derivation to this offered at McMaster. At least two other universities in the East are studying the possibility of following suit in 1966.

Course Content

A study of the undergraduate curricula at the Universities which offer three-or four-year undergraduate courses indicates that the content is such that approximately two-thirds of the courses included are drawn from academic disciplines while the remaining one-third are professional in nature. Despite differences in numbers of courses, lengths of programs, and types of degrees, a considerable amount of agreement on the type of courses which should be included in a program leading to a Bachelor's degree for physical education and recreation specialists exists.

HUMANITIES CONTENT Courses in English or French, and two or more additional courses in a modern language, philosophy, history, etc. are general requirements in Canada's professional programs. Particular emphasis is placed on English literature and composition at the freshman college or senior matriculation level, and on modern literature courses in the sophomore or junior year. The study of European, Canadian, and British and Commonwealth history is also a general requirement. Although introductory courses in philosophy are not required, nonetheless most programs do include them as elective offerings.

SOCIAL SCIENCES Both history and philosophy can, of course, be classified as humanities or social sciences. Mention has already been made of these two disciplines in the previous paragraph. A course in psychology and additional courses in either child psychology, adolescent psychology, or educational psychology, are required. Courses in economics, political science, and anthropology are usually listed among the electives. Sociology courses are, however, generally required, particularly for students who intend to proceed toward positions in private and public recreation.

MATHEMATICS Almost all curricula contain at least one full course in mathematics, and this is usually found at the freshman level. Those departments or schools which encourage students to develop a continuation series as an academic teaching minor normally make it possible for students to elect additional mathematics courses.

THE PHYSICAL SCIENCES Here again there exists a considerable amount of agreement. Senior matriculation or freshman college courses in chemistry and physics are required. In addition, students are either required or encouraged to take a course in kinesiology and organic chemistry. Since both chemistry and physics are subjects which are taught in the high schools, those institutions which provide for an academic teaching minor do attempt to clear additional courses in these two physical sciences as well as in mathematics, history, English, French, etc.

THE BIOLOGICAL SCIENCES Here again there exists almost complete agreement in that all professional schools or departments do require their undergraduate students to complete introductory courses in biology (or botany or zoology or both), human anatomy, human physiology, applied physiology (or physiology of exercise). In one or two instances, courses in genetics or comparative anatomy are included as well.

PROFESSIONAL COURSES IN EDUCATION Although the majority of professional schools do not include specific teacher education courses in the undergraduate physical education curriculum, McGill University, the University of New Brunswick, and Memorial University do require their students to enroll in a number of these courses so that they might qualify for provincial teaching licenses or certificates upon graduation. Courses in general methods of teaching, guidance, administration, school law, elementary education, secondary education, and statistics are most commonly included. Students who graduate from the professional schools in Ontario, Saskatchewan, Alberta, or British Columbia are required to attend a provincial teachers college or faculty of Education on campus for one full year in order to qualify for a teaching license or certificate.

PROFESSIONAL COURSES IN PHYSICAL EDUCATION (THEORY) In this area there exists a considerable amount of variety. The newer professional schools or departments, particularly those in Western and Eastern Canada, have quite obviously been influenced by the American system of term courses and credits. The original or older schools, particularly those at Toronto, McGill, and to a lesser extent, Queen's, have preserved the concept of offering one all-inclusive physical education course to each group of students each year. In the majority of institutions, however, most or all of the following physical education theory courses are offered:

> methods of teaching for physical education and recreation
> program planning for physical education and recreation
> kinesiology
> anatomy
> tests and measurements in physical education
> administration of athletics
> administration of recreation
> health education
> personal hygiene
> care and prevention of athletic injuries and first aid
> supervision of physical education
> history and philosophy of physical education and recreation
> physiology of exercise
> adaptive or corrective physical education

PROFESSIONAL COURSES IN PHYSICAL EDUCATION (PRACTICAL)   Skill content can, for convenience, be classified into five categories: acquatics, rhythmics, gymnastics, team sports, and individual and dual activities; and most are offered at two or three of the following levels: (1) basic skills and techniques, (2) advanced skills and techniques, and (3) coaching courses.

Under *aquatics* are included elementary and advanced courses in swimming, diving, life-saving and water safety, and synchronized swimming. In some instances, a coaching course is offered as well. Swimming standards as established by the Red Cross Society and the Royal Life Saving Society, or the Y.M.C.A. of Canada, are applied in the elementary and advanced skill courses.

Under *rhythmical activities* are included elementary and/or advanced courses in folk and square dance, modern dance, social or ballroom dancing, rhythmical gymnastics, and movement fundamentals.

Under *gymnastics* are included elementary and/or advanced courses in rhythmical gymnastics, movement fundamentals, tumbling, balance work, calisthenics, conditioning exercise programs, and heavy apparatus activities. A coaching course in gymnastics is offered as well by two institutions.

Under *team sports*, elementary and/or advanced courses in basketball, football, hockey, soccer, rugger, field hockey, softball, baseball, speedball, lacrosse, touch football, volleyball, curling, track and field, and low-organized games are usually included. Coaching courses in basketball, football, soccer, and hockey are commonly offered as well.

Under *individual and dual activities,* elementary and/or advanced courses in badminton, tennis, bowling, squash, golf, wrestling, track and field, and archery are usually included, as well as coaching courses in track and field. Skiing instruction is offered at six of the universities.

A rather recent innovation is the establishment of advanced activity and coaching electives. At least two of the professional schools have attempted to provide a totally elective activity program in the junior and senior years. Most of the other institutions provide for a limited choice insofar as advanced activity content is concerned.

PRACTICE TEACHING   This is the area of the undergraduate professional program in which there exists the greatest amount of difference. Four of the schools require almost no practice teaching since their graduates will be required to complete this phase of their professional education in the Faculty or College. A few others require only a token experience—one or two hours per week for a term or a year. Others require very little during the regular academic year but an extended period after the close of the university session in the spring or before classes reconvene in the fall. Finally, a few institutions require as much as nine or ten full weeks of practice teaching spread over two or three years. Whereas most of the universities confine their practice teaching to the junior and senior years, at least one, McGill, begins it in the freshman year. On the basis of the above, one can only conclude that no pattern has as yet been established which has national or even regional application.

OUTDOOR SCHOOLS   Three institutions, McGill, Alberta, and Waterloo operate a concentrated program of skill instruction during the month of May after the university has officially closed, or during the month of September before it reopens.

FIELD WORK   All of the universities require their students to gain additional practical experience in the field of physical education or recreation through summer field work at camps, with parks or playground associations, in public or private agencies, or during the regular academic year as assistant coaches, instructors, officials, or athletic administrators.

SUMMARY   On the basis of the above, it can be stated that the typical undergraduate program in physical education in fourteen of Canada's seventeen professional schools or departments is composed of courses in arts, science, physical education theory, physical education activities, as well as periods devoted to practice teaching and field work. Courses in English, chemistry, a second language, mathematics, biology, anatomy, sociology, psychology, physiology, and history are generally required. In addition, students are required to complete, on the average, approximately five hours per week of activity course work at the elementary, advanced or coaching levels each year. All are required to enroll in a number of courses (or parts of courses) devoted to the theory of physical education, health education, and recreation. Finally, most professional schools encourage or require students to follow what is commonly referred to as an academic teaching minor—a continuous series of courses in a specific academic discipline which is included in the secondary school program. The three other departments or schools concentrate the physical education theory and practical work in one academic year following the completion of an arts or science degree.

ADMINISTRATION OF THE PROFESSIONAL PROGRAM

One of the most interesting aspects of undergraduate professional preparation programs in physical education and recreation in Canada centers on the manner in which the program is administered. It was indicated earlier that the vast differences in the types of degrees awarded were indicative of differences in organization. Three different types of organizations exist each with its own peculiar advantages and disadvantages. For example:

(1) Four universities have placed the undergraduate and graduate professional programs and all phases of the athletic program under a single department or school: the University of Alberta Faculty of Physical Education, the McMaster University Department of Physical Education, the University of Saskatchewan School of Physical Education, and the Memorial University of Newfoundland Department of Physical Education.

(2) Two universities have placed all phases of the professional program and all phases of the athletic program except intercollegiate under one department or school: the University of Western Ontario Department of Physical Education and the University of British Columbia School of Physical Education.

(3) Four of the universities have separated for administrative purposes the professional undergraduate program and all phases of the university's athletic program: the University of Toronto School of Physical and Health Education, the McGill University School of Physical Education (Institute of Education), the Queen's University School of Physical Education and the University of New Brunswick Department of Physical Education.

The advantages associated with a type of organization which joins together administratively all aspects of the physical education and athletics program are rather obvious—a single department has a larger and more unified staff, a more equitable sharing of departmental responsibilities, avoidance of duplication of effort or expenditure, better use and control of facilities.

The disadvantages, though not quite so obvious, are nonetheless real. Possible overemphasis of one phase of the program to the disadvantage of other phases, and unnecessary or unavoidable pressure, particularly insofar as the intercollegiate athletic program is concerned, are two of the problems which might be faced by a department which is responsible for both the professional and athletic sides of the program.

Those universities which are so organized that the professional program is divorced from the athletic program are, in most instances, faced with problems relative to size of staff, use of facilities, and obtaining sufficient funds to purchase and maintain an equipment supply quite separate and distinct from that used in the athletic department program. In addition, this separation of these two phases tends to create for the director of athletics and his associates problems relative to rank, salary, tenure, and job security. It should be stressed, however, that regardless of the administrative system in effect, all phases of the professional and athletic program work in harmony in Canadian universities.

Insofar as policies relative to administering curricula, examinations, etc. are concerned, many of the physical education and recreation degree courses operate within the university's Faculty of Arts and/or Science. The notable exception is the Faculty of Physical Education at the University of Alberta, which has faculty status and autonomy. Physical education staff members do, in almost every instance, render asistance to the athletic department serving as coaches for one or more intercollegiate sports or as directors of one or more recreational activities. By the same token, individuals hired primarily by a university's department of athletics assist in the teaching of activity courses in the department of physieducation. With the exceptions of the University of Toronto and the University of Montreal, any relationships which might have existed between a university's Faculty of Medicine and School or Department of Physical Education no longer exist. Even the McGill University program which began as a school under the supervision and direction of the Faculty of Medicine at that institution is now established as a department within the Institute of Education of the McGill Faculty of Arts and Science.

Finally, it can be stated that a pattern has definitely been established whereby the physical education program is most intimately associated with the local Faculty of Arts and/or Science and that this type of organization will continue for many years to come. A review of the course content described in the previous section of this chapter would certainly validate this statement.

GRADUATE PROGRAMS

Only four Canadian universities in 1964 offered programs leading to master's degrees in physical education—the University of British Columbia, the University of Alberta, Saskatchewan, and Western Ontario. Since all of these programs are relatively new, it is impossible to assess their appeal and success. It should be stated, however, that their very existence, along with those announced in 1963 and 1964, would indicate the acceptance which the physical education professional program enjoys in these institutions. It can be concluded further that the inauguration of such programs would indicate the existence of superior facilities and equipment for the study of physical education at the graduate level. These institutions have been successful in obtaining the services of highly competent and enthusiastic staff members and have available to them exceptionally fine facilities for courses in athletics, physical education and recreation, and, more especially, for research.

The programs offered at Alberta and British Columbia are identical in most respects and similar in all others. The graduate student is required to complete five or six full courses and to prepare a thesis. At least half of the course work must be in physical education while the remaining work must be in a subject which normally falls within the university's Faculty of Arts and/or Science. Saskatchewan has oriented its graduate program mainly in the direction of research in applied physiology.

DIPLOMA COURSES IN PHYSICAL EDUCATION

For many years, the one-year and two-year teacher-training programs in Canada were the rule rather than the exception. Since 1950, however, teachers preparing for secondary school positions have generally been required to complete an undergraduate degree. A large number of provincial teachers colleges still exist offering one- and two-year programs for those interested in teaching at the elementary school level.

At the present time, the only diploma course being offered by a university in Canada to students interested in physical education careers is conducted by the McGill University Institute of Education, Macdonald College, in Ste. Anne de Bellevue, Quebec. This program is so designed that a student is granted a teacher's certificate at the end of a two-year course which is primarily professionally oriented. He may, if he so desires, remain at McGill for two additional years and thus qualify for the Bachelor of Education (Physical Education) degree.

This diploma course was reorganized in 1957 and was designed primarily to meet an emergency need for additional personnel in this field. In its 1962 submission to the Quebec Royal Commission on Education, the McGill staff indicated that they were most anxious to have the undergraduate degree become the minimum requirement for teachers in this field. One can conclude, therefore, that this diploma course for physical education specialists is strictly a temporary measure to meet an emergency situation.

The province of Nova Scotia for many years conducted a short course program for physical education personnel. Students were required to spend from three to four summers in this program in order to qualify for a Specialist's certificate. The program was abolished in 1964, and was replaced by a two-year diploma course at the Nova Scotia Teachers' College, Truro.

UNDERGRADUATE PROFESSIONAL PREPARATION FOR RECREATION PERSONNEL

Two Canadian universities offer undergraduate professional programs leading to degrees in recreation.

The University of Alberta offers a four-year course which leads to the degree of Bachelor of Arts in Recreation Administration, which includes courses in arts and science, physical education, art, drama, recreation administration, business administration, and with considerable emphasis on sociology and psychology.

The University of British Columbia also offers a program which is four years in length leading to the Bachelor of Physical Education degree with specialization in recreation. The course content is very similar to that of the Alberta program.

For many years the University of Western Ontario offered a degree course in recreation but this was abolished when a major curriculum revision took place in 1957.

A number of provincial Departments of Education offer short courses for personnel in the field of recreation which must be considered to be more technical than professional since they do not lead to a university degree. The one most worthy of note is that which is offered at the University of Guelph, Ontario, in co-operation with the Ontario Department of Education.

UNDERGRADUATE ENROLLMENT IN CANADA'S SCHOOLS OF PHYSICAL EDUCATION

The following are the enrollment statistics covering the period 1957 to 1965 inclusive for the undergraduate professional programs which were in operation during those years.

TABLE II

ENROLLMENT IN CANADA'S PHYSICAL EDUCATION UNDERGRADUATE PROGRAMS

University	1957-58	1959-60	1961-62	1963-64	1964-65
Toronto	115	149	160	198	238
New Brunswick	27	84	159	202	225
British Columbia	103	160	192	189	217
Alberta (Edmonton)	48	57	110	171	205
Western Ontario	49	67	86	201	204
Montreal	—	—	45	145	183
McGill	80	86	128	119	155
Ottawa	32	68	140	152	143
Queen's	87	111	130	154	148
Saskatchewan	—	33	73	121	129
Memorial	—	—	—	66	89
Laval	17	34	104	102	88
Manitoba	—	—	—	—	79
McMaster	7	16	35	64	75
Sherbrooke	—	—	—	20	40
Alberta (Calgary)	—	—	—	21	37
Waterloo	—	—	—	—	41
Totals	565	865	1362	1925	2296

Despite the increase in the number of schools, all have shown an increase in enrollment during the past five years. The inauguration of four-year honors degree programs at the University of Western Ontario and at the University of Toronto may result in slight intentional enrollment decreases in these institutions. Should McGill University decide to abandon its diploma course, then a decrease in the enrollment might be expected in that institution as well.

It is significant and indeed disconcerting to note that only one-third of the students in physical education or recreation are women. The Univeristy of Alberta's 1964-65 enrollment of 205 was made up of 133 men and 72 women. During the same year, the University of New Brunswick enrolled 170 men and 55 women, while Ottawa enrolled 139 men and only 14 women. The picture is almost identical from coast to coast with the exception of McGill University where a large number of women students are enrolled in the diploma course, and at Queen's University where the number of women students is greater than men. It is obvious that Canadian universities will have to take immediate steps to attract women students to their professional programs in physical education and recreation.

TRENDS IN PROFESSIONAL PREPARATION

The number of significant trends in teacher preparation for physical education, health education, and recreation are worthy of note since these may seriously change the type, quality, and number of professional undergraduate programs in the next ten years.

THE HONOR PROGRAM Since 1962 both the University of Western Ontario and the University of Toronto offered a four-year honors program in physical and health education. The result has been an increase in the number of courses in arts and science as well as a longer and more expensive program for the students enrolled in these institutions. Most other universities are increasing the number of academic courses in the curriculum in the hope that the academic qualifications of future graduates will be raised to an even higher level.

THE ACADEMIC TEACHING "MINOR" Almost all programs include a provision for an academic minor in an arts or a science subject which can be taught at the high school level. More emphasis is being placed on this minor in the hope that students will graduate with at least two teaching competences, an academic one and a professional one.

ELECTIVE ACTIVITY COURSES It was indicated earlier that at least two universities offer students in their junior and senior years an opportunity to choose their physical education activity courses from a long list of offerings. Other universities seem to be moving toward this type of organization. The net result should be a greater degree of specialization among physical education and recreation graduates.

THE ONE-YEAR COURSE IN PHYSICAL EDUCATION It was indicated earlier that McGill University established a one-year course in physical education for students who had previously completed the requirements for a Bachelor of Science or a Bachelor of Arts degree. This program, which was initiated in 1933 and abandoned in 1944, led to a certificate which was called "the Higher Diploma." The Queen's University program, established in 1946, has been quite similar in that students first earn a Bachelor of Arts degree with some physical education activity, and then in one additional year complete the requirements for a Bachelor of Physical and Health Education degree. McMaster University began its program in 1956 and the approach adopted was almost identical to that used at McGill. Sherbrooke and Waterloo Universities followed suit in 1964. At least two other Canadian universities have been giving serious consideration to just such a scheme. It may be that in the years to come this approach to teacher preparation may become the rule rather than the exception.

A CENTRALIZED CANADIAN INSTITUTE FOR PHYSICAL EDUCATION AND

SPORTS MEDICINE For many years some leaders in Canadian physical education have been pressing for the establishment of one large central institute which would be established specifically to train physical education teachers, coaches, supervisors, as well as specialists in rehabilitation, applied physiology, and sports medicine. Although nothing concrete has yet been done in this regard, the idea has gained some impetus in the light of recent developments at the national level in the areas of fitness and amateur sport.

SUMMARY

Programs designed to train professional physical education and recreation personnel in Canada have made tremendous progress since 1912, in that all regions of Canada are now served by one or more professional schools.

The degrees offered are many and varied but the course content is quite similar. Generally speaking, approximately two-thirds of the students' courses is in the areas of arts and science while the remaining one-third is in the area of professional physical education and recreation course work, both theoretical and practical.

Four universities—Alberta, British Columbia, Saskatchewan, and Western Ontario—offer both graduate and undergraduate work in the field of physical education and recreation. Thirteen universities offer only undergraduate work in the field of physical education.

In some institutions, athletics and physical education are united under one department, school or faculty; in others, these two areas are separated for administrative purposes, but in nearly every case a close relationship exists between the professional program and the local Faculty of Arts and/or Science.

The trends are few but are firmly established — a move toward honors programs, an increase in the academic content, increased emphasis on the academic teaching minor, and the establishment of one-year post-graduate courses for physical education personnel.

At least two problems of major significance confront professional physical education and recreation programs in Canada: the drastic shortage of female candidates and the large number of schools and departments with small enrollments. These two problems are now receiving a considerable amount of attention from leaders in the field and professional associations, and must be resolved if the next thirty years are to be as productive as the past thirty have been.

BIBLIOGRAPHY

1. Jackson, Dorothy N. R., *A Brief History of Three Schools*. Toronto: The T. Eaton Company, Limited, 1953.
2. Meagher, John W., "A Projected Plan for the Re-organization of Physical Education Teacher-Training Programs in Canada." Unpublished Doctor's thesis, The Pennsylvania State University, 1958.
3. ———, "The Status of Degree Graduates of Four Canadian Schools of Physical Education." Unpublished Master's thesis, The Pennsylvania State University, 1953.

Calendars, 1962-63:

1. Laval University.
2. McGill University School of Physical Education.
3. McMaster University Faculty of Arts and Science.
4. Queen's University Faculty of Arts and Science.
5. University of Alberta School of Physical Education.
6. University of British Columbia.
7. University of Montreal.
8. University of New Brunswick.
9. University of Ottawa Faculty of Arts.
10. University of Saskatchewan School of Physical Education.
11. University of Toronto School of Physical and Health Education.
12. University of Western Ontario Faculty of Arts and Science.

TEACHING METHODS 7

Lorne E. Brown

Associate Professor, College of Education
University of British Columbia, Vancouver

"Creative teaching must always present the child with a challenge. We must give our children the opportunity to do daring and challenging things. There is error in attempting to remove all elements of danger from our activities. The child must be given the opportunity to assume risk."

Golden Romney

WHAT ARE METHODS, TECHNIQUES, DEVICES?

These terms are often used interchangeably, so for purposes of clarity and better understanding it is important that they be defined more specifically.

Method can be interpreted as a relationship established by an institution with a body of participants for the purpose of diffusing knowledge, developing attitudes, and acquiring skills.

Technique can be interpreted as the ways and means of teaching skills, developing attitudes and diffusing knowledge.

Devices will include the use of visual aids, music, films, bulletin boards, and any other kind of environmental influence used in teaching.

As can be seen from the above the usual definition of *method* can now be referred to as *technique,* and *method* will always be used in terms of relationships. Actually the methods used traditionally in physical education can be summarized as follows:

1. The group method has been used almost without exception. Classes have been

formed administratively, either homogeneously or heterogenously, and are taught by a teacher with a certain body of content and material to be learned by the group within a certain prescribed time.

2. The amount of time has been decided upon and classes come regularly to take part.

3. Facilities and equipment are approved and made available.

For reasons that will become clearer as this chapter is developed the major discussion will center on methods as defined above. Not too much mention is made of techniques and devices because of the way "methodology" is developed.

What is meant by the terms "Child-centered program" and "program-centered program"? All across Canada there is every indication that changes are taking place in the teaching of physical education. Terms such as "formal," "informal," "traditional," "progressive," "teacher-dominated," "child-centered," "the "English method," all are used to point out that significant changes are gradually evolving, especially at the primary and lower elementary grade levels. It can also be added that greater changes have occurred in the girls' program than the boys'. Changes are also suggested in the general inclusion of circuit training, weight training, 5BX and isometric exercises, in the program at the high school and university levels. This has come about, in part at least, as the result of recent research in physical medicine and physical education, and the dissatisfaction that is found in many places with the old practices. A good deal is being claimed today about the value of sports and athletics in combating some of today's social problems. To some, an improvement in physical fitness seems to be the panacea for many of the ailments of man and his deviations from normal health. There is a restlessness and a genuine desire on the part of many professional educators to improve and justify more than ever the activity program.

One of the most significant changes taking place is the child-centered program, especially at the elementary grade levels. In order to avoid confusion, all the implications of the terms "informal," "progressive," "English method," "non-directive," will be included in the term "child-centered" method of teaching physical education. Terms such as "teacher-dominated," "traditional," "directive," will all be included in the general classification of "program centered."

Therefore, for purposes of this chapter only two types of method will be referred to: *child-centered* and *program-centered*.

Before getting into a more detailed discussion of the implication of methodology in the light of the definitions given, it might be well to suggest that perhaps there are a number of things that could be done to improve the physical education methods at all levels, keeping in mind that methods are a matter of relationships.

1. *Class sizes could be reduced so that more individual learning could take place.* If one accepts the notion that the child-centered method is what is wanted, then a greater individual contact with each student through direct observation is essential.
2. *In professional preparation of physical education teachers, greater emphasis could be placed on the understanding of the principles of growth and development.* The child-centered method of teaching physical education entails much more than competency in physical skills and an exposure to a prescribed curriculum. It means that teachers in training should come away from their professional courses in physical education with a deeper appreciation of the place of physical activity in the total development of the child, and with a willingness to develop this approach in their own teaching.
3. *Eliminate the present concept of what constitutes adequate physical education facilities.* In the child-centered approach to the teaching of physical education, it is necessary to plan quite differently for the facilities and the equipment required for the program. The present pattern of the facilities dictates one teaching station per class—usually a gymnasium, whose size is determined by the size of the basketball court, the number of badminton courts, and the provision of spectator space. A playground area for the playing of a team sport such as soccer is another necessity. The facilities are concentrated upon the program-centered method, with the teacher in direct contact with the whole class during the entire period. This, of course, is contrary to the child-centered method, and requires drastic changes in the planning of physical education facilities. A few brief suggestions are offered here.

   a. More multiple-use areas planned as part of the facilities: hard-top areas and turfed fields immediately adjacent to the gymnasium so that classes could be broken up and perform several activities at the same time.
   b. Plan for smaller areas for individual and small group activities related to fitness testing, recreational, corrective, and remedial work.
   c. An "applied health" room connected to the main physical education facilities where classes and individuals can see and study the other forms of physical activities which cannot be included in the activity program in school. This is where a health museum with models, charts, visual aid equipment, and reference materials could be found. Here is where discussions could be held on the health implications of exercise and could be carried on as part of the regular physical education lesson. Films on outdoor activities such as fishing, camping, sailing, mountain climbing could be shown.
   d. Plan playground area on a much more varied basis than is usually found at present.
   e. Include swimming pools as part of the physical education facilities.
   f. More equipment provided like the Crofton, Cave-Southampton, and similar agility and climbing apparatus as part of all facilities for elementary schools.

TEACHING METHODS AND PHILOSOPHY

Even more important than the mechanical aspects of methodology in the child-centered approach to teaching physical education is the actual contact with the child.

If one accepts the notion that method is a matter of something more than the mere traditional relationship of teacher and "taught," then it is clear that change and re-evaluation of what has been done in the past is essential. The following concepts may help to upgrade and justify the program. They could well be the foundation on which a modern physical education program with realistic educational objectives could be built.

The individual child within the group is the only important focus of the program. Every part of the program must be justified in terms of the needs of the individual and his relationship to others. Since these needs will vary considerably this demands a wide variety of activities. They must be determined by close scrutiny of those taught, observation of the community, and an application of the principles that come from the fields of pediatrics and child psychology. The gap must be narrowed between what is known in child growth and development and what is practiced in the field. Many school systems promote inter-school competitions at the elementary grade levels. Does this type of practice coincide with the findings of other disciplines such as medicine, anthropology, sociology, psychology, in terms of the needs of the child and society? If not, adjustments must be made.

Every individual child, irrespective of heredity or environmental background, deserves equal attention and opportunity to participate, at his own level of ability and need. How often is the aggressive, skilled boy or girl allowed to dominate the equipment? How important is it to notice those who have withdrawn, or are uncomfortable in the demands made by the activity? What happens to these children as the years pass by? Possibly nothing but dislike for physical education and a strong determination to avoid activity as much as possible.

Physical education should be more a part of the concept of total or optimal health of the individual. Professionally and traditionally physical educators have included health education in their field of endeavor but have almost always given it a minor or secondary place. Health education has also been considered a responsibility of health departments of government, medical organizations, nursing and home economics groups. It has struggled to gain a rightful place for itself through many other disciplines and this has led to its having relatively low status, especially in physical education. Never has there been any clear understanding or acceptance of health education by schools or departments of physical education. Why has this been so?—perhaps because many have tended to make physical education an end in itself, in a context separate from the health of the individual. It may be that this was justified because health was thrust on the educational system as a "subject" dealing with many trivial health rules and with a factual content (the structure and functions of the human body) little related to actual behavior and attitudes. Its small appeal for children and teachers alike has resulted in its becoming in many respects a "hated" subject in schools. Criticism has come from many sources about the effectiveness and accuracy of the health education program. Little attention has been paid by teacher training institutions to preparing people to teach this "subject."

Although health education, in its modern concept, can stand on its own feet as a justifiable field of competency, physical educators have paid little attention to the health implications of the physical education program. Seldom have the effects of various physical activities been related to the actual health of the child. Generally all children have been expected to participate equally in any given activity. They have been asked to take part in a strenuous period with little thought given to whether they have had adequate nutrition, or are rested, or are recovering from some minor illness. Often inadequate provision is made for showering and changing clothes for the physical education lesson. Whole classes may be given a common assignment such as running a long-distance run, "lapping" the gym a given number of times, doing a set number of push-ups, with little consideration given to individual differences, or environmental influences.

It is not the purpose of this chapter to enlarge on this point except to suggest that if method is part of a relationship, then it is important to move toward a recognition of the total child in relation to activity, and come more to recognize the inadequacies of the program-centered approach in teaching physical education. If physical education is part of the concept of the total man, then its health implications must be recognized and applied more than they have been in the past.

If these two points are accepted then it follows that the child-centered concept could well become the essential approach to the methodology of teaching physical education. This in no way suggests that no good has accrued from the program-centered approach. It is simply a matter of realizing that no method is perfect, and that experimentation is necessary for progress. From the present perspective it seems that the child-centered method should produce a better result than the program-centered approach.

A re-evaluation of the objectives and a courageous and drastic change in techniques is demanded. No longer can the traditional attitude be held of the program as merely a break from the inactivity of the classroom, where the physically literate get most of the attention. Activities must be selected with thought and understanding. Should calisthenics be taught? Why? Are team games desirable or even good for children? What values come from these activities and do teachers teach for these values? Is sportsmanship a natural outcome of team competition or must it be planned for? So often the assertion is made that boxing develops courage, contact sports toughen boys, gymnastics increases self-confidence. On what basis are these assertions made? The behavior of teams after games, the attitudes of spectators at games and tournaments often leaves much to be desired. Should there be a compromise with standards to win games? Rationalization is often to excuse lower standards. Is there really a code of sportsmanship?

Who are the people who sponsor Little League competition? Many undoubtedly are genuinely interested, give time, energy, and money, and have the very best of intentions. But can it always be said that these persons are fully aware of the problems that arise when immature boys are placed in highly emotional situations? Is it good enough to leave the development of attitudes toward games and sports to well-intentioned people who are not able to use these situations for desirable learning experiences? Perhaps educators must first set their own program in order and then assist all those who are engaged in the development of sports and games in communities, by organizing leadership training programs which will help them do a better job.

IMPLICATIONS OF THE CHILD-CENTERED METHOD IN TEACHING PHYSICAL EDUCATION

That teacher training institutions and professional schools of physical education must start now to prepare their graduates for a better under-standing of the child-centred method. Those same graduates must have the understanding and attitudes that will enable them to go before groups of young and old alike with confidence and enthusiasm to use this method at every suitable opportunity. This means the elimination of biases and prejudices for the traditional beliefs, the courage to experiment with new ideas even though there is often failure to reach the hoped-for goals. Children and teachers can learn through failure as well as success.

Many say that children are not ready for this approach to teaching physical education. This is probably true, but unless teachers take the initiative no one will ever know if it will work. There should be an honest effort to let children explore and experiment with equipment and apparatus. They should be encouraged to discover the best way for them to perform a game skill. A climate should be provided which is comfort-able so that whatever the students do will be looked upon as being worth while, because *they* did it. Any genuine effort, no matter how simple or trivial, must be commended at first, until the child realizes that he is not working in a situation where adult standards are going to be expected, but his own best effort recognized. This involves the whole matter of being able to work individually in a group, work with a part-ner, and also work with the whole group.

If this approach or method has not been attempted, there is no basis for saying it will not work. Of course, it cannot be foisted upon an older class which has been steeped in the traditional methods, and expected to work. Traditional groups must be exposed with great care to new-found freedom and opportunity. They will soon learn to respond and grow in the improved atmosphere.

The idea of giving responsibility to children, of having them make decisions, and providing the opportunity to be original is somewhat new and will be difficult, especially in the adult-dominated world where the child has been curtailed and directed by older people since birth. However, it is suggested that the child-centered concept is sound and is worthy of every effort at all levels of teaching physical education. This method also suggests that children should share in the planning of the program much more than they have done.

In continuing with the idea of the child-centered method it is interesting to look at the intellectual side of the present program to see where it stands in terms of the thinking process. The program-centered approach has been to demonstrate, explain, and have the child perform the exercise, stunt, or skill under teacher direction. The "correct" way to kick a ball is explained, the details of the gymnastic stunt are carefully taught and demonstrated by a skilled performer and the child does it exactly the same way and may even be marked and rated on his ability to reproduce the stunt. Undoubtedly there is value in this if the goal is to participate in a highly competitive game or gymnastics where standards are predetermined and the child strives to attain those standards. However, how can this be justified in a heterogeneous group of boys and girls in any typical physical education class?

Regardless of the type of method employed it seems highly doubtful that there has been enough stress on understanding the reasons for doing the activities. Do children know why they are required to exercise? Do they understand and appreciate the effect of exercise on the body? Do they relate the eating of a suitable meal to their ability to perform easily or effectively in the activity program, or any other program for that matter? In other words, has the use of the intellect been encouraged along with the activity? In what ways has the participant been expected to think while performing a skill, or even given the opportunity to create new ways of doing it? Perhaps teachers need to ponder the above questions and decide if they can improve methods of teaching physical education by expecting as much mental activity from the boy or girl in the gymnasium as in the classroom.

The following outline includes the main features of the two methods of teaching physical education as suggested in this chapter.

Program-centered method

1. Mainly teacher-directed approach.
   — formal
   — teacher is the focus of attention

2. The concept of "drill" inherited from the military maneuver.

3. Little use of small equipment and apparatus.

4. Formal commands used.

5. External discipline imposed.
   — passive obedience by pupils
   — lack of initiative by pupils
   — alert response

6. Not much provision for individual differences, if any.

7. Rigid class formations used.

8. Little chance to observe children as they really are.

9. Greater physical demands on the teacher.
   — more demonstrations
   — more participation by the teacher required in order to lead exercises and activities.

10. Children likely to be hampered through adult fears.
    — overemphasis on caution: "be careful now"
    — lack of adventure
    — "safety" achieved by restricting many activities.

Child-centered method

1. Mixture of teacher direction and pupil initiative and enterprise.
   — more scope for independence, exploration, and experimentation

2. Physical education based on what is known about child growth and development.

3. More abundant use of apparatus both large and small.

4. More use of natural voice.

5. Mixture of external and self-discipline.
   — stress on developing self-control
   — more scope for initiative and independence
   — alert response

6. Progressive stages of activities.
   — opportunities for each one to progress at his own rate and level.

7. Freer grouping—child develops a sense of spacing for himself and his apparatus without bothering others.

8. Pupils can be themselves, more natural.
   — teacher must be an astute observer to guide and help each child's development.
   — children can display and develop their own personality traits.

9. Less physical demands on the teacher.
   — more mental activity required by the teacher to plan, to observe and to give scope to pupil development.

10. Wider opportunity for activity.
    — more adventure
    — more challenge
    — less need for safety admonitions
    — greater skill at each one's level reduces need for stressing safety.

Program-centered method	*Child-centered method*
11. Physical development held back because of restrictions. —formal mass activities tend to pull skilled children down and discourage and frustrate unskilled children.	11. Promotes physical development of the class to the limit of each individual child. — more freedom for children to select their own activities with or without apparatus.
12. Teacher takes a prominent part in handling and placing apparatus.	12. Pupils arrange own apparatus. — learn to take things out and put them away. — learn to manage their own affairs as much as possible.

It must, of course, be added here that many of the learnings in the child-centered method can also be found in the program-centered approach with a good teacher. It can also be said that the child-centered program will fail in many respects in the hands of a teacher who is both unskilled and uninformed in the handling of children. It is suggested, however, that the child-centered method of teaching physical education can produce better results than have been produced in the past.

Here are two examples which will in some way show the practical application of the child-centered method of teaching physical education. The first outlines a number of gymnastic tasks or challenges which are given to any class, and the second presents an introductory lesson on soccer.

GYMNASTIC TASKS OR CHALLENGES[1]

General challenge: Find different ways of balancing

(Teacher's suggestion: Can you balance on your knees, shoulders, one hand, and one foot?)

Suggestions for developing the general challenge

1. (a) Select two of the balance positions and practice them until you can hold them steady.
   (b) Find a way of moving from the first balance position to the second and back to the first.
   (c) Practice this sequence of movement.
   (d) Using the same two balance positions find a different way of moving from the first balance position to the second and back to the first.

(Teacher's suggestion: Can you make the change by rolling or twisting?)
   (e) Practice this sequence of movement.
   (f) Combine these two movement sequences (b, d) in any order you like.

---

[1] Prepared by Miss Shirely Nalevykin, Miss Anne Tilley, Miss A. L. Meredith, British Columbia Faculty of Education, University of British Columbia.

2. (a) Find different ways of balancing on your hands.

(Teacher's suggestion: Can you balance in a curled position, horizontally extended position, vertically extended position?)

(b) Select and practice one of these balance positions.

(c) Find different ways of transferring your weight back to your feet.

(Teacher's suggestion: Can you roll, turn?)

N.B. The teacher can suggest other parts of the body as a basis for similar movement sequences.

3. (a) Choose a way of supporting the weight of your body and then find different body positions while balancing.

(Teacher's suggestion: Can you find an extended, curled, or twisted position? Can you show a symmetrical or asymmetrical position?)

(b) Select two of these positions and find a way of changing from one to the other.

(c) Working with a partner make a movement sequence by combining, adapting, or integrating the balance positions you have just practiced.

(Teacher's suggestion: Can you work in unison with or in opposition to your partner?)

INTRODUCTORY LESSON TO A GAME OF SOCCER[2]

I Aim Exploration of ball control techniques with the feet.

II Equipment and Facility

(a) An outdoor lesson; suitable field space; no goals required.

(b) Balls; soccer and playground, as many as possible (see N.I).

III Teaching Points (see N.2)

(a) Dribbling: use of the inside and outside edges of the foot; keeping the ball close to the foot for control.

(b) Passing: use of the inside and outside of the foot; speed of the pass suitable for a controlled reception; value of a rolling pass— keep ball on the ground.

IV Introductory Activity (on the field) (see N.3)

Question 1. (a) How many have played or have seen soccer played? (see N.4)

(b) What are some of the things players do in a game of soccer? (run, kick, shoot, head, block)

(c) Which one do you think occurs most often? (desired response: running)

Activity 1. (Exploration)

To run a designated distance, e.g. around the field.

Question 2. (a) Is that the way you are likely to run during a soccer game?

(b) You say "No." All right then, how would you run? What would you do that is different? (desired response: stop and start, changing speed, change direction)

---

2 Prepared by Norman Watt and Reid Mitchell, Faculty of Education, University of British Columbia.

Activity 2 (Exploration)

> To run at random using changes of speed and direction of their own choice.

V Development

Activity 3 (Exploration with a ball)

> To execute maneuvers similar to Activity 2 with each student or pair using a ball (see N.5).

Question   3. (a) Which part of the foot did you use to move the ball? (desired response: toe, instep, inside edge, outside edge)

(b) Which part do you think would be the best way to move and control the ball? Why? (Desired responses: inside and outside edges of the foot; they are broad flat areas that allow for better control. The inside is useful when passing the ball from one foot to the other, which is dribbling. The outside edge of the foot is good for changing direction while dribbling.)

Activity 4 (Exploration) (see N.6)

> To practice further maneuvering with the ball, concentrating on the use of the inside and outside of the foot.

Question   4. (a) In a game of soccer, what is it that prevents you from having the freedom to move the ball about as you have been practising? (desired response: an opponent who is trying to take the ball away)

Activity 5 (Competition—"1 on 1 drill") (see N.7)

> To work in pairs with one ball so that students take turns trying to dribble past one another.

Question   5. (a) What are the important things to keep in mind when you want to dribble past an opponent? (desired response: keep the ball close, advance slowly, fake, change pace)

Activity 6 (Competition—"1 on 1 keep-away")

> To repeat Activity 5 introducing the continuous effect of "1 on 1 keep-away," where the player immediately tries to regain possession of the ball when it is lost.

Question   6. (see N.8)

(a) Is there another way to get the ball past an opponent and keep the ball in your team's possession?
(desired response: passing)

(b) Before you try passing to a partner can you suggest ways of passing to a partner keeping in mind what you have discovered so far about ball control?
(desired response: use of the edge of the foot; rolling rather than bouncing the ball; speed and direction of the pass suitable for controlled reception)

Activity 7 (Co-operation—"passing in pairs")

> Two students working with one ball, select an area of the field within which to practice stationary and short range passing maneuvers.

Activity 8 (co-operation and competion)

> Since we have discovered from our dribbling practice that the presence of an opponent adds difficulty to the performance of a skill, let us now try to pass the ball with a partner past an opponent.
>
> (a) ("2 on 1")
>
>> One player takes a position approximately 15 feet from the other two players who act as partners and will attempt to advance the ball past the single defender by dribbling and passing. The single and partner players should interchange frequently.
>
> (b) ("2 on 2 keep-away") (see N.8)
>
>> This is similar play to Activity 6 except that players work in partnership.

Activity 9 (Application of Learned Skills)

> Team Game ("3 pass keep-away")
>
> The class is divided into two equal teams. A defined area similar in size to one half of a soccer pitch is advisable. The objective of this game is for a team to successfully pass the ball three times without the opposition touching it. Any contact with the ball by the opposing team nullifies the passes of the team in control at the time.
>
> Scoring: 1 point is scored for the team completing a series of three successive passes.
>
> The game is started by the instructor dropping or throwing the ball anywhere on the field of play. Continuation of play from out of bounds or scoring situation can be handled in a similar manner. (see N. 9)

SPECIAL CONSIDERATIONS FOR THE SOCCER LESSON

N.1. Soccer balls should be used if possible. However, at this stage of skill development it is probably more important to have a ball for each student in the class. The type ball is not of great importance—play balls, rhythm balls, old volleyballs, softballs or even tennis balls could be used. If there is a shortage of balls then one ball between two pupils would be satisfactory.

N.2. There are many other teaching points involved in dribbling and passing. Again, for an introductory lesson only two or three basic techniques need be emphasized. The other features of these skills could be brought out in subsequent lessons.

N.3. The free practice period is an important part of each lesson. For this type of outdoor lesson it may be limited by the local class organization, e.g. the class may move freely from locker-room to field or pupils may be moved as a class. In the former situation the balls should be made available for a free practice, in the latter the instructor may want to start the period immediately on arrival at the field.

N.4. The success of this initial question obviously depends on the experience of the pupils. In situations where the class had little or no experience with the game it is recommended that a film on soccer be shown before the introductory lesson is given.

N.5. In the individuals exploration phase of this lesson it is important that each pupil be allowed to work on his own. This shows the importance of having a ball for each one. If this is not possible individual exploration is still recommended even if one or two have to wait for their turn.

N.6. More time should be given for individual exploration during this part of the lesson. Because both the instructor and the pupils have contributed their ideas on how the skill can best be performed, an appreciable amount of time should be allowed for practice.

N.7. This activity should be somewhat structured in that the defending player should stand at least fifteen feet away from the person with the ball. This allows sufficient space for the dribbler to start moving before the defender moves to intercept the ball.

N.8. Keep-away can be a strenuous activity. It may be desirable to have a rest period when a review could be made of the points covered, and perhaps introduce such things as the number and position of players.

N.9. This game can be further refined by counting only those passes which are deliberate. This eliminates "fluke" touches or passes by a team and gives greater emphasis to the passing skill. It is futher suggested that this game could be used as a warm-up or introductory activity for the next period. By doing this you are engaging in a game-like review of previously practiced skills. It also provides an opportunity to bring out new skills to be covered in later lessons—tackling, trapping, and team-play.

The two specific lessons just cited are examples of a suggested approach to the teaching of physical education and incorporate the principles found in the child-centered method. No further elaboration is possible in a general text of this kind, but these examples should be enough to illustrate some of the main features of the child-centered method outlined previously in this chapter.

CONCLUSION

It is the sincere hope of the author that the spirit of the foregoing will in some degree be caught by the reader and will perhaps result in a courageous re-appraisal of the methods used in the present physical education program in schools and elsewhere; and that out of this re-appraisal will come methodology which will be so attractive and meaningful to all those taking part that physical education will be raised to new heights of acceptance and will take its equal place with all other areas of the curriculum. If this chapter accomplishes such re-appraisal then it will have been very worth while.

The following quotation is most suitable to close this chapter on methods in physical education:

"Movement is not simply an affair of strong muscle, supple joints, but, part and parcel of personality."

"Movement may be both a means towards, and a reflection of, maturity."

BIBLIOGRAPHY

1. Andrews, Gladys, Jeannette Sauborn, and Elsa Schneider, *"Physical Education for To-day's Boys and Girls."* Boston: Allyn and Bacon, Inc., 1960.
2. Billrough, A., and P. Jones, *"Physical Education in the Primary School."* University of London Press, Ltd., 1963.
3. Caillois, Roger, *Man, Play and Games.* New York: Free Press of Glencoe, Inc., 1961.
4. Curtiss, Louise M., and A. B. Curtiss, *Physical Education for Elementary Schools.* Milwaukee: Bruce Publishing Co., 1957.
5. Davis, Elwood C., and E. L. Wallis, *Toward Better Teaching in Physical Education,* Englewood Cliffs, N.J.: Prentice-Hall Inc., 1961.
6. Knapp, Clyde, and E. P. Hagman, *Teaching Methods for Physical Education.* New York: McGraw-Hill Book Company, 1953.
7. Kozmon, H. C., R. Cassidy, and C. O. Jackson, *Methods in Physical Education.* Philadelphia: W. B. Saunders Co., 1958.
8. Miller, A. G., and V. Whitcomb, *Physical Education in the Elementary Curriculum.* Englewood Cliffs, N.J.: Prentice-Hall Inc., 1959.
9. Murray, Ruth L. and Delia P. Hussey, *From Student to Teacher in Physical Education.* Englewood Cliffs, N.J.: Prentice-Hall Inc., 1959.
10. Ontario Department of Education, *Junior Division Physical Education.* Toronto: Canadian Association for Health, Physical Education and Recreation, 1960.
11. *Physical Education in the Primary School,* Part 1: "Moving and Growing." London: Her Majesty's Stationery Office, 1952.
12. *Physical Education in the Primary School,* Part 2: "Planning the Programme." London: Her Majesty's Stationery Office, 1953.
13. Randall, M. W., and W. K. Kaine, *Objectives of the Physical Education Lesson.* London: G. Bell & Sons, Ltd., 1960.
14. Sehon, E. L., *et al., Physical Education Methods for the Elementary Schools.* Philadelphia: W. B. Saunders Co., 1955.
15. Smithells, Philip A., and Peter E. Cameron, *Principles of Evaluation in Physical Education.* New York: Harper and Brothers, 1962.
16. Vannier, M. H., and Mildred Foster, *Teaching Physical Education in the Elementary Schools.* Philadelphia: W. B. Saunders Co. ,1959.

Hugh A. Noble

*Provincial Director
Physical Education and Recreation
Province of Nova Scotia*

THROUGH THE Y.M.C.A.

Canada possesses a long tradition of an active interest in those vigorous activities of sport which, in themselves, contribute to the physical development of the participant.

Physical education, however, was first cradled in Canada through the Y.M.C.A., and to a lesser degree the Y.W.C.A. These two organizations, along with a few notable athletic clubs, such as the Wanderers Athletic Club of Halifax and various Highland Societies, were the first agencies to take an active interest in the physical development of the youth of Canada.

The Y.M.C.A., in particular, blazed the trail by opening up community centers in many of the larger towns and cities just prior to, and immediately following, the First World War. Many who received their first training at the "Y," or at the Athletic Club, are now among the leading physical educators of the present day.

It would appear that one of the greatest contributions of the Y.M.C.A. has been trained leadership. The Y.M.C.A. Training College at Springfield, Massachusetts, sent into the provinces of Canada a number of men who have left an indelible mark upon the life of their times. These men were stalwarts, not only physically, but also mentally and spiritually. They imparted their high standards and horizons of sportsmanship and achievement to succeeding generations.

In later years, as physical education gradually became part of the school program, the Y.M.C.A. and the Y.W.C.A. turned their attention to the field of recreation, and set an equally high standard in that area. Along with this service of recreation, they also developed camping to a high degree and have made it easier for those who would follow them in this field of outdoor education.

Now that the responsibility for recreation is being assumed more and more by individual communities, a further pioneering venture is engaging the attention of these two social agencies. They are now directing their energies into the field of group work among the students of high school age. It is certain that they will continue to lead the way along paths on which the coming generation will tread, and find the best road carefully marked.

Almost from the beginning, in the Maritimes, practically every town and city had its club that sponsored sports of all kinds, and at the same time, provided facilities for its members. Some excellent playing fields and running tracks, some still in use today, were built at the turn of the present century.

These clubs played the game for the game's sake; they not only promoted a high degree of fitness on the part of those who trained faithfully, for the sheer joy of achievement, but rendered good entertainment for their supporters as well. The loyalty of communities to their teams was a binding force uniting the people. It is perhaps regrettable that there is not the same degree of unanimity behind the important "greats" of the present day.

Paralleling the promotion of physical education through the Y.M.C.A., Y.W.C.A., and the athletic clubs of the country, an effort was made at the various provincial normal colleges to introduce a course for teachers in training. These courses received their impetus from the Trust Fund established by Lord Strathcona.

During the years from 1908 to 1940 the graduates of the provincal normal colleges, most of whom taught in elementary schools, tried to carry out a physical training program based on the British Syllabus, insofar as facilities and inadequate equipment would allow. This program, taught by the class teacher, was successful only in proportion to the interest and enthusiasm of the individual teacher. The drill lessons were relatively easy to conduct, and were performed more or less as a break from the regular classroom routine. The only physical education program carried out at the secondary school level during this period was the program of games played by the representative school teams. The lack of facilties and staff time did not permit a wider program of intramural activities.

One can readily gather from the foregoing that physical education in Canada has been markedly influenced by two main sources. It is difficult to say which of these came first or which has had the more profound effect.

UNITED STATES INFLUENCE

In any case, it must be recognized that Canada has been, is, and will continue to be influenced in the development of its physical education program by American developments. This is particularly true up to date because of the number of Canadians who have received professional training in American colleges and universities. Many of these men and women have returned to Canada to assume responsible positions as leaders in universities and other teacher training institutions.

Thus the influence of the American-trained educator is felt from coast to coast in Canada. The Americans are noted for their interest and proficiency in skill training associated with sports and their desire to test and measure physical performance and efficiency. As a result of this interest on the part of the American physical educator, Canadian programs, particularly at the secondary school level, have leaned rather heavily toward sports.

Gymnastics, in the traditional sense has enjoyed spotty popularity based in some degree on the ethnic background of training of the teacher. Ethnic groups, which have immigrated to Canada, have enriched the culture particularly in the area of folk dancing, and to a lesser degree by introducing their respective national games and customs to the communities in which they reside.

THE UNITED KINGDOM

It is evident that the British Syllabus of Physical Training must be considered another major influence, particularly at the elementary school level.

The Board of Education Syllabus of Physical Training, 1933, met with an enthusiastic response from the teachers throughout the United Kingdom. The syllabus, although based on the Swedish system, was carefully adopted to meet the requirements of the Canadian national character, climate, and facilities. This syllabus showed a steady advance in technique from the rather rigid course of 1904, and even from the broader course of 1919.

Brief mention should also be made of the influence of Niels Bukh, of

Denmark, on physical education in England at this time. Bukh visited England in 1927, bringing with him a gymnastic team of girls and boys, whose approach to gymnastics was far more rhythmical than the established pattern of the Swedes. In Sweden, however, at this same time, an effort was being made by Elin Falk to make exercises more appealing aesthetically, without losing any of the physiological benefits.

Niels Bukh had a profound effect on gymnastics for men, and it was not many years before the rhythmical approach to exercises, or calisthenics, was commonly accepted by men in Canada.

The British Syllabus of 1933 served as the basic course for physical training in most, if not all, teacher training institutions in Canada up until very recent times. The valuable contribution this syllabus has played in the development of physical education is well recognized throughout Canada. The book is often referred to today by teachers throughout the land and is acclaimed as an excellent volume of reference material.

Probably the most recent trend in program content might also be considered significant as a direct influence from the United Kingdom. To this end a brief description of physical education in the United Kingdom might be in order. The outbreak of World War II brought any significant advances in physical education at the secondary level almost to a standstill. It was inevitable that staffing difficulties, during this period, should result in lowering of standards, particularly on the boys' side in the secondary schools.

It is also interesting to note that, while the work at the secondary level was restricted during these war years, and despite the upheaval caused by so many children being moved out of the target areas, some new approaches to physical education were taking place in a good many junior schools in different parts of the country.

Specially designed, and often improvised apparatus captured the interest and imagination of the children and their teachers. One might, in a conservative way, say that this equipment resembled very realistically the type of apparatus used in training the service personnel on the obstacle and other similar courses. The objectives were obviously not the same, but this type of experience did much to enrich the children's training in physical activities. The result was a greater development of strength, agility, and co-ordination in keeping with the maximum potential of the individual. Many consider this to be one of the most significant forward steps taken in physical education in the United Kingdom.

The above reference to physical education "holding the line" during the war years refers particularly to the work for boys. Although the girls' program was also affected by a depletion of trained staff, this was not as serious as it was in boys' schools. Here again, despite the upsets of war, the program for girls continued to expand and many innovations of that period remain as a challenge and inspiration for the girls' secondary schools today.

The war years brought about not only changes in legislation affecting physical education (section 53, Education Act, 1944), but also some creative thinking on the fundamental principles of physical education as well. New experiments were tried out in different parts of the country, particularly with apparatus at the primary school level. The end of the war found many communities and areas promoting various types of climbing and moveable apparatus. The communities of Essex and Bristol must be regarded as among the first pioneers in these experiments. Other areas, such as Halifax, Manchester, and Southampton, however, promoted special apparatus of their own.

The basic principle behind the introduction of this new type of apparatus was in keeping with the newer educational philosophy of the rights of the individual and, at the same time, satisfied the basic physical needs of children for individual and free experimentation in climbing and balancing skills.

To the women must go the credit for the expansion in physical education during the years of war, and indeed, during the post-war years as well. They not only pioneered in the field of primary physical education, but also realized that basic movement was the foundation of all activities (for all ages) in physical education.

Here again the objectives of the child-centered curriculum were very much in the minds of those responsible for the development of this more creative approach to physical education. The accepted philosophy, that emotions should be expressed in a constructive and satisfying manner, rather than repressed, challenged the women to abandon the more formal and rigid approach to physical education; and to seek ways and means by which the activities would be more meaningful and helpful to the individual.

It was perhaps logical that the dance, which has always been a basic form of art should present an excellent medium through which the individual could learn to discipline his feelings and, at the same time, share in a real emotional experience. The dance then took on more significance in the physical education program, particularly with secondary school girls. The women, however, did not confine their knowledge of and enthusiasm for movement merely to the dance. If movement was fundamental to all activities, then it was fundamental to gymnastics. As the pattern of freedom was more and more developed at the primary stage, so did gymnastics for secondary school girls become less formal and more free. In this newer approach to gymnastics, the girls found an opportunity for self-discovery and self-expression, and at the same time, maintained and in most cases improved their high standard of efficiency in the skills involved.

It would seem that the purpose of the Education Act has been to give all children the broadest possible education in learning and living so that at whatever age they might leave school, they would be equipped to meet the demands of society, earn a living and realize the possible scope of their own potentialities. Education, rather than instruction, has been the keynote throughout.

The quality of this phase of the work is extremely high. The approach to basic movement or movement in education introduced into the United Kingdom by Rudolph Laban and primarily designed to assist those who were concerned with the dance, has nevertheless had its influence on gymnastics.

Many teachers have recognized that movement as a means of education is concerned with the blending of individual freedom and discipline. Through movement the initiative of the individual is expressed within the framework of a given formation or pattern, at the same time that the individual must work co-operatively with others.

It is perhaps in the field of gymnastics that the women have made the most outstanding advances. Gymnastics has long been regarded in England as fundamental to any physical education program for girls. The passage of time and the introduction of games and the dance has not in any way lessened the importance of gymnastics.

In summary, the boys' secondary school program is trying to meet the challenge of modern educational philosophy. The program for girls is coming even closer to meeting the objectives of a modern physical education program. The girls have a wider and more comprehensive selection of activities and the relationship between teacher and pupil is at its best.

The secondary schools, for the most part, are blessed with an abundance of well-equipped and well-cared-for playing fields. One cannot help but be impressed by the great heritage which England has given to the world of sport through its love of games. Such a tradition, which has motivated the philosophy of "playing the game for the game's sake," is continually being cherished, fostered, and nurtured by the men and women teachers of physical education.

Since World War II, many teachers from the United Kingdom have moved to Canada. They have brought with them a fundamental interest in the child and in education. They have been critical of Canada's lack of interest in physical education and yet they have been most helpful in their desire to adjust and assist in the development of physical education in all parts of the nation.

SUMMARY

The Y.M.C.A., the Athletic Clubs, the Army, various ethnic groups, the British Syllabi of Physical Training, the post-war program of the United Kingdom, and the closeness of the United States, all have had a marked influence on the development of physical education in Canada.

Canada's program has also been influenced by the growth of international competitions in almost every form of sport and athletics.

It is obvious that young athletes have improved and refined their skills as they have tested their abilities against more-seasoned opponents from around the world. This improvement in performance, the tendency to overemphasize coaching skills at an early age, and the vast publicity given to the skilled athlete have been at the same time assets/and liabilities.

The principles of fair play and good sportsmanship, and the opportunity for the individual to grow in strength, personality, and character, through games, gymnastics, dance, and the many avenues of outdoor education should be obvious in a good physical education program. These principles, and the degree to which they are being accomplished, are a reflection on all those working in the field of physical education. This is a heritage from the United Kingdom and the United States which Canada will forever cherish.

BIBLIOGRAPHY

1. Ainsworth, Dorothy, *History of Physical Education in Colleges for Women.* New York: A. S. Barnes & Co., 1930.
2. Binfield, R. D., *The Story of the Olympic Games.* London: Oxford University Press, 1948.
3. Bryant, Rachel, "World Trends in Physical Education," *Journal of the American Association for Health, Physical Education, and Recreation,* XXI December, 1950), 32.
4. Darwin, Bernard, *British Sports and Games.* London: Longmans, Green & Company, Ltd., 1940.
5. Forsythe, Charles E., *The Administration of High School Athletics.* Englewood Cliffs, N.J.: Prentice-Hall, Inc., 1948.
6. Griffin, F. W. W., *The Scientific Basis of Physical Education.* London: Oxford University Press, 1937.
7. Henry, William, *An Approved History of the Olympic Games.* New York: G. P. Putnam's Sons, 1948.

8. Kandel, I. L., (ed), *Educational Yearbook of the International Institute of Teachers' Colleges*. New York: Teachers' College, Columbia University Press, 1940-44.

9. Knapp, Maud L., and Frances Todd, *Democratic Leadership in Physical Education*. Millbrae, Calif.: The National Press, 1952.

10. Krout, J. L., *Annals of American Sport*. New Haven, Conn.: Yale University Press, 1929.

11. Leonard, Fred E., and G. B. Afflect, *A Guide to the History of Physical Education*. Philadelphia: Lea & Febiger, 1947.

12. McCloy, C. H., "Physical Education Around the World, What We Can Learn from Other Nations?" *Journal of Physical Education*, XLV (November, 1947), 28.

13. ———, "The Pan-American Institute of Physical Education," *Journal of the American Association For Health, Physical Education, and Recreation*, XXII (March, 1951), 30-31.

14. Ministry of Education, *A Guide to the Educational System of England and Wales*. London: His Majesty's Stationery Office, 1945.

15. Murray, William D., *The History of the Boy Scouts of America*. New York: Boy Scouts of America, 1937.

16. Oberteuffer, Delbert, *Physical Education*. New York: Harper and Brothers, 1951.

17. Plewes, Doris W., "Affiliated Organizations v. The Canadian Physical Education Association," *Journal of Health and Physical Education*, XVII (May, 1946), 273.

18. Rice, Emmett A., and John L. Hutchinson, *A Brief History of Physical Education*. New York: A. S. Barnes and Co., 1952.

19. Schwedener, Norma, *A History of Physical Education in the United States*. New York: A. S. Barnes & Co., 1942.

20. Scott, Harry A., *Competitive Sports in Schools and Colleges*. New York: Harper and Brothers, 1951.

21. Shann, F., *Canberra System of School Athletics*. Melbourne: University Press, 1948.

22. Lester Smith, W. C., *Compulsory Education in England, Studies on Compulsory Education*, UNESCO, 1951: "To Whom Do Schools Belong?" London, 1945.

23. Stumf, Florence, and Frederick W. Cozens, "Some Aspects of the Role of Games, Sports and Recreational Activities in the Culture of Modern Primitive Peoples," *Research Quarterly*, XVIII (October, 1947), 198-218.

24. Valentine, P. E. (ed.), *Twentieth Century Education*. New York: Philosophical Library, Inc., 1946.

25. Von Szukovathy, I., "Some Notes on the History of Sport Bibliography," *Research Quarterly*, VIII (March, 1937), 3-14.

26. Walters, M. L., "The Physical Education Society of the Y.M.C.A.'s of North American," *Journal of Health and Physical Education*, XVIII (May, 1947), 311-312, 357-358.

27. Wuerfel, Theodore, "An International Laboratory," *Journal of Health and Physical Education*, II (November, 1931), 14.

Publications and Pamphlets
1. Ministry of Education, *A Guide to the Education System of England and Wales*, Pamphlet No. 2. London: Her Majesty's Stationery Office, 1955.

Reports:
1. National Association of Physical Education for College Women, *Report of International Congress of Girls and Women*. Washington D.C.: American Association For Health, Physical Education, and Recreation, 1949.
2. National Association of Physical Education for College Women, *Report of International Congress of Girls and Women*. Washington, D.C.: American Association For Health, Physical Education, and Recreation, 1950.
3. *Physical Education in the Schools Today and in the Future*. Scottish Joint Consultative Committee on Physical Education, 1954.
4. Report of the International Congress, *Physical Education, Recreation and Rehabilitation*. London: Ministry of Education, 1948.
5. *The Teaching Profession Today and Tommorrow*. Report by Oxford University, Muffield College, 1944.

9

Audrey M. Carson

Assistant Professor
Faculty of Physical Education
University of Alberta (Edmonton)

Jean M. Leiper

Assistant Professor
Department of Physical Education
University of Alberta (Calgary)

INTRODUCTION

Canada has, in a brief two hundred years, developed from a savage culture through a rural farm-oriented society to a modern urban society. The population has been mainly concerned with survival and assuring the future development of the country. The growth of cities and towns, first in the East and finally in the West, changed the pattern of living for all, but particularly for children. As leisure time increased in the urban setting, the opportunities for physical activity decreased. Open spaces, trees, and the natural environment disappeared for the urban population. A change took place in the rural areas as well. Mechanization had arrived. Some educators saw the need for physical education within the school program. As has been noted in other chapters, early programs and teacher training institutions relied upon men trained in the armed services to provide leadership, and therefore a formal calisthenic approach was in use at all levels. "Physical training" was the term appropriately used to describe the activities. The methods employed did not make any provision for individual differences or individual expression. Recess and noon-hour activities included games which were informally passed down from child to child. Perhaps the most important step prior to 1939 was the recognition that the development of the physical should be included in the school curriculum.

The advent of World War II and the testing programs following the War effected gradual changes in the elementary school program. Large numbers of young men were rejected as being unfit for service in World

War II. It was assumed that the rejects were physically unfit. Following the War, the results of the Kraus-Weber tests were cause for concern in Canada. It was assumed by many that the findings were a true measure of physical fitness and that the findings applied as well in Canada as in the United States. As a result, increased emphasis was given to fitness-centered activities. However, trends in the United States during this period helped to maintain a "play" and "games" approach.

CURRENT DEVELOPMENT IN ELEMENTARY SCHOOL PHYSICAL EDUCATION

In the past ten years, we have developed an approach to elementary school physical education that combines the best of the British and American systems. Ellen Reid in Montreal has developed a truly magnificent primary grades program; the Nova Scotia Department of Physical Education has done wonders with its rural schools program; New Brunswick has taken a leaf from the Ontario book and has adopted the Nora Chatwin and Junior Divisions program; Andy Martin of New Brunswick Teachers' College has won at least two awards from his "Playtime" school broadcasts; the West has kept pace as well with vital new comprehensive elementary school programs.[1]

Influences affecting elementary school physical education since World War II have been the natural population explosion along with large numbers of emigrants from Europe, increased urbanization, centralization of schools, automation and specialization, increased facilities, and a severe teacher shortage.

The population explosion experienced across Canada resulted in a tremendous building program. In a questionnaire circulated across the nation, all provinces indicated an increase in gymnasium facilities. Manitoba reports the building of 150 gymnasia in the past five years, Alberta 632, British Columbia states that all larger schools have gymnasia. Urbanization and centralization, however, have tended to increase the total number of classrooms in each school without increasing the number or size of gymnasium areas available. This has reduced the time available for each class for physical education. A gymnasium built to serve twelve classrooms is now serving sixteen to twenty. Administrators find it impossible to schedule more than two physical education periods per week per class in these situations. Outdoor programs could provide the necessary time needed to achieve the objectives of physical education, but weather conditions and the lack of guidance in the selection of suitable activities practically preclude this solution. The physical education pro-

---

[1] Meagher, "Our Successes," p. 34.

gram at this level normally consists of from one to three twenty- or thirty-minute periods per week.

Although increased population, urbanization, and centralization have seriously affected facilities and time allotment for physical education, most provinces have indicated that they are hoping to institute programs which make use of small individual equipment, climbing apparatus, and outdoor facilities. These factors should increase the total participation.

In all provinces the onus of time allotment for physical education seems to rest upon the local authorities or the school principals. Department of Education regulations only recommend minimum times.

Too frequently local administrators appear to disregard curricula developed by a professional committee. Students are required to take physical education at the junior and senior high school level and administrators must include physical education for all students for stipulated amounts of time at this level. With the wide variation of elementary schools it would appear that there still exists, at the local administrative level in many areas, a lack of understanding of the role of physical education in the total educational program at the elementary level. Physical educators and teacher training institutions are helping to increase the understanding of the values of physical education. Parents, within the past five years, have become very conscious of fitness through the 5BX and XBX programs. While this interest is strong, a program of public relations designed to educate the parents continues to be necessary. As parents and teachers alike become fully convinced of the value of physical education time allotment, facilities and equipment are likely to be provided by the authorities.

Organization and supervision of physical education at the local or the provincial level progresses very slowly. Only three provinces have provision for physical education at the provincial level and only two provinces have actual supervision at this level. Ontario, which is far in advance of other provinces, has a special curriculum superintendent in physical education with district inspectors in this field. Two of the inspectors are elementary specialists. In New Brunswick, physical education is under the guidance of the Adult Education and Fitness Branch which consists of a director and two supervisors. Nova Scotia employs a provincial supervisor of physical education. Saskatchewan has a Fitness and Recreation Division which employs a number of field supervisors whose responsibilities include assisting with physical education programs throughout the province. Physical educators in Manitoba will undoubtedly receive assistance from the Fitness and Amateur Sport Division of the Department of Welfare. The Recreation and Cultural Development Branch of the Department of the Provincial Secretary in Alberta has established an Athletics and Outdoor Education Division. Unfortunately, most of the aid provided in Manitoba, Saskatchewan, and Alberta is aimed at the secondary level. Across Canada, at the local level, some urban centers and a very few rural areas have supervisors or consultants. Within the schools themselves, very few resource teachers are available to co-ordinate a total program or to provide valuable in-service training.

The teaching profession, in this age of specialization, has experienced difficulties. The philosophy of physical education and the methods and materials employed require specialized training. However, as a result of the vastly increased population, a severe teacher shortage in all provinces has forced provincial authorities to shorten the period of training for teachers at all levels. Several provinces have not recovered from the shortage and still require only one year of training to teach in the elementary schools. The majority of teacher training institutions have included only one course in physical education. The one course varies from thirty to fifty hours of instruction, but in some instances philosophy, methods and materials specifically related to elementary schools are not included at all.

The typical elementary school teacher in the past has been the older married woman with one year of teacher preparation. The teacher shortage in the junior and senior high school has caused the administration to concentrate on training secondary school teachers, and this has resulted in the necessity of relying on married teachers in the community to staff the elementary schools.

More and more young men are being attracted to teaching at the elementary level and more and more men and women are remaining at the university to complete degrees in elementary school education. The professional attitude is bound to improve and with it will come an improvement in physical education. In-service training, which has existed on a hit-or-miss basis in most areas, is gradually improving. Convention programs are increasingly emphasizing the area of physical education. Special interest courses at the universities are being offered to improve the qualifications of experienced, competent teachers. Canadian, American, English, and German publications in the area of elementary school education, and physical education in particular, continue to improve and increase in number.

All but the most recent texts and publications from the United States have stressed the "play" or "games" approach exclusively. Canadian texts are virtually non-existent, and the majority of elementary school teacher-preparation courses across Canada makes use of American texts. Many departments of education outline the physical education curriculum and still list American books as primary references, with the recent inclusion of the Ontario Department of Education publications *Primary Division Physical Education* and *Junior Division Physical Education*.

The pressures brought to bear as a result of scientific advances, coupled with the teacher shortage, have made it difficult for universities and teacher training colleges to increase specialization in non-academic areas. Two universities now offer a major in elementary school physical education. The Faculty of Physical Education, University of Alberta, is the most recent, with a program put into effect in September 1963. Some provinces provide certification courses in this area. Several provinces are encouraging elementary teachers to take courses in physical education at summer sessions. These practices are likely to increase in the near future as the demand for specialists in physical education in the elementary schools increases.

RECENT DEVELOPMENTS The immigrants from Europe since World War II have tended to shape programs to some degree, but the large influx of teachers from England has probably exerted the greatest influence on elementary school physical education in Canada during the past eight years. Many Canadian physical educators were prompted to visit England and further explore the methods and activities employed. The British Empire and Commonwealth Games held in Cardiff in 1958 attracted many physical educators from Canada, who were given an opportunity to attend the Annual Conference of the British Association of Organizers and Lecturers in Physical Education. They returned to Canada convinced that the methods and activities demonstrated at the Conference were superior to either the formal approach or the games approach, both of which were then being used in Canada. The physical education program as witnessed by Canadians in Britain was influenced by the work of Rudolph Laban, who evolved a modern dance approach with its "own vocabulary and techniques applicable to the school child."[2] This vocabulary and technique were applied to movement and are now termed *movement* education.

> The emphasis in this work therefore is on each individual boy, developing daily at different rates and different ways, growing physically, maturing mentally, emotionally and socially. It is our duty to know, not only that there are basic similarities but that there also many fundamental differences between individuals, in physique, in ability and in attitude, and our work must be so planned that we can accommodate each individual to the full.
>
> With this in mind, the methods we employ should:
> (a) Provide opportunities for each boy to experience a real sense of achievement.

---

[2] Munro, *Pure and Applied Gymnastics*, p. 240.

(b) Appeal to all boys—such appeal being inherent in the activities performed and produced, and enjoyment a by-product of well planned, well chosen, well taught and well executed work, based on sound educational principles.

(c) Make the most of the potential ability of each boy. This applies equally to those not so gifted and the work must be planned to ensure that each boy is making the maximum progress of which he is capable.

(d) Develop in the boys a greater understanding, not only of what they are doing but also how they are doing it and so make them conscious of the many factors which influence all that they do.

(e) Provide opportunities for the boys to make positive contribution, mentally as well as physically, and to exercise the natural learning processes of enquiry, discovery and consolidation. To do this they must be allowed to explore, to experiment, to use their imagination and initative in many varied situations, and to be given the opportunity for the release and development of creative ability.

Can we say with real honesty that our more traditional methods accomplished all these aims? Surely, somewhere, sometime, and as often as possible, each boy must be given a chance to experience the thrill of doing something really well, and of satisfying not only us as teachers but himself also.

FEATURES OF THE WORK Amongst the more important features of a lesson taken on these lines are:

1. The activities themselves—which are based on the natural movements and activities such as running, jumping, climbing, hanging, heaving, rolling, stretching, twisting, etc.

2. Informality—which has replaced the regimentation of "drill".

3. A conversational teaching manner instead of the command-response type of instruction.

9. The use of varied methods of presentation.

5. The various methods of individual, group and class coaching.

6. The use of demonstration and observation as teaching aids.

7. A simple lesson plan which can be easily modified and adapted to the particular situation.

4. Free practice— practising in one's own time instead of in class unison.

8. The more varied use of portable and fixed apparatus.

9. The use of varied methods of presentation.

10. A realization by the teacher of the individuality of each member of the class.[3]

Some educators, prior to 1958, had been experimenting with movement education and the indirect approach to the teaching of elementary school physical education. The publication in Ontario of Nora Chatwin's book *Primary Division Physical Education* was the first real indication of a

---

[3] Jones, "Educational Gymnastics," p. 27.

change in emphasis. The book was adopted for experimental use in Ontario schools in 1956. This was followed in 1959 by *Junior Division Physical Education,* prepared by the Physical Education Branch of the Ontario Department of Education. Since that time, the Canadian Association for Health, Physical Education and Recreation has purchased the plates for these two books and made them available across Canada. Many provinces list these books as primary references and supply them to teachers, while others have adopted one or the other as the official curriculum. Alberta, as recently as May 1963, adopted *Junior Division Physical Education* as the curriculum for Grades IV, V, and VI. These books are designed to help the classroom teacher whose background does not include study in the methods and materials of the new approach to elementary school physical education.

Recently, physical educators across Canada were asked to comment on trends in elementary school physical education in relation to methods and course content. The following terms were repeated innumerable times: "child-centered," "individual activity," "non-directive," "problem-solving," "movement training." This would seem to indicate that the future of elementary school physical education in Canada is more secure presently than at any previous time. The elementary school physical education programs of the future are being planned to meet the needs of young Canadians.

A BASIC PROBLEM   Instruction in the elementary schools is a unique area of the physical education profession. High school and college programs are handled by trained physical educators, but the responsibility for program administration in the elementary schools is held largely by non-professionals—classroom teachers, principals, and school boards. This state of organization is the norm in Canada with the exception of a few advanced areas. The introduction of elementary physical education supervisors and specialist teachers is comparatively recent even in those more forward-looking sections of the country. The methods and program content of elementary physical education contrast vividly with those of the high school. The characteristics of younger children prevent the acquisition of highly developed skills and discourage the use of standard methods of teaching. Physical education teachers prefer to employ their training at more advanced levels than the elementary schools. Therefore the concern of the physical educator has been concentrated at the junior and senior high school level and the elementary schools have received little attention.

THE AIM OF EDUCATION   The fundamental aim of democratic education is the optimum development of the individual within his own pattern of growth. To achieve this purpose consideration must be given to all facets of the individual: mental, social, emotional, and physical. Education in the classroom is primarily geared to educating the student intellectually, with emotional and social learnings of secondary importance. Little opportunity is presented for physical growth of the child.

THE AIM OF PHYSICAL EDUCATION   Physical growth is the area of education where physical education becomes important. The development of the total individual which is begun in the classroom is extended to include physical growth when physical education enters the program.

Because the atmosphere of the gymnasium and playground, of sports, games, and dance is the world in miniature for the child, natural opportunities exist in the physical education class for experiencing situations which can lead to best learning. This suggests that physical skills learned in physical education are not only ends in themselves but also means through which the aim of education may be achieved. Therefore, the broad aim of physical education is identical with the aim of education.

THE OBJECTIVES OF PHYSICAL EDUCATION IN THE ELEMENTARY SCHOOL   It is an interesting observation that when lay critics of our school systems are searching for "frills" to throw out of the curriculum they often point a finger at physical education. This is curious when one considers the possible all-round developmental advantages of physical education to the child. It would appear that those involved in physical education instruction at all levels are failing to acquaint the general public with the relationship between objectives and course content or with concrete examples of the achievement of these objectives. The possibility exists that teachers do not note the success of their striving, being too much involved in the striving process. Every good instructor knows what he is attempting to achieve, but does he define his achievements with the same detail? The teacher *must* be able to explain with complete clarity concrete examples of the values accruing to the children when objectives are fulfilled.

At any specific level of instruction in the school system some objectives are emphasized more than others. In a system where trained personnel are operating at all levels and a complete progression is attained, each of the objectives will obtain its due emphasis somewhere in the progression, depending on the needs of the children of each age group. In the elementary school all objectives are considered in program and lesson planning but several are spotlighted with greater intensity.

The discussion of objectives which follows will make three points. Main objectives will be listed as they apply to all levels of physical education instruction. Comments will be made on the degree of emphasis placed on each objective in the elementary curriculum. Specific examples will be given of the value of each objective in the experience of a child or class.

1. To develop fundamental skills of movement. These skills are the racial skills of humanity—walking, running, climbing, throwing, rolling, jumping, twisting, swinging, bending, stretching, etc. These movements are the basis of the activities of daily life. Working life, recreational life, and home life require implementation of all of these skills to some degree.

The development of fundamental skills of movement should be the prime goal of physical education in grades I to VI. At this stage in physical growth the development of a great range of basic physical abilities is most desirable. A child's "vocabulary" of movement skills is important to his future abilities in games and sports. In the lower grades students are taught how to run with agility and control speed and direction, how to jump effectively and land safely and how to throw efficiently and catch securely. Much time is spent in encouraging the child to investigate how his body parts move in space, how to take his weight on various parts of his body, and how to work with various types of apparatus. A realization that all movement initiates a "feeling" which depends on the use made of time, space, and force factors is invaluable to future skill. Many ways of walking, leaping, curling, stretching, climbing, hanging, and skipping are explored. This gives each child a range of movement possibilities from which to choose when more specific skills are required later in his school life.

ILLUSTRATION #1   The concentration of the grade two class was complete. Oh, there was noise, not very loud, but a grunt of effort, an indrawn breath, an excited "I did it!" or the chatter of one child explaining to the other a discovery made. The problem on which they were all working was "shapes" and "spaces." One child made a shape with his body and the other was to discover all the methods he could of moving in and out, over and under and around the parts of the shape. It was definitely a problem requiring concentration. First, the "shape" had to think up a position that would leave lots of spaces and, also, had to be able to stay in the chosen position until the partner had finished moving around. Then, the performer had to try not to touch the shape. A little brush against a leg didn't really matter, but if the shape was touched very hard it might collapse.

At this point in the activity Mr. Donovan, the principal, entered the gym. He often came in while Miss Terry's grade two's had physical education. He appreciated the problems of movement on which they worked, and particularly enjoyed overhearing the comments the children made to Miss Terry.

"Miss Terry, Miss Terry—look at how I found to get under Sharon's leg. I rolled! That's easier than pulling with my arms."

At the other side of the room Jack was sizing up the space between Henry's head and the arm holding him off the floor. The two boys were discussing the problem.

"There's not much space, Henry, guess I could get my head through if I lean on my arms. Hold still while I try it. Hey, it works if I move from one arm to the other!"

Beside them Paul, who usually hated to do anything slowly, was on his back inching cautiously along under a bridge shape Marion had constructed. Miss Terry asked him why he was going so slowly.

" 'Cause I tried running and sliding under and I bumped her over every time so I got to go this way to do it."

The next couple were equally fascinating if one knew these children as well as did Mr. Donovan. Annie was the direct contrast to Paul. She seldom moved fast or jumped around but there she was jumping over an outflung leg and scooting back under the shape as fast as though this were natural to her.

This was the type of thing that pleased Mr. Donovan so much that he tried to slip out of his office to see this class—Annie and Paul finding new sensations and experiences of movement. The most satisfying feature was that the children made these discoveries for themselves. Miss Terry didn't tell them how to move, she provided opportunities for them to make their own explorations and decisions. Mr. Donovan made plans to be free to come in again next day to watch this class tackle a new problem.

2. To develop athletic and game skills. Fundamental skills are refined and combined to produce advanced athletic skills as used in activities such as basketball, tennis, swimming and gymnastics.

Athletic and game skills are taught at simple skill levels only. Basic skills required for this type of activity are taught as refinements of fundamental movements, but high levels of skill development are left to be stressed in high school. Lead-up games to adult athletics are included as part of grade V and VI programs but the sizes of fields and equipment are reduced and the rules are simplified.

ILLUSTRATION #2   Pat was the first child to arrive at school this morning. That might not appear to be an unusual occurence unless one knew Pat. Normally, she flew in out of breath just as the bell rang. But, here she was, forty-five minutes early, standing on the deserted play field beside the long jump pit.

If Miss Hudson, the grade five teacher, had been present she might have explained the phenomenon. Pat had discovered track and field, and had come early to practice. The grade five girls had begun track and field two weeks ago. Pat hadn't seemed very interested at the beginning, and Miss Hudson had noted with interest the growing enthusiasm Pat was putting into her class practice. This was noteworthy because Pat had never been eager for physical education activities before. She took part and performed very well but her attitude was primarily one of indifference. Pat hadn't become this involved in track and field last year.

As she drove into the school yard early, to get some work put on the board before the bell rang, Miss Hudson wasn't too surprised to see the lone form at the pit. After parking the car Miss Hudson walked across the field to where Pat crouched, investigating the mark made by her foot at the take-off line.

"Miss Hudson, why do I always step over the line? What can I do to get it right?"

"Have you tried starting your take-off just a trifle farther back?"

"No, will that fix it?"

"Well, it might, if you are running at the same speed and with the same size steps every time. Pat, you're working very hard at track and field. Why do you like it so much this year?"

"I'm not sure, Miss Hudson, but I do like it. And I like practicing to get better at it. It seems to be more important that I do well this year."

Miss Hudson thought she knew what Pat meant. Skills were taught more thoroughly in grade V than in earlier grades and Pat was just at that stage of her development where she had the perseverance to apply herself to practice. Being able to perform activities skilfully was important to children of this age. Miss Hudson walked into the school feeling encouraged with Pat's reception of track skills.

3. To develop and maintain physical fitness through vigorous physical exercise.

Usually less specific emphasis is placed on fitness development in the elementary school than in high school and college. This does not mean that no attempt is made to keep the elementary school child fit, but rather, that such efforts are not readily recognizable, particularly in the first three grades. Stunts, animal walks, and movement challenges are the basis of the fitness program for strength, agility, and co-ordination in the lower grades. Vigorous activity is stressed as a component of every lesson to build endurance. The later grades of elementary school may gradually move toward a more formal mode of fitness training as children become more interested in specific activities. However, even in grades IV, V, and VI an informal approach can be highly motivating and successful. (Illustration listed after objective 4.)

4. To develop knowledge and attitudes. The study of game strategies and rules, the encouragement of creative abilities in movement, and the appreciation of the values of physical skills for leisure and recreational use require intellectual growth.

The knowledges and attitudes developed at the elementary age level are basic and rarely complicated. The children are taught the necessity for rules and how to play by the rules, rather than studying complex game regulations. Much time is spent on the encouragemnet of safety appreciation at all levels. Great emphasis is placed on creative abilities especially in the early elementary grades. Grades I and II are given many opportunities to put their vivid imaginations to work to create stories, movements, and situations of their own devising. In the elementary school most movement and play require mental as well as physical effort. Physical education can be integrated with classroom activities and general knowledge, particularly in the higher elementary grades.

ILLUSTRATION #3 The grade five boys were going on a trip. It was a fairly long trip to make, particularly when everyone had to run all the way. They were going to the animal farm fifteen miles out of the city. It was Don's idea first, really, but everyone added suggestions until it was hard to remember who had started it. Don had driven out to the animal farm with his family on Sunday and in school the next day he told about seeing two men in baggy clothes running along the road. His father had told him they were athletes out practicing running and they were wearing "sweat" clothes to keep them warm. Don's suggestion had really been that the class go to the animal farm for a field trip but Mark had laughed and added, "Yeah, and we'll run all the way." The whole class had laughed at that, but Mr. Jamieson had suggested a way they *could* go to the farm running all the way there. "Each day everyone in the class does some running and keeps note of how far he ran. Each day add that day's distance to the distance you've accumulated so far. When everyone has run fifteen miles then we'll really go to the animal farm, but by car."

Everyone had an idea to add and pretty soon there were so many things to think of and do that Mr. Jamieson suggested that teams be formed, each responsible for a part of the planning. The boys named heir teams according to the jobs they had. The "Measuring Worms" vere to get the big tape and measure the outside of the school grounds and then figure out how many times around would add up to fifteen miles. The "Pencil Pushers" got a chart ready with every boy's name isted down the side and columns for each day for the next three weeks along the top. They also decided to draw a map to show where they were oing. Another team called themselves the "Researchers" and looked up nformation on the famous distance runners in the world and how they rained themselves to be good runners. They decided to find out about he best runners in the animal world too, so they could tell the class bout cheetahs and gazelles when they saw them at the animal farm.

Everyone worked out well and thirteen days after they started everyone ad completed the fifteen miles. The boys got so used to running and rying to run a little farther each day that they didn't want to stop. In act, after the last day of running, Johnny said, "Now let's start running o the lake, it's only 150 miles!"

5. To develop social awareness and abilities. Group interaction, team vork, and learning to accept the responsiblities inherent in leadership nd followership are areas of individual development affected by the hysical education program.

The effort to develop in children acceptable social practices is one of he most challenging objectives for the teacher. To take small grade I hildren who are basically "I" oriented and lead them to the "we" con- ept required of games is an exciting experience. Some children have lifficulty learning to wait for their turn or to share equipment. Creating . class atmosphere of self-responsibility and co-operation in the primary rades is a task of some magnitude. The concept of several children ooling their ideas and abilities to produce a total single result is entirely lien to the lower elementary age group and situations must be carefully et up to encourage group interaction and co-opertion. Older children ave a tendency to brush off those with poor skills or handicaps unless hey are guided to an understanding and acceptance of such children.

ILLUSTRATION #4   Steve was worried. There was to be a meeting of the our captains in Mr. Cox's room after school. Mr. Cox said they would hoose the teams for the grade VI physical education class soccer games. teve didn't understand how they could do that in a classroom. At his old chool the captains had stood in front of the class and called out the ames of the boys they wanted and if you could sneak in a name out of urn and get that boy lined up behind you before anyone realized, you sually got away with it. Oh sure, there was an argument, but he was retty tough and no one wanted to fight him. Doing it that way he always ot the best team and the dumb-bells who weren't good players were on the other team. Steve was suspicious about what was going to happen after school. This was a funny school, they even let the kid with the leg brace play the games. He was all right, Steve guessed, except he sure couldn't kick a ball very well. There's the bell, time for that stupid meeting.

Bill, Tiny, and Skip were already in room 12 when Steve walked in. Mr. Cox was writing the names of the class on the board. Steve already knew the ten boys he wanted, but he had a feeling he wasn't going to get his way. Funny, the first thing Mr. Cox said was, "Now, boys, what do we want to keep in mind while we choose the teams?" Steve just wanted to get started choosing, but that was an easy question. "Get the best players," said Steve. "Heck, no," said Skip, "that's why we're here. We want good games and we won't have them if any one team is too good. We want to get teams that are fairly even, it's a lot more fun." Steve was silent, he'd never thought of that, but still, why else did they play if not to beat everyone else? He decided to ask the question. Tiny answered that one. "Sure we want to win, but winning isn't really any good if you don't have to work for it. What have you proved? Everyone knows you'll win before the game starts if your team is a lot stronger. And it's no fun for the weak team. What chance have they got? No, we want our teams of even strength. Then if we win it's because we practiced and leared how to play together."

"Come on you guys, let's get started," said Bill, "I have to catch my bus." Steve kept still and listened. Mr. Cox said, "Let's rate the players, then we can get the same number of players of the same ability on each team." "Boy," thought Steve, "That'll even the teams out okay, but who gets stuck with Peter who has two left feet, and Tubby who's as slow as molasses, and Jack with the leg brace?" Bet I get them all 'cause I'm new here." But by the time the teams were arranged, after much discussion, he discovered that Peter was the only poor player he had. His team wasn't as good as he had planned but it was as good as the others. This would be a tough series of games.

"Steve," said Mr. Cox, "I want to make sure you know what happens now. We have two more days of practice before we start the games. Tomorrow you and your team decide the position each man plays. Then you can practice attacks or defence or specific skills, depending on each player's weakness. I'll help any time someone is having trouble. Okay?" "Sure," said Steve, and picked up his books and headed home. "Boy," he thought as he ambled along. "I'd better get hold of Leo to plan what we have to practice. You know, that Peter might not be so bad if we helped him. This might be all right after all. If we can get good enough to beat those other guys we'll really have done something."

6. To develop emotional stability and control. Physical education

presents many opportunities, through sports and physical challenges, for the student to develop his emotional reactions to a socially acceptable state.

The development of emotional control goes hand in hand with group work. It is a sudden change for the child to discover at school that the world no longer revolves around him. His reactions to being one of many are often violent and anti-social. He may cry or become extremely angry when his wishes are thwarted. This energy and desire to be first must be channelled through control and understanding to acceptable behavior. Through partner work, small group work, and practice in accepting decisions of others the child can achieve stable emotional reactions.

ILLUSTRATION #5   After some "fussing" around while everyone tried to get Mrs. Dodge to let them be "it," the tag game got under way. Mrs. Dodge watched with some apprehension. These grounds were certainly not the best surface for grade ones playing tag. But what else to do? Children needed to run and chase instead of spending physical education time standing still. She would just have to start teaching them responsibility for each other immediately. If the children didn't learn how to control their excitement they would forget about that depression across the field and trip trying to flee the tagger. And if there were problems with "its" tagging too hard because the children wouldn't admit being touched, someone would end up face down in the dirt. Oh, dear, someone crying so soon.

"What's wrong, Jenny?"

"Sammy pushed me down! He didn't need to push!"

"Did not push, all I did was tag."

"Did so, my knee's got blood."

"Yeah, but when I tagged you, you said I hadn't, so I got to do it harder. Mrs. Dodge, she said I hadn't tagged her but I had."

"Children, everyone come here and sit down and we'll talk about rules. Do you like playing tag?"

"No," "Sure," "Yeah, its great," "Its okay part of the time."

"Billy, why don't you like it?"

"Aw, no one will say so when they're tagged. We fight too much. And the girls screech."

"Yes, I think that's what is wrong. Has anyone any ideas as to what we could do to make it fun for everyone? Danny?"

"Well, we could make a rule that if you're tagged you have to say so."

"That's supposed to be the rule now, you dope."

"But maybe now we've talked about it everyone will try hard. Can you do that, boys and girls?"

"Sure, let's try."

"Any other suggestions?"

"Mrs. Dodge, maybe we won't screech if we're sure we won't be pushed."

"Yes, that should help. If everyone tries to be very honest about being tagged then no one will have to tag so hard that you fall. And if you think about where you're running maybe you won't get so excited. Screeching and squealing doesn't help you to be safe, does it? Now, let's try again and remember the things we talked about."

Well, it's better this time, less panicky running, easier tagging. Jim and Margie are arguing about a tag, I hope I don't have to step in there. No they've solved it. Whoops, Tommy's down—wasn't watching where he went. However, even one self-solved argument and three minutes without a scream is a satisfactory achievement for one lesson. Next time will be better.

THE CHARACTERISTICS OF CHILDREN

The preceding discussion of objectives has taken into consideration the characteristics of children. This is a desirable and necessary emphasis. The total program in schools should be based on the needs, interests, and characteristics of the pupils and on the type of society in which they are growing up. Curriculum materials and methods are selected on the basis of the nature of the individual and the nature of the society in which he lives. It is important, therefore, that the teacher of physical education be aware of those characteristics of children which have a bearing on her selection of experiences for her class. Although each individual child is like no other, there are patterns of growth and development which can be identified and are normally present at certain age groupings. The following outlines give a concise summary of the physical, mental, and socio-emotional characteristics of elementary school children and present important implications for the establishment of a sound physical education program.

Grades I-III

Characteristics of children and the implications of these for physical education programs and methods.

Characteristics	Implications
1. Energetic and restless.	1. Provide opportunity for vigorous physical exercise.
2. Heart growing rapidly, fatigues easily.	2. Balance vigorous exercise with less energetic activities to provide a recovery period.

3. Large muscles quite well developed.

3. Include activities requiring use of large muscle groups; e.g. running and climbing for legs, pushing and pulling for arms, twisting, bending, and stretching for trunk, etc.

4. Manipulation of small objects difficult because eye-hand co-ordination poor.

4. In early grades use large equipment, gradually introducing smaller equipment and activities requiring fine muscular co-ordinations.

5. Curious, interested in everything that happens.

5. Make explanations clear, encourage children's ideas. Plan for special events.

6. Like to do, not listen.

6. Keep explanations short, let the children try activities, and insert specific skill instructions periodically during their practice.

7. Attention span short.

7. Provide a variety of activities during each lesson—don't practice too long on one problem.

8. Creative, imaginative.

8. Provide opportunities for children to create and improvise movements, with and without equipment.

9. Crave attention and approbation of adults.

9. Give each child some praise for effort or achievement. Encourage improvement, spread opportunities to demonstrate, etc., around so all get a chance.

10. Individualistic.

10. Work best on their own or in small groups of two or three. Ignore team efforts until grade three.

11. Love repetition if activity is enjoyable.

11. Provide plenty of opportunity to repeat the skills and activities they enjoy, but continue to encourage improvement during these sessions.

12. Boys and girls play well together.

12. No necessity for separating classes. Performance levels similar, interests not yet too divergent.

Grades IV-VI

Characteristics	*Implications*

1. Extremely active.

1. Present opportunities for much vigorous activity.

2. Strength is greater than previously, but not equal to growth.

2. Provide activities requiring greater stress on strength and work to develop this factor.

3. Endurance improved, but still not adult level.

3. Length of time spent on vigorous activity can be increased, but don't impose adult standards.

4. Co-ordination better. Girls may be equal to or better than boys.

4. Expect development of specific skills in boys and girls.

5. Desire to perform well, can persevere.

6. Attention span lengthens.

7. Interest varied and broad.

8. Enjoy competition.

9. Hero worship, particularly sports heroes for boys.

10. Desires approval of his fellows.

11. Ready to work in and for groups.

12. Can carry responsibilities.

13. Sexual differences and antagonisms developing.

14. Tendency to be boisterous, rowdy, (many boys, some girls).

5. Children will want to improve their skills, so provide opportunity for much practice and guidance.

6. Ability to concentrate for longer periods permits more complex instructions and longer periods spent without change of activity.

7. Include many activties and skills in program; e.g. swimming if possible, gymnastics, etc.

8. Use competitive games and relays. Lead-ups to adult athletics.

9. Physical education teachers must be good examples. Be aware of sports happenings, stars. Can use skills of heroes to stress practice and good learning.

10. Be alert to assist poorer performers to improve, to become more knowledgeable about rules, etc., to gain group's approval.

11. Begin team games, lead-ups to sports, relays. Provide opportunity for squad work.

12. Gradually turn more of the routine organization over to students. Students can help teacher plan.

13. Classes should be separated at grade IV or V for most of the program.

14. Provide opportunity for activities vigorous enough to use up some of this energy. Give boys rough and tough activities (under close control).

BIBLIOGRAPHY

1. Alberta, *Bulletin 4: Elementary School Physical Education*. Edmonton: Department of Education, 1951.
2. ———, *Fifty-Fourth Annual Report of the Department of Education,* Edmonton: Legislative Assembly, 1960.
3. American Association for Health, Physical Education and Recreation, *Children in Focus*. Washington, D.C., 1954.
4. Breckenridge, Marion, and Lew Vincent, *Child Development*. Philadelphia: W. B. Saunders Co., 1956.
5. British Columbia, *Health and Physical Education: Programme of Studies for the Elementary Schools of British Columbia*. Victoria: Department of Education, 1951.

6. Bucher, Charles A., and Evelyn M. Reade, *Physical Education in the Modern Elementary School*. New York: The Macmillan Company, 1958.

7. Chatwin, Nora, *Physical Education for the Primary Grades*. Toronto: The House of Grant (Canada) Ltd., 1956.

8. Cowell, Charles C., and Helen W. Hazelton, *Curriculum Designs in Physical Education*. Englewood Cliffs, N.J.: Prentice-Hall, Inc., 1955.

9. Detroit Public Schools, *Exploration of Basic Movements in Physical Education*. Detroit: Publication Department of Detroit Public Schools, 1960.

10. ———, *Spotlight the Children in Physical Education*. Detroit: Board of Education of the City of Detroit, 1951.

11. Diem, Liselott, *Who Can*. Frankfurt a M. solidus Germany: Wilhelm Limpert, 1955. (Copyright U.S.A., Chicago: George Williams College, 1957).

12. Eckert, Helen, "The Development of Organized Recreation and Physical Education in Alberta." Unpublished Master's thesis, University of Alberta, 1953.

13. Halsey, Elizabeth, and Lorena Porter, *Physical Education for Children: A Developmental Program*. New York: The Dryden Press, 1958.

14. Jersild, A. I., *Child Development and the Curriculum*. New York: Columbia University Press, 1947.

15. Jones, P., "Educational Gymnastics," *Journal of C.A.H.P.E.R.*, XXVII, No. 4 (1961).

16. Leiper, Jean M., "A Course of Study Supplement for Physical Education in Small Elementary Schools of Western Canada." Unpublished Master's thesis, State University of Iowa, 1962.

17. Ludwig, Elizabeth A., "Basic Movement Education in England," *Journal of Health, Physical Education and Recreation*, XXXII, No. 9 (1961).

18. Manitoba, *Physical Education Grades I-VI*. Winnipeg: Department of Education, 1951.

19. Meagher, J. W., "Our Successes in Physical Education," *Journal of C.A.H.P.E.R.*, XXVII, No. 4 (1961).

20. Munro, A. D., *Pure and Applied Gymnastics*. London: Edward Arnold [Publishers], Ltd., 1955.

21. Ontario, *Educational System of Ontario*. Toronto (mimeographed), 1957.

22. ———, *Physical Education. Junior Division: Grades 4, 5, 6*. Toronto: Department of Education, 1959.

23. ———, *Physical Education Supplement*. Toronto: Department of Education, 1960.

24. *Physical Education in Rural Schools*. Toronto: Strathcona Trust Committee (Ontario), 1954.

25. Saskatchewan, *Elementary School Curriculum Guide II for Health and Physical Education*. Regina: Department of Education, 1956.

26. Schneider, Elsa, *Physical Education in Small Schools*. Washington, D. C.: National Education Association, 1954.

27. Steckle, Ward Allan, "An Historical Survey of the Growth and Development of Interscholastic Athletics in the Public Schools of Calgary." Unpublished Master's thesis, University of Washington, 1955.

28. United Kingdom Ministry of Education, *Physical Education in the Primary School. Part I: Moving and Growing; Part II: Planning the Programme*. London: Her Majesty's Stationery Office, 1952, 1954.

29. Van Vliet, M. L., "A Guide to Administrative Policies for Physical Education in Canadian Public Schools, Grades One Through Nine." Unpublished Doctor's thesis, University of California, 1950.

Helen Bryans

Professor of Physical Education
Ontario College of Education

* EDITOR'S NOTE—The curriculum for girls was selected by design for inclusion in this book. It was felt that a chapter on both boys and girls would be necessarily repetitious and at the same time, that the vast experience of Miss Bryans and her long years of observation of both boys' and girls' programs might best allow for portrayal of Canadian program development in the broader general sense, even though the approach was through a review of the girls' programs.

With relatively few exceptions, there seems to be very little difference between the history of curriculum development of the boys' and girls' programs. With the exception of contact sports in the inter-school program and hockey, touch football and some wrestling in the class programs, most of the activities are the same. There is, of course, more emphasis on dance in the girls' program and, depending somewhat on the school, perhaps more emphasis on individual sports by the girls.

INTRODUCTION

Each of the present ten provinces has developed its own educational system, in its own unique manner, beginning in its own time, and progressing at its own tempo. The physical education curricula reflect these differences in growth and development. There is, for instance, a lapse of some years between the appearance of the first course of study in each of the provinces. There have been no less than eight revisions of the original course in one province.

A casual glance at the word *curriculum* suggests merely a list of items to be taught, but more thoughtful consideration provokes such questions as:

For what reasons were these items selected for the courses of study?
Of what value will they be to those for whom they are planned?

In what sequence and by what methods will they be taught?
How successful has the procedure been?
How could the curriculum be improved?

A curriculum is more than a list of items. It is a continuous cycle involving the whole educational process of setting up the objectives, planning the procedure, proceeding according to plan, evaluating the results, and re-planning to achieve better results. Consciously or unconciously, a growing curriculum follows this continuously repeated cycle.

THE GROWING CURRICULUM

Physical education today is a compulsory subject in most secondary schools in Canada, and each one of the ten provinces has developed its own course of study in the subject. This achievement represents the culmination of more than a century of experimentation, growth, and thought, through which has emerged a philosophy of physical education and a recognition of the need for it in schools and its final acceptance as an essential part of the school curriculum.

Early development in each individual province has been outlined in Chapters II and V. The pattern of development is well exemplified in Ontario, one of the four provinces in Canada at the time of Confederation. Landmarks art easily recognizable and there is reason to believe that the pattern is not dissimilar in other provinces.

THE GROWTH OF A PHILOSOPHY It is the nature of children to experiment, to explore, to move. Childhood is associated with mental curiosity and physical restlessness. Children learn to think as they solve problem after problem by a process of exploration, experimentation, and selection. They learn to manage their bodies, growing in health and strength and self-confidence as they respond to its need to move.

THE ACCEPTANCE OF PHYSICAL EDUCATION IN THE CURRICULUM A public demand for physical education in the schools was increasing "as illustrated by an article in the *Journal of the Board of Arts and Manufacturers* for Upper Canada in 1865, and two articles in the *Journal of Education* for Lower Canada in 1873 and 1874, all pointing out dangers in the neglect of physical culture in schools or benefits to be secured by its introduction." The *Canadian School Journal,* in 1886, makes the comment that "drill for boys and calisthenics for the girls are among the excellent new inventions."

The first official recognition of physical education as an important school subject was the offer of grants in 1884 for "the promotion of physical culture by means of gymnastics, drill and calisthenics, a sum not exceeding $10,000 to be apportioned—among such high schools and collegiate institutes as are considered worthy." This did not produce startling results, however. According to Phillips, there was an increase of only $50,000 in the value of gymnasia over the twenty-year period 1889-1909.

In addition to establishing grants, the Ontario Department of Education in 1890 took its most important step in its recognition of physical education by placing it on the course of study and allotting it a minimum time of an hour and a half a week for drill, gymnastics, and calisthenics, not less than one additional hour each week for "other forms," and additional provision for practice by pupils under efficient supervision. The regulation did not make physical education compulsory in all grades. The statistics show the effect of these regulations; in 1889 the percentage of pupils taking drill and calisthenics was 32, and by 1894 the percentage had increased to 57. The inspectors' reports for some years following do not suggest any firm insistence on the regulations.

In 1909 a regulation was passed requiring that gymnasia be built in collegiates by 1911, on penalty of forfeiting collegiate status. By 1929 all the collegiates and half the high schools were built with gymnasia.

THE CHANGING CURRICULAR CONTENT Having achieved recognition and acceptance as a subject in the school program, the shaping and reshaping of the curriculum has been a continuing process, a fact which augurs well for its future. Its growth has been marked by occasional spurts due to outside influences, inside enthusiasms, and the shocks of wars. As with Canada's neighbor to the south, Canada tries this and that, changes, adapts, and discards. Unlike the United States, Canada tends to be conservative. The pendulum swings from philosophy to philosophy, from system to system, and from activity to activity, but the range of the swing is more restrained and seldom goes to extremes.

The early curriculum for the Normal Method School in 1851 was "gymnastics, calisthenics and drill." From this beginning, the present provincial curricula have grown. It is possible to trace through the past hundred-year period general trends in the development of the Canadian curriculum of today.

Calisthenics was apparently the first form of physical education recommended for girls. It has been defined as "free exercise without apparatus, and light gymnastics which are exercises without apparatus, and light gymnastics which are exercises with light apparatus such as dumbbells, bean bags, wands, rings, and clubs." Whether this form of exercise owes its popularity to European or American influence is not clear, but its use in American schools had been advocated ever since Catherine Beecher adapted European exercises into a system to meet American needs. In her book entitled *A Course of Calisthenics for Young Ladies* published in 1832, her system was designed "to develop the health, strength and beauty of the physical system." By 1850 some American cities had progressed so far as to allow a few minutes of calisthenics in the daily curriculum.

Calisthenics in Canada continued as a basic part of the curriculum for girls well into the 1920's. For those who can remember, it calls up a picture of girls and women in voluminous bloomers to the knees, middies, and long black stockings, moving through elaborate routines with clubs, and contortions with wands; of lunging, bending, and twisting. For displays, the apparatus was frequently colored, bedecked with flowers, streamers, or lights. Since that time it has been replaced by a succession of other systems of body conditioning and education, but through the years, though the name, the form ,and the methods may change, the pendulum has never swung completely away from the philosophy of exercise to develop "the health, strength and beauty of the physical system."

With the establishment of the Strathcona Trust Fund in 1911, the "Strathcona system" as it was popularly labelled, made up the curriculum. It was in reality a "watered-down" version of Swedish exercises, performed in response to command, with emphasis on precision, uniformity of movement, straight lines, squared corners, and tensed muscles. There were movements for each part of the body, performed in an unalterable sequence. In time, with the acceptance of games, dance, and swimming in the programs, Strathcona exercises were replaced, but with each war and the revival of interest in physical fitness, there was a return to exercises strongly reminiscent of the Strathcona system.

The next two decades (1930-50) were marked by a swing away from the militaristic precision and formalism of Swedish gymnastic exercises and the set patterns and drills of calisthenics, to more plastic, rhythmic forms of movement. It was a period of experimentation, probably initiated by the wave of enthusiasts who travelled and studied abroad, and returned to teach and to make, unknown to themselves, a contribution to the growth of the physical education curriculum. These new systems had much in common. They were developed primarily for women and girls, not only for their beneficial physiological effects but also for their contribution to such feminine qualities as grace, poise, sensitivity, and rhythm. They are freer, more natural, flowing, and expressive. The systems followed one another in quick succession: Bukh, Bjorksten, Bertram, each with an individual interpretation and development of Swedish gymnastics; Medau, Logis, Bode, and others of the German school, with flowing swings, less localized and more natural movements, exhilarating and imaginative in their use of balls, clubs, hoops, and percussive accompaniment.

Almost stealthily on the heels of this succession of systems followed modern dance, modern because it knows no restrictions of technique and no limits to the creative and expressive use of movement. With roots in Germany, developed by Mary Wigman (a pupil of Rudolph Laban, often referred to as the "father of modern dance"), nurtured in the United States by generations of dancers into an American art form, it is not surprising that its influence should have been felt in Canada. Primarily an art form, it has nevertheless left its imprint on physical education. One of the unique contributions of modern dance is an increased awareness of body movement with respect to space, quality, dynamics, and rhythm. This kinesthetic sensitivity which results from a wide variety of movement experiences provides a vocabulary of movement and an understanding which leads naturally into creative activity and composition. Another contribution which is reflected in the conditioning programs for girls is the wide variety of interesting and challenging techniques designed to maintain and increase the range in joints, and the strength and efficiency of the body.

Gymnastics in the early Canadian curriculum meant heavy apparatus work—on the horse, box, buck, parallel bars, horizontal bars, the flying rings, travelling rings, wall bars, and horizontal ladder apparatus—which has continued in common practice until the present day. It will be remembered that in 1861 a visitor from the States found that for girls at the Normal Model School, needlework had been substituted for the "more rigorous and unsuitable gymnastics." Although the apparatus was standard equipment for boys, there is no evidence to show that it was taught to girls until several years later. With the introduction of gymnasium costumes the interest of girls in the twenties increased in this form of activity.

Undoubtedly apparatus work was taught in conjunction with Bjorksten and Bukh exercises when these systems were in vogue. Both systems of "gymnastics," as they were called, retained the Swedish plan of including in the regular lesson a series of exercises followed by apparatus work and mat work, usually in squads. This pattern was adopted in Canadian schools for some time, until it was found to be impractical, in part because of the short periods and in part because most pupils entering high school, having had no previous experience in this type of activity, made very slow progress.

The trend has therefore been to revert to the previous concept of gymnastics (heavy apparatus work) and to teach it as an isolated activity rather than in combination with exercises. It has been common practice to begin with tumbling and stunts, and activities at a low level until the necessary control was gained for the more vigorous forms of jumping and vaulting. Various methods have been developed, but squads, student leaders, and "spotters" have been in general use. There is evidence of effort to develop suitable progressions for girls, rather than to follow the pattern of the boy's work as has too often been the practice. Also there is a marked trend toward suiting the activity to the individual and letting pupils work at their own level. As elementary pupils gain experience on apparatus suited to their age and development, greater progress should become apparent in the secondary school program, and the methods and materials become better adapted to the adolescent girls.

Dance In the early nineteenth century, dancing was frequently found in the curriculum of private schools for girls, where it was taught for its social and aesthetic values. In 1840 Mrs. Huret's school in Saint John offered "music, painting, French, Italian, dancing and deportment." In the same city in 1843 the Misses MacIntosh taught a much greater variety of accomplishments, "and also offered as contributions to gracious living: 'drawing—transferring—writing (round and square)—music—dancing (Victoria and Lowe's quadrilles, lancers, cotillions, and other fashionable dances).' " The modern counterpart for such dances is the ballroom dancing which is taught for the most part in privately run dance studios. It has, however, found a small place in the physical education curriculum since 1930, where it is frequently taught as a co-educational subject.

It would be difficult to say when dance first gained a foothold in the secondary school curriculum, but probably about the same time as games. Now and then there has been occasional opposition to dance for religious reasons. While its position has remained unchallenged, a concession has sometimes been made in name if not in content, by substituting "rhythmics" for dance. Like calisthenics, dance has appeared in many forms throughout the period under consideration. Not all provinces have experienced all the transitions, but there is a fairly clear sequence of dance forms, most of which are associated with the efforts of individual teachers. Proximity to these influences has shaped the local programs in each part of Canada.

Probably the first vogue was aesthetic (or classic) dance about 1900 to 1925. It was developed in the United States by Melvin Ballou Gilbert, at the suggestion of Dr. Sargent of Harvard, who told Gilbert that "from the physical educator's point of view dancing ('fancy steps' with little action) was weak because it involved only the legs and not the trunk and arms." First taught at the Harvard summer schools in 1894, it became exceedingly popular, and its popularity spread to Canada in part through the influence of Mrs. Ada Seikle, who taught for several years in Canadian summer courses for teachers.

Other dance forms followed during the next two decades (1920-40), most of them having a very transitory existence. Some ballet, modified for use in schools and colleges, crept into the program where it probably merged with the aesthetic dance. This came through the influence of Louis Chalif, a Russian dance teacher in New York, who was invited by Dr. Gulick to develop a course for teachers. Chalif's chief contribution was made through his five volumes of national and folk dances. Gymnastic and character dances were particularly useful for demonstrations and school concerts. Clog and tap dancing which followed were popularized largely through the teaching and publications of Hinman, Frost, Hillas, and Duggan.

Aesthetic dance and its successors have from the beginning found a strong rival in folk dancing. About 1900, folk dancing was in the curriculum of the Normal Model School and was taught by Mrs. Somers, an outstanding teacher in her day. For many years Mrs. Somers put on fine displays of folk and national dancing, club swinging, and ball routines at the annual field day. Every girl participated, looking her best in white middy and skirt. To the accompaniment of the bagpipes the girls marched onto the field two by two, toes turned well out in the so-called graceful walk of the day. During the 1920's Miss Mary G. Hamilton of the Margaret Eaton School made a notable contribution by inviting to Canada such leaders as Elizabeth Burchenal and Cecil Sharp. Elizabeth Burchenal, the author of ten volumes on folk dancing, based on much original research in the United States and other countries, became a frequent visitor in Canada, where her influence has been widespread and continues to this day. Cecil Sharp promoted English country dancing, Morris and sword dances. During the period of Bjorksten and Bukh gymnastics, Scandinavian dances were popular chiefly due to the enthusiasm and vital personality of John Madsen from Denmark.

After World War II there was an unprecedented wave of enthusiasm for square dancing in the schools, in extracurricular and co-educational groups and as recreational dancing for young and old. As Canada's adopted form of folk dance, it is not surprising that the enthusiasm has been long-lived and widespread from coast to coast. With the influx of new Canadians, dancing has again taken on a more international character in the schools, but this time it has come from the people and from within, rather than through individual efforts and from without.

Games and Athletics Pupils were playing games and competing in athletics long before "gymnastics and calisthenics" were introduced into the school curriculum. They played in the recess period and at noon, before school and after school, and so it continued after gymnastics and calisthenics were established as a school subject. It is reported that in 1877 the first sports day was held in the Toronto Collegiate Institute, and that in 1880 the principal of Dundas High School in addressing the Teachers' Association, urged them to encourage outdoor games and take part in these games with the pupils. It is not easy to specify just when games were officially added to the curriculum. The records show that in Ontario some time after 1912 school teachers in training at the Faculty of Education were taught games, athletics, swimming, and dancing. One may be certain that from that time, officially or unofficially, games became a regular part of the physical education course in secondary schools. The growing importance with which games and play were regarded after World War I is brought out in the Minister of Education's Report of 1920 which read:

> The value of play as a factor in intellectual and moral education—perhaps even in physical education—has not been fully recognized. Its full meaning and significance for life is one of the lessons of the war which has also strangely taught us to place less reliance than formally on military drill and exercises. Play in the past has assumed too much the character of sport, in which all the prizes go to the strongest. Its great value would rather appear to lie in the possibilities, when properly managed, which it opens up for the development of the puny and feeble into a sturdy and healthy and happy childhood.[1]

The 1920's were marked by an upsurge of interest in games, both for their educational value in the physical education program, and for their recreational value in after years. There was a growing emphasis on intramural activities and the slogan "a team for every girl and every girl on a team" became a common objective. Track and field, possibly the oldest of competitive activities, continued in popularity. Softball, with its origin back in the early eighteenth century in England in rounders and cricket, was included and has become traditional in Canadian schools. Basketball, invented in 1891, and volleyball, in 1895, became immediately popular in the United States and soon afterwards were introduced into Canada where they have remained the most popular indoor team games to this day.

The growing participation in games and the increase in competition brought their problems. Chief among these was girls' sports coached and controlled by men, involving the conflict between girls' and boys' rules. Standards for girls' and women's sports were established and as more women became trained in the competitive activities, conditions improved. In 1945, the rating of women officials was introduced and this has

---

[1] Quoted in Copp, "History of Physical Education," p. 27.

further raised the standard of competition. The struggle between girls'
and boys' rules has been dominion-wide. Rampant in the Maritimes in
1933 it has since been resolved by the wholesale adoption of girls' rules.
The three western provinces still use boys' rules more than girls' rules.
The central provinces use mostly girls' rules.

After World War II there was a decreasing interest in physical fitness
and another upsurge of enthusiasm for games and sports. The physical
education curriculum was expanded to include a wider choice of team
games: soccer, fieldball, speedball, and field hockey. With the advent of
more leisure time and increasing interest in adult recreation, preparation
for this was made by introducing more individual games into the cur-
riculumn—badminton, tennis, golf, and archery—particularly for the upper grades.

Swimming Since the place of swimming in the curriculum is determined entirely by the facilities, the only major development has been in
Ontario, where the first swimming pool was built about the year 1920.
The number has increased to about fifty pools at the present time. The
primary emphasis in the program has been on teaching beginners to
swim, on water safety, and on life-saving methods. Hundreds of pupils
are qualified annually for Canadian Red Cross and Royal Canadian Life
Saving Certificates. As the standard of swimming has improved, synchronized swimming, diving, and speed swimming have received increasing
attention. In a few schools quite elaborate programs of synchronized
swimming have become annual affairs.

Two schools in Edmonton, Alberta, have indoor pools and two more
are being built. Much swimming is given as a part of the school physical
education program in outdoor pools throughout Western Canada in May
and June. Montreal schools have free entrance to fifteen municipal pools,
which makes an extensive program possible.

THE CHANGING ATTITUDES In reviewing the "changing curricular content"
one cannot but realize that it is a reflection of the times, and that one of
the notable features of the century under discussion has been the revolt
from the Victorian point of view. This is apparent in the changing attitude to women, their dress, their education and activities. The Victorian
type of girl has been described by Dr. Jesse Feiring Williams as one "with
a well developed headache and a poorly developed body." Pre-Confed-
eration schools for young ladies, according to Phillips, "were designed to
emphasize female dependence," differing "only in the greater variety of
useless skills they offered to impart." Sussex Vale Academy in 1819 taught
"drawing, painting on paper or silk, all kinds of plain and ornamental

needlework, embroidery with silk or gold, embroidery flowers, figures, or pictures, filago work, etc."

"By 1880, the revolt had reached steam roller proportions." This is the year that Harvard girls led the fashion in gymnastic costumes as they blossomed forth in the divided skirt or bloomers and middy blouses, which later became a universal favorite. The bloomers in time grew shorter and briefer and were replaced by short pleated skirts, shorts, knickers, tunics, and occasionally leotards. Long black stockings were eliminated about 1930. Running shoes which have been singularly unaffected by the metamorphosis of costumes are now discarded for the soft dance shoe or no shoes at all for many activities.

As girls' bodies were freed from the restrictions of tight clothing and voluminous skirts, their interest and participation in sports increased. To croquet, hiking, and bicycling were added more vigorous sports of tennis, track and field, basketball, and volleyball. Dancing progressed from the "fancy steps" with little action, to aesthetic dancing. Ballet was modernized to exercise the body as well as the arms and legs, and folk dancing grew in popularity. As late as 1920 there were still vestiges of doubt concerning the wisdom of vigorous activity for girls, as indicated in Major Kirk's address to the School Health Section of the Ontario Education Association, in which he remarked that he was "not at all sure that the more robust games for girls are of benefit either to the individual woman or the future of the race." Today there are no restrictions other than the individual's strength and desire, and the present trend in the physical education programs is toward more and more vigorous activity.

THE CHANGING CONCEPT OF PHYSICAL EDUCATION The twentieth century has also been marked by a change in the philosophy and concept of physical education, a change which is reflected in the terminology. In the early years of the nineteenth century, when physical education was commonly referred to as "gymnastics and calisthenics," it was generally considered that "a systematic and well developed course in exercises would produce trained symmetrical body development with strength and grace," or as Miss Catherine Beecher quaintly expressed it in 1832, "health, strength and beauty of the physical systems." The transition to "physical training" with its strong suggestion of formality and purely physical development, and to "physical culture" with its more aesthetic and intellectual significance, was almost imperceptible. These less specific names, which appear to have been used interchangeably from as early as 1886, are less limiting with respect to content, which by this time included a considerably wider variety of activities.

In 1923 Dr. A. S. Lamb, in an address on objectives to a group of teachers, listed these as "corrective, educational, hygienic and recreative," suggesting that already the concept of "physical training" had outgrown the current name. With the growing realization of the possible contributions of the subject to the objectives of general education, it seemed right and natural that it should become "educational in name as it is in purpose." To those in the profession it was no doubt encouraging to find some understanding of this viewpoint as early as 1929 when an inspector reported that "the value of well-conducted physical exercises, gymnastics and games is now universally conceded, not only as a means of making and keeping the body fit, but also as a means of training the characteristics essential to a virile manhood and womanhood."

The Curriculum Today

By tracing the development of the curriculum through the past century, the continuous cycle of the "educational process" becomes clearly defined. The objectives of physical education have broadened from the narrow physical concept to the general objectives of all education, the development of the child as a whole. To a restricted program of calisthenics have been added other activities more in keeping with the change in objectives. The implementation of the program has been conducted with less formality and more self-direction on the part of the pupils, with the help of more and better-qualified teachers, with an assured time in the curriculum, and under steadily improving conditions. There has never at any time been complete satisfaction with the results, as evidenced by the number of curriculum revisions to date, and the several curricula currently undergoing revision.

THE SCHOOLS OF TODAY Over the last fifteen or twenty years the schools in Canada have mushroomed almost faster than they can be counted. Many of them are not only functional but unbelieveably beautiful. Facilities for physical education are now recognized as essential and schools without these facilities are becoming the exception.

There is usually one gymnasium shared by the boys and girls in the smaller schools, and one gymnasium with dividing doors in the larger schools. In the large centers most schools have two or more gymnasia, and in one overcrowded suburb a school is currently building a fifth gymnasium. Swimming pools are still most numerous in Ontario schools. All provinces have established minimum standards for equipment.

THE CURRICULAR CONTENT The curricular content represents the procedures planned to achieve objectives which have been acknowledged as acceptable to all provinces. Despite the variation in nomenclature, classification, and organization, the material selected by each province is aimed at achieving their common objectives.

It is obvious that comparative studies in this area present difficulties. However, for purposes of simple analysis the activities of the different curricula may be grouped under five comprehensive headings as follows:

a) Movement: exercises, conditioning exercises, techniques, fundamental movements, modern dance (American or English), rhythmics.
b) Gymnastics: tumbling, student-pyramids, apparatus activities, free movement.
c) Dance: folk dance, ballroom dance.
d) Games and athletics: team games, individual games, track and field.
e) Swimming: strokes, water safety, life-saving, synchronized, diving, speed swimming.

Movement The fact that some form of movement education is included in the curriculum of every province suggests that there is general agreement regarding the need for body development and that this cannot be completely achieved through the other four program areas. There is *no* agreement, however, as to what form it should take, nor what it should be called, what place it should have in the program, how much time should be devoted to it, nor by what method it should be taught. It would appear that at the present time Canadians have no common philosophy in this area.

Three provinces recommend that a few minutes at the beginning of *every* lesson be devoted to "conditioning exercises." Another recommends the use of specific tables of exercises, probably as a guide for those who need help. Nova Scotia requires that 50 per cent of the time be spent on "physical fitness activities" and is careful to list these as "exercises, group games, tumbling, apparatus, testing and certain rhythmic activities." The other 50 per cent of the time is for "games, gymnastics, rhythmic activities, including modern dance, track and field."

"Fundamental movements" and "movement education" are terms growing in importance across the country. They represent an attempt to provide a frame of reference within which teachers educated in different systems of movement, with widely divergent backgrounds and with varied levels of skill, can *work together with some unity of purpose* toward a common goal—that of teaching girls how to use their bodies efficiently, with sensitivity, understanding, body pride, and self-confidence. This may involve a wide variety of movement experiences, observation, selection, problem solving, creative activity. It includes systematic conditioning to maintain and increase mobility, strength, and body control. It sets minimum standards of skill—good static and dynamic posture, conditioning exercises for present and future needs, skill in the basic locomotor movements (walking, running, hopping, jumping, leaping, galloping, sliding, skipping) and steps (step-hop, schottische, two-step, polka, waltz) . For those teachers whose ability and training enable them to set higher goals there is no limit to what they may aspire to:—the intriguing skills with balls, hoops, clubs; movement combinations and sequences; movement studies and creative activity based on "the factors related to movement, i.e. space, quality, rhythm and dynamics," *or* on the principles of "time, weight, space and flow." The possibilities are endless, limited only by the imagination of the participant and the teacher.

Gymnastics   The position of gymnastics in the girls' program is probably more strongly established today than at any previous period in its history. It is included in all the courses and allotted a not inconsiderable amount of time. The introduction of new types of apparatus designed specifically for the elementary grades and the change to informal methods of teaching ("educational gymnastics") with freedom and guidance to explore, select, and create is already having repercussions at the secondary level. It will in time enable secondary school girls to progress further and faster and with greater satisfaction and confidence.

The nature of the individual programs is determined in part by the equipment. In all provinces, tumbling has been the activity most consistently taught, probably for three reasons: most schools have mats, the only essential equipment; the activities are relatively simple to teach; and they are introductory to apparatus work, since through tumbling, body control and many of the principles of movement may be stressed.

Dance   Dance is included in the programs of oll provinces but it receives a relatively smaller percentage of time than either of the two preceding areas.

All provinces teach American, folk, and ballroom dance. Ballroom and square dancing are taught co-educationally in all provinces, in both the regular class periods and after school. All agree that dance is taught primarily for enjoyment, and that skill is an important component of enjoyment. Teachers usually choose the dances from their personal repertoires but in a few courses of study, classified graded lists are included for those who need guidance. Records are used almost exclusively for accompaniment.

Games and Athletics   More time is allotted to games and athletics than to any other one area of activity. Within the individual provinces there is a range of about 49 per cent between the least and the greatest amount of time devoted to this subject.

Basketball and volleyball are the most popular team games and are played in all provinces. Softball is next in popularity. Others mentioned are speedball, soccer, and field hockey (5 times), ice hockey (3 times), fieldball (twice), lacrosse (once).

Badminton and tennis are taught in all provinces. Other games mentioned are golf (4 times), bowling (twice), handball (once), and curling (once).

Track and field is emphasized in all provinces.

Swimming Where swimming is included in the program it is usually taught once a week. This amounts to one-third or one-half of the entire program. In some situations where facilities permit, a more balanced program is obtained by discontinuing this activity for two-thirds of the winter months.

The first responsibility of the physical education department is to teach every non-swimmer to swim, and second to this, the elements of water safety and life-saving. Recreational swimming skill comes last— diving, speed swimming, and, most popular of all at the present time, synchronized swimming.

In the large centers where swimming is taught in elementary schools, a large percentage of pupils are able to swim before entering secondary school. It is then possible to specialize in synchronized swimming where pupils find scope for their creative ability and increase their recreational skills.

It is common practice to have those who are temporarily excused change into gymnastic costumes to participate in the land drill when new skills are taught and to assist with coaching under the direction of the instructor. In this way, the pupil keeps abreast of the class in understanding, and may even make useful contributions.

THE EXTRACURRICULAR PROGRAM This is considered by all provinces as an integral part of the physical education program in schools. The fact that it is conducted after regular class periods, that it is recreational and voluntary, that no credit is given for participation other than simple awards, and that it is not ordinarily specified in a teacher's contract, does not alter the fact that the profession has accepted the additional responsibilities entailed, probably because of the inherent satisfactions that accompany it.

The co-ordination of curricular and extracurricular activities is common practice, the application of the skills taught in daily classes being a natural follow-up that consolidates learning and increases enjoyment. All provinces report that activities are scheduled before school, at noon, and after school, which would indicate that facilities carry a peak load. All students are encouraged to participate and the programs are planned to meet the varied interests of the students. It is usual for the intramural program to take precedence over the extramural competition. (Too frequently this cannot be said of the boys' program.)

Regulations and Common Practices

a) Physical education requirements   Physical education has long been a required subject in most Canadian high schools. Lack of facilities and the widespread shortage of qualified women teachers are the chief reasons for not requiring the subject in all grades. In Saskatchewan, Quebec (Protestant), and Prince Edward Island, it is compulsory in all four high school grades. British Columbia and Manitoba require it in three grades (IX-XI). Alberta in two grades (IX-X). Nova Scotia in Grade IX only. Theoretically the subject is compulsory in the Roman Catholic (English) schools of Quebec, but teachers and facilities for this are lacking. Newfoundland has not yet made physical education a compulsory subject though in some of the larger schools it is required.

Most provinces specify two periods a week for this subject; Saskatchewan requires only one period per week; Manitoba, Nova Scotia, and Prince Edward Island one or two periods per week; Ontario four periods per week.

b) Marking   Departmental regulations in the three western provinces require a mark for physical education. In all other provinces the schools are free to determine their own policy with respect to marking and grading. All provinces suggest that no more than 5 to 10 per cent of the time be devoted to marking. Five provinces give marks for attitudes (one as much as 25 per cent) ; four give marks for attendance and costumes; all base marks on a combination of objective tests, knowledge tests and skill ability.

c) Costumes   Costumes for physical education classes are now standard equipment in all provinces, but vary in type. Shorts with blouses or jerseys appear to be the most popular; one-piece romper suits are favored by three provinces, Ontario, Quebec, and Nova Scotia. Teachers wear tunics, tennis-style costumes, or short skirts and blouses.

Barefoot work is becoming increasingly common for dance, exercises, and gymnastics.

Conclusion

A curriculum is evaluated by its results. These cannot be scientifically measured for the whole of Canada at the moment. They can, however, be imagined and hoped for. It might be hoped to see girls rushing eagerly to the gymnasium, dressing with lightning speed that they might have a few moments of practice before class; to see every girl participating, dressed in a clean, colorful, attractive costume. There should be purposeful activity in every lesson; lessons packed full of activity and fun, learning and achievement, pupils challenged to extend themselves physically and mentally; self-control, initiative, and good work habits. Further, on leaving school, every girl should carry herself erect and with body pride, moving with grace and poise; she should know how to play two or three team games and two or three individual games with skill and enjoyment, be able to participate in a folk dance group with confidence, swim with safety and be prepared to assist others when needed. These are a few of the results hoped for from physical education for girls in the secondary schools of Canada.

BIBLIOGRAPHY

1. Copp, Harold W., "The History of Physical Education and Health in Ontario Schools." Master's thesis, University of Michigan, 1933.
2. Donaldon, Darryl, "Physical Education in the Elementary and Secondary Schools of Ontario to the Year 1911." An unpublished historical essay, 1937.
3. *Journals of C.A.H.P.E.R.*, 1933-61.
4. Ontario, *Courses of Study and Examinations*, 1885-1936. Toronto: Department of Education.
5. ———, *Courses of Study in Physical Education*, 1937-55. Toronto: Department of Education.
6. ———, *Inspector's Reports*, 1870-1930. Toronto: Department of Education.
7. Phillips, Charles E., *The Development of Education in Canada*. Toronto: W. J. Gage, Limited, 1957.
8. "Physical Education," *Encyclopaedia Canadiana* (1958).
9. Reports of the Minister of Education for the Provinces, 1930-40. Newfoundland, 1949-50.
10. Van Dalen, D.B., E. D. Mitchell, and B. L. Bennett, *A World History of Physical Education*. Englewood Cliffs, N.J.: Prentice-Hall, Inc., 1957.

LEADERSHIP TRAINING

11

Hart M. Devenney   *Inspector of Special Services (Physical Education)*
                                    Ontario Department of Education

A DEFINITION

To ask the question "What is a leader?" may seem trite, but there is no quick or single answer to such a question. Is leadership of the same type or the same quality in all situations? When is a "leader" leading or exercising leadership? When he is "first" in a race? When he is the "strongest" member, physically or mentally, of his organization or class? When he has the "highest" rank? When he is the "instructor"? Does it always mean that the individual best equipped, mentally or physically, will be the leader?

Obviously from such queries it should be apparent that there are different kinds of leaders and different kinds of leadership. Even the words will have varying connotations to all who would carefully pursue the topics. In recent years researchers in the fields of human behavior have been investigating the subject of leadership. These social scientists have been concentrating on the functions of the leader rather than on the consequences of leadership behavior; or, as in the early days of such study, on the personality traits which were thought to be the embodiment of good leadership potential. Much new information has, therefore, come to the attention of those professional and business people whose primary work responsibilities bring them close to the related problems of leadership training, the newer methods of leadership training, and the new approaches to the organization of potential leaders. Furthermore, these are too often being experimented with, conducted, and developed through what might be called "crash" empiricism.

Leadership is exerted when those who follow are influenced in some manner to do three things; to listen to the leader and to agree on common goals; to follow a leader or his advice; and to go into action on these goals.

All three of these conditions must be present before it can be said that leadership is in operation or is really effective. There can be no leadership without followers and there can be no effective leadership unless the followers go into action.

In the exercise of his leadership in these terms, then, the experienced leader makes use of a great variety of complex and subtle means to influence and stimulate those toward whom he directs his leadership to be creative and productive respecting goals or efforts. Most typical of these means are considered to be telling, selling, testing, consulting, and joining.

What has actually been said thus far is to intimate that in its essence leadership is the influencing of others to the point where there has occurred, or will inevitably occur, some change in behavior patterns. Behavior is a changeable manifestation (either in a positive or a negative direction) of a reaction to knowledge, values, skills, and relationships.

If behavior is to be changed positively—i.e., for the further advancement or the improvement of the individual through the efforts of the leader—then there must be a personal and involuntary acceptance by the follower of suggestions, instructions, or directives. But it has been said that behavior can also be changed negatively. Leadership in this respect has been wont to impose conditions which, although accepted by the followers out of fear of loss of prestige, status, or salary, or even fear of punishment (mental or physical), are totally and undeniably rejected as voluntarily assumed, and therefore the behavior change is transitory.

In consequence of all this, it might be said that a leader is an exceptional person. He must be prepared for opposition and for hard work. He must be, to a degree, self-reliant, not to the point of smugness or arrogance but with a quiet confidence in his ability and desire to lead. As such he will have great inner strength. He will have a need to know his environment, and this need becomes more obvious when he recognizes the forces which impinge upon him. If leadership is related to the needs of others (the followers), then the leader must also recognize his own relationships with others. Thus a second set of forces will be present to influence his own behavioral reactions.

Besides these needs, there are qualities which affect leadership and which may make the leader a total failure in terms of results. Bad programs carried out by recognizably good but irresponsible leaders may be given as examples of one of the most difficult phases of the leadership problem. What one leads in and where he leads his followers is more important than the efficiency of the leadership itself. The historical accounts of the bizarre, hysterical, and disastrous leadership of Hitler and Mussolini are prime examples of this.

It has already been pointed out that there are limits to leadership and that a leader in one area of activity is not, *ipso facto*, a leader in all areas. There are definite limits to areas of leadership, to leadership goals, and to the time that is available for the exercise of leadership.

TWO LEADERSHIP TRAINING PROJECTS

It is with these general views of leadership in mind that one may find it profitable to review the development of leadership training projects in certain fields of education in Ontario.

Before narrating the growth and the development of the two leadership training projects of the Ontario Department of Education, it is important and timely to outline the history of these two schemes, formerly under the direction of the Department's Physical Education Branch.

The Ontario Athletic Leadership Camp and the Ontario Camp Leadership Centre have been in operation since 1946 and 1947 respectively. In 1963, 360 girls and 360 boys attended the Athletic Leadership Camp at Lake Couchiching, while 160 girls and 120 boys were registered at the Camp Leadership Centre, familiarly known as Bark Lake. There is very little difference in the basic purpose of the two programs; both are designed to develop volunteer leaders who have the potential to inspire their peers. Couchiching provides leadership development for high school students, generally in Grade XI, who are committed to assist the physical education teachers of their schools throughout the next academic year. Bark Lake Camp participants are trained to take leadership responsibilities in non-profit camps and are expected to assume these duties for one summer as unpaid volunteers. Since the inception of the camps the total number of trainees for the two camps is estimated at over 6,000 girls and 5,000 boys. These young people were all carefully selected after going through a screening process which included such things as leadership potential, swimming ability, academic standing, age, and willingness to give service after they completed the course. All candidates had attained at least a Grade X academic standing and were sponsored by either their respective high schools, or, if they were selected for Bark Lake, a non-profit children's camp. Acceptance for the training periods meant also the assumption of a service obligation, i.e., an obligation to their respective sponsors for a period of service previously agreed upon by the sponsor and the trainee. It is interesting to note that in this respect these young people, whose average age would be seventeen years plus, fulfilled their service agreement with a less than one per cent reneging record. Usually there is a long waiting list or applicants, particularly of girls; and a considerable number of those who are accepted go on into teaching or social work.

It was the far-reaching insight of one of the great Chief Directors of Education for Ontario, the late Dr. J. G. Althouse, which led to the acquisition of facilities upon which the physical assets—buildings, play space, and so on—were constructed, and which inspired the efforts of the early pioneers in the two projects. The former Director of the Physical Education Branch in Ontario, Gordon A. Wright, worked indefatigably on improving and developing the two projects. This work is being continued and expanded to meet further needs by the present administration. With one or two exceptions, staff have been drawn from the teaching profession, both elementary and secondary branches. The success and the enviable reputation that both Couchiching and Bark Lake enjoy throughout Ontario is in no small measure due to the interest and enthusiasm of these professional teachers. Indicative of the success of this program is the fact that each new season sees former trainees returning as staff members. In nearly all cases their continued interest in leadership and the incentive to go into teaching were motivated by their training for leadership responsibilities while they attended one of the two camps.

The whole theory of the two programs stems from the fact that if one is to become a leader, then opportunities for the practice of leadership must be immediately at hand during any period of training. Another way of saying this is that only as there is a need for leadership can there be any opportunity for practicing leadership. In the camp programs there are daily—almost hourly—many opportunities for the practicing of leadership created by the members of the staff. The primary assumption in this regard, and one which is borne out by researchers and students in the field, is that leaders can be trained. This assumption also has been accepted by the Department of Education officials responsible for the operation of the two leadership centers.

In reviewing the methods employed by the staff of these two leadership projects, it is hoped that evidence of the application of the theories outlined in the opening paragraphs of this chapter will be revealed.

In selecting trainees for the highly concentrated and intense period of training, the Department has a definite purpose and definite objectives in mind. Those individuals who successfully complete the Couchiching courses return to their respective high schools to give service in the physical education departments of those schools, by acting as officials in extramural activities and demonstrators in class activities, and aiding in various other areas where their service is needed. The graduates of the Camp Leadership Centre serve in non-profit camps. This is important to keep in mind, for while the general objectives for the camps have been developed *intra muros,* as it were, by the Physical Education Branch, the specifics are fully discussed by the staff at pre-camp get-togethers, and later on by the trainees when they first arrive at camp. Whatever evaluation or assessment is attempted is only done in the light of the objectives which have been accepted by all concerned before the actual time of training begins. There can be no changing horses in midstream once the training period is under way. Adaptions to new situations, yes; but no new or strange objectives can be inserted halfway through or at the end of the program. Only in this manner can a valid assessment of progress be made.

Earlier it was suggested that the behavior of an individual may be changed, either positively or negatively, insofar as four fundamental human competencies are concerned—knowledge, values, skills, and relationships. The leader will function mainly, if not wholly, with respect to these competencies.

Generally speaking, one may also assume that it is in the functioning of a group or organization that leadership plays its most useful role. If this is so, then in the act of leadership the aspiring leader will be required to have knowledge, which may be described not only as a range of information but also as rudimentary to an understanding of the situation in which his leadership ability is to function. Usually one thinks of this as being acquired in the more formal environment of the classroom. It is best to remember, however, that there are many ways to acquire knowledge; in other words, that knowledge is perhaps the easiest competency for the leader to acquire. But unless it is correlated with the other competencies mentioned above, little behavioral change is effected. There must be insight and understanding as well as attitudes and feelings about the knowledge. This means the development of a system of values and value priorities.

Much success is achieved at the two leadership training camps of the Department of Education in Ontario. This is especially so because those who come to the centers are specially selected young people with a background of qualifying prerequisites. It is interesting to examine some examples taken from the procedures followed at Bark Lake.

A core of leadership spheres within which there are demanded particular and entirely different techniques of function from the leader are included in the course of study: swimming (water safety), canoeing, outtripping, woods lore, and crafts. There are other fringe areas touched upon, but these are basic to the course. Involving all of these is the basic subject called Counsellor Training. The knowledge of leadership procedures that must be acquired by the trainee will be different in each sphere; the insight and the understanding required will deepen with each new experience depending upon the value assessments consciously or unconsciously made at the time of the experience. Old attitudes and feelings will give way to the new only when the leader experiences greater success with the new.

This has been recognized at Bark Lake and the method of approach to the newly-arrived trainee is to place him almost immediately into the core situations called for at any one particular time during the instructional day. The organizational format calls for four sections of twenty-two to thirty trainees, depending upon whether the program is dealing with girls or boys. Since the administration is worked on a rotary schedule, no two sections are doing the same thing at the same time. The staff members assigned to each section follow through as guides and critics only. There are no specialists. All are competent for the task given them.

The fledgling leader is thrust, as it were, into the "cold water" of experience in any one of the core areas. He may fumble, struggle, dawdle, or be in a complete "funk." At the end of the leadership assignment, there is a period of evaluation. What was done by the leader? How was it done? What has to be improved upon if really productive leadership function is to be forthcoming? In other words, what behavioral changes are to be desired? And finally, what are the methods, the techniques, the procedures which are needed in order that the so-called improvement might be realized?

Knowledge, yes; values (insight, understanding, attitude, and feeling), yes; but in order that there may be an advance, a change, there must be a learning process in operation. This is the job of the neophyte working with the counsellor.

It might be expected that trainees who come to either Couchiching or Bark Lake would already have developed certain skills, mainly physical, which they have been able to practice in their home communities. For this select group, skills such as swimming, canoeing, track and field, game skills of various types, and so on are perhaps the most developed of all the competencies for the simple reason that there has been more practice time given to them. But the acquirement of physical skills is not a guarantee of a leadership function which will be productive of the kinds of results which are positive in meaning and of value to the development of good citizenship. The performance of physical skills must not be allowed to supersede or in any way detract from the main objective, good leadership. Performance on this basis, as opposed to leadership and/or training, is purely personal and is not directed toward group instruction or improvement.

There are other skills of the leadership function which are given high priority at the two leadership centers in Ontario and these should not be overlooked in developing such a program as is carried on. Practice is

given the trainee in leading discussion groups, in planning programs and
co-ordinating experiences, in being a good listener, in helping others
with their performance, in diagnosing group problems by using typical
case situations, in role-playing, and in performing various leadership
functions concurrent with participation in other aspects of the program.

Leadership is developed and is best learned in a group setting where
interaction constantly provides learning situations. Action within a
group or a "group process" may be thought of as the way people arrange
themselves and their relationships with others in order to get something
important accomplished either for themselves or society generally. When
this is fully understood by the trainees leadership goes much beyond
the mere organizational aspects of sports, recreation or physical educators' programs and begins to focus on acceptable behavior patterns in
today's society. Leadership is exerted when those who follow are influenced in some way to listen and to agree on common goals; to follow
approved and acceptable advice; and then to go into action on these
goals. The importance of the facts, therefore, respecting the leader's need
to maintain good relationships with others cannot be overemphasized.
Leadership does not function *in vacuo*. There must be communication.

Glib comments have been made in the last two or three decades about
democracy. Much, too, has been written about the need for training
leaders to work within the democratic system of values so that its future
functioning will be assured. Most people will agree, however, that democracy in any sense involves the relationships of many individuals and
groups of individuals. Few people realize that the wrong kind of relationships or a questionable type of participation may result, not in democracy, but in what might be called a disguised, although perhaps benifi-
cent, totalitarianism.

In the process of a leadership training program, if there is no provision
for implementing some conception of what is common to all members of
a group, then there will be no opportunities provided for developing
attitudes and feelings about democracy. This will mean that participation must be fundamental to the process, but it can only be regarded as
such when three basics are considered: first, a recognition that participation must be motivated from within the individual and in areas of concern to him; second, a recognition that some sort of opportunity must be
provided which will allow for "feedback" or in other words some way to
get accurate information about the difference between what he is trying
to do and how well he is doing it; third, a recognition that further action
in regard to opportunities is possible and permissible.

All of this calls for positive relationships among those who are engaged
in the training process. In all the leadership projects which have been
developed and promoted by Ontario in its leadership camps, it might

well be asked, "What experiences are the trainees being provided in relationships?"

The samples of leadership opportunities which follow are provided in the centers because it is recognized that there is need to encourage these relationships. Even in the short training periods available the carefully selected trainees can and do make progress. For this reason it is felt that positive attitudes and feelings toward the democratic process are being encouraged.

The organization of the projects is such that experiences are provided whereby these young people are given responsibilities as section or cabin leaders. They serve on activity committees of various kinds. They take responsibility for planning, conducting, and organizing "cook-outs" and "out-trips." They assume teaching assignments in activity areas to help in instruction sessions by teaching lessons in nature lore, in woodcraft, canoeing, swimming, athletic games, and many other types of programs. Special projects are chosen in which selected leaders-in-training (L-I-T's) carry out organizing chores which also will bring them into close relationships with their fellows. They do service assignments relating to the health and the hygiene of their little communities. Interest groups provide opportunities for specialist leadership interests which supplement the more formal assignments. Individual trips are set up for small groups.

Where five or six teen-age students live together for up to three weeks in a closely-knit family cabin group there is bound to be an awareness of those intangibles which go to make up the good community. All of this actually takes place in situations where theory is put into practice. Because of the great variety of leadership situations it is important for all members to realize that although they may be leaders in one situation, they will often be required to be followers in others.

THE PROGRAM

A generalized outline of what goes on in these specialized leadership training projects may be put more in focus by taking a more concentrated look at the Ontario Camp Leadership Centre program of training.

The objectives of the Centre are related to the non-profit camps of the province, i.e. the Church and Association camps, the Scouts and Guides, and the agency camps. It is from these camps, most of them short-term, that the sponsored trainees come and it is to them that the L-I-T returns after the leadership course has been completed. The objectives are thus related to the specifics of leadership. Specialized camp programs include water safety, canoeing and boating, out-tripping, camp craft and woods lore, nature lore and crafts, the nature of leadership, and a realization of how "on-the-spot" or "at hand" facilities and equipment can be used to meet camp purposes.

Within this format, then, every L-I-T is offered, either by assignment or through volunteering, leadership opportunities.

John Jones, a seventeen-year-old with Grade XI academic standing, may be cited as a typical camp trainee. The process of his training in one phase of the program may be outlined as follows:

Upon arrival he is given a physical examination by the camp doctor, takes an induction swimming test, and is tested on his ability in handling canoes. Such tests are the only formal tests he is required to take on a strictly pass-or-fail basis. Failure in either of the first two would have meant that he could not have continued the course of training.

From this point on John is under constant challenge. He is assigned to a section of twenty-nine other boys of varying age range (16½-19), which for the balance of his stay at Bark Lake is his community group. Although he follows the same format as L-I-T's in the other three sections, the rotary schedule means that he and his fellows do not do the same things at the same time as these sections.

Space does not permit a detailed exposition of all of John's opportunities for leadership experience during his three-week stay at the Centre. His effort as trip leader for the long out-trip of five meals has been chosen and this example is offered in support of the method of training which has already been described in general terms.

A few days before the trip was scheduled to leave, John was chosen as trip leader in open vote by his section, during the preparatory meeting in the section lodge. His was to be the responsibility for arranging all the details of the trip. He could not even rely on his counsellors, as he had done when he was simply a follower. The staff members would be going with their section but only as guests. During the trip they would be making mental notes of John's techniques of leadership, but would not have any direct responsibility for what happened unless an emergency situation of serious proportions developed, such as sickness or accident. Their impressions would be saved for the evaluation session which would be held upon the return of the section to camp.

The out-trip plan which it had been John's responsibility to develop required him to make provision for various essential jobs to be filled by members of his group. He assigned one person the responsibility of checking canoes and paddles; another food requirements; another tents; another fires; another three or four wood, and so on. The over-all responsibility was John's: he was held accountable for the success of the trip. When out on the trip, assignments were made to certain group members o teach lessons—on nature lore, woodcraft, and other activities in which he group will participate.

The five meals for which the trip would be away from camp, the canoeing route, the orienteering and map reading, the nature knowledge, the environment of the forest; all of these are the areas for which practice in leadership is possible. After it is over, the period of evaluation takes place. No doubt mistakes have been made. The members of the expedition, very serious about the discussion, will spend an hour or so on this process of assessment. Criticism will be constructive but incisive. When the final summation has been made, with comments, by the staff members, John Jones, and all members with responsibilities during the trip, will have learned something of the techniques of leadership. This has been the real purpose of the trip.

In each area of training, the L-I-T's will have somewhat similar experiences, accepting responsibilities, working on them with others, assessing and evaluating what has been done, making mental decisions as to what might have been done differently or what might have been improved upon so that the next time an opportunity for further experience will be presented, some evidence of progress will be seen. This, then, is what is known as "leadership training" by the staff at the Ontario Camp Leadership Centre.

Henry L. Stimson, one of the great American Secretaries of State, once wrote: "No private program and no public policy, in any section of our national life, can now escape from the compelling fact that if it is not framed with reference to the rest of the world, it is framed with perfect futility." If the implications and the seriousness of this statement are recognized in relationship to others, then perhaps training for leadership responsibilities will take on an entirely different look. Canada has a serious bicultural problem which must be solved. In fact, the entire world must face the struggle to improve interracial conditions and situations.

Is it not possible that efforts at leadership training, even within the framework of professional interests of physical educators and recreationists, may be turned toward helping to provide leaders who will accept and be able to meet the challenges that Canada and the world face now and in the future? There is evidence to suggest that what is being done in the Ontario Department of Education's two projects is a step in the right direction.

The Ontario professional people in the field of recreation and physical education like to think that they are helping to improve the potential of the leader by the training methods which have been described and which are being practiced. At least, a carefully planned attempt has been made to do this and the Department is committed to further efforts to expand this contribution. There is no suggestion that the Ontario leadership training program has been perfected. There is still much to be learned. But, generally, one must appreciate the fact that this program has been under way long enough to have discovered and dealt with the usual difficulties. Procedures are constantly being revised to prevent recurrence of such difficulties. Intensive and sometimes soul-searching sessions are held by the staff members of both the girls' and the boys' camps for this very reason—in order to make a realistic evaluation of the season's work. These staff reports have been of great help to the Department of Education in making preparations for a new season.

PLANNED-FOR RESULTS

In summary, the premise underlying the two projects has been that leaders are made, not born, and that the functions of leadership can be and are learned. The process is continuous and co-operative. If learning occurs when an individual experiences a problem or recognizes a gap between where he is and where he wants to be, then he will proceed by a self-inquiry in which he will draw on all available resources. This is where the staff finds its chief responsibilities. As critics, as guides, as observers of action, the staff members help the leader-in-training to learn leadership.

By setting goals beforehand and by attempting to have them clearly understood it may be expected that the learning will be efficient and purposeful. Students at the two training centers are thus not put through a series of "hoops" nor are they marked or examined in the formal school fashion. Almost from the beginning, the L-I-T's diagnose their needs for further development. This maks it possible to legitimately assess progress.

Learning, as has been intimated, involves a change in behavior and it should always be emphasized that change of any sort tends to be resisted. Leadership means the translation of knowledges, insights, attitudes, skills, and values into one's everyday conduct. Each new year at the Centres, the acceptance of this is reaffirmed by putting it to the test in the deliberate planning that is always a part of the preparation for the new season. Aids such as a leader-in-training "log book" have been given at times to the newly-arrived trainee at the Camp Leadership Centre at Bark Lake. In this log book may be recorded by the trainee, without compulsion, his own day-to-day observation of his experiences as they reflect changes in outlook, skills, knowledge, or relationships.

Nearly all of the leaders-in-training show evidence of progress during the time that they are within a center. This additional motivation makes for the investment of additional energy. These young people who attend

Bark Lake or Couchiching work hard from the early rising bell to the 10 P.M. closing, harder than they have ever worked before. It is purposeful hard work, self-imposed and to a large extent self-motivated. They are accepted, when they arrive at the camps, as young people who, by and large, are mature for their age and thus they are judged as willing to accept responsibility. They are not treated as children but as individuals with a potential for leadership which can be further developed by proper guidance. The staff fully recognizes that a finished product cannot be sent out in a short time. As a matter of fact, to accept such a premise in any length of course would be self defeating because learning is a continuing process which in reality never stops. These young people, then, have merely been helped and guided a little further along the road toward the ultimate realization of their full potential—and no one actually knows when this comes.

In a recent publication, the author stated that, "The greatest type of satisfaction to the leader-in-training comes from the self-respect developed by having gone through a rigorous high-quality program successfully." This is the aim and hoped for role of the two camps in leadership training in Ontario.

In an address to the Ontario Association for Curriculum Devolpment in October 1951, the late Dr. J. G. Althouse raised some very poignant questions regarding educational objectives which might well be considered today as educational progress continues. There is little disagreement among teachers, administrators, coaches, and researchers that part of their professional responsibilities lie in the field of leadership training. It is important therefore to be certain of the position which is advocated. It is necessary to be certain and satisfied as to the direction taken and the methods used.

Dr. Althouse made these points clear when he said, "When your ideas on this subject [educational objectives] have begun to crystallize, I am sure that you will feel the need of going on to consider how these shall be taught . . . [you will have] a continuing and profound concern over who shall teach [the subject]." He then goes on to propound the most important question, "What is the purpose of public education?"

Perhaps one should suggest that this same question phrased in a little different manner should be of major concern today. What is the purpose, the real purpose of professional efforts in leadership training? What is a leader? When is an individual exercising leadership?

For the past two decades the study of leadership has greatly increased in importance. As evidence of this are the many references now available in this field. The brief bibliography appended at the end of the chapter is very selective in respect to specific areas and is only a slight indication of the type of material available. New publications are appearing almost monthly and should be carefully read and discussed by those who desire to pursue the study of leadership. Leadership is not static: it is dynamic in the truest sense of the term.

Today's environment is one of rapid change. Technological changes, changes in the mores of the people, changes in relationships, in values, in knowledge, even in skills, all affect a populace not quite willing to break away from tradition, but being forced into new situations for which they often find themselves ill equipped.

More than ever leaders are needed. Industry and management have been realizing this for years, but only within the last decade have they turned to specifics as to how their leadership can be improved. The church, the school, and the social sciences have begun to study ways and means with varying degrees of experimentation and success. The resistance to change involving a new look at leadership training can be traced, in part, to the psychological "sets" which are developed by individuals and which determine many human reactions to particular situations.

The experiments in leadership training being carried out by the Ontario Department of Education at Lake Couchiching and at Bark Lake have amply demonstrated that leaders can be trained and that leadership can be learned. This being so, the fact may be accepted that leadership training is of pre-eminent importance in any breakdown of educational objectives.

Leadership under legal authority and with power concentrated in the hands of a dictator is a relatively simple matter. Leadership under democratic conditions is a subtle and difficult procedure. A good leader must be conscious of effective procedures and recognize the influence of the forces within himself, the forces within the group he is trying to lead, and the forces within the situation he faces.

It is difficult, in fact quite impossible, to deal properly and fully with the subject of "leadership" and "leadership training" in one brief chapter. It is to be hoped that what has been described as the experiments of one province in Canada may motivate others to further experiment in this field of leadership training. A permissive climate is not easily achieved. Those who would engage in such programs must abandon traditional concepts of power and dominance insofar as leadership is concerned. They must place their faith in the willingness, the sincerity, the enthusiasm, and the ability of young people to solve problems which are real to them. The traditional urge to dominate them should be displaced by the more civilized urges to aid, to encourage, and to inspire. The success of others—which means their growth—is the reward of the status leader who may be given the initial opportunity of establishing a leadership program. Therefore such a program will be most successful with long-term results when it is recognized that leadership is effective in direct proportion to the extent to which the trainees are involved in solving problems which are important to them; that best results can come when members of the training group recognize the need for group action in the solution of problems common to the group; that the leadership learning process is started at the point where the group is; that real progress and development will come slowly; that the training program must be one of action and not just the enervating procedure of continuous chatter and discourse; that insofar as is possible, the leadership activity should involve wide participation from all concerned in the training project—staff, students, and other members of the training community; that the leadership program should be such as to release energy, not bottle it up; that a thread of creativity should run through the program; that everyone in the training program should be given leadership responsibilities of some nature in a wide variety of opportunities; and that, finally, democratic procedures should supplant authoritarian ones. For a discussion of other areas of leadership function the reader is referred to the bibliography, particularly Auren Uris' book, *The Techniques of Leadership.*

BIBLIOGRAPHY

1. Althouse, J. G., *Addresses*. Toronto: W. J. Gage, Limited, 1962.
2. Andrews, J. H. M., "The Practical Function of Research," *Canadian Education & Research Digest*, III, No. 3 (1963).
3. Beckhard, Richard, "Consultative Process," *Looking into Leadership Monographs*. Washington D.C.: Leadership Resources, Inc., 1961.
4. Bennett, T. R., "Process of Change," *Looking into Leadership Monographs*. Washington D.C.: Leadership Resources, Inc., 1961.
5. Blansfield, Michael G., "Appraisal of Personnel," *Looking into Leadership Monographs*. Washington D.C.: Leadership Resources, Inc., 1961.
6. Bradford, Leland P., "Devolping Instructional Leaders," *Journal of the Association for Supervision and Development*, XX, No. 3 (1962).
7. ———, "Human Forces in Teaching and Learning," *Selected Reading Series #3*, National Training Lab. Washington, D.C.: National Education Association, 1961.
8. Brown, David S., "Authority & Hierarchy," *Looking into Leadership Monographs*. Washington, D.C.: Leadership Resources, Inc., 1961.
9. ———, "Decision-making," *Looking into Leadership Monographs*. Washington, D.C.: Leadership Resources, Inc., 1961.
10. Browne, C. G., and T. S. Cohn, *The Study of Leadership*. Danville, Ill.: Interstate Printers & Publishers, 1958.
11. Buchanan, Paul C., "Individual Motivation," *Looking into Leadership Monographs*. Washington, D.C.: Leadership Resources, Inc., 1961.

12. Burton, Wm., and L. J. Brueckner, *Supervision, A Social Process* (3rd ed.), New York: Appleton-Century-Crofts, 1955.
13. Frazier, Alexander, ed., "Freeing Capacity to Learn," *4th Research Institute, Association for Supervision & Curriculum Development.* Washington, D.C.: 1960.
14. ———, ed., "Learning more about Learning," *3rd Research Institute, Association for Supervision & Curriculum Development.* Washington, D.C.: 1959.
15. Gordon, T. L., *Group-centered Leadership.* Boston: Houghton Mifflin Company, 1955.
16. Klein, A. F., "Developing Democratic Human Relations." *First Yearbook,* American Association for Health, Physical Education, and Recreation, 1951.
17. ———, *Society, Democracy & the Group.* New York: Women's Press and Wm. Morrow & Co., Inc., 1953.
18. Knowles, Malcolm S., "Self-development," *Looking into Leadership Monographs.* Washington, D.C.: Leadership Resources, Inc., 1961.
19. Laird, D. A., and E. C. Laird, *The Techniques of Delegating.* New York: McGraw-Hill Book Company, 1957.
20. Lippit, Gordon L., "Leadership in Action," *Selected Reading Series #2,* National Training Lab. Washington, D.C.: National Education Association, 1961.
21. ———, and Edith Whitfield, "Group Effectiveness," *Looking into Leadership Monographs.* Washington, D.C.: Leadership Resources, Inc., 1961.
22. Luszki, M. B., *Inter-Disciplinary Team Research, Methods & Problems,* National Training Lab. Washington, D.C.: National Education Association, 1958.
23. Miles, M. B., *Learning to Work in Groups.* Bureau of Pub., Columbia University Press, N.Y., 1959.
24. Montgomery, Viscount, *The Path to Leadership.* New York: G. P. Putnam's Sons, 1961.
25. Pollock, Ross, "Staff-Line Relations," *Looking into Leadership Monographs.* Washington, D.C.: Leadership Resources, Inc., 1961.
26. Ross, M. G., *Community Organization, Theory & Practice.* New York: Harper & Brothers, 1955.
27. ———, and C. E. Hendry, *New Understandings in Leadership.* New York: Association Press, 1957.
28. Schmidt, W. H., "Leadership Dilemma," *Looking into Leadership Monographs.* Washington, D.C.: Leadership Resources, Inc., 1961.
29. This, Leslie E., "Communication," *Looking into Leadership Monographs.* Washington, D.C.: Leadership Resources, Inc., 1961.
30. Tracker, H. B., *New Understandings of Administration.* New York: Association Press, 1961.
31. Uris, Auren, *The Techniques of Leadership.* Toronto: McGraw-Hill Book Company, 1964.
32. Waetjen, Walter, ed. "Human Variability Learning," *5th Research Institute ASCD.* Washington, D.C.: 1961.
33. ———, ed., "New Dimensions in Learning," *6th Research Institute, ASCD.* Washington, D.C.: 1962.
34. Warren C. Gilbert, *The Counsellor in a Changing World.* Washington, D.C.: American Personal Guidance Association, 1962.
35. Weschler, Irving R., "Creativity," *Looking into Leadership Monographs.* Washington, D.C.: Leadership Resources, Inc., 1961.

PHYSICAL EDUCATION AND RECREATION FOR GIRLS AND WOMEN

12

Winona E. Wood

Chairman, Physical Education Division
Institute of Education
McGill University, Montreal

GENERAL DEVELOPMENTS

As the twentieth century progresses, Canadian women are finding they have more and more leisure time. They also have more money to spend, not only because of the general affluence of Canadian society, but because women have become major wage-earners themselves. Many of the hobbies, club work, and different phases of community services engaged in by women exhaust neither time nor money. Alert commercial recreation interests, such as bowling syndicates (and on their heels, billiards) have moved quickly to offer their services to this new leisure group. Glamorous new "bowladromes," air-conditioned, decorated in eye-catching colors with handsomely carpeted and draped lounges, complete with baby-sitting services as well as automatic pin-setting equipment, and hushed by acoustic tiled ceilings, have sprung up in all parts of the country, designed to lure the feminine trade. Women, properly flattered by this assiduous attention to their tastes and comfort, have responded in droves and quickly profited from the courteous, excellent instruction provided.

During the last decade women have become fitness-conscious. The pursuit of fitness has led many to sports, others, in flocks, to "Keep-Fit" classes conducted by the "Y's" and community recreation organizations. It has pushed the XBX booklet to the top of the best-seller list. The XBX plan is a series of ten basic exercises for women, prescribed in such a way as to condition the body gradually and safely. Originally designed as

155

a program for women serving in the Royal Canadian Air Force, the XBX plan was received by the public with the same enthusiasm as had greeted the earlier program for airmen, the 5BX.

In the 1930's, the League for Health and Beauty, which had branches in most Canadian cities, catered to those women seeking the benefits through physical exercise of improved figures and general well-being. The Pro-Rec Program in British Columbia offered mass programs in fundamental gymnastics. During the war years, whether they were serving in the armed forces, in munitions factories, or in the home community, some women marched and exercised valiantly in mass, regimented programs. The post-war years restored citizens to the status of individuals, and as individuals women showed a wide range of interests in their choices of physical recreation—noticeably avoiding any mass activities. Some took to the air, piloting small craft, or gliding, or parachuting. Judo and yoga arrived to claim devoted practitioners, as did the dance in various forms: ballet, modern, square, and folk.

The prosperity of the post-war years furnished Canadians with thousands of miles of new and improved roads, thousands of automobiles, and unrationed gasoline, factors which turned a restless population into a mobile one. Canadians discovered how much of their land was actually water, and what fun could be had on it or in it or under it. Canadian women with their families took to motor boats, water-skiing, skin and scuba diving. Attracted by the clean, gleaming fiberglass boats which supplanted the traditional wooden craft, women became interested in, for one thing, angling. Of the 2,500,000 registered anglers in 1961, fifteen per cent were women.

The unsurpassed scenic beauty of Canada's vast wilderness areas, its magnificent forests and lakes, streams and mountains, have an irresible appeal for nature lovers and those who seek rugged outdoor living. Women are numbered among the pioneers who established organized camps before the turn of the century. Canoe tripping was and still is a featured activity of many of these camps. The Canadian Youth Hostel Association was founded in 1933 by two Calgary women, Catherine and Mary Barclay. From one unit it has grown to national stature, the organization now comprising six regional districts. Its membership includes over 1,000 girls and young women. Limited financial support over the years has resulted in an inadequate number of suitable and attractive hostels, which in turn has seriously hampered the growth of membership among girls. However, governments are now making commendable efforts in improving networks of trails and hostels in parks. The Fitness and Amature Sports Advisory Council, realizing that hostelling offers one of the best and most permanent means of enticing large numbers of Canadians into the ways of physical fitness, has provided some financial assistance under the terms of Bill C-13[1]. Interest in hostelling among Canadian girls has been quickened by the influence of European girls, who continue their tradition of hostelling as a means of becoming acquainted with the new country.

The Alpine Club is another organization which has introduced women to the rigors and deep satisfactions of outdoor recreation. Forty per cent of the 2,500 members of the Canadian Alpine Club are women, many of whom have enviable climbing records spanning some twenty-five to thirty years of active participation. In Canada women may join the Club independently, whereas in many European countries membership is open to women only if male members of the family are Alpinists. Trail skiing enables these lovers of nature to maintain contact with the outdoors in winter months. Although the numbers have dwindled, *touring* introduced the infant sport of skiing to this country and the faithful few, including women, stubbornly pursue their beloved sport in the face of discouraging obstacles erected by urban sprawl over many of the hillsides originally used.

The diversity of activities available to Canadian women and girls is matched by the diversity of agencies engaged in making the activities available. In total numbers involved, commercial interests undoubtedly surpass all other agencies. But this does not necessarily represent continued participation by the same individuals. The outstanding record of the Y.W.C.A. in providing soundly constructed and wisely administered programs commands special tribute. The needs of young women, particularly those entering careers, have always been its special concern, but programming has been kept flexible so that facilities and services have been extended to other groups. Throughout the years the Y.W.C.A. has given leadership in designing programs appropriate for girls. The Y.M.-the Y.W.C.A. in providing soundly constructed and wisely administered for women. From the early 1800's to the present, private clubs have enabled many girls and women to become proficient sportswomen. Sports clubs, with or without affiliation with sports governing bodies, have been tireless in their efforts to promote sporting activities. Organizations such as the Girl Guides, Canadian Girls in Training, various church clubs, the Women's Institute, the Canadian Red Cross with its water safety and swimming instruction programs, the Royal Canadian Legion through its sponsorship of track and field programs, welfare organizations, and, of course, educational institutions at all levels have all shared in developing physical education and recreation programs for girls.

Despite this apparent wealth of opportunity, Canadian women and girls are not noted for their avid eagerness for athletic activity. On the contrary, they are frequently reproached for their presence in the grandstands and for thus adding to over-indulgence in "spectatoritis." The opportunities for participation are not without some limitations. A complete lack of uniformity or equality of distribution of physical recreation facilities exists. Some communities are almost devoid of facilities for girls, while others abound in them. The majority of Canadian communities plead guilty to providing for boys and men first and concede the inadequacy of provisions for women. Almost universally, the lack of good leadership for girls' programs is cited as the basic cause of this situation. Faced with this difficulty, the expediency of offering modified boys's programs or nothing has become standard practice. The community problem steadily becomes more pressing as girls' school physical education programs have improved and become more common. Yearly, more and more girls on leaving school turn expectantly to the community for the continuation of the sports activities introduced to them in the schools. Lack of dynamic leadership, capable of arousing and sustaining interest, seems to be the factor which impedes the growth of girls' programs, both in communities where facilities are abundant but ignored, and in those which have not yet bestirred themselves to acquire facilities.

However, voluntary participation in physical recreation by Canadian women, steadily on the increase since 1940, suddenly soared in the 1960's. Exact statistical evidence cannot be produced, but two examples of unprecedented growth spurts point to a startling trend. Figures released by the Royal Caledonian Curling Club indicate that during the preceding decade (1950's), women curlers in Quebec and the Ottawa Valley increased their ranks from 2,609 to 6,220, and the number of private women's clubs rose from 53 a decade ago to 100. Participation has nearly tripled. The Report on the Survey of Fitness and Amateur Sports Activities in Nova Scotia (1961-62) revealed that within the previous two years the number of women bowlers leaped from a negligible figure to 17,000. Nor are these isolated incidents confined to one section of the country. The same phenomenon was observed from coast to coast and has given rise to much discussion. Optimists regard this as the beginning of a new era in sports participation by women. Less sanguine onlookers believe it to be merely a fad.

Within the protective framework of an educational institution, physical education programs in universities have prospered and grown in size and quality. Lacking the stability of tight organization and control, sports clubs show a more uneven growth pattern but by no means a discouraging one.

PHYSICAL EDUCATION FOR WOMEN IN THE UNIVERSITIES

Women's physical education departments in Canadian universities.

offer striking evidence of the recognition accorded to women students in university life in the twentieth century and to physical education as a desirable component of the total university experience. The tremendous growth in size of the women's student body, particularly since the late 1940's, is reflected in a parallel growth and expansion in women's physical education departments. The early typical department, inadequately staffed and equipped, offering a very limited program of formal gymnastic activities with a few sports (basketball predominating), was tolerated, and at the same time eclipsed, by the men's department. The modern counterpart, virtually autonomous, conducts an extremely varied program in accordance with policies of meeting professional standards for women's activities.

The austerity of the war years forced curtailment and regimentation of activities. In the post-war years, new and equally challenging problems arose, posed by the unprecedented influx of students. These years, in many ways trying and frustrating, were marked by the constant struggle to procure sufficient staff and facilities to enable departments to function efficiently despite overcrowded conditions. Fortunately, post-war prosperity has solved seemingly insoluble problems. It has contributed to the increase of professionally well-qualified teachers, as well as to the erection of new buildings and the acquisition of more facilities.

In most Canadian universities the Director of women's physical education is responsible to the Director of the men's department, but as facilities and equipment are to a large extent shared jointly, the organization and administration, on broad outlines, are interdepartmental matters. With respect to budget, selection of staff, planning of program, and specific policies, the men's and the women's departments are administered separately. The University of Toronto is the first Canadian university with a Women's Physical Education Department enjoying its own building and complete parity with the men's department.

The program offered by women's physical education departments can be classified under two headings: compulsory and voluntary. The compulsory program, also known as the service program, requires, on most campuses, participation in physical education classes two hours a week throughout the first year by all medically approved students. Although credit toward graduation is not granted, fulfilment of the requirement is a condition of graduation. Only one university with an enrollment of over 1,000 women students and two with an enrollment of under 1,000 do not have such a requirement.

A wide choice of activities exists within this requirement, with as many as twenty-six different activities being offered by the largest institutions, and as many as fifteen by some of the smaller ones. One restriction on choice which is almost universally enforced is the provision that non-swimmers must take instruction in swimming. Some also require one course in body mechanics. The core of the required program in all universities comprises the traditional sports: basketball, volleyball, tennis, badminton, swimming (including life-saving), some type of gymnastic "keep-fit" work, and dance. Where climate and facilities permit, curling, skating, skiing, and field hockey are offered. But program planning is far from being static. New trends are seen in the frequency with which synchronized swimming and modern dance are offered. Two institutions reflect contemporary society by including modern jazz dance and skin diving and scuba diving.

Voluntary participation by all students is encouraged by a program organized in three sections which recognize varying levels of ability and accommodate a wide range of interests. These three sections are recreational, intramural, and intercollegiate.

The activities which predominate in the recreational program are the individual and dual sports, many of which are conducted on a co-recreational basis. Recreational activities are organized on a club basis, and instruction is provided for those desiring it. Thus a student may indulge in a favorite sport, just for the sheer fun of playing, or she may join a club to learn a new skill and so benefit from the instruction provided. Swimming is the most popular choice in all universities, with skating, curling, badminton, and bowling also being prime favorites. Dance clubs are included in the recreational program of seven universities, and it is interesting to note that modern dance draws as many participants as folk and square dance.

The intramural program involves the greatest number of participants (two-thirds of the total enrollment in some institutions), providing as it does enjoyable competitive play for the girl with average skills. Basketball and volleyball dominate the intramural program, particularly in the smaller institutions, where the size of staff and limited facilities restrict the range of choice. Broomball, ice hockey, field hockey, curling, swimming, badminton, all rank high in popularity. Archery, bowling, tennis, and golf are commonly offered in the intramural program; fencing, riflery, and squash much less frequently, and judo by only one institution. Little emphasis seems to be placed on track and field or softball, possibly because these are seasonal events which do not coincide with the university term.

Intercollegiate competition is organized on a geographical basis. The Western Canadian Intercollegiate Athletic Association governs competition among universities in the prairie provinces and British Columbia. For the larger institutions in Ontario and Quebec, it is the Women's

Intercollegiate Athletic Union, while a separate body functions for the smaller colleges. The universities in the eastern provinces compete in the Maritime Intercollegiate Association. Telegraphic meets make it possible for all Canadian universities to compete against one another in such sports as archery, bowling, swimming, and a few use this form of meet for track and field as well.

The major consideration in setting the policies governing all competition for university women has always been the welfare of the competitor. For example, an intercollegiate competition, whether in team or individual sports, takes the form of a weekend tournament, thus reducing to a minimum the amount of travelling required and the loss of time from academic studies. Some universities enter teams in as many as sixteen different sports, but the average is about ten. Participation in leagues and invitation meets in the home city enable teams to maintain a satisfactory level of performance. Climate and terrain are determining factors with respect to outdoor activities. Field hockey is of major importance on the West Coast, where climatic conditions are favorable, as in the University of British Columbia. It is also important in the Maritime universities. But it is curling on the prairies and skiing at those institutions with easy access to the ski slopes of the Rockies or the Laurentians. Where marked fluctuations in interest in various sports have occurred, the determining factors have been the quality of competition and instruction available. Stimulating competition and enthusiastic, highly-skilled instruction outweigh factors such as superior facilities in maintaining a high level of participation. Competitive sports as conducted by the universities offer women the opportunity to experience competition in its most desirable form, where the mastery of skills and the matching of them in friendly rivalry are as important as winning.

Women's physical education departments view their role as an educational one rather than as producer of champion athletes. Policies are guided by a keen sense of responsibility for assisting all women students to realize as fully as possible the potential values inherent in physical education activities. A sincere effort is made to equip them with physical skills which can be enjoyed for many years, and to develop the conviction that such enjoyment and abilities are a part of the good life. Better prepared, both in physical and psycho-social attributes as a result of participation in the physical education program, women graduates leave the universities to take up the many-faceted roles awaiting them in contemporary society. Women physical educators will continue to operate a flexible program to meet the changing needs of the students in future decades, a program founded on sound educational principles and resistant to transient popular pressures.

The Organized Sports of Canadian Women and Girls

The organization of women's sports clubs has been of necessity very loose. The vast distances, accentuated until recent years by the lack of easy communication; the uneven distribution of population centers; the tendency of ethnic groups to cluster in pockets in the new country; the hazards of climate; the decentralized form of government: all these factors combined to foster the formation of sports groups entirely independent of each other, and even ignorant of each other's existence. Eventually most clubs did unite under one governing body, sometimes at the national level, but often only at the regional or provincial level. In the 1960's, with the hurdles of poor communication long since cleared, the habit of independent action lingers so that it is possible for two regional units (they can even exist in neighboring provinces) to busy themselves exclusively with their own concerns, indifferent to the operations of any affiliates. Geography and climate frequently have led clubs into international competition before experiencing it at the interprovincial or national level. For numerous reasons it was more convenient for most sports to be included in, or to be branches of, the men's organization. Thus it happened that only four women's sports, organized at the national level, are administered solely by women. These are the Canadian Ladies' Golf Union (founded in 1913), the Canadian Ladies' Curling Association (1955), the Canadian Women's Field Hockey Association (1962), and the Amateur Synchronized Swimming Association of Canada (1950). One sport, bowling, has no Canadian governing body, and participants are under the jurisdiction of the American body, Women's International Bowling Congress (1960).

The Women's Amateur Athletic Federation of Canada

The Women's Amateur Athletic Federation of Canada (W.A.A..F of C.), founded in 1925, was composed of provincial branches which controlled athletics (track and field), hockey, baseball, and basketball. General supervision of these sports included the issuing of amateur cards, and organization of meets and championships. The Federation was affiliated with the Amateur Athletic Union of Canada, and thus had international recognition of world sports groups. Baseball (softball) severed connections because it became so large that separate control seemed more efficient; basketball became affiliated with the men's organization of the sport, and hockey for women almost ceased to exist nationally. Fencing and gymnastics gained in prominence, however.

Because of the lack of sustained interest by women officials, the

W.A.A.F. of C. in 1953 asked to become part of the A.A.U. of C. This was effected in 1954, with one woman to be an executive member of the A.A.U. of C. This executive member was to be elected by the vote of the women representatives from each branch, one for each A.A.U. sport in which women compete. These branch representatives formed the Women's Advisory Committee. The organizational structure thus set up still functions. Mrs. Jean Calder of Montreal has frequently held the post of women's executive member, as has Miss Margaret Lord of Burlington, Ontario, who also served as Chairman of the Honours and Awards Committee.

VELMA SPRINGSTEAD MEMORIAL TROPHY

The late Alexandrine Gibbs of Toronto, one of the W.A.A.F. of C. founders and one-time president, gave a trophy in memory of Velma Springstead of Hamilton, who was a member of Canada's first international track and field team. It was first awarded in 1934 and has been awarded annually since that time. No stipulation was made that the sport must be under the jurisdiction of the Federation, but it was stipulated that the award be made on the basis of performance, sportsmanship, and behavior.

Nominations, accompanied by a substantiating citation, must be submitted prior to the Annual Meeting, when the Honors and Awards Committee weigh them and award the trophy. The trophy is displayed in the Hockey Hall of Fame at the Canadian National Exhibition Grounds, Toronto, together with photographs of the winners (see Appendix C).

THE SPORTS: INDIVIDUAL; DUAL; TEAM

ARCHERY Archery has had a limited following across Canada since 1920. The Canadian Archery Association has 5,000 registered members in some 200 clubs. The most active groups are in Ontario and British Columbia, although provincial tournaments are held annually and National Championships biennially. Target competition appeals equally to all age groups and is the main interest of women archers, although some do hunt with the bow and arrow. Because of the difficulty of obtaining suitable indoor ranges for winter participation, archery is predominantly a summer sport in Canada.

BADMINTON Badminton is not indigenous to Canada but has become Canadian by wholehearted adoption since the 1920's. Women have been enthusiastic participants for forty years, forming a substantial proportion of the total membership—approximately 15,000. Virtually every church basement, school hall, and vacant warehouse has housed informal clubs in villages and hamlets across Canada, in addition to the formally organized badminton clubs in the cities. Annual tournaments are held by provincial organizations, and open and closed tournaments by the Canadian Badminton Association. Thrice winner of the Canadian Women's Singles Championship, and also the British Ladies' Singles in 1939, Dorothy Walton of Toronto is the only badminton player ever to be awarded the Velma Springstead Memorial Trophy. Toronto has produced another outstanding player, Margaret Shedd, who has also won the Canadian Women's Singles three times.

BASKETBALL   Since basketball is probably the most universally played team sport in Canadian schools, few girls leave school without some playing experience. The form of the game familiar to a Canadan girl is determined largely by where she happens to live. Westerners usually play A.A.U. of C. rules, while Easterners play Canadian girls' rules. This came about because educational institutions in Eastern Canada (until recently more numerous and larger than those of Western Canada) have for many years had qualified women instructors and referees, who used only girls' rules. The more modest institutions in Western Canada with smaller staffs frequently depended on male instructors to handle the girls' programs. These instructors used the rules with which they were familiar, the traditional A.A.U. of C. rules. (The game according to the A.A.U. of C. rules is considered much more strenuous, as each player is permitted to play the whole court instead of being restricted to two-thirds of it, and also because five instead of six players compose a team.)

This tradition was further strengthened, in fact raised almost to a sacrosanct position, by the amazing performance of the Edmonton Grads in the 1920's and 1930's. The Grads, a succession of teams formed by the graduates of a technical school, coached by J. Percy Page (later Lieutenant-Governor of Alberta) established records never since approached by girls' basketball teams. In the period 1924-35 the Grads won 409 out of 421 games and frequently had to compete against men's teams in order to find teams of playing caliber equal to their own.

In recent years the Canadian Amateur Basketball Association has been the governing body for women's basketball, A.A.U. of C. rules. The regulation requiring that two vice-presidents on the governing board be women ensures that women control their own branch of the game. Provincial organizations are found in most provinces. Team membership comes largely from girls in their late teens who have gone directly to work from high school, or are in short vocational training courses. Industrial centers such as Hamilton, Ontario, where there are large numbers of young women in various trades, as well as the Air Force and Army bases, have flourishing leagues.

Enthusiastic and purposeful leadership provided by members of the women's physical education departments in eastern universities and high schools has produced a marked increase in the number of leagues playing under the Canadian girls' rules. Within the framework of C.A.H.P.E.R., a committee on women's sports has drawn up and published a new rule book. A vigorous program of clinics and officiating courses has been successful in establishing uniform standards of play at an improved level of performance.

BOWLING The only organized form of bowling is the ten-pin game. This is a new departure for Canadian women who have, over the years, indulged in the occasional game of bowling: five pins in the West, candle pins for the Easterner, and probably duck pins in Quebec. Until the recent transformation of bowling alleys into bowladromes, the game was largely the prerogative of men, but now there are approximately 2,000 Canadian women participating regularly in organized competition. Bowling can be and is enjoyed by all age groups.

CURLING The Canadian Ladies' Curling Association has been in existence only since 1955 when it was formed principally to arrange the Dominion Curling Championships known as the "Diamond D," but curling itself is the oldest organized sport for women in Canada. A glimpse of its history is provided by an excerpt from the program of the Fiftieth Anniversary Bonspiel of the Ladies' Curling Association of the Canadian Branch of the Royal Caledonia Curling Club, held at the Seingnory Club in 1954:

> The Ladies Curling Association was formed in 1904 and held its first meeting on February 4, 1904, with Mrs. E. A. Whitehead as its first president.
>
> However, ladies were mentioned in 1874 when Lady Dufferin was elected a member of the Vice-Regal Club as a member of the Men's Club.
>
> In 1894 we find first mention of a Ladies' Club, the Montreal Ladies' Club, but it was only in 1903 that the Ladies' Clubs, as follows, participated in play: Montreal, St. Lawrence, Lachine. That same year ladies were admitted to membership in the Canadian Branch of the Royal Caledonia Curling Club. In 1905 they had their own Bonspiel and played for their first trophy. As time went on the game gained in popularity. Today (1954) the Ladies' Curling Association is composed of 61 clubs with a membership of approximately 3000.
>
> Probably the first iron ever put up in a rink in Canada by a lady was at the Thistle Club on Monique Street by Lady Meredith, then Miss Brenda Allan. Apparently this was with one of the men's irons, as later Mr. George Brush made lighter irons for the ladies.

Ladies' curling clubs have a long history in Ontario and in the Maritimes as well. Surely curling irons (both kinds) must have weighted down settlers' effects as they trekked westward. The prairies became the second home of curling, and the curling rink became as familiar a landmark in the villages as the grain elevator. Now that artificial ice has become a commonplace, the curling fever sweeps the country from coast to coast. Canadian women, from teens to grandmothers, literally sweep away the winter months as they curl in bonspiels in local clubs, at provincial meets, or in the Dominion Championships. Invitation meets are held with American clubs, and teams of Canadian and American women curlers have visited Scotland and entertained the Scottish teams in return. Sociability and curling are inseparable, which probably accounts in part for the enduring popularity of the game.

FENCING Fencing associations exist in most provinces under the jurisdiction of the provincial branch of the A.A.U.of C. This sport was most popular for a period immediately following the First World War and again had a surge in popularity after the Second World War. The immigration of many Europeans, for whom fencing had been a major interest in the homeland, did much to stimulate and sustain interest in the sport in Canada. Fencing is most popular in Montreal, Toronto, and Vancouver, cities which have a cosmopolitan population.

Compared with other sports, fencing has never attracted large numbers of participants. It has suffered from lack of competition, lack of financial support, and indifference on the part of the press. In spite of these drawbacks, women fencers of international caliber have been developed: Betty Hamilton, Rhonda Martin, and Jeanne Gilbert have all been Canadian champions and have competed in the British Empire Games. Betty Hamilton and Rhoda Martin competed in the 1948 Olympics, Betty Hamilton winning a silver medal.

FIELD HOCKEY The mild climate of British Columbia provides the long season and the excellent turf that favor field hockey. It has long been a prime favorite in the schools and the university, and of the twenty-eight member clubs in the Canadian Women's Field Hockey Association, eighteen are in British Columbia. The Maritimes and Toronto account for the rest. Two teams from the British Columbia league have been sent to Australia and Europe to compete internationally. This league has also established a Rating Board for Umpires. In 1962 it was successful in getting a national body, the Canadian Women's Field Hockey Association, formed.

FIGURE SKATING During the early days of figure skating it was controlled by the Amateur Skating Association of Canada, along with speed skating. In 1914 the two activities, in reality so dissimilar, established separate organizations. In 1939 the figure skaters took the name of the Canadian Figure Skating Association and in 1947, was selected as the Canadian member for figure skating to the International Figure Skating Union of Davos, Switzerland.

In 1947-48 Barbara Ann Scott won all the world championships including the Olympics. She became the idol of small girls all over Canada, and the vogue for figure skating swept the country. From a very few clubs in the early days, the Association has grown to 240 member clubs which take care of approximately 100,000 skaters. The membership is predominantly girls and women. The annual meeting of the Association brings together 100 delegates from all parts of Canada, representing the seven sections into which the Association is organized. The Canadian Association can boast of the largest membership in the world, including many outstanding performers. Three times the pair championships—Canadian, North American, World, and Olympic—have been won by Canadians: Frances Dafoe and Norris Bowden; Barbara Wagner and Robert Paul; Maria and Otto Jelineck and eighteen-year-old Wendy Griner, who captured the Canadian championship for three successive years (1960-62), and added the North American Championships in 1963.

A great many Canadian girls skate their way into a career, joining one of the commercial shows. The glamorous costumes and settings combine with the graceful skating to transport audiences into fairyland—powerful influences in maintaining the high interest in figure skating.

GOLF   More than fifty years of extremely successful operation lie behind the Canadian Ladies' Golf Union, founded in 1913.

Whether owing to some quality inherent in the game of golf, or to some magic practiced by the national and provincial governing bodies, the percentage of membership competing seriously is much higher in golf than in any other women's sport. The Canadian Ladies' Golf Union has 385 member clubs in the ten provinces, two-thirds of them in Ontario and Quebec. The playing membership totals over 35,000 and includes all ages from twelve years up. The greatest increase in both club and player membership has occurred since 1955. This may be attributed to greater emphasis being placed on encouraging junior membership. A recent grant from the Fitness and Amature Sports Advisory Council made possible a Junior Development Program which produced immediate and gratifying results. The Canadian Open in 1962 was won by an eighteen-year-old junior, Gayle Hitchens; and another eighteen-year-old, Sue Hilton, won the Ontario Junior Open and the National Junior Closed, topping it off with a hole in one!

National Championships are held each year in a different province.

The competitions include senior and junior team matches in conjunction with the Closed Championship, which is followed by the Open Championship. Internationally, Canada entered both Commonwealth Tournaments, the most recent held in Australia in 1963, and the first (1959) at St. Andrews, Scotland, where it placed second.

Through the years Canada has had two outstanding competitive women golfers, both of whom have brought honors to Canada in international play and have been named Canada's Outstanding Woman Athlete of the Year: Ada Mackenzie in 1933 and Marlene Stewart in 1956. Miss Mackenzie's golf career is remarkable, not only for the number of trophies won, but for its duration of thirty-five years.

GYMNASTICS Competitive gymnastics for women received considerable impetus from the publicity following Ernestine Russell's outstanding performance: Canadian champion for ten years, 1950-60; three times winner of the United States all-round women's championship; and a Gold Medal recipient at the 1959 Pan-American Games. Then, too, European-trained coaches have provided stimulus and strength for gymnast enthusiasts. Participation is quite widespread with the activity being conducted in schools, "Y's," and ethnic groups, such as the Sokols. Although the numbers who continue to the level of serious competition are small, dedicated clubs do function in most provinces, especially Quebec and Ontario.

LAWN BOWLING Lawn bowling is one of the exceptions to the prevailing trend to larger membership, as the number of participants appears to be decreasing. Few young people are drawn to this sport, so that it has tended to become the older woman's game. Lawn bowling clubs exist in every province, but British Columbia with ideal conditions for the game claims the majority of the clubs and the greatest activity. No national governing body has ever been formed.

LAWN TENNIS The Canadian Lawn Tennis Association with affiliated branches in every province is the official governing body for the sport. Lawn tennis, seldom actually played on lawns, is most popular on hard courts throughout Canada, having 300 registered clubs with a total membership of 25,000, half of whom are women. The most enthusiastic players are in the age groups from the teens to the thirties. Canadian women have not yet equalled the caliber of play displayed by American and British women in tournaments. A flourishing Junior Development Program, which has recently benefited by a Fitness and Amateur Sport Advisory Council grant, as well as financial assistance from a commercial company, is providing excellent instruction and opportunities for competitive play. A bright future is opening up for Canadian girls in the tennis world, but players of international championship caliber can be developed only if an extended playing season can be provided. In Canada, this means either indoor courts (very rare) or wintering in a warm climate, also rare for aspiring athletes.

SAILING Sailing is not a sport in which women have ventured on their own. Approximately 1,000 Canadian women are active participants, and a Women's Committee of the Canadian Yachting Association has charge of arrangements for a women's competitive event, the Adams Trophy, a North American meet.

The most active women members have belonged to clubs in the Ontario and Quebec water areas, but increased interest has been observed in British Columbia clubs. Some outstanding women crews have been developed, but the expense in maintaining the boats, the time involved, and the necessity of spending part of the winter in southern climes in order to lengthen the season, restrict this sport to a minority of Canadian women. A vigorous junior program may show noticeable increases in the women's membership shortly.

RIFLE AND PISTOL SHOOTING There are fewer than one dozen ladies' rifle or pistol clubs in Canada, but most clubs accept women members, some even having ladies' sections. This is most frequent in the smaller centers where social activities are a feature of the club. About 1,000 women between the ages of fifteen and thirty-five are active in this sport. A goodly number of the outstanding performances were achieved in Calgary clubs, but the Canadian Ladies' Rifle Champion, Mrs. M.V. Thompson, belongs to a Toronto club.

TRAPSHOOTING AND SKEET SHOOTING Trap and skeet shooting, relatively expensive sports, seem to attract women only after they are married and between the ages of thirty and fifty. Not more than 200 women participate in either sport, and these are members of the men's clubs. Western Canada, Ontario, and Quebec have produced some very creditable performers, notably Mrs. V. Holdsworth of Calgary, Alberta, who was Canadian Lady Champion trapshooter from 1956 to 1962 inclusive, and a member of the 1962 All-American Trap Team (women). Skeet shooting devotees seem to be concentrated in Ontario and Quebec, so it is not surprising that the outstanding scores have come from these regions, nor that the 1962 lady champion is from Westmount, Quebec, Mrs. D. V. Robertson.

SNOWSHOEING Snowshoeing, that mode of transportation so vital to the fur trade and to the exploration of Canada in the seventeenth century, associated so firmly in Canadians' minds with the romantic *coureurs de bois* and Indians of the Canadian History textbooks, can by no means be relegated to the role of vestigial activity. A million-dollar industry in

Loretteville, Quebec, where the best moccasins and snowshoes are still produced by Canadian Indians, is eloquent testimony to the vitality of this sport.

The Canadian Snowshoe Union, which comprises some 130 clubs, nineteen of which are in Montreal, organizes competition on the national and international level. The latter is confined to competition with the New England States, especially New York. Competitive events for women, including the one-mile march, 60-, 100- and 200-yard dashes are held regularly every weekend by local clubs. The competitors are usually between the ages of sixteen and thirty, but general participation includes all ages.

Women have played a very active part in maintaining the lively spirit of the sport, which was one of the most colorful and characteristic features of the late 1800's and early 1900's in Montreal and Quebec. Since the heydey of the sport, membership has remained fairly constant, with a total of about 2,500 women. Traditional costumes, songs, and the camaraderie remain as much a part of the enjoyment as in olden times. To the women members goes much of the credit for the warm sociability which pervades all the gatherings. No snowshoe convention would be complete without the traditional "Canadien souper" of pork and beans, tourtière, pea soup habitant style; without the folk dances and songs. The famous Torch Parades appear at some conventions, but modern highways have almost eliminated this event. The revival of the Winter Carnival during the past ten years has been a great incentive and has resulted in the formation of new clubs and heavy commitments for all members. Schedules have to be drawn up in the autumn and rigidly adhered to in order that every carnival may have its fair quota of snowshoe events.

Strictly amateur in the sense of being non-professional, the Snowshoe Union has received financial aid from the Fitness and Amateur Sport Advisory Council. Fervent "amateurs" in the original meaning, snowshoers provide Canadians with one of the outstanding examples of joyful participation by all the family, including grandmère.

SOFTBALL This game, played extensively in recreation programs in large industries and at bases of the armed forces, is often featured in the municipal recreation program of small cities and towns. The popularity of the game has decreased since the 1930's, when it was almost a national craze with Canadian girls. With other team sports, it has yielded to the rising interest in individual sports.

SKIING The Wurtele twins, Rhoda and Rhona, first attracted attention to Canadian women as competitive skiers when between them they retained the Canadian and United States championships from 1947 to

1952. Lucille Wheeler followed with a Bronze Olympic Medal in 1956 and in 1958 two Gold Medals in the World Championships. In 1960 Anne Heggtveit returned from the Olympics and the World Championships with three Gold Medals.

This meteoric rise from nonenity to world champion status has had an electrifying effect on the interest in and attention paid to competitive women skiers. The example of these competitors has aroused in potential skiers and in the officials of the Canadian Amateur Ski Association the belief that outstanding performers can be developed regularly in Canada. Determined to realize this belief, the Ski Association has developed a strenuous training program demanding year-round, all-out effort on the part of the participants; has organized challenging competition to season the untried competitors; and is developing an ever-expanding program for juniors to discover talent early. The athletes have responded wholeheartedly and the dedication of competitive skiers has become a byword.

The excitement has spread to the general public, which is not only rallying to support the Ski Association, but has taken to the hills itself. Two hundred clubs with a registration of 25,000 members distributed in six divisions supervise the organized phases of the sport. Some 100,000 other skiers, from pre-school age up, flock to take ski lessons, covering the slopes practicing and enjoying the skills. Since World War I, tremendous developments have taken place in skiing facilities, both in the Rocky Mountains and in the Laurentian and Gatineau areas. Ski lifts of every type have multiplied as new slopes are opened to accommodate the ever-increasing throngs of skiers.

The average age of the woman competitive skier is eighteen, but there are no age limits for pleasure skiing, as many a grandmother knows.

Swimming (Speed)   Competitive speed swimming for women is governed by the Canadian Amateur Swimming Association, which has provincial branches in most provinces and has 3,700 registered members. British Columbia and Ontario vie for the honor of producing most participants, both provinces having devoted considerable attention to young swimmers. Top performance comes early in this sport, so that the majority of the outstanding performers are found in the teens or early twenties at the latest. Participation in competitive swimming is increasing rapidly now that Canada is experiencing a swimming pool boom. Facilities and expert instruction are now available to almost anyone, anywhere. Clinics held at the sectional and national level have, of course, caught the interest of many more potential performers.

Canadian women swimmers have competed in the Pan-American, British empire and Commonwealth Games, and the Olympics, acquitting themselves creditably. Twice at the British Empire Games every girl on the team brought home a medal. Some of the outstanding performers include Beth Whittal and Helen Stewart Hunt, record holders at the Pan-American in 1955; Sara Barber, Jenny Grant, and Margaret Iwasaki; and Mary Stewart (sister of Helen), who established in 1962 the world record in the butterfly 100 meters and was named outstanding woman athlete for the year.

SWIMMING (SYNCHRONIZED)   Competition in swimming skills has not been confined to speed events. As early as 1926 the Gale Trophy was offered for competition in figures at the national level. These competitive figures, derived originally from the basic Royal Life Saving Society figures, evolved into the slate of events comprising a synchronized swimming meet: solos, figures, strokes, aggregate. This development was subject to diversified influences: the rhythmic swimming featured by Catherine Curtis in the United States in 1933; the popular success of Billy Rose's Aquacade in 1938; followed by the equally popular Esther Williams water ballet films; and the precedent of figure skating with its set competitive figures and routines. In 1947 the Dempsey Trophy (Quebec) was awarded for a duet routine and figures.

Under the able leadership of Peg Sellers of Montreal, this branch of swimming developed rapidly. In 1949 standard rules of competition were established, and at the annual meeting of the Canadian Amateur Swimming Association in 1950 the proposed constitution of the Canadian Synchronized Swimming Association was accepted. Thus a new governing body for a women's sport was instituted. Provincial sections have been organized in most provinces and synchronized swimming has grown steadily in popularity in universities, Y.W.C.A.'s, and private clubs.

Marjorie Cochand was one of the first Canadians to reach the heights of stellar performance. In 1952, Canadian champion Joan Orser of McGill University demonstrated synchronized swimming at the Olympics in Helsinki, and again at the British Empire Games in 1954. Canadian swimmers have competed at the Pan-American Games in 1954, 1958 and 1962. An outstanding performer, Pauline McCullagh, held four Dominion Championships at once and was awarded First Class Honours by the Academy of Aquatic Art (International).

TRACK AND FIELD   The achievements of the first Olympic team, that of 1928, with three gold medals captured by Bobby Rosenfelt, a high jump record set by Ethel Catherwood, and the fine showing of the relay team have not since been equalled by Canadian women in international competition. Creditable performances have been recorded in British Empire and Commonwealth Games, and the Pan-American Games, as well as in Canadian championship meets by Eleanor Haslam, Rosella Thorne,

Maureen Rever, and Abigail Hoffman in track, and Jackie Macdonald and Marie Dupré in field, but world records have eluded Canadian women.

Provincial track and field associations, affiliated with the provincial branch of the A.A.U. of C., conduct activities for both men and women. Participation by women in track and field reached its peak in the 1930's. Then, until the 1960's, when a marked increase in club membership showed a revival of interest, relatively few women and girls took part in this sport. The dearth of training facilities, especially in winter months, and scarcity of experienced coaches, coupled with the lack of emphasis on this sport in school programs, have been hampering factors. Although women athletes did participate in the annual clinics for competitors sponsored by the Royal Canadian Legion from 1954, the numbers were insufficient to produce a noticeable improvement in the sport across Canada. The problem of making good coaching available to potential athletes in all parts of the country had to be solved. In 1962, a clinic for Coaches was sponsored by the Royal Canadian Legion, with financial assistance from the Fitness and Amateur Sport Advisory Council. Some twenty women coaches, many of them high school teachers, attended. The success of the venture, with the attendant favorable publicity for the sport, greatly strengthened the cause of track and field. Continued emphasis must be placed on supplying scientific coaching and training to young potential athletes throughout the nation.

THE CANADIAN SPORTSWOMAN—DILETTANTE OR SERIOUS COMPETITOR?

The records attest that Canadian women can achieve superlative performance whatever the dominant quality demanded may be. The test of endurance was ably met by Marilyn Bell in marathon swimming; the ability to release explosive power is demonstrated by skiers, swimmers, and track sprinters; superb control in intricate skills by Ernestine Russell in gymnastics, and by figure skaters and golfers. Despite the emphasis on team sports in schools, it is in individual endeavor that Canadian women have won world recognition. Not since the Edmonton Grads have Canadian women distinguished themselves in a team sport. They have been startled and interested by the game of volleyball, as played by European women, but they have shown little inclination to emulate this vigorous style of play.

That such a small minority of Canadian girls is motivated to excel in sports has long puzzled enthusiastic sports administrators, who have devoted time and effort to the promotion of sports programs for girls. Many theories have been advanced to explain the persistent indifference. A society which has emerged relatively recently from pioneering conditions, and is reveling in the effortlessness of gadgets, of ready-made entertainment, is not apt to focus the attention of its young on personal effort, on demanding challenges. A generation to which so much comes so easily finds it difficult to understand the individual who intentionally puts himself to great personal effort and even hardship.

Canadian society does little to encourage girls to seek recognition in athletic achievements. True, each medallist returning from international competition is greeted with a jubilant ovation—a mixture of surprise and delight. Success for women athletes is never really expected by the public. As many inches of news reports are devoted to bemoaning the lack of male medallists as to congratulations to the successful women athletes. When a Canadian speaks of an athlete, he is referring to a man, not a woman.

Girls who have shown promise early, and who have had the benefit of continuous concentrated training and coaching during their developmental years, suddenly lose interest when on the verge of substantial achievement. They have discovered that Canadians expect their young women to possess slim silhouettes, sufficiently fleshed to be shapely, but never to suggest muscle! It dawns on them that Canadian girls are expected to play well enough to be pleasant playing companions for the male (should he desire feminine company), but never to be a threat to his superiority and never to be more interested in her own achievements than in his.

Employers have a tendency to be benevolent should a request be made for time off by an employee to play the role of "Queen," no matter how inconsequential the occasion. Such a request would be regarded as appropriate and not unreasonable. The same employer, asked to release an employee to train for an athletic competition, would in all likelihood be astounded that such a request should be made seriously, and would not view it in the same benevolent light.

The adjective "casual" is frequently used to describe the quality of life on the North American continent—etiquette, manners, clothes, are casual. And casual clothes are usually sports clothes to which fashion designers have given of their ingenious best. Sports clothes, whether for "spectating" or for participating, are a must in every girl's and woman's wardrobe. So attractive have sports costumes become that frequently the participants have been drawn first to the clothes and thence to the activity. Skiing, which enjoys the position of a prestige sport, owes no small debt to the sports clothes designers. Swimming has also benefited from the attention of bathing suit and accessory designers.

The combined influence of designers and advertisers, which has accustomed the Canadian woman to soft colors and glamorized equipment in her home and in her car, has worked its magic in attracting her to feminized sports equipment. Jewelled pistols have been created for her pleasure; light synthetic materials in pleasing color combinations have made many adjuncts of various sports more appealing; the decor of bowling alleys was not planned with the gentlemen in mind.

From her earliest sorties into various games, the Canadian girl has seldom had pressure exerted on her to play seriously, or to be intensively competitive. She has been encouraged to regard physical recreation as a source of fun and sociability, the open door to new friendships, or perhaps to a more desirable social circle. Canadian girls, elite performers excepted, are not brought up to value the personal testing which competitive athletics and sports offer. The ideal of the ancient Greeks, that joy in participation is directly proportionate to the amount of effort and toil demanded of the athlete, is an unfamiliar concept. Consequently, they do not respond as girls of some nations do to the challenge of constantly striving to excel in physical performance.

As mothers, many Canadian women are very conscious of the value of sports as a medium for a family participation. Some make a point of either continuing or resuming an activity when the children are old enough to join in. Some mothers are even bold enough to take up a new sport that will interest the family group as a unit.

All communities reflect the importance accorded to sports in the life of the Canadian boy, by the efforts made to provide sports programs for boys. The same national attitude is reflected in the annual government grants which are made to boys' programs, while only spasmodically are grants allocated to girls' programs. When the federal government appointed the Fitness and Amateur Sport Advisory Council to administer the Act to Encourage Fitness and Amateur Sport, only two of the thirty members were women. If the actions of the government mirror popular opinion (which it is not unreasonable to suppose) then the conclusion can only be that sports for women in Canada are not regarded very seriously.

Whether Canadians take their sportswomen seriously or not, and whether Canadian women take their sports seriously or not, one thing seems assured: the trend of the 1950's and 1960's for more and more women and girls to enjoy active participation in some form of physical recreation will continue. Bolstered by the support of sports organizations which are sagely using the grants from the Fitness and Amateur Sports Advisory Council to develop the junior program, this trend is not only firmly established but promises to accelerate in future years. Canadian girls will turn to serious competition in great numbers only when Canadian society makes it seem important enough.

BIBLIOGRAPHY

1. Canada, Department of National Health and Welfare, Physical Fitness Division, *Recreation, Physical Education and School Health Education in Canada.* Ottawa: The Queen's Printer, 1952.
2. ———, Department of National Health and Welfare, Research Division, *Activities of the Federal Government Related to Recreation.* Ottawa: The Queen's Printer, 1955.
3. Canadian Youth Hostel Association, *The Handbook of Canadian Youth Hostels.* Calgary: 1962.
4. Nova Scotia, *Report on the Survey of Fitness and Amateur Sport Activities in Nova Scotia.* Halifax: Department of Education, 1962.
5. Tuttle, George, *Youth and Recreation.* Toronto: Ryerson Press, 1946.
6. ———, *Youth Organizations in Canada.* Prepared for Canadian Youth Commission. Toronto: Ryerson Press, 1946.

COMPETITIVE ATHLETICS **13**

Ivor Wynne

Director, School of Physical Education
McMaster University, Hamilton

ATHLETICS

This is not intended to be a history of "athletics" in Canada but rather an attempt to describe and explain them as they exist in Canada in this seventh decade of the twentieth century.

The term *athletics* is a rather nebulous one but is commonly used to include all sports and games, whether of the individual, dual, or team variety. The team further reflects its Greek derivation (*athlos*, contest; *athlon*, prize), for it appears always to denote a competitive ingredient. That is, recreational hunting or fishing are classified as sports but not as athletics, but if these were organized on a competitive basis the Canadian would probably regard them as athletic events. There are no specific criteria to determine what is or what is not a sport or game, but it is customary to expect an activity to involve skill and physical exertion in a "play" context. Again, the contest seems to be a vital component.

Dr. J. Howard Crocker wrote:

> Canada is a land of sports and sportsmen. Out of the hard years of pioneer life, as this country advanced toward nationhood, there grew up in the villages, towns and cities a love of sports and competition which had been transplanted from the many motherlands of our people. On the village green, games had been the test of strength and courage for centuries. Now in Canada the spirit and love of competition began to express itself in many lines of athletic endeavour.
>
> These new Canadians adopted from the Indians their game of baggataway and made it the national game of lacrosse. Rugby, hockey, basketball and many other games have the stamp of the maple leaf upon their rules and

177

development. Boxing, wrestling, skiing, swimming, fencing, gymnastics, weight-lifting, badminton, golf, cricket, skating, snowshoeing—all of these sports have been highly developed and men and women everywhere enjoy the recreation and competition that brings its full measure of health to all.[1]

Although Dr. Crocker's words are unquestionably true, it should be stated that the development of many sports was the result of the interest, enthusiasm, and opportunities of a relatively privileged class of men. Douglas Fisher, M.P. points out that:

> Most Canadian games and pastimes go back into the nineteenth century. The common factor in almost all of them is that they reached an organized or codified form under the leadership of men from the military or the universities or from the business world; that is, men who had time, money, and one assumes, intelligence. Baseball fits this pattern badly but before it came to Canada it had taken shape on cricket grounds of gentlemen clubs rather than on corner lots. The turning of lacrosse from a pell-mell Indian frolic into a coherent game was largely the work of a prosperous Montreal dentist, W. C. Beers, and clubs of well-to-do young men of the Montreal English community. Hockey has an ancient ancestry through shinty but its introduction to Montreal was largely the work of James Creighton, a Dalhousie graduate studying law at McGill. Basketball was the brainchild of a brilliant McGill graduate.
>
> The initial rowing fame of Canada was first earned by boatmen of St. John and Halifax harbours in the late 1860's but it developed on a large scale through clubs at Lachine, Toronto, and Winnipeg whose membership comprised the social and business elite of those communities. They made the performance of Canadian oarsmen notable throughout the world by 1900.[2]

It appears that a fusion of the two general concepts indicated by Dr. Crocker and Mr. Fisher has determined the course of Canadian sports. Their development has been characterized by the tremendous influence of individuals and voluntary groups and associations, consistent with the democratic nature of the society. A typical example is that of the Amateur Athletic Association of Canada (later to become the Amateur Athletic Union of Canada). This Association was instigated by the Montreal Amateur Athletic Association in 1883 in a letter to various clubs.

Subsequently, at a meeting held at the Toronto Fencing Club on April

---

[1] *Amateur Sports.*
[2] "The Cult of Sport."

11, 1884, a constitution was accepted. An interesting excerpt from the minutes of that meeting reads:

> The President stated that the object of the Association was to regulate such athletic sports as are not now under the control of other associations. The Canadian Cricket, Lacrosse, Rowing, Football, and Wheelmen's Associations cover these various branches of athletic sports already. The aim of our association is mainly to regulate amateur competitions on the cinder path.

To this day individual sports still control their own destinies. More and more of them have formed their own associations, and their strengths and weaknesses are very much at the mercy of well-meaning voluntary leaders. In fact, to tell the story of the development of Canadian athletics would be to trace the development of each sporting activity as a result of the enthusiasm of participants and in some cases promoters. In general, it would be a series of tales of the struggle against the forces of geography and related expenses. And here lies the basis of the great dilemma of Canadian athletics, the relationship between diversified athletic mediocrity on the one hand and specific excellence of attainment on the other. There has never been significant governmental assistance or control of athletics in Canada. Only the passing of Bill C-131 (Appendix A) indicates a somewhat new approach, but even the financial support involved does not contravene the traditional laissez-faire attitude toward each sport, and grants to athletics are only given to existing sports governing bodies.

The aforementioned diversity and philosophy may be shown by referring to the Canadian Sports Advisory Council, established in 1951 and incorporated in 1959. This body, having changed its name in 1963 to the Canadian Amateur Sports Federation, consists of the sports governing bodies across the country.

The President's Report at the Twelfth Annual Meeting on January 11, 1963, contains the following:

> First I would like to welcome the delegates of our members to our Annual Meeting. Many of you have come long distances to be here. This is evidence of the time and effort so willingly given by you and many others to the cause of Amateur Sport in our country. The meeting is open to all. No other organization in Canada can say this in the same way. We control no sport, yet provide a common meeting place to discuss our problems to advance our cause and to speak with a united voice.
>
> Some have felt and expressed the feeling that with the creation of the new National Council on Fitness and Amateur Sport, our council had outlived its usefulness. This is a curious attitude and difficult for me to understand. The Government neither represents nor is responsible to sport as ours is. It expresses the opinion of individuals, no doubt capable and no doubt

interested, but still individuals, appointed geographically, who in no way represent or are responsible for the plans and ideas of organized sport. Our Council's part in the past in selling the Government on the necessity and value of assisting sport has been a leading and important one. In continuing to give all organized sport a place to discuss together its problems we still have an important and valuable role to play. It will remain undoubtedly true that the voice of amateur sport will have more volume and impact when we sound together.

It is significant to note that this meeting had delegates from a large number of organizations (see Appendix D).

SCHOOLS, COLLEGES, AND UNIVERSITIES

The original Canadian Intercollegiate Athletic Union was formed in 1906 with just three active members; Queen's University, McGill University, and University of Toronto. In 1910 came the Maritime Intercollegiate Athletic Union and in 1920 the Western Canada Intercollegiate Athletic Union. Since then, there have been additions and divisions, until in 1961 a truly Canadian Intercollegiate Athletic Union came into being, a union of the Western Intercollegiate and Maritime Intercollegiate Unions and the Ontario–Quebec and Ottawa–St. Lawrence Athletic Associations. In 1963, the Ontario Intercollegiate Athletic Association was accepted as a fifth member; so colleges and universities from coast to coast are now united organizationally, although only hockey, basketball, and cross-country events have been conducted on a C.I.A.U. level up to 1964.

At both the secondary school and university level, intramural athletics are an integral part of the program. Although some institutions give only lip service to the importance of intramural participation, most athletic facilities are taxed to capacity by the demands and desires of a large school population.

Elementary schools, except those in large towns and cities, do not usually have gymnasiums, but within limits of facilities children are encouraged to play, and more and more recognition is being given to the importance of the introduction of physical education by qualified teachers at an early age.

Although it would appear that the school system is a strong contributing factor in stimulating interest in athletics, there are some serious limiting factors. One of these is a lingering scholasticism which regards athletics with some suspicion as a dangerous threat to scholastic performance. Schedules in team sports are often curtailed for the apparent protection of the student, and the "all or nothing" aspect of the final examination in Canadian schools affects the student's desire for athletic participation. The British "way of life" concept of the place of sports is not evident in Canadian schools; nor is the United States 'semester organization of the school year, which makes examinations more frequent and in a sense less important.

There were no athletic scholarships in Canadian universities until the 1964 announcement of Simon Frazer. To some extent, this fact has affected the caliber of play in Canadian Intercollegiate athletics with many of the best athletes being siphoned off into United States colleges. This had hampered the promotions and acceptance of university sport. Lack of public interest, however, has made Canadian intercollegiate athletics one of the last bastions of amateur sport.

CHURCHES

Many churches include athletics as a part of their youth program, and leagues in sports such as basketball, badminton, and softball are found in most cities and large towns. The Catholic Youth Organization has athletics as a strong component of its developmental program. In general, however, the influence of the churches on the development of a particular sport or in skill development is not great as their purpose is mostly social and religious-educational.

INDUSTRY

Most large industries sponsor leagues or teams in sports such as softball, hockey, basketball, and bowling. Again, these are of a recreational nature and normally do not include specialized instruction or coaching.

MUNICIPAL RECREATION

Most municipalities now have a Recreation Commission or similar organization which promotes a wide variety of sports. The community arena or recreational center with trained personnel gives young people the opportunity to play organized hockey, baseball, and other sports at a very early age, and service clubs and other local organizations often cooperate with recreational directors to share the responsibility for a large volume of participants. Thousands of young people become interested in athletics through these opportunities.

AMATEUR SPORTS CLUBS

Organizations dedicated to a specific athletic activity give opportunity to pursue a particular skill under expert coaching and usually to provide participation at a highly competitive level. These range from the badminton club of a village to the Argonaut Rowing Club of Toronto. Track and field clubs continue to emerge as do those of many other sporting activities but not to the extent essential to the maintance of the interest begun in the school and local recreational organizations. Financial problems are acute as interest wanes among individuals continually faced with the expenses of travel and equipment.

PROVINCIAL SPORTS ORGANIZATIONS

Local sports clubs and municipal recreational programs develop in so many centers that usually interested individuals in a particular sport combine to form provincial bodies. So it is that for each sport belonging to the Canadian Amateur Sports Federation there is a corresponding provincial organization which combines with its counterpart in other provinces to develop a national governing body for that sport. It is interessting to note that softball and baseball, which are so popular in Canada, have had strong provincial associations but have never had a national governing body. This is a rare exception on the Canadian scene.

BILL C-131

The passing of this bill (outlined in detail in Appendix A) may prove to be the greatest factor in advancing sport in Canadian history. However, its degree of effectiveness and lasting qualities will directly depend on its acceptance as a regular division of the federal government. It is hoped that all political parties will recognize it as providing services of major importance to the Canadian people and allow these services to expand and grow into a unit which produces maximum results in both fitness and athletics.

PROFESSIONAL ATHLETICS

It is significant that a high level of athletic skill involving many participants is only seen in Canada in hockey and football, which have a strong professional influence. Except at universities, adults in general compete at a highly competitive level in these two sports only if they are paid. So it is that Canada periodically has a world caliber athlete in track anf field, skiing, or figure skating, but perenially its basketball players, baseball players, soccer players, swimmers, and gymnasts suffer by comparison with those other countries. Meanwhile, hockey and football as entertainment or spectator sports dominate the Canadian scene and the revered sports heroes of the day are usually from these highly televised sports. Professional soccer is emerging but as yet is not affecting the sports aspirations of many Canadians.

COMMERCIALIZED SPORTS

Golf, curling, skiing, and bowling may be combined to epitomize the most recent trend in Canadian athletics. The "affluent society" appears to have brought with it the desire to combine the physical with the social and to some extent to develop family participation. In general, these activities involve substantial membership fees or payment for participation. Even the "status symbol" is a factor here. Thousands each year take up these sports for the first time, and small children are introduced to the golf swing or ski-tow at a cost considered prohibitive a generation ago.

SUMMARY

From the earliest history of the country to the 1960's Canadian athletics have relied upon the enthusiasm of the participant and usually that of former participants of a particular sport or sports for their development and maintenance. The nature of amateur sport in 1883 and in 1963 indicates little change in fundamental attitudes in what has been and still is a basic private-enterprise, democratic society.

Most countries in the world have come to think of athletics as important for prestige and the basis of national pride. Some countries still lacking in adequate educational facilities for the masses give governmental financial support to emphasized teams and athletes; others control athletics. Canada, with one of the highest standards of living in the world and with ample opportunity for its citizens to obtain secondary education, has no system of controlling or promoting athletics. The United States also lacks a government-directed system, but motivation for winning at all levels of competition is sustained mainly through the school and university. Canadians are athletically dwarfed by their neighbors to the south and appear to have rationalized their status as an athletic nation by international standards. They are pleased to win but fundamentally do not appear to feel that hard work is justified when applied to play. The large numbers of fishermen, hunters, curlers, golfers, bowlers, skiiers, campers, and boating enthusiasts, attest to the zeal of Canadians for recreational pursuits. In individual sports only the dedicated few apply themselves diligently. In team sports, school and community pride continue to stimulate the teenagers, but graduates soon lose their enthusiasm when faced with the inadequately supported sports clubs as their only means of continuing their interests.

The success of the far-flung hockey "farm systems" indicates what can be done with monetary and organizational support and control, if excellence is the main purpose. But Canadians in general do no see any urgency about producing excellence in athletics. Meanwhile, the youth play with joy, enthusiasm, facilities, and freedom. Perhaps Canada almost unwittingly has the most comprehensive and sensible athletic program in the world.

BIBLIOGRAPHY

1. Canadian Sports Advisory Council, *Proceedings of the Twelfth Annual Meeting*, Ottawa (January, 1963).
2. Crocker, J. Howard, "Amateur Sports and Games in Canada," Unpublished pamphlet prepared for the sixtieth anniversary of the Amateur Athletic Union of Canada (October, 1953).
3. Fisher, Douglas, "The Cult of Sport in Canada," *Journal of the Canadian Association for Health, Physical Education and Recreation*, XXX, No. 1 (1963).
4. Loosemore, J. P., "Intercollegiate Athletics in Canada," *Journal of the Canadian Association for Health, Physical Education and Recreation*, XXVIII, No. 2 (December 1961—January 1962).
5. Canada, The House of Commons of Canada, Bill C-131, *An Act to Encourage Fitness and Amateur Sport*. Ottawa: The Queen's Printer, 1961.

Fernand Landry

Director
School of Physical Education and Recreation
University of Ottawa

Rev. M. Montpetit, o.m.i.

Advisor and Administrator
Physical Education Summer Camp
University of Ottawa

THE PAST

The daily struggle of man against nature and the skirmishes with the Indians were harsh facts of life for the North American pioneers, including the early French Canadian settlers. For a few centuries, the population of French Canada had to concern itself with the essentials of survival, the betterment of general living conditions, and the development of the young colony. Until the late nineteenth century, the population was mostly rural, there was hardly any end to the working hours, and the rest periods barely permitted recuperation.

The necessity of hard work had a strong bearing on the philosophy of life of the people. Often misunderstanding the true meaning of the Christian doctrine concerning the value and place in their life of material things, joy, beauty, art, and love, people were inclined to measure them by incomplete, exaggerated, and even false moral principles. Things that had to do with leisure and physical activity of a recreational nature were generally considered a waste of time and effort—sterile amusement, if not downright sinful.

The basic social structure of the French Canadian people was for a long time the parish. Geographical location and poor means of transportation, as well as the civic and religious structures, have in the past more or less isolated parishes from one another. The community and the parish were for all practical purposes identical. Sport, recreation, and physical education consequently developed within the parochial structure.

The gradual and slow rise of industrialization in French Canada, at the turn of the last century, favored the multiplication and grouping of the basic social unit, the parish. The educational and cultural patterns soon began to change at a more marked pace. After having been the nucleus of community life, the parish saw its auxiliary services such as parochial schools, adult education, public welfare, playgrounds, and sports clubs gradually withdrawn from its sphere of influence to become more systematically organized into wider networks of education, welfare, and related services.

The contemporary rise of sport, physical education, and recreation as a social reality in French Canada appears to have been based less on the recognition of their necessity and value than on the coming of age of an entirely new and different way of life. As in many other areas of western civilization, the wise utilization of rapidly increasing leisure hours has convinced French Canadians that various forms of physical activity do have positive values in the self-realization of the individual. If it seems rather difficult to follow the new process of evolution of sport and recreation in French Canada, one can at any rate see that they have become prominent everywhere in the last fifty years.

While individuals, families, schools, and community organizations were gradually taking a more active interest in them, the various levels of authority remained indifferent and did not give the necessary guidance and support. As a consequence, amateur and professional sport, physical education in the schools, sports clubs, and community recreation programs evolved more or less independently of each other.

World War II helped to focus public interest on the utilitarian values of physical education and sport for fitness and recreation. Subsidized school military training in French Canada replaced a large part of the existing sports and recreational programs in secondary schools and colleges and brought activity where there had been little or none before. A number of private sports clubs and associations were either formed or improved their framework of operation considerably as a result of the war effort.

The world of sport and recreation exploded with activity during the Second World War. The situation was all the more confusing in French Canada in that there was no over-all planning or control at any level. Amateur sport soon was suffering from the domination of professional sport and from the exploitation of young athletes and the greed for money. The valuable progress of private sport and recreation associations had to be accomplished on mediocre budgets. Financial assistance from the various government levels was often given without preconceived plan and was not sufficient to meet the large needs. Physical education could not expand its program in the schools because of a serious lack of facilities and staff.

In an effort to remedy the situation, pressures were exerted to bring about provincial legislation on sport and physical education. In 1939, the "Loi Instituant le Conseil provincial des Sports" was passed. Executive power was to be vested in a Sports Council under the Ministry of Municipal Affairs, Commerce and Industry. Composed of five members named by the Lieutenant-Governor, the Council was to be given the powers:

— to govern and supervise professional, semi-professional, and amateur sport:
— to establish regulations for the staging of sports contests,
    through the development of sport associations:
— to determine the forms of player contracts and to investigate all irregularities.

Application of the law was judged too difficult because of its own intrinsic complexity and because the public was unprepared. Even though it received a favorable vote, the law did not receive royal assent and consequently was never applied. Many believe that powerful influences intervened to shelve the project.

Professional sport remained in the hands of the existing athletic associations and financial magnates, and school physical education did not receive a much-needed impetus at the time. The publication in 1942 by the Départment de l'Instruction publique of a physical education manual borrowed entirely from the 1933 British physical training syllabus illustrates the school authorities' lack of appreciation of the situation.

The physical education programs in the elementary and secondary schools of French Canada continued to lack sufficient scope and structure to serve the growing needs and interests of the children. By contrast, commercial sport in the urban centres was rolling successfully with excellent organization patterns and adequate financial backing.

Some schools in the public sector of education took it in their own hands to organize their own physical education activities. In the vast majority of public schools, however, programs as well as facilities remained in a primitive state. A considerable number of city and town councils compensated for this deficiency by encouraging, under the guidance of the best available volunteer leaders, year-round sports programs in the public parks, playgrounds, and recreation centers.

In a parallel manner, the *Collèges classiques* (private schools combining a four-year program secondary school with a four-year liberal arts college education), assumed total responsibility for providing their students' needs for physical education. They became the first institutions of French Canada to initiate sports programs, leading to modern intramural and interscholastic leagues, and paving the way for total physical education programs in the other sectors of education.

Other private organizations such as L'Œuvre des Patronages (commonly referred to as "Les Patros" in Quebec), and La Confédération des

Œuvres de Loisirs (known as the C.O.P.), have made outstanding contributions to the development of physical education and recreation in French Canada.

Founded in France and directed by the Order of Les Frères de Saint-Vincent-de-Paul, the Patros came to French Canada as early as 1884 and ever since have promoted successfully out-of-school sports, physical education, and other types of leisure-time activities for children and youth.

In 1946, at the request of the Catholic Bishops of Quebec, "La C.O.P." was founded with the aim of bringing together, from the viewpoint of a Catholic education, the various *Fédérations diocésaines* already in existence, which grouped at the time hundreds of local, parochial, and municipal organizations such as playgrounds, recreation centers, sports clubs, and summer camps. In fifteen years, the C.O.P. was to become one of the most enterprising and representative bodies of sports and recreation in French Canada.

Notwithstanding the efforts and successes of volunteer physical education and recreation leaders at the time, they could no longer cope with the demands and responsibilities of fast-expanding and increasingly complex organizations. The rapid urbanization and industrialization that followed the start of World War II had already given a much larger place to sports and leisure-time activities in French Canada. To anwser the demands for more instructors, coaches, and professional leaders, training centers had to be established.

In the course of six years, three universities started physical education and recreation degree courses in the French language: the University of Ottawa in 1949, Laval in 1954, and Montreal in 1955. The efforts of graduates from these schools have contributed largely to the integration of physical education in the school curriculum and also to the expansion of community and parochial recreation programs. At the request of the public, summer extension courses in physical education were offered soon afterward by the same three universities as a crash program aimed at filling the new acute needs for specialist leaders in all sectors of physical education and recreation.

A number of colleges and school commissions began to depend on the professional services of private and influential institutions for the organization or management of their physical education and recreation programs. The more active in that respect have been Le Centre d'Education physique in Trois Rivières, L'Institut Kebedgy and L'Institut Coutu, both of Montreal. The latter Institute today groups more specialist teachers than any organization of its kind and extends its services to amateur sport and community recreation as well as to the three levels of education.

Concrete results mostly proved to be very difficult and were achieved only as the result of laborious effort. Thus, only after an inquiry into the physical fitness of students of both sexes in the *Collèges classiques* that the Faculty of Arts of Laval and Montreal Universities established compulsory physical education as an integral part of the curriculum with the same status as all other academic subjects. Strong recommendations were made to the colleges to provide as soon as possible the facilities and staff needed to conduct the newly-approved program.

For a long time only tolerated in the framework of elementary and secondary education, physical education and sports have recently been making rapid progress toward complete integration in the regular school program. A marked trend in the last few years has been the hiring by many city school commissions of full-time directors of physical education responsible for the development of programs and facilities adapted to local needs and financial means. The School Commission of the City of Quebec is considered one of the finest examples of its kind.

Public interest and opinion have forced the hand of the school commissions to the point that Le Départment de l'Instruction publique has deemed it necessary to appoint a committee to revise its physical education program and requirements. The development of out-of-school sport and physical education in French Canada is to a large extent due to the dedicated efforts of service and welfare clubs as well as parochial recreation committees. These organizations, often the originators of sport in their respective localities, they still bear the entire burden in many places. While these various bodies interested in sport and physical education do not all have the same seriousness of purpose and educative aims, their efforts have nonetheless fostered better co-operation among groups of similar, but often conflicting, interests. The C.O.P. is credited with having best understood the urgent need for closer collaboration between interested groups at the parochial, municipal, and provincial levels, and to have acted in that direction.

The Present

The traditional way of life of French Canadians is undergoing profound changes, especially in urban and industrial centers. A fast-expanding economy, increased technological aids, and better management are molding new social, cultural, and educational patterns.

The contemporary needs of the population in physical education, sport, and recreation can no longer be satisfied with improvisation and urgently call for new patterns of legislation, organization, and operation. The first action taken by the Quebec government in that direction was the appointment in March 1962 of a special study committee charged with the duty of recommending to the provincial government ways and means of establishing coherent sports, physical education, and recreation policies and programs.

The three fields of physical education, sports, and recreation, mingled as they were in the past, are beginning to operate separately, and even to compete openly. Almost everywhere in French Canada, groups and associations are concentrating their efforts to serve the needs of the public more effectively and also to gain stronger representation to the municipal and provincial authorities. Le Service des Loisirs du Diocèse de Montréal, representing forty-nine municipalities and a population of over one million, is campaigning for government legislation and structures in the areas of physical education as well as sport and recreation.

The recent inquiry of La Commission Laroche (charged by the civic autorities of Montreal to investigate the status and practices of professional and amateur sport in the greater Montreal area; their report was made public in the spring of 1962) has created such a stir in Quebec that it will undoubtedly influence future municipal and provincial legislation. The pressures from independent sources are now reinforced by the specific recommendations made to the government by political groups throughout the province. Occurring at the time when the royal commission on education in the province of Quebec is in full swing, these pressing recommendations are expected to acquire more meaning.

The voice of the C.O.P. is carrying more and more weight throughout French Canada. Over two million children and adults of both sexes profit yearly from its extensive network of services in more than 100 recreation centers and 800 playgrounds. Its hockey, baseball, and playground organizations, along with those of the Parks and Recreation Department of the City of Montreal, are among the most extensive and successful in North America. Where school physical education is not organized, they serve as excellent substitutes.

The Patros, more dynamic than ever before, are extending their own services to other areas of French Canada and are now offering one of the best multi-elective types of physical education and recreation programs to girls as well as boys. La Centrale des Patros (central administration offices, located in Quebec City) houses one of the finest sports and physical education libraries and a recently formed technical information service on the same subjects for the use and benefit of their thousands of members and the public at large.

Efforts have been made in the last two years to group together physical education and recreation leaders with common interests and problems. In the fall of 1960, L'Association des Diplômés en Education physique et Récréation (familiarly known as A.D.E.P.R. in professional circles of

French Canada) was incorporated and became the first official association of its kind ever to exist in French Canada. The same year La Ligue canadienne de l'Education physique (which has recently changed its name to "La Ligue canadienne-francaise de l'Education physique") came into existence as a branch of the International Federation of Physical Education (F.I.E.P.). Its bulletin, written in the French language, serves for the promotion of the Federation's ideas as well as for open discussion of current controversial physical education problems in the French-speaking community.

It appears that the impetus given to fitness and amateur sport under Bill C-131 has not been fully felt as yet in French Canada, mainly because of incomplete federal-provincial agreement on these matters. A manifestation of the impatience of needy groups can be seen in the recent foundation of a national association of French-speaking recreation centers for the primary purpose of meeting the specifications for receiving federal grants directly.

Simple observation can detect many disparities still restraining the evolution of physical education and clouding its issues. It is too soon to judge whether the manifestations described above will have temporary or more permanent effects. One fact remains, however: physical education and sports are every day becoming a more integral part of the French Canadian culture.

Until very recently, the fate of these fields was almost exclusively in the hands of men of action. That time is passed. The contributions of eminent philosophers and pedagogues such as Ramunas and Tremblay have already cast new light on the intricate socialogical, economic, cultural, and philosophical implications of contemporary concepts in these fields. Their solid, deep, and refreshing thinking is guiding accomplishments of ever-widening scope and depth in the French-speaking community.

BIBLIOGRAPHY

1. L'Action Catholique Canadienne, *Voies nouvelles du loisir*. Montreal: Editions de l'Action Catholique Canadienne, 1961.
2. Bélanger, Yves, "Le Sport dans les institutions d'enseignement publiques C.O.P.," *Le Sport dans la societé*. Quebec: Editions C.O.P., 1961.
3. Confédération des oeuvres de loisirs de la Province de Québec, *Le Comité paroissial de loisirs et la municipalité*. Quebec: Editions C.O.P., 1962.
4. ———, *Le Sport dans la societé*. Quebec: Editions C.O.P., 1961.

5. Journées Nationales d'Etudes, *Les Loisirs des jeunes*. Paris: Secrétariat de l'Union des Religieuses Enseignantes, 1958.
6. "Le Loisir," *Revue Esprit*, No. 274 (June 1959).
7. Médéric, Paul, *Loisir et loisirs*. Quebec: Ministère de la Jeunesse, Service des Cours par Correspondance, 1961.
8. Mouroux, Jean, *Sens chrétien de l'homme*. Paris: Editions Montaigne, 1945.
9. Paplauskas-Rumunas, Antoine, *L'Education physique dans l'humanisme intégrale* (2nd ed.). Ottawa: Les Editions de l'Université d'Ottawa, 1960.
10. "Texte intégral du rapport de la Commission Laroche," *Le Devoir*. Montreal, 17 January, 1962.

THE INTERRELATIONSHIP OF HEALTH EDUCATION AND PHYSICAL EDUCATION

15

E. June Frache

Assistant Professor, Health Education
Faculty of Physical Education
University of Alberta, Edmonton

A survey of the universities and colleges concerned with teacher education revealed that nowhere in Canada is it possible for potential teachers to choose health education as their major field of study. However, specialization in physical education is possible in most provinces, and includes in its program one or two courses in health education. While methodology is the basic constituent of these health courses, many areas of study which are basic to physical education are essential for health education. These subjects include anatomy, physiology, kinesiology, and care and prevention of athletic injuries. Hence, many provinces are meeting their responsibility for school health education in this way. There is talk, however, of instituting a School of Public Health in association with one of the leading universities in Canada which would eventually offer a Master of Public Health degree in Health Education.

In all but one province, health education in elementary schools is the responsibility of the classroom teacher. This is reasonable, since the classroom teacher is aware of the needs and interests of the class and therefore able to provide an effective program. With this fact in mind, some universities and colleges provide health pedagogy to prospective teachers in the elementary route. Manitoba offers a compulsory half-year course in health education. Alberta has recently decided upon a half-year methods course in which physical education and health education are combined. A few lectures in health are included in a one-year program of teacher education in Quebec, while the teachers' colleges of Ontario offer a compulsory full-year course in health to all teachers preparing for the elementary school (Grades I-VIII). Candidates in the elementary pattern in

British Columbia can elect a health course in their third year.

The size of schools too, determines who will teach health education
Provinces such as Prince Edward Island and Newfoundland have pri
marily one-teacher schools. In larger schools, (particularly junior and
senior high schools with greater specialization of subject areas) health
education becomes the responsibility usually of the physical education
instructor, sometimes of the guidance personnel, and occasionally of the
science teacher.

History of Health Education in Canadian Schools

The term "health education" was not commonly used before 1910 to
describe the formal health courses existing in Canadian schools. Anatomy, physiology, and hygiene comprised most of the health content prior
to this time. Patricia Kahr, Consultant in School Health Education for
the British Columbia Department of Health Services and Hospital Insur-
ance, has reported that anatomy, physiology, and hygiene were required
subjects for pupils in that province as early as 1877. Newfoundland saw
school health instruction under way in the 1890's and most of the other
provinces claim initial health programs in elementary schools between
1900 and 1910.

A knowledge of bacteriology was urgently needed to improve sanitation measures and to combat communicable diseases. Voluntary health
organizations, particularly the Canadian Tuberculosis Association,
played a major role in encouraging health education in the schools. The
gap between health science and public knowledge needed to be closed,
and the successes of these early school health programs played a major
role. A secure place for health content in school curricula was won.

In 1918 a commission of the National Education Association of the
United States published the "Cardinal Principles of Secondary Education."[1] Of the seven major objectives of education, health was given a
prominent place.

In 1938, the Educational Policies Commission, in its discussion of "objectives of self realization," stated three primary aims for health education:

1. The educated person understands the basic facts concerning health and disease.
2. The educated person protects his own health and that of his dependents.
3. The educated person works to improve the health of the community.

---

[1] N. E. A., *Health Education.*

THE PRESENT STATUS OF HEALTH EDUCATION IN
CANADIAN ELEMENTARY SCHOOLS

Eight of the ten provinces make health instruction compulsory for each level of elementary school. Two other provinces report that school health is treated incidentally; that is, no specific time is allotted, but health problems are dealt with as they arise in the natural setting of school life. A feeling of pseudo-security is reflected in two provinces where elementary health education is reported to exist only in theory. Since habits and attitudes toward health are more easily influenced at the elementary school level than at the secondary, a very propitious opportunity presents itself. But perhaps the communicable diseases that prompted instruction in health habits no longer are considered a threat. Smallpox, pertussis, diphtheria, tetanus, poliomyelitis, and other death-dealing ailments are being effectively controlled by immunization or bacteriological procedures. Hence many teachers do not feel the need to use class time for the discussion of health habits. George Bernard Shaw disapproved of immunization because it undermined the need for upgrading the quality of life, and allowed people to live in filth and still be safe from disease. Education should consider the dangers of painting over grime when a lasting brightness is desired. Contagion is always a threat and new vaccines are far from providing complete control. Industry, hoping to keep its highly-skilled workers on the job, has taken the forefront in the use of influenza vaccines which have shown themselves to be 80 per cent effective. Yet an epidemic of Asian flu raging in Eastern United States in 1963 which moved into Eastern Canada left a 20 per cent absentee rate in some high schools. "Cocktails" of vaccines will soon be available to control many respiratory infections as well as influenza; but public knowledge is lagging badly.

A recent epidemiological report from the Department of National Health and Welfare in Canada, called attention to Ontario's diphtheria epidemic involving twenty-four carriers and resulting in the death of a two-year-old girl. Alberta's public health personnel were shocked by an outbreak of salmonella food poisoning in a large city hospital which affected 116 persons and was a result of commercially manufactured meringue powder. Dangerous procedures in food handling were observed, and corrected, in the process of investigation. Custards were being placed in large containers to cool before refrigeration, thus providing opportunity of time and medium for the swift growth of disease-producing bacteria. It is hoped that the irradiation process which would eliminate salmonella growth in commercial egg mixtures will soon be perfected by Atomic Energy of Canada Limited and others throughout the world. The odor of irradiated cake mixes completely disappears when the cake is baked, but convincing the public to purchase cake mixes on the basis of safety rather than smell will be no small task for health educators. The report went on to mention staphylococcal food poisoning following a wedding party in Saskatchewan and acute botulism occurring in Newfoundland. Infectious hepatitis seems to be common to all provinces and of growing concern in many other parts of the world. Until a satisfactory vaccine is produced it will be necessary to rely upon preventive health measures, namely personal and community sanitation. W. W. Stiles has stated that

> Sanitation is a way of life. It is the quality of living that is expressed in the clean home, the clean farm, the clean business and industry, the clean neighborhood, and the clean community. Being a way of life, it must come from within the people; it is nourished by knowledge and grows as an obligation and ideal of human relations.[2]

THE STATUS OF HEALTH EDUCATION IN CANADIAN SECONDARY SCHOOLS

Most provinces offer compulsory health education in grades VII, VIII, and IX. The average time allotment is 50 minutes per week, per year; the range being 30 minutes in Nova Scotia to 60 minutes in Prince Edward Island, New Brunswick, and an average of 60 minutes in Newfoundland. British Columbia's grade IX and X health course is elective and included in three periods of physical education, in keeping with the recommendations of the Chant Commission. High schools in Quebec begin in grade VIII. Some offer compulsory health in grade VIII, others in grade IX, some in both, and still others in neither. In view of the Cameron Commission's report in Alberta, compulsory health education has been terminated at the grade VIII level and a guidance course encompassing mental health content is now offered in grade IX.

Nova Scotia, Newfoundland, Prince Edward Island, and Quebec have no health education program beyond grade IX. New Brunswick sometimes includes health content in secondary physical education classes. Saskatchewan provides a compulsory course in grade X, Manitoba in grade XI, and Ontario in grades X, XI, and XII. Alberta and British Columbia have an elective course at the grade IV level.

Specialization of subject matter tends to occur in secondary schools, and when it does, health education most often becomes the responsibility of the physical education teacher. Obviously, the number of students that

---

2 Stiles, *Individual Health.*

each teacher supervises daily has become much larger, and individual student needs become somewhat masked.

However, such an arrangement does have some merit. There is a built-in rapport between the physical education teacher and the student. As Chancellor Nutting says: "It requires a degree of sophistication to worship a science master, whereas it is natural for youngsters to idolize the physical education teacher." With the emphasis in health swinging toward mental health, no one will deny the need for an atmosphere of mutual respect, in order that group discussions of real problems can take place within the classroom. Now deep-seated attitudes, fears, and resentments can be expressed, seriously considered, and perhaps altered.

The findings of the Denver Report on the Health Interests of Children in 1947, clearly indicate the need for a relationship between health education and physical education. A questionnaire survey consisting of 250 pre-tested questions over twenty-eight areas of health was given to 3,600 pupils in all grades from I to XII. A list of twelve items of greatest interest and twelve items of least interest for each grade was derived. There would of course be many differences in the interests of children in different parts of Canada, but there would also be some basic similarities that typify children of a given age. Interest in muscular prowess is characteristic of boys in grades VII through X; therefore, it does not take much ingenuity to realize that a health topic will take on real significance if it is "hung on muscles." Physical education, therefore, has become the motivation for health education. According to the report, personal appearance is not the primary area of concern for boys. At no age level does it score more than 20 per cent of the items selected as of greatest interest.

From grade VI up, the topic of mental health appears of vital concern to girls. The seven items of greatest interest for girls, in order of preference, are:

1. To find out why some people like you and others do not.
2. To learn the activities boys and girls enjoy together.
3. To discuss how to be popular with your classmates.
4. To find out ways to make yourself more interesting to other people, including personal appearance.
5. To learn how you should act if you spill a glass of water at a party.
6. To read a book on how to be popular.
7. To learn what a girl likes in a boy and what a boy likes in a girl.

These topics may not appear on the surface to be related to health, but a discussion of personal appearance is not possible without some mention of hair and skin care, figure control through diet and exercise, grooming, and in general, the sparkle of health. Girls in grades VII to X showed very little interest in muscular ability. For them, health education can provide motivation for physical education. Jean Mayer's (25) work illustrating the relationship of exercise and appetite and the subsequent control of weight should motivate girls to welcome opportunities for physical activity. Balance, grace, and efficiency of movement, so much a part of personal appearance, are dependent upon some sort of regular activity program, to say nothing of the opportunity to broaden interests, stimulate conversations, and increase popularity.

The Denver study was repeated in 1954 with many significant changes reflecting the precociousness of youth each decade. This earlier maturation of both boys and girls necessitated the shifting of certain health topics to the grade level preceding the 1947 placement.

A discussion of teaching health would not be complete without some mention of the role of guidance personnel in health education over the past few years. Concern about mental health is stimulated in the wake of reports such as that delivered by the Alberta Mental Health Association to the 1962 Royal Commission on Health Services. Eight per cent of the children in Alberta schools are maladjusted to the point of requiring a change of environment while one-half of one per cent require psychiatric care. The 8 per cent figure may seem high until compared with other parts of the world, reporting 10 to 15 per cent.

For those advocating a neglect of the psychological aspects of health education and a return to instruction in anatomy and physiology alone, the book entitled *Stress and Disease* by Dr. Harold C. Wolff, Professor of Medicine, Cornell University, is highly recommended.

Roy Sorenson, General Secretary, Y.M.C.A. of San Francisco and speaker at the 1962 Joint Conference on Children and Youth in Washington, D.C., has this to say concerning goals that educators should hold in relation to teaching youth about drinking.

> I think the major goal should be one larger than the specific subject matter—namely, to help young people to understand their generation, the things they do, and why they do them. You know, copying mechanisms can be pretty powerful forces, but often when they become cognitive (when the individual understands why it is he is doing a particular thing) they just don't work anymore. . . . So Education should focus on the many patterns of drinking and non-drinking that exist in this country and on the many motivations for doing so. The purpose here would be to enlarge the youth's view of his world and of this particular phenomenon, drinking, so that the choice he makes for himself may be of a free nature.[4]

Dr. Margaret Nix, Health Educator with the federal government of Canada, found that only 24 per cent of the Toronto teachers of grade V and VI were ready to include mental health in the instructional program.

---

[4] "Alcohol Education."

When asked about course content for professional improvement 33 per cent of the teachers desired help in mental health.

Guidance personnel have a rich background in social sciences (sociology and psychology) and should be recognized for their particular role in public health education. Physical education instructors, who are naturally familiar with student activities and problems, are often encouraged to choose options in areas of social science and frequently become very successful guidance counsellors in addition to their physical education responsibilities.

HEALTH EDUCATION AND PHYSICAL EDUCATION OBJECTIVES ARE PREVENTIVE IN NATURE

Obviously it is more economical to prevent a disease than to treat it. Why have a disease if it can be prevented? On the other hand, how can one prove that a disease has been prevented? Perhaps it would not have occured anyway. This factor, plus man's natural reaction "it can't happen to me" is responsible for the spending of dollars for treatment and pennies for prevention. Immunization and purification of water are examples of preventive measures that have been publicly accepted with due process of health education. However, fluoridation of public water supplies has been delayed in some provinces because of legislation, and is still a lively topic of debate in many areas. Fluoridation in Canada can be introduced by either a decision of municipal council on recommendations of health authorities, or by plebiscite. Some provinces require as high as a $66\frac{2}{3}$ per cent majority, making its introduction exceedingly difficult.

Health preventive measures demonstrate their value promptly and directly with the decline in the incidence of such things as smallpox, typhoid fever, and dental caries. Neither can health education and physical education neglect their responsibility to combat mental illness through preventive measures. Unfair criticism, thriving upon the prejudices of the public toward mental illness, has tended to ridicule health education and physical education for their efforts in this area.

Large segments of the population have chosen to mitigate tensions through the dangerous use of tranquilizers or other depressants. If education should teach wise choices and appropriate action, then surely instructors have a responsibility to present alternative methods of tension reduction. Physical activity relieves tension; also beneficial are relaxation exercises, being introduced into physical education programs throughout the country. Psychologists claim that mere vocalization of feelings reduces tension. Therefore, opportunity must be available for students to experience and consider conflicting attitudes and to gain skill in dealing with difficult social pressures.

Preventive medicine involves changes of attitudes and habits in selecting goods and services and in taking action when necessary. Evaluation of programs then, must measure attitudes. However, the only kind of evaluation which is acceptable is that which is factual and capable of measurement immediately, or very soon after, instruction is given. Although facts can be memorized and reiterated with accuracy in a short time, attitude changes are usually not immediate. Factual knowledge must be digested, and if too unrelated to a person's existing knowledge, it will be rejected. Pre-tests are necessary in order to determine present attitudes of students, so that progress and effectiveness of instruction can be evaluated. Knowledge of facts is an important ingredient in attitude-changing, but these facts must be related to familiar situations of concern to students at the present time. The students must feel emotionally involved if attitudes and habits are to be significantly altered. The dangers of developing alcoholism or lung cancer in twenty years appear a little too remote to control the smoking and drinking habits of grade VII students, although some films can bring the possibility close to hand. A discussion of the effect of ethyl alcohol on the performance of motor skills, and how to refuse a drink and not look like a "square," should guarantee emotional involvement among boys and present an opportunity for changes in attitudes and habits.

The cosmopolitan character of Canada requires that instructors of health and physical education become aware of the customs and values of the various racial and religious groups in her domain. Post-high school interest in physical fitness is dependent upon a health and physical education program which is adapted to the cultural background of the student, and which uses familiar equipment and terms.

Food patterns are extremely difficult to change and are also closely related to the home culture. However, if one takes the time to examine at close range the foods usually consumed in a particular commmunity, slight alterations may be made which would improve the nutritive quality of the native diet. Immigrants are often unfamiliar with Canada's highly refined foods. Many Italian babies in Toronto exhibit iron deficiency anemia; as the result of a diet of milk and macaroni instead of the iron-rich baby cereals. The Vitamin and Nutrition Section of the Food and Drug Directorate of the Canadian Department of National Health and Welfare is constantly on the alert for situations favoring malnutrition. Iron-rich macaroni products have now appeared on the market, but this information must be distributed through education.

To conclude the blueprint for changing of attitudes and habits, effective learning requires opportunity for the practice of health habits or the practical application of the new knowledge. For a long time health knowledge was provided in schools but these same schools had common drinking cups, cold water, and usually no soap. The realization by the school boards of the importance of a healthful school environment brought remarkable changes. Warm water is much more conducive to washing before eating and after going to the toilet. Teachers in northern areas of Canada are enthusiastically giving stars to encourage students to wash frequently. Because water is very often difficult to obtain in these areas, usually costing one dollar a barrel, the child's parents may consider it a colossal waste to use this precious commodity for bathing.

Healthful school environment is vitally related to mental health. Frustration and discouragement resulting in early withdrawal from school has been threatening the economic future of the nation. Jobs for unskilled workers are diminishing because of automation but school drop-outs are prepared for little else. Many drop-outs have college potential. Incidentally, it is interesting to observe that Milwaukee, which boasts an ungraded school system, has the lowest drop-out rate in the United States. Pre-empt programs were tried across Canada to improve mental health, by giving students an opportunity to talk out their problems and to see themselves in a much larger context than family or neighborhood. Here again, knowledge is important but opportunity for practical application is equally vital. More and more counsellors are inviting parents to schools in order to improve home environment. Winnipeg School Division No. 1. has instituted a "Higher Horizons" program designed to stimulate pupils, particularly in culturally deprived and economically depressed areas, to stay in school until they have qualified for admission to college or acquired a trade or marketable skill. Money has been provided for additional services and greater opportunities including intensive pupil and parent guidance and cultural activities which are normally not available to underprivileged children, with a view to creating enthusiasm and appreciation for fine arts. The experiment is currently confined to one junior high school and its five feeder schools in central Winnipeg.

The "Whole Child" Concept Means Greater Recognition for Physical Education and Health

The unity and interdependence of mind and body is rarely questioned or criticized in contemporary thinking; hence many provinces are enlarging their health and physical education program. However, this unity of mind and body seems to have been overlooked in some provinces where health and physical education have lost certain status. Perhaps it would facilitate understanding of just why the pendulum swings uneasily from one extreme to the other, if one were to look at concomitant factors that affect education generally.

Eloquent, well-educated, vocal persons have had a decided impact upon public thinking and educational policies over the years. The medieval philosopher St. Augustine believed the body was an impediment to the soul; "a muddy vesture of decay [which] doth grossly close us in."[5] The French philosopher Rousseau (1712-78) reversed the trend to isolate the mind from the body, and the serious thinkers today allude to the strong mind usually found in a strong body. Late nineteenth century saw educational research from Britain (Galton and Pearson) reflected in Canada's concern for individual differences. Canada also felt the influence of Germany's interest in natural science and experimentation and was not unaware of Binet's and Freud's work in France and Austria concerning the maladjusted child. Next came the period of testing and counting. In 1904 Thorndike's book on mental measurement stated "everything that exists, exists in some amount and can, therefore, be measured." I.Q. scores were thought to be mirror images of mental potential and the child became an ambulant mind to be treated accordingly.

The stock market crash of 1929 announced a re-appraisal period as far as techniques were concerned. Emphasis was upon democracy and equality. Homogeneous grouping and acceleration lost favor. No longer was intellectual excellence of primary concern. The theme of progressivism was "the whole child." "Adjustment" and "emotional maturity" were terms often repeated but rarely explained. Inadequate interpretations led to unbelievable school programs. As Dr. J. D. Ayers stated "the whole child" proved to be a lot more difficult to pin down and measure than his academic aptitude and achievement.[6]

The wave of criticism hit in the late 1940's reached a peak in the middle 1950's, and made itself heard through royal commission investigations into education. The Cameron Commission in Alberta and the Chant Commission in British Columbia are notable examples. The Chant Commission found the course entitled "Family Life" a stimulus for controversy. The Cameron Commission reported that "Health and Personal Development," the title of the course of study in Alberta at that time, received the majority of complaints, which specifically queried portions termed "personal development." Recommendation 75 requested that a committee including a majority of medical practitioners and health authorities review present health content at all grade levels to judge its accuracy and value. Unnecessary overlapping and repetition has

---

5 Shakespeare, *Merchant of Venice*, V, 1, 64-65.

6 "Emerging Trends," p. 288.

long been the blight of school health education and should certainly be removed to make room for other essential topics.

Changes go on, motivated by the pressure of power, eloquence, or need. But if the basic product, or body of knowledge, remains essential to the growth and development of human beings, then the changes occurring are only in appearance, not in ingredients. Just as the ingenuity of a mother leads her to add strawberry flavoring to her child's previously refused plain milk, so do those persons responsible for public education present health content in another form, more acceptable to the people at that time. Because education is for people, it should see people first as persons, secondly as citizens, and thirdly as vocational possibilities. Public pressure, based upon artificially conceived ideas of human needs makes this process function in reverse. Employment is the major concern and motivator for the layman; a man must have a job. Then his role as a citizen comes to the fore when employment is threatened. If citizenship were considered by the public as a primary objective of education, then perhaps schools would not be so timid in their approach to the issues of fluoridation and medicare.

Since employment prospects are of vital interest to the public, needed personal health knowledge, so related to successful living both on and off the job, can easily be presented in a vocational setting. Of the seven units in British Columbia's new Guidance 20 course for Secondary Schools, five units contain health content:

Unit 1—Medical Science
          The Battle with Disease
Unit 2—Community Health
Unit 3—Alcohol and Other Potentially Harmful Substances
Unit 4—First Aid
Unit 5—Safety Education in Driving

As the nation spotlights physical fitness as necessary for the health and vigor of its citizens, the natural relationship of physical education and health education becomes even more evident. Obesity, with its concomitant aspects of susceptibility to cardio-vascular disease, diabetes, and diminished longevity, demands both reduction in caloric intake and increased physical activity. The controversial cholesterol content of the blood is similarly affected by both diet (the importance of fruits and vegetables) and exercise.

Many curriculum designers have been motivated to combine health and physical education within the same timetable block, or under the same cover in course of study (Saskatchewan and British Columbia), or to approve textbooks which recognize this special relationship, e.g. *Health in Work and Play* and *Good Health Today*. The following statement is taken from the Saskatchewan Elementary School Curriculum Guide II:

> . . . teachers will note a strong emphasis on both physical activity and personal development, the aim being to ensure well-developed bodies and sound attitudes towards health and life generally. Formal classroom instruction will come alive by well-designed physical activities and healthful living throughout the school day. . . . Health education and physical education are not two separate subjects. It is possible to isolate each from the other but the result is that both lose a great deal of their purpose and meaning.

The interrelationship of health education and physical education is both natural and necessary; each affects the other, reinforces the other, and depends upon the other for success. In accordance with the age and sex of the students receiving health instruction, physical education can provide the motivation, the content, and the practical application of acquired knowledge. However, the relationship of health and physical education is not exclusive; the contribution of other fields of study in the fight against disease is well recognized. It may be said that health education today is like an animated octopus with tentacles reaching into many fields of research. Some even compare the role of health education with that of the general practitioner in an ever-increasing world of specialists. Effective health education must be willing to consider all aspects of disease, not overlooking relevant psychological and sociological factors.

In some provinces health education is still the "runt" of the family of school subjects. Small, not because its potential is insignificant, but thwarted in growth, perhaps because of insufficient nourishment at the university level, and perhaps because it may appear to infringe upon the rights of the home to determine the health of the child. Then too, health education is different from other members of the family in that it insists upon influencing attitudes and habits—it wants to involve students in concrete situations that will provide opportunity to practice knowledge learned; and finally, the problems it faces are extremely complex, subject to many variables, and require an inter-disciplinary approach. If health education fails to thrive, governments will have to make the important decisions about public health, since citizens will lack sufficient knowledge to exercise freedom in making wise choices.

BIBLIOGRAPHY

1. Alberta, *Occupational Trends and Employment Opportunities*. Edmonton: Department of Education, 1960.
2. ———, *Report of the Royal Commission on Education in Alberta*. Edmonton: Department of Education, 1959.
3. Armstrong, Iva L., and Barbara McLaren, "We Are What We Eat," *Health* (October, 1962).
4. Ayers, J. D., "Emerging Trends in Education Research in Canada," *Canadian Education and Research Digest*, II, No. 4 (1962).
5. British Columbia, *Secondary School Guidance* (Experimental Edition). Victoria: Department of Education, 1961.
6. Canada, *Epidemiological Bulletin*. Ottawa: Department of National Health and Welfare, VI, No. 1 (1962).
7. Canadian Education Association News Letter, No. 171 (January, 1963).
8. Castaldi, C. R., G. H. Ball, et al., *Dental Health Socio-Economic Level and Voting in Fluoridation Plebiscites*. A project supported by grants #608-7-22 and #608-7-13 from the Department of National Health and Welfare, Canada, 1959.
9. Commission on Philosophy for School Health Education, "A Point of View For School Health Education." *Journal of Health, Physical Education, Recreation*, XXXIII, No. 8 (1962).
10. Cornely, Paul B., and Stanley Bigman, "Some Considerations in Changing Health Attitudes," *Children*, X, No. 1 (1963).
11. Denver Public Schools, "The Health Interests of Children." Denver, Colo.: Denver Public Schools, 1947, 1954.
12. Frappier, Armand, "Recent Advances in Immunization," *Canadian Journal of Public Health* (December 1962).
13. Hallock, Grace T., et al., *Health in Work and Play*. Toronto: Ginn and Company, Ltd., 1956.
14. Hein, Fred V., and Allan J. Ryan, "The Contributions of Physical Activity to Physical Health," *The Research Quarterly*, XXXI, No. 2 (1960).
15. Hickman, W. Harry, "Education for the Future," *The Canadian Nurse*, LVIII, No. 10 (1962).
16. Kohler, Mary Conway, "We Waste a Million Kids a Year," *The Saturday Evening Post* (March 10, 1962).
17. McCarthy, T. F., "Influenza," *Occupational Health Bulletin*, XVII, Nos. 11-12 (1962).
18. MacIver, John, "An Industrial Psychiatrist Looks at V.D.," *Health* (December, 1962).
19. Mayer, Jean, "Exercise and Weight Control," *Exercise and Fitness*. Illinois: The Athletic Institute and the University of Illinois College of Physical Education, 1960.
20. National Education Association and American Medical Association, *Health Education*. Washington, 1924.
21. Nix, Margaret E., Unpublished survey.
22. Phair, J. T. and N. R. Speirs, *Good Health Today*. Toronto: Ginn and Company, Ltd., 1958.
23. Robertson, Elizabeth Chant, "Nutrition Problems in Canadian Children," *Canadian Nutrition Notes*, XVIII, No. 2 (1962).

24. Rose, Dr. Dyson, "Irradiation of Food Products," *Canadian Nutrition Notes*, XIX, No. 1 (1963).
25. Saskatchewan, *Elementary School Curriculum Guide II for Health and Physical Education*. Regina: Department of Education, 1956.
26. Sorenson, Roy, "Alcohol Education and its Relationship to Teenage Culture of Today," *Bulletin of the Association for the Advancement of Instruction about Alcohol and Narcotics*, VIII, No. 2 (1962).
27. Stiles, W. W., *Individual and Community Health*. New York: McGraw-Hill Book Company, 1953.
28. Tanner, J. M., *Growth at Adolescence* (2nd ed.), Springfield, Illinois: Charles C. Thomas, Publisher, 1962.
29. Tyler, Ralph W., "Implications of Behavioral Studies for Health Education," *The Journal of School Health*, XXXIII, No. 1 (1963).

OUTDOOR EDUCATION

16

W. Donald Smith

Professor, Faculty of Physical Education
University of Alberta, Edmonton

INTRODUCTION

During the present era of increased costs for education and a steadily rising student population, outdoor education has failed to take its rightful place in the school curriculum in Canadian provinces. Even with the advent of an awareness by citizens and school authorities that the fitness of youth is a contemporary challenge, little has been done to stimulate teachers to take an active interest in the important role of outdoor education. Provincial curriculum guides do little more than mention outdoor education and camping as part of the physical education program. Whether or not outdoor education is introduced to school children remains up to the individual interests of teachers, principals, or board members.

Julian W. Smith, Director of the Outdoor Education Project for the American Association for Health, Physical Education and Recreation has done a great deal to stimulate an awareness of the great possibilities in outdoor education for American youth. He conceives outdoor education to mean

> learning in and for the outdoors. . . . it is simply a learning climate which offers opportunities for direct laboratory experiences in identifying and resolving real-life problems. . . .[1]

Two relatively important facets of outdoor education are the learning

---

[1] Smith *et al.*, *Outdoor Education*, p. 19.

by doing, and the human relationships that are involved in the social living.

Most authorities on the subject hold the concept that outdoor education can and should play an important role in the school curriculum. The principal theses underlying the implications of outdoor education are described by L. B. Sharp, Executive Director of the Outdoor Education Association Inc. (Carbondale, Illinois). He states, "That which can best be learned in the out-of-doors through direct experiences, dealing with native materials and life situations, should there be learned."[2]

Although programs of outdoor education, school camping, and resident camping are similar in content, the particular emphasis placed upon segments of each varies a great deal. The broad, general aims of all three are closely related. In its broader sense, outdoor education implies school camping in a setting where the school curriculum is integrated with direct experiences in living in the out-of-doors.

The American Camping Association in its Standards for Resident Camping describes camping as "an experience in group living in a natural environment . . . it is sustained experience under the supervision of trained leadership and provides a creative educational experience in cooperative group living."[3]

Little is being done in outdoor education on a formal basis in Canada. Classes experience field trips to study conservation, geology, forestry, and biology in many of the science programs within the school systems. But all too often these are short, afternoon or one-day outings where the only expenses involved are those of transportation. School camping over a prolonged period of time in which an entire grade may go for three days or a week is a relatively rare occurence. Usually it is stimulated by the foresight, interest, and enthusiasm of a dedicated teacher working in a cooperative venture with parents, other teachers, and school authorities.

When delegates were questioned at a Canadian Camping Association Conference held in Banff, Alberta, in January 1963, only one province represented could definitely state that school camping was a reality in at least one area. Although many of the delegates were involved in resident camping and only a limited few were teachers, it is fair to assume that either there is little long-term school camping or that the members of the camping association are not familiar with the programs in operation.

OUTDOOR EDUCATION

Catherine Scholes, former Head of the Department of Health and

---

[2] A. A. H. P. E. R., *Outdoor Education*, intro.
[3] A. C. A., *Resident Standards*, p. 1.

Physical Education, York Memorial Collegiate Institute, York Township, in an article published in 1954, stated, "In Ontario four schools have pioneered in school camping within the last four years . . . upon investigation we find that no other province in Canada has school camps."[4] The four schools listed were Forest Hill Junior High School of Forest Hill Village, Toronto; Pickering College, Newmarket; King George School, Guelph; and York Memorial Collegiate Institute, York Township.

Forest Hill Junior High School and Pickering College used Limberlost Lodge near Huntsville as a site and students studied the natural resources of a northern county of lakes and woodland, and what had happened to them over the years. The King George School camping projects took place at the Lutheran Church Camp in Wedgewood Park near Guelph and studied subjects related to that particular environment. York Memorial Collegiate students went to the Humber Glen Camp near Bolton and used the Humber Valley Conservation Area as a project theme.

A more detailed description of the preparatory work, programs, expenses, and evaluation of objectives for the school camping may be found in the booklet *Now We Suggest*[5] published by the Ontario Teachers' Federation in 1955. A useful series of articles on camp schools was published in June of 1959 by J. Bascom St. John in the Toronto *Globe and Mail* in the column "The World of Learning." St. John elaborates on one aspect of city life which he calls "the remoteness from contact with the natural sources of life" and utilizes the information on school camping to illustrate his basic premise. The articles are entitled "Camp Schools Beat Urbanization," "Camp School Aids City Pupils," "Find Classrooms and Camp Schools are Different," and "Province Lags on Camp School Idea."

Miss Blanche Snell, who has taken a leading role in the school camping of York Memorial Collegiate, has also made a valuable contribution to physical education in Ontario as Chairman of the Ontario Teachers' Federation Committee reporting on eight problem areas in physical and health education (8). The two booklets *Let's Talk It Over* and *Now We Suggest,* which present an excellent over-view of physical and health education in the elementary and secondary schools of the province of Ontario, each contain a section on school camping.

It is rather disturbing to note that the Ontario Camping Association, with one of the largest memberships in the Canadian Camping Association, lists no standing committee on outdoor education or school camping in its 1963 Directory of Member Camps. For a province that has done more in school camping than any other in Canada, it merely emphasizes

---

4 Scholes, "School Camping," pp. 15-17.
5 pp. 47-55.

the lack of close co-operation between school authorities and camping associations necessary to foster the growth and development of school camping.

The most outstanding example of school camping in Canada, in the writer's opinion, is that of the Island School for Natural Science sponsored by the Toronto Board of Education. Utilizing the resources of Toronto Island the school provides, on a year-round basis, a very worthwhile experience in natural science for grade VI school children. A report on the school activities illustrated with 35 mm. color slides was presented at the Outdoor Education section of the 1961 C.A.H.P.E.R. Convention at McMaster University in Hamilton. In 1962, ninety grade VI classes of boys and girls spent a week of the school year in residence at the School for Natural Science. In addition to classroom sessions, much of the time was spent in observing and reporting on marine, bird, and animal life from an all-weather pond on the island and a bird refuge. Integrating actual experiences in a natural habitat with the science course of the school curriculum provides an interesting and informative experience for elementary school children. Other school systems in the provinces across Canada would do well to follow the foresight and imagination of the Toronto Board of Education by establishing similar projects.

CAMPING IN CANADA

Organized camping in Canada is fostered on a national basis by the Canadian Camping Association. Made up of provincial associations or sections, it operates under a constitution incorporated by letters patent issued by the Secretary of State for Canada (10). The objects of the association are:

1. To further the interests and welfare of children, youth and adults through camping as an educative, character-building and constructive recreational experience;
2. To act as a co-ordinating body for camping throughout Canada;
3. To develop and encourage high standards in camping and the maintenance thereof;
4. To study all aspects of camping and to interpret and disseminate knowledge concerning developments and regulations pertaining thereto;
5. To acquire and own assets, property, privileges, real estate and other rights by purchase, donation or legacy for the purposes of the association; to sell, alienate and exchange the said properties and to acquire other properties in their place.

As of December 31, 1962, there were seven provincial associations with more than 700 members in the Canadian Camping Association. They were Alberta, 47; British Columbia, 40; Manitoba, 52; Nova Scotia, 23; Ontario, 328; Quebec, 207; and the recent addition of Saskatchewan, 15. Nearly one-half are camp members (308), with individual members (248), student and commercial members making up the remainder.

Prior to 1963 the president and executive were either from the Ontario or the Quebec Camping Associations. For the first time in its history, the Canadian Camping Association elected an executive for 1963-64 from elsewhere. The complete slate of officers is from Alberta, and follows such well-known camping names of former presidents as Taylor Statten, Dais L. Gass, Anne I. Vail, W. E. (Ted) Yard, Irwin Haladner, F. M. Van Wagner, and Kenneth H. Murray.

The official publication of the association is *Canadian Camping*, published four times a year by the Canadian Camping Magazine Co. for the Canadian Camping Association at 170 Bloor Street West, Toronto, Ontario.

In Canada, the majority of private camps are located in Ontario or Quebec. There are few private camps west of the Lakehead (Fort William and Port Arthur). British Columbia has three and the prairie provinces none. Most of the camps in Western Canada are sponsored by agencies, church groups, or youth service organizations. The Maritimes are similar to Western Canada in this regard, although there are four private camps in Nova Scotia.

In the brief resumé of camping across Canada that follows, it becomes apparent that participation is increasing and that camping is playing more of a vital role in contributing to the development of Canadian youth than ever before.

BRITISH COLUMBIA   There is no school camping as such. The B.C. Camping Association is being revitalized at present. Members have participated as a planning committee for the Camp Leadership Conference conducted by Lorne Brown on the U.B.C. Campus. The Community Programs Branch of the Department of Education assists financially with leadership training. There are three private camps and over 100 agency or church camps registered under the Welfare Institutions Act of the Department of Health. The Greater Vancouver Parks Board operate three day camps as an extension of their program for playgrounds at Camp Capilano, about forty minutes from Vancouver.

ALBERTA   There are northern (Edmonton) and southern (Calgary and District) sections of the Alberta Camping Association. There is some weekend camping by school groups of the Edmonton Public School System, mainly through the interest of individual teachers. There are no private camps except the dude ranch version. All camps are agency-, church-, or club-sponsored. The Recreation and Cultural Development

Branch of the Provincial Secretary's Department provides financial assistance for leadership training at the Camp Directors' Seminar, Senior Counselors' Conference, and Junior Counselors' Course. In addition, the Branch provides camp leadership training as part of its Recreation Leadership Course at summer session. Other government departments that provide services are Highways, by establishing picnic areas, Forestry, through provincial parks and the conservation area of the Eastern Slope of the Rockies, and Health, through local health units on camp sanitation.

SASKATCHEWAN   Church camps, Y.M.C.A. and Y.W.C.A., other youth agency groups, and special camps (music) are the most common. The provincial association is in the early stage of development, centered in the Saskatoon and Regina areas. There is some leadership training assistance given by the Continuing Education Branch of the Department of Education and its staff of field supervisors.

The Regina Public Schools sponsored an Outdoor Education Experiment in June 1963 when fifteen boys and twelve girls of the Grade VI class from Birchwood School spent four days at Cypress Hills Provincial Park. The Director of Physical Education for the Regina Public School Board and the Director of the Continuing Education Branch of the Department of Education initiated the experiment by presenting the proposal to the School Board in 1962.

With an emphasis in program patterned after the Natural Science School of the Toronto Board of Education, the experiment was carefully planned and co-ordinated by many interested groups. The participants included the following: the superintendent, six principals, the director of physical education, the home room teacher and school principal of Birchwood School, the Regina Home and School Association, the Conservation Information Services Division of Natural Resources, Fitness and Recreation Division, and the parents of the participating students.

MANITOBA   There is no school camping as such or private camps. The Manitoba Camping Association holds eight monthly meetings and conducts a weekend institute in April at Winnipeg. The Department of Agriculture Extension, Manitoba Federation of Agriculture, and the recently created Physical Fitness and Amateur Sport Division of the Department of Welfare provide leadership and some financial assistance. Church camps form the largest group of the association with agency camps a close second. The northwest section of Ontario (west of the Lakehead) meets with the Manitoba Camping Association. One of the important influences on leadership training has been that of the School of Social Work at the University of Manitoba.

ONTARIO   The Ontario Camping Association is the largest and probably the most comprehensive of the provincial associations. Its camps have been established longer than any others in Canada. The association has standing committees on the conference, on education, finance, membership and directory, nominations, public relations, and standards. Special projects include canoeing standards, conservation, legislation, sales tax, and staff training. A well-attended annual conference is held each spring.

There are probably 900 summer camps of various types, 168 to 175 of them privately owned and operated. There is a tremendous use of outdoor facilities by family groups throughout the summer. The Department of Lands and Forests operates Junior Warden Camps for training in conservation. The Federation of Ontario Naturalists conducts a week-long camp in conservation, bird life, etc. for its members. The Ontario Community Programmes Branch and Department of Lands and Forests conduct two camps at Quetico Provincial Park for training of guides in woodsmanship. Through the Physical Education Branch, the Department of Education has carried out relationships with summer camping as follows:

1. Grants-in-aid to non-profit camps numbering about 400.
2. Operation of the Ontario Leadership Camp Centre in which about 280 high school boys and girls attend the seventeen-to twenty-one day course.
3. Co-operation with non-profit camps in the promotion and conduct of a week-end workshop presently in its seventh year of operation.
4. Summer visitation of non-profit camps by summer staff to help in matters of program, administration, etc.
5. Co-operation with the Ontario Camping Association concerning desirable practices.

QUEBEC There are two sections or associations in the province of Quebec, one French-speaking and the other English-speaking. The English-speaking section represents Quebec in the Canadian Camping Association. There are many private camps and church-operated camps in the province. Many of the camps that operate in the area north of the Montreal area, or north of the Ottawa-Hull area are bilingual, and the opportunity for conversational French is an added attraction. The provincial association meets annually in March and has done a great deal of preliminary work in studying camp standards, employment opportunities, and preparing a camp registry.

NOVA SCOTIA There are about seventy camps, including five day camps and four private camps, in the Nova Scotia Camping Association. School camping has been discussed but, so far, not carried on for long-term periods. There is an annual spring conference on leadership training for counsellors, directors, and committee members. It is usually held at Big Cove Camp and is financed in part by the Department of Education. A special co-educational camp for 110 campers is held during the last ten days of August and is called the Junior School of the Arts Camp. The Federation of Home and School Associations and the Department of Education sponsor the camp, which specializes in music, art, drama, and recreation.

The Trade and Industry Department of the Government of Nova Scotia construct and service provincial camp sites.

FUTURE IMPLICATIONS

Although the provincial associations in Alberta, Manitoba, Ontario, and Quebec are doing camp visitations based on desirable practices or standards, there is a need for co-ordination of the program on a national scale. Standards for day camps and family camping would be the next two logical areas for consideration.

The Canadian Camping Association should investigate the possibility of publishing a national information booklet on provincial camping areas, resources, accommodation, hiking and canoeing trips, etc. Statistics should be compiled on the number of camps, campers, and camper-days serviced by the association through its members.

Provincially, more of the associations should be doing preparatory investigations of such items as a provincial charter, legislation for tax relief, conservation, provincial parks, school camping, year-round use of facilities, family camping conferences, day camp courses to train leaders, camp sites for tourist families in towns and cities, and travel camps.

Camping, in its variety of forms, is big business today. Millions of dollars are spent annually in North America on equipment, facilities, and leadership. Co-operating groups must work closer together in a unified effort to cull the full benefit from individual resources. The most important task for the Canadian Camping Association is to assume its rightful place with biology, agriculture, forestry, conservation, social work, public health, physical education, and recreation as a potent force in giving a well-rounded education to all youth.

The Executive of the Canadian Camping Association has the responsibilities of informing sections across Canada of what is happening on a national scale, getting them to assume some responsibility for initiating conferences and leadership training, and co-ordinating the present organizations that have some contribution to offer.

BIBLIOGRAPHY

1. American Association for Health, Physical Education and Recreation, *Outdoor Education for American Youth*. Washington, D.C.: 1957.
2. American Camping Association, *Resident Standards*. Bradford Woods, Pa., 1960.
3. Canadian Camping Association, *Constitution*. Montreal, 1949.
4. ——, *"Report of Membership for 1962,"* Annual Report presented at Banff, Alberta, January, 1963.
5. Ontario Camping Association, *1963 Directory of Member Camps*. Toronto, 1963.
6. Ontario Teachers' Federation, *Let's Talk It Over*. Toronto, 1952.
7. ——, *Now We Suggest*. Toronto, 1955.
8. St. John, J. Bascom, "The World of Learning," Toronto *Globe and Mail*, June, 1959.
9. Scholes, Catherine, "School Camping in Canada," *Canadian Camping*, VI (April, 1954).
10. Smith, Julian W., Reynold E. Carlson, George W. Donaldson, and Hugh B. Masters, *Outdoor Education*. Englewood Cliffs, N.J.: Prentice-Hall, Inc., 1963.
11. Students of Blanche Snell, "School Camping in Ontario," *Canadian Camping*, VIII (April, 1956).

17

John Farina

Associate Professor
School of Social Work
University of Toronto

PROBLEMS OF COMMUNICATION

In Canada communication failure is a critical barrier to a united approach to the challenge of leisure. There are physical educators, recreationists, social workers, Y.M.C.A. secretaries, boys' club workers, parks administrators, and adult educators all stating claims as professionals in the field of leisure services. Most of these groups interpret their particular discipline as broad and inclusive of a wide range of leisure pursuits as contrasted with the relatively narrow ranges of all others. All these groups communicate on the basis of a common terminology, yet each loads terms with subtly different values yielding a variety of connotations and surplus meanings.

This barrier to communication is especially relevant to any discussion of the private agencies for physical education in Canada.

Physical educators view recreation as an essential area of concern of their discipline. By implication, other workers in the field of leisure believe that physical educators consider themselves the mentors of recreation. On the other hand, workers from a variety of disciplines within private agencies tend to derogate physical education as only one, and perhaps the most abused, aspect of recreation. It is probable that in most instances of such differences of opinion, the two sides, although using the same terms, are not addressing themselves to the same concept. It is not the purpose of this chapter to deal with this problem of interpretation, but rather simply to draw it to the attention of the reader interested in the role of private agencies.

In general, the private agencies in the field of leisure services have never viewed their activity programs as ends in themselves. Rather they have seen activities as a medium through which the stated purpose of the agency can be achieved. In none of the private agencies has the focus been exclusively on physical activities (or physical education), nor has any agency program regularly excluded physical activities. Indeed, for many agencies this has been the dominant form of activity.

IDENTIFICATION OF AGENCIES

When one speaks of a private agency in the traditional sense, reference is being made to a service organization in the broad field of community welfare, which is under the direction of a board of private citizens who are acting voluntarily for the betterment of the community. This, however, is no longer an adequate basis for differentiating public and private agencies in modern Canadian society. There has been a great increase in the number of public agencies acting for the welfare of the community and directed to a large extent by private citizens acting voluntarily. Municipal recreation commissions or committees, library boards, museum boards, and local historical boards are typical illustrations. There are, however, three other criteria by which public and private agencies have been identified.

The first and most easily measured is source of finance. A public agency is financed by public funds, that is, by the financial resources of the Dominion, provincial, country, or local government. In essence this means that public agencies are tax-supported by private or voluntary funds—United Funds, Community Chests, donations, bequests, fees, and charges. This means that theoretically, private agencies are not a charge on the tax-paying public. This in essence is their justification for private control and operation—by virtue of their independence of the public purse they have the right to operate outside the framework of government services.

The second criterion of identification of agencies as public or private relates to agency program support."The public agency program must have the support of the general public and be backed by legislation, while the private agency may offer a program based on the support of only a small group of citizens who recognize a specific need."[1] The implication, of course, is that the line between public and private programs is not fixed. A need recognized by a small group of socially responsible citizens yesterday may be accepted by the general populace today or

---

[1] Thompson and Farina, "Two Way Lane," p. 116.

tomorrow. For example, programs of recreation for the aged in Canada were pioneered by such agencies as Gordon House in Vancouver and the Toronto Second Mile Club. In addition, where the need for service to this selected group was recognized by socially conscious community leaders, new private agencies were formed to provide programs for the aged. The Friendship Clubs in Edmonton, growing out of the concern of women's club leaders, are a typical example. The developments noted above occurred in the decade following World War II. During the 1950's, however, general public acceptance of the need for recreation programs for the aged was manifest in many Canadian communities. Public agencies in some instances gave support and assistance to private programs. For example, the City of Edmonton Recreation Commission introduced into its community center programs specific activity sessions for the aged. Thus, programs that were originally offered on the basis of support by a small group of citizens soon came to be recognized and supported by the general public.

The third criterion by which the public and private agencies may be distinguished relates to the clientele to be served. The public agency, which receives its mandate from the general populance, is obliged to offer services to every citizen who is eligible and seeks service, whereas the private agency, which has a more limited mandate, can be selective in offering service.

Obvious examples of this selective offering of services are the Boy Scout and Girl Guide programs which serve only boys and only girls, and the Catholic Youth Organization which is designed specifically to serve Catholic youth.

These criteria for differentiating the public and private agencies in the field of leisure are sound in theory. They are, however, less than adequate for assessment of the present *de facto* situation in Canada. Every so-called private agency in the field of leisure services in Canada today has some obligation to the general public, as they do not clearly meet the first criterion listed above. All receive financial support from the public either in the form of grants of money or concessions that are in effect a charge against the taxpayer.

Financial grants to private agencies exist at all levels of government and appear to lack any logical pattern. There is no apparent relationship between the size of grant and the size of the agency, the type or the quality of service offered, the financial status of the agency, the extent to which the agency fills an unmet need, or the purpose of the agency. It might be speculated that the critical variable is the potential of agency board members for influencing legislators at various levels of government or the extent to which appeals for grants are based on emotional rather than logical factors. This perhaps provides the rationale for the lack of any logical pattern in the disbursement of government financial grants.

The federal government seems most inclined to offer direct financial aid to private agencies, apparently on an unconditional basis.

A study by the Research Division of the Department of National Health and Welfare published in 1955 listed "Selected Grants made by the Federal Department of Finance" for fiscal years 1950-51 to 1954-55. The following table suggests a continuation of the policies (or lack thereof) underlying such grants.

SELECTED FEDERAL GRANTS TO VOLUNTARY AGENCIES,
FISCAL YEARS 1950-51, 1954-55, 1958-59, 1961-62.*

Agency	1950-51	1954-55	1958-59	1961-62
Boy Scouts	$15,000	$65,000†	$15,000	$15,000
Girl Guides	9,000	12,000	15,000	15,000
Boys Clubs of Canada	—	10,000	10,000	10,000
Royal Canadian Academy of Arts	2,025	4,025	4,025	5,000

* Source: Research Division, Department of National Health and Welfare, Ottawa (personal letter, April 18, 1963.

† Including grant of $50,000 toward defraying a portion of the operating costs of the Eighth World Jamboree and International Conference held in Canada, 1955.

In addition to direct financial grants the federal government, through a variety of departments, gives direct aid of uncalculated value to private agencies. The Canadian Citizenship Branch of the Department of Citizenship and Immigration has assisted in, or been associated with, a wide range of recreational and cultural events throughout Canada. Staff members have given direct assistance to leadership training camps in all parts of the country. The Canadian Broadcasting Corporation co-operates with a wide variety of private agencies in presenting special radio and television programs. The most significant assistance to private agencies comes from the Council on Fitness and Amateur Sport of the Department of National Health and Welfare. These services are dealt with elsewhere in this volume.

One other form of federal support of private agencies is through conditional grants to provincial governments for disbursement to, or for the provision of services to, provincial and local agencies.

Provincial governments are more inclined to assist private agencies by conditional grants and supporting services. In some instances both the grants and services involve disbursement of federal as well as provincial funds. The organization of services at the provincial level usually involves several government departments often operating without reference to or, — indeed communication with — one another. The primary division of responsibility appears to be that between the branch of government responsible for provincial parks, the branch responsible for program services, and the department responsible for municipal affairs. The involvement of agriculture departments varies from province to province. These and other agencies of provincial governments are directly involved in giving supporting services to private agencies and in some instances handing out financial grants. The Recreation and Cultural Development Branch of the Department of the Provincial Secretary in Alberta will finance the training of leaders for private agency work and then subsidize the activity sessions they lead by contributing to the leaders' salaries. The Community Programs Branch of the Ontario Department of Education will conduct training institutes for private agency personnel in a wide range of activity and program media. The Youth and Welfare Department of the Quebec Government makes direct financial grants to private agencies. The departments of agriculture in most provinces make grants and services to a variety of rural and farm organizations most of which could be otherwise classified as private agencies.

Government involvement does not, however, stop at the provincial level. Local governments present an equally confused and illogical pattern of subsidizing of private agencies. Direct grants, services, and tax concessions to private agencies are common in all parts of Canada and in all types of local government. Indeed, in many small communities the local government will subsidize an otherwise private agency for the specific purpose of carrying out the essentially public function of providing a playground program. In larger Canadian cities both grants and tax concessions to private agencies are common.

A relatively recent development in Toronto is the provision, at public cost, of recreation facilities and maintenance cost to private agencies who undertake the program operation in those facilities. The example best illustrating this approach is University Settlement of Toronto. University Settlement, founded in 1912, is one of the oldest independent private agencies in Canada. It operated its program from old houses, redesigned for the purpose, continuously until 1957. Up to that time, the program had been focused on small club groups, arts and crafts, adult education classes, and a music school. In 1957, the agency, renamed University Settlement Recreation Centre, moved into its new premises. This was a new $750,000 recreation building containing the essential facilities for the traditional program of the agency but also a large modern gymnasium and a swimming pool of standard competitive dimensions. Two fully qualified physical educators were added to the staff at a senior level and a significant program development in the public sector of responsibility was undertaken.

While University Settlement Recreation Centre continues to carry and expand its traditional program, the agency also accepts responsibility, under the terms of its agreement with the City of Toronto, for the provision of a public recreation type program in the downtown area served by the agency.

An opposite approach to the subsidization of private agencies is taken by the City of Edmonton in relation to the Edmonton Community Leagues. It may be argued whether the Community Leagues are in fact private agencies. They do, however, appear to meet the essential criteria. They are primarily financed by voluntary funds, they operate on a membership basis, and they are directed by public-spirited citizens acting on a voluntary basis. In essence they combine the functions of a Neighborhood Center Association and a local Ratepayers' Association. While they cooperate extensively with the public authority they do not hesitate, but rather see it as their function, to criticize constructively any public policy related to recreation planning, development, and program. Yet the City of Edmonton subsidizes its avowed critics!

Community Leagues lease land for community and recreation uses from the City on ten-year leases at one dollar per year. They receive capital grants for the construction of facilities and operating grants for the maintance of facilities. The City provides playground equipment and a variety of play materials. Finally, the City through the Parks and Recreation Department makes recreation leadership available to the Community Leagues. The Community League as lessee maintains control over property, facilities, and program. This, in theory, assures a community base rather than a centralized service.

These illustrations point up the contrast between the approach to subsidization of the cities of Toronto and Edmonton. University Settlement Recreation Centre was built and financed by the City of Toronto on land owned by University Settlement; program leadership comes from the University Settlement professional staff and is financed by voluntary funds. In Edmonton, on the other hand, the Community Leagues develop their buildings and facilities on land owned by the City of Edmonton and professional leadership for programs is provided by the City Parks and Recreation Department. In one city subsidization is directed primarily towards facilities while in the other it is directed primarily towards program staff.

Neither of these approaches is typical of patterns of subsidization. The contrast, however, is characteristic. Each Canadian community has developed its own pattern of subsidy based to a large extent on the local history of recreation program development and also on financial expediency. For it must be emphasized that while public subsidy of private agencies is common in terms of financial aid, tax concessions, and program assistance, private agencies in fact subsidize the public authorities by undertaking responsibilities in the field of public recreation that otherwise would be borne by the public authorities. In communities where private agencies have been strong and operated extensive programs, the scope of the public agency program tends to be limited although the public type of program *may* be quite extensive.

The development and extension of subsidies and the evolving philosophy of service of private agencies make it increasingly difficult to differentiate between public and private agencies on either basis.

PIONEER EFFORTS

During the second half of the nineteenth century and the first quarter of the twentieth century private agencies were identified with pioneering new services in the field of leisure activity. The early Y.M.C.A.'s in Canada, in addition to their emphasis on evangelism, introduced library and reading-room services for members and sponsored lecture series and classes on a wide variety of subjects. The programs of many Canadian Y.M.C.A.'s in the 1850's, (Halifax, Montreal, London, Kitchener) "were, perhaps, among the earliest experiments in adult education in this country."[2] In the last decade of the nineteenth century, before the general establishment of public schools, the Y.M.C.A.'s in Canada offered night-school classes in a wide variety of subjects including languages, singing, Bible study, shorthand, and physical training. The Boy Scout movement received its original impetus in 1903 from Lord Baden-Powell's concern for enriching existing training schemes for boys. He wished to demonstrate the efficiency of "a syllabus of training in self-sufficiency in and knowledge of the out-of-doors."[3]

At the time, all of these were exciting new programs representing creative and responsible reactions to existing social conditions. In essence, these programs were exploratory, experimental, or demonstrative. Those noted are simply illustrative. Significantly, both the Y.W.C.A. and the Y.M.C.A .had by the close of the nineteenth century accepted responsibility for "a four fold program" embracing the spiritual, intellectual, physical, and social condition of members. The concern for the "physical condition" most certainly represented pioneering work in physical education in Canada. In terms of the modern definition of physical education, the program of the Boy Scouts remains as progressive today as at its inception at the turn of the century, especially in its championship of outdoor camping and hiking activities.

While there are many other pioneering programs of private agencies

---

2 Davis, *The Y.W.C.A.*, p. 26.
3 Milne, "Volunteer Leaders," p. 21.

that could be cited, the examples given are representative. There is, however, a further point relative to pioneering services in the field of recreation and physical education in Canada. It must be noted that pioneering effort has not been limited to private agencies. As early as 1885 the Dominion government established the first recreation and scenic National Park at Banff, Alberta. By the close of the nineteenth century there were four such parks, comprising a total area of approximately 3,800 square miles. This indeed was a pioneering and demonstrative program of significant proportions. In a rare burst of intuitive foresight, municipal authorities in several cities reserved large, desirable sites as municipal parks (e.g., Montreal and Vancouver), while others forbid commercial development of scenic ravines and gullies within their jurisdiction (e.g., Toronto and Edmonton). In more recent years public authorities have experimented with or demonstrated the effectiveness of programs of creative dramatics (Ottawa), for the mentally retarded (Edmonton), ballet classes (Forest Hill), Theatre Under The Stars (Vancouver), 5BX (R.C.A.F.), multiple use of conservation areas (Metropolitan Toronto Conservation Authority), etc.

In some instances these programs have been initiated and sponsored by the public authorities alone while in other instances the programs have been developed in co-operation with other agencies. Suffice it to say that pioneering in physical education and recreation is not limited to the private agencies.

There is one other type of social institution involved directly in the development of physical education and recreation programs in Canada. That is the service club. These are not public agencies, nor are they specifically private agencies in this particular field. Leisure services are only one area of concern of such organizations. Their interest in comunity services ranges over the whole spectrum of welfare, education, health, public affairs, and recreation. They have played in the past, however, and continue to play, a significant role in the total picture of leisure services in Canada.

Experimentation and demonstration have been the chief distinguishing features of programs offered or supported by service clubs. The first national survey of recreation services in Canada was completed in 1936, and goes under the heading "Service Clubs."

> Activities of a more purposeful and objective nature and that make a more lasting contribution to the community vary widely. Often it is one substantial effort of a *supplementary* nature, making possible the initiation of services that otherwise might not get under way. It may take the form of equipping a playground or camp, buying a camp site for a boys' club, or building a wading or swimming pool. . . . Usually gifts of this type are accompanied by definite encouragement to civic authorities or to

private agencies to undertake recreational programs. In the western provinces there are many municipalities where the beginnings of community recreation may be traced back to the active *encouragement* of service clubs.[4]

The initiation and encouragement of supplementary services has been the dominant policy of service clubs throughout their history in Canada. The playground programs of many communities in Western Canada owe their introduction and encouragement to the Gyro Club; in Ontario the Lions Club and Rotary International have provided similar services. The Kiwanis, Kinsmen, and Optimist Clubs have all been associated with the initiation and support of club activities and camping for boys, while the Knights of Columbus have sponsored club programs and other recreation services for boys of the Roman Catholic faith. While there have been some notable exceptions, services to girls and young women have been largely mere adjuncts to men's service clubs. In this age of near equality of the sexes this neglect appears to represent a cultural lag. The growth of women's service clubs in recent years, though, has to some extent closed the gap between services to boys and girls.

One of the strongest forces in pioneering new areas of service in the broad field of welfare is the Junior League. This is a national organization of young women (under thirty-five years of age) affiliated with the United States organization of the same name. There are branches in most major Canadian cities. In recent years Junior Leagues have strongly supported the introduction of high quality Children's Theatre into community recreation programs. At present the Toronto Junior League is sponsoring a demonstration project in co-operation with Central Neighborhood House related to the problem of school drop-outs. The major focus of these organizations is, however, the provision of voluntary service to social agencies in their communities.

TYPES OF AGENCIES

In any discussion of leisure services the contribution of private agencies to the field of recreation and physical education can only be put in perspective by an explicit statement of the position of private agencies vis-à-vis the provisions of public agencies and of commercial agencies. In terms of financial commitments made by the consumers of leisure services, the private agencies are of little significance. In the commercial field, for example, expenditure on alcoholic beverages alone probably surpasses the total income of all private agencies combined. The Canadian Broad-

---

4 Canadian Welfare Council, "Recreation," p. 40.

casting Corporation, one public agency, on occasion spends more on a single one-hour television program than the total annual income of most private agencies. Other commercial recreation expenditures that loom large in comparison with private agency budgets are commercial sports equipment, the boat building and servicing companies, the entertainment industry, and book and magazine publishing. In the public field, huge expenditures are involved in the operation of the Canada Council, the Council on Fitness and Amateur Sport, Community Programs and similar branches of provincial government, and municipal parks and recreation authorities. In terms of volume, measured in dollars and cents, the private agencies are a poor third and are steadily losing ground.

Yet this is not, in fact, a true measure of the social significance of the contribution that private agencies make. Preventive, restorative, and therapeutic approaches to social problems of individuals all receive attention in the statements of purpose of private agencies. Therefore results should not be measured in terms of numbers served but rather in terms of positive outcomes for individual participants. Traditionally this has been the stated orientation of private agency service.

Private agencies in the field of recreation and physical education may be divided into two general classes. On the one hand are those agencies which have aimed to serve a specific clientele wherever it may be found. Examples of such agencies indicating those whom they serve are The Boy Scouts Association (boys), The Girl Guides Association (girls), The Young Men's Christian Association (Christian young men), The Young Women's Christian Association (Christian young women), The Boys' Clubs (boys) and the Young Men's and Young Women's Hebrew Association (Hebrew young men and women). At the time of their organization each of these agencies specifically focused on serving the clientele noted. For example, the Constitution of the Montreal Y.M.C.A., as adopted in 1855, read, "Any young man under forty years of age, who is a member in good standing of an Evangelical Church in this city, may become an Active Member."[5] (10:12) The constitution of the first Y.W.C.A. in Canada, in Saint John, New Brunswick, stated that, "Active members of the new Association had to be members in good standing of some church."[6] The Act of Parliament incorporating the Canadian General Council of the Boy Scouts Association in 1914 defines the first purpose of the Council as "The instructing of boys in the principles of discipline, loyalty, and good citizenship. . . ."[7] The purpose of the Girl Guides

---

5 Ross, *The Y.M.C.A.*, p. 12.
6 Ross, *The Y.M.C.A.*, p. 10.
7 Tuttle, *Youth Organizations.*

Association is "To develop good citizenship among girls. . . ."[8] While individual Boys Clubs vary somewhat in their stated purposes, in general their aims are consonant with the statement of purpose of Boys' Clubs of America. "The purpose of Boys' Clubs of America is the social, vocational, and character development of boys."[9] Although they aim at a specified age group and are primarily serving boys, the Boys' Clubs also are concerned with serving defined geographic areas in most cities. This to some extent indicates their inclusion in both classes. For convenience, however, they have been included in the class of agencies which aims to serve a specific clientele wherever it may be found.

The second class of private agencies is that where service is aimed at the general population rather than a defined sector thereof but tends to focus its services within a specified geographic area. Typical of this class are the Settlements and Neighborhood Houses found in major Canadian cities. The National (U.S.A.) Federation of Settlements state that,

> We believe that our primary concern should be neighborhood life and its development. . . . A settlement fulfills this purpose by providing the opportunity for a variety of individual, group and inter-group experiences for people of all ages, regardless of race, creed, nationality or political belief, living together in a circumscribed geographical area.[10]

This statement is subscribed to in general by all Canadian Settlements and Neighborhood Houses. Some agencies in this category maintain a close association with a church and are influenced by a religious point of view.

The foregoing classification is broad, general, and not too precise. While the Y.W.C.A. is primarily providing programs for girls and women, there are provisions for the participation of boys and men; Boys' Clubs do provide programs to which girls are welcome; the Y.M. and Y.W.H.A. does not limit its services entirely to Hebrew young men and women; and the Settlements freely accept members from outside their primary area of service. The essential criterion for differentiation is whether the *primary* focus is on a particular constituency or on a specified geographic area.

The six agencies mentioned in the first category—the Boy Scouts, the Girls Guides, the Y.M.C.A., the Y.W.C.A., Boys' Club, and the Y.M. and Y.W.H.A.— have several features in common. First, all of them are nation-wide agencies with local branches affiliated with a national and international association. Second, none of them is indigenous to Canada

---

8 Tuttle, *Youth Organizations.*

9 Boys' Clubs, *Manual.*

10 Social Planning Council, *Needs*

but rather represent Canadian adaptations of foreign inspiration. Finally, although all six of these agencies are heavily involved in what appear to be recreation programs, all disclaim being recreation agencies; and while all of them conduct a large proportion of their programs in gymnasia and swimming pools they do not claim to be physical education agencies. The general public and lay leaders of these agencies will frequently refer to them as "character-building" agencies.

Within this category of agencies, a further division can be made which should clarify discussion of their operations. The Boys' Clubs and the three "Y's" are primarily building-centered agencies. Except for a small headquarters building in some of the large cities the Boy Scouts and Girl Guides do not have any investment in recreation or physical education facilities or property. Rather, these agencies are primarily concerned with the development and operation of explicit programs and make use of any available and suitable community facility. Programs of Scouting and Guiding operate from church halls of all denominations, synagogues, school buildings, public recreation facilities, armed forces camps, other private agency facilities, and commercial and industrial properties. "The Boy Scouts and Girl Guides have never felt the need for proprietary rights to the facilities they use."[11]

The "Y's" and Boys' Clubs, on the other hand, have always had a direct concern for the provision of facilities which would offer a broad base for program development. The physical structure has served these agencies as a concrete symbol of their concern for community betterment. Further, the buildings and properties developed by private agencies have provided to a significant extent the model and the impetus to subsequent development of public recreation facilities and community centers. This, then, is one way in which these building-centered agencies have fulfilled their traditional role of experimenters and demonstrators.

Many of the early Y.M.C.A.'s in Canada listed as an early objective the acquisition of a room for the association that would serve for meetings, Bible reading, lectures, and a library. Certainly, in these early years (1850-70) the Y.M.C.A.'s did not seek facilities for recreation. The Y.M.C.A. Convention in 1867 at Montreal passed the following resolution:

> Resolved: That this Convention regards the introduction of games into the rooms of Young Men's Christian Associations, for the entertainment or amusement of young men, as fraught with evil, dangerous to the best interests of Associations, compromising to Christian integrity, and dishonouring to the blessed Master and Teacher, the Lord Jesus Christ.[12]

---

11 Canadian General Council, *Canadian Boy Scouts*, p. 2.
12 Ross, *The Y.M.C.A.*, p. 35.

Today one can only speculate on what games those convention delegates had in mind.

It was not until a decade later that the physical aspect of the program of the Y.M.C.A.'s received attention. Murray Ross reports that while there had been early attempts in individual associations to promote a physical program, " 'gymnasium programs' were not encouraged before 1880."[13] By 1890, however, the Toronto Y.M.C.A. reported that "the Physical Department attracts more young men than any other Department of our Association."[14] At the same period various Y.M.C.A.'s were introducing boys' programs, and in 1891 an "Annual Boys' Summer Encampment" was started in Nova Scotia which was probably the first of its kind in Canada.

The evolution of a program of physical activities in the Y.M.C.A. had a pervasive influence on building development. In 1873 six "Y" buildings were under construction and by 1889 twenty-one buildings were opened. In 1935, seventy-four local associations throughout Canada had property valued at $8,731,200.00 which included forty-seven gymnasia and forty-three "indoor swimming tanks."[15] The 1962 *Y.M.C.A. Yearbook* reports 116 associations in Canada owning 105 buildings, including fifty-one gymnasia, fourteen auxiliary gymnasia, and fifty indoor swimming pools, with a total value of $32,869,300.

The first Boys' Club building in Canada was that of the Griffintown Boys' Club of Montreal which was established in its own quarters in 1905. In 1929 when the Boys' Club Federation of Canada came into being there were sixteen separate clubs in seven different Canadian communities, and by 1947 there were thirty clubs representing ten different communities. During 1947 the movement was reorganized under the name Boys' Clubs of Canada with thirty member clubs. Only one, however, Griffintown, had its own building. Since that time affiliation has grown to eighty-one clubs. Twenty-seven of these occupy buildings designed and constructed specifically as Boys' Clubs, while nine are located in buildings remodelled for the purpose. All the new buildings have gymnasia, and seven have indoor swimming pools. The total value of Boys' Clubs buildings is between six and seven million dollars. This equity has been built up over the astonishingly short period of fourteen years!

The first Y.W.C.A. in Canada, founded in Saint John, started its work in 1870 from two rented rooms. In 1873 the Toronto Y.W.C.A. rented two houses to serve as "boarding houses for young women." In 1890 a

13 Ross, *The Y.M.C.A.*, p. 87.
14 Ross, *The Y.M.C.A.*, p. 88.
15 Ross, *The Y.M.C.A.*, p. 52.

new building was opened which included the boarding house, reading room and library, a large parlor, classrooms, and a gymnasium. While a residence was the first building consideration of local Y.W.C.A.'s, physical education classes were from the start an important part of programs. In 1907 there were twenty-six City Associations and twenty-three Student Associations in Canada. In 1910 the Y.W.C.A. pioneered camping for girls and women with the opening of a school Girls Camp instituted by the Dominion Council at Geneva Park, Lake Couchiching. This development grew out of the positive experience for girls resulting from the loan in 1890, by John Ross Robertson, of a furnished summer cottage.

Although perhaps the first agency in Canada committed to a program of physical education, the Y.W.C.A. was relatively late in the development of gymnasium and swimming facilities. By 1932, however, the value of Y.W.C.A. property and furnishings was $2,250,000, and by 1948 twelve Y.W.C.A.'s had their own swimming pools and there were two others in joint Y.M.-Y.W.C.A.'s. In 1964 there were in Canada sixty-eight branch associations. They had thirty-six buildings with thirty-six gymnasia and twenty-six swimming pools.

The terms "Y.M.-Y.W.H.A." and "Jewish Community Centre" are synonymous. Early in 1963 these agencies, at a meeting in Hamilton, formed a national association. Montreal, Toronto, and Winnipeg have had vigorous associations for the past fifty years. The type of facility provided and the commitment to physical education has not differed significantly from the Christian Associations. In 1964 there were nine Y.M. and Y.W.H.A.'s in seven different Canadian communities with several new associations in prospect. These associations own nine buildings valued between six and seven million dollars. They all have gymnasia and six have indoor swimming pools.

The Boy Scouts and Girl Guides are representative of program-centered agencies. Both are Canadian branches of world-wide organizations.

The Dominion Headquarters Council of the Boy Scouts Association was established in 1910, two years after the foundation of the parent council in England. The Honorary Secretary of the Canadian Council wrote in 1912, "It was necessary to evolve a plan of *control* which, without hampering the growth and freedom of individual troops, would secure *uniformity* on broad lines."[16] The purpose of the organization is "The instructing of boys in the principles of *discipline*, loyalty, and good citizenship."[17]

The program of the Boy Scouts focuses on preparation for life, service

---

[16] Tuttle, *Youth Organizations*, p. 226.
[17] Tuttle, *Youth Organizations*, p. 211.

to others, and getting out of doors as much as possible. While the program was conceived in Britain it has been modified in Canada. The uniform, however, is definitely of British design and this has frequently been considered by officials of the Association as a possible factor contributing to resistance to membership. It is probable that a program titled *scouting*, if conceived in Canada, would have found garb reminiscent of Radisson or Hearne more representative of what the term "scout" implies when divested of the connotations associated with Boy Scouts.

The Girl Guides Association, dating from 1910, is organized on essentially the same pattern as the Boy Scouts Association. In Quebec there is the sister agency Federation Des Guides Catholique De La Province De Quebec (Federation of Catholic Guides of the Province of Quebec) founded in 1939.

The purpose of the Girl Guides is "To develop good citizenship among girls; to develop character; to encourage habits of observation, obedience and self-reliance."[18] Of note is the fact that approximately 15 per cent of the leadership in the Boy Scouts is female, while there are no male leaders in the Girl Guides. It would appear, then, that while either male or female leaders may competently "instruct boys in the principles of discipline, loyalty and good citizenship," only females can "develop good citizenship among girls, etc." Actually, though the situation results from an insufficient number of men interested in the program. It seems unfortunate in view of the amount of female supervision experienced by most boys that at this particular period in the social history of Western civilization a very masculine boys' program is greatly influenced by the feminine viewpoint.

The six agencies dealt with above carry out the bulk of private agency programming in Canada. There are, however, a small group of agencies, confined to a few major cities, which until recently have lacked any national organization or common statement or purpose. These are the Settlements and Neighborhood Houses. They are found only in Montreal, Toronto, Winnipeg, and Vancouver, the country's four largest cities.

Like the Y.M.C.A., Y.W.C.A., Boy Scouts, and Girl Guides, the settlement movement had its origin in England. Toynbee Hall, the first Settlement, was established in the East End of London in 1884. Subsequently similar agencies have been established in many parts of the world. Evangelia, organized in 1899, was the first Settlement in Canada, although University Settlement (Montreal), organized as a Settlement in 1910, has roots going back to 1891. University Settlement (Toronto) was founded in 1910, and two years later Central Neighborhood House, St. Christopher House, and Memorial Institute were organized. Not one

---

18 Social Planning Council, *Needs*, p. 5.

Settlement has been organized in Toronto since. In Hamilton, a Neighborhood House was organized in 1922, and in Winnipeg, Norquay House in 1927. Gordon House (1939) and Alexandra House (1935) in Vancouver are relatively recent Settlements. Evangelia, Memorial Institute, and Hamilton Neighborhood House no longer function as Settlements, while Ivenley (Montreal) amalgamated with the Old Brewery Mission some thirty years ago and functioned subsequently as a community center. There are a number of agencies on the Settlement pattern which operate with a missionary zeal that makes it difficult to distinguish them from missions doing recreational work. Woodgreen Community Centre in Toronto is representative of this type of agency.

The work of the Settlement is essentially to serve a specific neighborhood in a depressed part of a city. The service offered is not limited by age, sex, or creed. Basically, the program is one of informal education, recreation, and the development of indigenous leadership. Programs have been directed toward the enhancement of the social functioning of the clientele. This early commitment to professional social work leadership, made by most Canadian Settlements, has not precluded effective contributions by physical education, nursery school teachers, and fine arts instructors.

A significant development in the organizational pattern and program of Settlements was the amalgamation in 1962 of such services in the city of Winnipeg into the Neighbourhood Service Centres. Thus one agency with one board of directors is now providing service to four different neighborhoods in the city. Extensive use is made of existing facilities and programs are specifically geared to the specific needs of each neighborhood.

> This agency is unique in at least two respects: it was born out of the marriage of two former Neighbourhood Houses; and its service is "mobile," always focussing on local needs and problems, but adjusting its attention to unserved neighbourhoods as concerns rise and decline in the ever changing texture of a growing city.[19]

In addition to these developments in Winnipeg, 1962 was the year in which the thirteen Neighborhood Houses and Settlements in Canada formed the Canadian Association of Neighbourhood Services. This national association soon initiated a quarterly newsletter devoted primarily to an exchange of information between the agency members.

During the past half-century there appears to have been a significant degree of institutionalization in the organization and operation of all these agencies. Status tends to be given to the holders of specific positions

---

[19] Canadian Association of Neighbourhood Services, *Newsletter*, Vol. 1, No. 1, September 1963, p. 1 (mimeographed).

in the formal structure rather than on the basis of excellence of role performance in any position. Expectations and norms of behavior of staff members are quite rigidly prescribed and lines of demarcation between areas of staff responsibility are clearly drawn. Program planning, development, and administration evolve from agency structure. In many agencies personnel is trained and developed within the philosophic framework of the agency. This constitutes job training in many instances as opposed to professional training.

The process of institutionalization is frequently characterized by the reverence of traditions and a frequent backward look to past achievements. Ideas and purposes tend to become identified with concrete symbols, such as buildings, rather than the services designed to achieve purposes.

A blanket condemnation of all private agencies as institutionalized systems is not warranted. There are, however, evidences of this process in most private agencies in the field of leisure services in Canada.

Fortunately there are indications of creative new programs developing in some communities that are not bound by existing structures and traditions.

CLUB EXPANSION

Perhaps the most important recent development is the burgeoning of small private membership clubs in and around large cities. These clubs usually offer recreation opportunities for the whole family in sports, games, and social activties. Such clubs have been a part of the Canadian scene for many years, but until recently membership has been limited to a relatively elite few. Now, with increased affluence and hence discretionary income, the great middle class is enthusiastically embracing the family membership club such as the Granite in Toronto, the Royal Glenora in Edmonton, and the Winter Club in Winnipeg.

A related phenomenon has been the increase in the number and scope of clubs which had traditionally focused on one specific form of recreation. This is particularly apparent in the fields of golf and curling. Whereas for many years these activities were operated on a separate club basis, there is today a strong trend toward consolidation on a year-round basis with each activity synchronized with the Canadian seasons.

The traditional private agencies in Canada have long been concerned with the promotion of family recreation. Working within their established structures they have not been able to achieve as significant an impact on patterns of family recreation as have the more flexible membership clubs.

PLANNING GROUPS

Private agencies have always reacted responsibly to the need for effective relationships between all agencies and organizations responsible for
services in the broad field of recreation. In the early years of public
recreation development, the private agencies assisted public authorities
by sharing their experiences and frequently supplying or assisting in the
training of staff for new public services. With the post-war growth of
public recreation services the private agencies adjusted to the role of
equal partners in planning the development of services with the public
recreation authorities. The machinery which evolved for this co-operative
approach is the Social Planning Council, Council of Social Agencies, or
Welfare Council.

These Councils are made up of both lay and professional representatives of social agencies in a given community. In larger centers those
agencies whose primary field of services is recreation are frequently organized as a recreation division or section. Councils were initiated and
supported by private agencies from the beginning. Public agencies have,
however, frequently been reluctant to join. There has been a tendency
for some public leaders to view the Councils as "them" rather than "us"
and to see them as no more or less than their members.

There is no appropriate body in any of the provinces performing a
planning and co-ordinating function at the provincial level. A basic
value of the local planning council is that it is a non-operating agency.
As such, it does not have a vested interest in any program of direct
service. The only provincial body meeting this criterion is the Ontario
Welfare Council, but to date it has hesitated even to attempt to fulfil a co-
ordinating function with recreation agencies. Rather, such co-operative
effort as does exist at the provincial level is on the initiative and with the
support of provincial government agencies. The Recreation and Cultural
Development Branch in Alberta, and the Community Programs Branches
in B.C. and Ontario are illustrative. All three of these governments
offer direct services in the field of recreation. Thus their potential as co-
ordinating agencies between public and private agencies is drastically
limited. It is analogous to being one of the players in a game and at the
same time being the referee.

A second limitation on effective provincial co-ordination is the organizational patterns of many of the private agencies. These patterns are
typified by a strong national body and relatively autonomous local
branches, but with no provincial structure. The three "Y's" and Boys'
Clubs of Canada are organized on this pattern.

At the national level in Canada there is a strong coterie of private
agencies dedicated to serving their own local branches on the one hand

and fulfilling their world-wide commitments on the other. And government services are hopelessly fragmented by an ever-increasing number of departments, divisions, councils, and Crown corporations. A major problem, then, appears to be the co-ordination of services within both the private agencies and the public authorities; only then can co-ordination of the two be profitably discussed.

As early as 1929, "The Canadian Welfare Council"—then "The Canadian Council on Child and Family Welfare"—established a Recreation Division. Even prior to this, the Council had published a sixty-page booklet, "Play and Materials for the Pre-School Child." During the early thirties, Mr. Eric Muncaster was engaged by the Council to prepare recreation literature. He wrote thirteen pamphlets entitled the "Challenge of Leisure Series." This material was distributed by the Canadian Welfare Council until 1947 when the stock was depleted. In 1935 the Canadian Welfare Council completed the first national survey made on recreation services in Canada.

The Canadian Welfare Council was the first national organization to express and act upon its concern for the over-all development of recreation services in Canada. Organized on a pattern similar to that of local councils, the Council is well suited to fulfilling a co-ordinating function. In essence, it is a research and enabling agency eschewing any direct service function.

From its earliest beginnings the Council has attempted, patiently, and, for the most part, unsuccessfully, to fulfil its role as enabler of co-ordination in the field of recreation. Recreation leaders have been reluctant to grant this role to the Canadian Welfare Council. They are suspicious of and reject the implication that recreation is a welfare function. The subsequent hesitance of the Council about making a worth-while investment of finances in its attempts to fulfil a meaningful role on the national scene is understandable.

The apparent inadequacy of efforts to provide a co-ordinated, comprehensive approach to recreation in Canada reflects a number of current problems in the field of leisure services. The resolution of these problems is in the interest of public and commercial recreation but is perhaps vital to the continued existence of private agencies as we know them today.

AGENCY RESPONSIBILITY

Private agencies were initiated to meet felt needs in society during the Victorian era. Leisure was a scarce and valuable commodity; there were practically no public leisure services; educational services were restricted and limited; and commercial recreation sought to serve the small leisure class or to provide questionable pastimes with only the profit motive in mind.

The fact that these are no longer the prevailing conditions in Canadian society must be understood, accepted, and acted upon as a first principle in addressing the challenge of leisure. With this in mind the following is an evaluation of existing patterns of private agency services and public services, with statements of guiding principles for the delineation of agency responsibility.

1. The provision of services intended to make possible the natural expression of human interests through pursuits freely decided upon with no ulterior compulsions and with no commitment to behavioral change is a public responsibility. Such services are utilized primarily for enjoyment, creative expression, and release rather than to solve a personal problem or to learn a skill.

This type of service may, of course, be provided by private groups on a membership or fee basis—e.g., golf clubs, tennis clubs, social clubs, religious organizations—or may be provided by commercial interests—e.g., bowling alleys, driving ranges, billiard halls.

There is no justification, however, for tax support for such private or commercial groups providing this type of service. Further, there is no justification for the solicitation and use of charitable funds for facilities and services that are the responsibility of public agencies or that are public type service for a private group.

This statement is intended to make explicit the area of responsibility of public agencies.While limitation on private agencies' scope is implicit it is not suggested that there is no private responsibility. Rather, all agencies in the field of leisure services have a responsibility to press for public acceptance of the above-noted services.

2. Informal education services concerned primarily with the inculcation of moral values, the development of social and personal qualities, and the acquisition of technical skills customarily have been the responsibility of private agencies. Moral values and personal qualities tend to be closely associated with religious beliefs. Governments are reluctant to enter such fields of service. Because of our convictions concerning the value of diversity and the protection of the rights of minority groups to programs inculcating their own value systems, the need for the provision of these services through private agencies is recognized.

Increasingly, however, the responsibility for some of these services is being assumed by public education authorities through both formal and informal education programs. Where the service is directed towards the whole community, tax support is justified. Where the constituency is limited, sponsorship by private agencies is indicated with support from fees and charges, or from voluntary donations.

3. Agencies which use recreation as a tool and a medium by which to affect individual change are not recreation agencies. They may function under public support—e.g., hospitals, psychiatric clinics, correctional institutions—or under private auspices—e.g., childrens' homes, adolescent treatment institutions.

4. Increasingly, the provision of facilities for a broad, organized activities program is accepted as a logical function of the public authorities. Auditoria, gymnasia, swimming pools, and playing fields are provided in towns and cities by park, recreation, and school authorities. Much of the pressure on available voluntary funds has possibly resulted from the financing of voluntary services which essentially are the responsibility of government. We should no longer expect voluntary funds to finance physical plants that duplicate public facilities or that are the responsibilty of government.

The notion that ownership of the operating plant is essential, as held by many private agencies, is open to question. Such a principle has never been held in the world of business and in recent years industry has found that the specialized function of real estate management and maintenance detracts unduly from its primary function. Private agencies might well evaluate their policies and practices in this regard.

While the provision of recreation facilities is a primary concern of public agencies, the provision of service should be the dominant concern of private agencies. The diversion of funds from real estate development and management to direct service would go a long way toward meeting the current budget demands of such agencies.

It should be noted that by tolerating and encouraging the private financing and operation of facilities and programs that are essentially public in character, municipal governments are able to evade a significant proportion of their responsibility in the field of recreation. While there is public subsidy of private agencies there is also private subsidy of public agencies.

5. All private agencies have statements of purpose. These tend, however, to be vague and undifferentiated. There is a need for clear statements of function by all agencies indicating how that function relates to purpose. This is needed for interpretation to recipients of agency service, for the public, for donors, and for Planning Councils. Effective results consonant with stated purpose should be a measure upon which to base community support.

These five principles are intended to provide a framework within which it will be possible for private agencies to grow and to strengthen their unique community services. Paradoxically, while there is no longer any real need for private agencies to provide a continuing program of recreation services *per se*, there has probably never been a greater need for them to work in and effectively use recreation as a medium for the transmission of moral and social values and norms. With the memory of the Hitler Youth and Young Blackshirts still fresh, leaving this responsibility solely to government is not a comfortable thought.

BIBLIOGRAPHY

1. Boys' Clubs of America, *Manual of Boys' Club Operation*. New York: Dodd, Mead & Co., 1956.
2. Canada, Department of National Health and Welfare, Research Division, *Activities of the Federal Government Related to Recreation*. Ottawa: The Queen's Printer, 1955.
3. Canadian Association of Neighbourhood Services, *Newsletter*, I, No. 1 (1963).
4. Canadian General Council, The Boy Scout Association, *Canadian Boy Scouts*. Ottawa, 1911.
5. Canadian Welfare Council, *Recreation and Leisure Time Services in Canada*. Ottawa, 1936.
6. City of Edmonton Recreation Commission, *Annual Report*, 1949.
7. Davis, Helen E., *The Y.W.C.A. and Public Recreation, Informal Education, and Leisure Time Programmes*. New York: Association Press, 1946.
8. DuMoulin, Ann, "Gordon House Serves Its Senior Citizens," *Canadian Welfare*, XXV, No. 6 (1949), 26-30.
9. Etobicoke Recreation Commission, *Annual Report*, 1956.
10. Innis, Mary Quayle, *Unfold the Years*. Toronto: McClelland and Stewart Ltd., 1950.
11. "Interest in the Aged" (editorial), *The Social Worker*, XVII, No. 3 (1949), 1-2.
12. McAdam, Vernon F., "The Nature of The Boys' Clubs of Canada," Address to Boys' Club Workshop, Toronto, November 7, 1959 (lithographed).
13. McEwen, E. R., "List of Provincial Government Recreation Services," prepared for *Resources for Tomorrow Conference*, 1961 (mimeographed).
14. Milne, Donald R., "Volunteer Leaders in Scouting." Unpublished Master's thesis, University of Toronto, 1950.
15. Ross, Murray G., *The Y.M.C.A. in Canada*. Toronto: Ryerson Press, 1951.
16. Social Planning Council of Toronto, "Report of the Technical Committee on Recreation and Informal Education," *Needs and Resources Study*. Toronto, 1961 (mimeographed).
17. Thompson, Lillian, and John Farina, "The Two Way Lane to Leisure," *Proceedings, Canadian Conference on Social Work, 1950*. Vancouver, 1950.
18. Tuttle, George, *Youth Organizations in Canada*. Prepared for the Canadian Youth Commission. Toronto: Ryerson Press, 1946.
19. Unpublished Report of the Secretary of the Recreation Division to the Executive Director of the Canadian Welfare Council, 1948.

THE FITNESS MOVEMENT

18

William A. R. Orban

Professor and Director
School of Physical Education
University of Saskatchewan, Saskatoon

THE FIRST RECOGNITION

Awareness of, and subsequent interest in, physical fitness on a national level began during the Depression years. In order to provide the unemployed youth with an opportunity for learning new skills, an agreement was made between the Dominion and provincial governments to provide money for a scheme to train the unemployed in new skills. It was not long, however, before it was discovered that although skills were learned, the youth were unable to apply them because of an inadequate level of physical fitness. Subsequently, another schedule was introduced with emphasis on leadership training in exercise and sports. Those participating in this scheme were exposed to one hour of exercise which was followed by one hour of sports activities. Thus began the first official national physical fitness program.

As a result of this interest in physical fitness, two provinces, British Columbia and Alberta, initiated their own fitness programs in order to develop and maintain physical fitness. Thus the Pro-Rec in British-Columbia and the Y.T. Movement in Alberta were born. The success of these programs was reflected by the length of time that they were supported and operated by the respective provincial governments. They not only survived the Depression era, but flourished until the passage of the National Fitness Act in 1943. Moreover, they left an impact in these provinces which was not quickly forgotten.

THE FIRST NATIONAL LEGISLATION

Not unlike other countries, Canada saw a renewed interest in physical fitness during World War II with attention again focused on the low level of physical fitness as revealed by the large number of rejects for military service, the federal government became concerned about the problem of fitness. The result was the passing of the National Physical Fitness Act on July 24, 1943. The Fitness and Recreation Division and the Fitness Council were established in the Department of Pensions and Health, under the Health Branch in order to administer the Fitness Act. Subsequently, the department was changed to Health and Welfare, and the division and council were placed under the Welfare Branch, where they remained until the repeal of the act on June 9, 1954.

It was repealed simply because it was ineffective, which was the result of ill-conceived legislature, ill-defined objectives, and a lack of leadership and direction.

Although the act never achieved its general objective of promoting physical fitness among the population, it did stimulate interest in physical fitness in seven provinces where it was directly responsible for the development of provincial agencies of physical fitness.

The primary reason for the act's failing to achieve its primary goal of improving the level of fitness nationally was that it never received full government support on either the Dominion or the provincial level. There was insufficient money, and the federal government indicated a lack of interest by not making an effort to get co-operation from the provincial governments. The conflict which inevitably followed caused the council to disband.

Agreements between the Dominion and provincial governments were made on an insufficiently high level to effectively establish policies. However, all the blame for the failure of this act cannot be laid on the shoulders of the government agencies. The population never acknowledged the need for fitness and no serious or systematic efforts were made to inform them about it. Thus, because of the lack of popular support and necessary funds, the provinces were not able to expand their present programs, much less to start new programs. It was but a matter of time till the small initial programs shrank with loss of public interest and attention. The dissolution of the council soon followed.

However, in spite of these many shortcomings, the act cannot be called an absolute failure. As has been said, it did stimulate interest in and concern about physical fitness in at least several provinces. Furthermore, it provided an example of inherent weaknesses which had to be avoided in subsequent legislature. Two consequences of this act of great weight in the fitness movement in Canada were the establishment of the Division of Fitness under the Welfare Branch and the appointment of Dr. Doris Plewes as the assistant to the National Director.

The Division of Fitness was created by the act to look after the interest of the Department of Health and Welfare in the field of fitness and to provide secretariat services for the Fitness Council. Under the direction of Dr. Plewes, the division published several series of pamphlets dealing with posture and exercise between 1946 and 1948. In this way it endeavored to promote the cause of physical fitness through explicit guidance.

Undoubtedly, the National Fitness Act and the subsequent interest in physical fitness which it produced were instrumental in the inauguration of professional training courses in physical education. The first degree course began in the fall of 1940 at Toronto, to be followed closely by courses given at McGill and the University of British Columbia.

It was not long before graduates from these courses made their presence felt locally by initiating definite steps to develop physical fitness programs. One example of this was the Teachers College at Fredericton, New Brunswick. Until 1954 there was no provision for physical fitness in the teacher training program. However, when Andrew Martin, a graduate of McGill, took over the Teachers' College program, he inaugurated some changes in the course of studies which emphasized the development of physical fitness.

Nevertheless, interest in physical fitness programs remained relatively localized and sporadic, with only limited national movement taking place before 1956. At this time the publicity given by the United States concerning the unfitness of children in that country began to make Canadians more conscious of the need of physical fitness.

FEDERAL AWARENESS

The physical fitness movement up to this time was limited, but not without ferment. The ferment which gave momentum to the present trend for physical fitness on a national scale began in 1949 in the Fitness Division of the Department of Health and Welfare in Ottawa. More specifically, the fountainhead of the physical fitness movement as it is known today was Dr. Plewes, who served as Fitness and Recreation consultant up until 1962.

It was Dr. Plewes with her untiring energy and enthusiasm for physical fitness who not only made Canadians more aware of physical fitness, but inspired them to do something about it. In the beginning she accomplished this by writing many pamphlets and booklets, holding conferences with sports governing bodies to interest them in this area of deficiency. She untiringly campaigned to inform the public about the need for a high level of physical fitness.

It was generally assumed that Canadians possessed the same level of fitness as their United States cousins because of similarity in the standards of living. Probably in a flash of nationalistic pride many determined that Canadians would not be quite so badly off as Americans. Directly and indirectly this aroused a great deal of enthusiasm to develop a physical fitness test to measure present physical fitness standards and exercises to develop the necessary levels.

All the physical fitness tests used in Canada up to this time were from the United States. Furthermore, all the standards were based on the United States population.

This fact as well as the lack of one simple comprehensive test, prompted Dr. Plewes to initiate work to develop the Canadian Physical Efficiency Test. This battery of seven tests and the subsequent standards were based on physique category (age, body weight, and height).

Whereas earlier attempts to develop such standards had failed because of the scarcity of professionally trained persons, as well as lack of interest, this project did develop some grass roots and showed some signs of sprouting.

Once the basic tests were developed, several provinces showed interest in exploring the physical fitness status of their citizens. Consequently, a large number of co-operative projects were initiated whereby large groups of children and adults were tested with the assistance of local and provincial teachers. The evidence that Canadians were not as physically fit as had been thought prompted an increased demand to know what actually could be done.

INTEREST BY THE R.C.A.F.

The Air Force about this time, stimulated by Dr. Plewes, began to be concerned about the physical fitness of their personnel. It was natural, therefore, that the Department of Health and Welfare should co-operate with the Air Force in evolving a program of exercises to develop adequate levels of physical fitness. The result of this co-operation was basic principles underlying the 5BX plan of physical fitness published by the R.C.A.F.

During this time a growing demand by local and provincial organizations for testing of children and adults initiated a surge of interest and indicated that the movement was picking up momentum. But the tests themselves never were completely accepted; there were two reasons: the large amount of space and equipment required for their administration, and the large number of personnel with specialized training.

Paralleling the development of these tests since 1956 was the development of the 5BX program of physical fitness. In order to determine the reason why Air Force personnel were not exercising, a survey was made in the fall of that year. Officers and men at different R.C.A.F. stations were asked just why they did not exercise. An attempt to resolve these objectives laid the foundation for the Five Basic Exercises Plan for Physical Fitness. Although the basic concept of the 5BX as it is known today was objectively a result of this survey, the person who provided the inspiration was Dr. Plewes.

In order to develop the details of the concept and to design the program, a research project was undertaken. Assisted by seven professional people from various universities, the Air Force physical fitness specialists conducted the necessary research. The pressure for providing a type of program to develop and maintain fitness by the Air Force was so great that the plan was written before the necessary research was completed. Consequently, even though the charts and age levels were based on inadequate numbers for validity, the book was printed.

The desire to achieve adequate levels of fitness was reflected by the fact that this booklet was almost immediately accepted by the public with unprecedented enthusiasm. Since it first appeared it has been exported to many countries and translated into foreign languages.

Across the Nation

Concurrent with, but stemming from, the interest created by Dr. Plewes, were increased activities to improve fitness in local areas. An example of this was the Citizens' Committee on Children in Ottawa. As a result of the publicity of the lack of fitness in the States and assistance from Dr. Plewes, they began advocating more emphasis on physical fitness in the public school physical education program. Donald Purdy, Physical Education Supervisor of Ottawa, determined to do something about the problem. Working very closely with the Citizens' Committee sub-committee, he set about developing a series of tests which could objectively evaluate and grade the students. The purpose of this was twofold: to make parents aware of the level of fitness of their children; and to stimulate interest of the students to become more physically fit. He kept at this task doggedly for several years before his work was accomplished, for which effort he received national recognition.

Another person who made no small contribution to the interest and stimulation of physical fitness in Canada was Lloyd Percival. By his weekly programs, Sport College of the Air, he created a great deal of interest in fitness for sports, particularly among youngsters aspiring to become athletes. His advice to youngsters during his radio broadcasts was supplemented by pamphlets on methods of keeping fit. However, it was not until 1957 that he published a booklet on a plan to develop physical fitness. The purposes of this booklet were to give some concrete guidance on how to develop and maintain fitness, and to provide information about the various benefits of fitness. In spite of the title, "Fitness is Easy," the booklet never achieved popularity. Although a layman, Percival's efforts to stimulate the general populace, particularly children, to develop higher levels of fitness were influential only in making people conscious of the present lack of fitness and thus adding to the momentum of the movement.

One of the first provinces to incorporate fitness into the physical education program in the schools was New Brunswick. This took place in the spring of 1957 after the Canadian Physical Efficiency Tests were administered to a number of urban and rural schools, involving approximately 2,000 students. Thus the physical fitness movement in New Brunswick and the rest of the Maritimes began. Two years later Stanley Spicer, the Director of the Fitness Division, prepared the Fitness and Sports Efficiency program for the New Brunswick Command of the Royal Canadian Legion. The program became very popular, so that even today there are from 8,000 to 14,000 students who are benefiting by it.

In the same way, physical fitness gradually permeated through all regions of Canada. Key people in physical education across the country began experimenting with methods of measurement and evaluation, and incorporating physical fitness activities into their programs. School boards became more aware of the need for physical fitness and began to legislate policies on physical education which would emphasize it. An early example of this is the Brandon School District Board, which set up a policy to include and emphasize more physical fitness activities in physical education.

However, the interest in physical fitness was not restricted to children, but included adults as well. This interest was reflected by what happened in the public recreation program in London, for example. A fitness program of exercise classes and tests for adults expanded rapidly to encompass five centers in the city. The program started several years ago and is still so popular that at the present time there is a long waiting list.

Saskatchewan, in the meantime, under the enthusiastic direction of Bill Ross, a field worker for the Division of Fitness and Recreation in Saskatchewan, tested thousands of school children with the Kraus-Weber Test. Precisely because this test is only a minimal tolerance test for use in low back clinics, it strikingly revealed the low physical fitness status of children in Saskatchewan.

In spite of the vigorous opposition to the emphasis of physical fitness in physical education which came mainly from within the professional ranks, whose major interest was sports and sports skills, interest in fitness was increasing. This interest was reflected at the 1957 Biennial Convention of the Canadian Association for Health, Physical Education and Recreation, which was held in Halifax. At this conference there were several panels and talks on physical fitness. However, a substantial number of professionals were not completely receptive to the concepts that there was a lack of physical fitness and that physical fitness should be the primary concern in the physical education programs. This was reflected by the very critical attitude of some of the leaders during and following these meetings. But the movement which had begun in 1949 and received an impetus in 1956 kept on gaining momentum. The uninterested people who attempted to resist were carried along with the tide of public opinion.

Not long after the repeal of the National Fitness Act in 1954, Melvin F. Rogers, with the assistance of Dr. Plewes, convened a meeting of all the interested national sports governing bodies at Ottawa and formed the Canadian Sports Advisory Council. Rogers took an active interest in fitness and subsequently presented briefs to the Minister of Health and Welfare requesting assistance to take some positive measures in the problem of physical fitness. It was not until March 1957, however, that the third presentation made to the Honorable Paul Martin was officially presented by the representatives of the Canadian Sports Advisory Council. This brief focused attention on the problem of physical fitness in Canada, indicating that the situation was grave and deserved immediate attention. Although there was very little information concerning the fitness of Canadians contained in the brief there were some startling statistics concerning the lack of fitness of Americans.

It had been hoped that this brief, like the report written to President Dwight Eisenhower in 1955, might move the Canadian government to take similar action. It urged as well that the government co-ordinate all available services related to physical fitness in order to make people aware of the need to promote activities to raise the level of fitness in Canada. Although a great deal of interest was shown by the government officials and interested parties toward the brief as reflected by speeches in the House of Commons, no immediate action was taken, probably because of impending elections.

No further action was evident until 1959, when the newly-elected stable government began to act rapidly. The quickness of the action cannot be completely unrelated to remarks made by the Duke of Edinburgh about this time. In his presidential address to the Canadian Medical Association in Toronto on June 30, 1959, he made some rather startling statements that will go down in the annals of physical education in Canada as a milestone in the fitness movement. Quoting extensively from a report by Dr. Plewes published in Britain the previous year dealing with the level of physical fitness in Canada, he rebuked Canadians for their complacency and at the same time challenged the doctors to take some positive steps to improve the situation.

This speech set off a spark which lit the public interest and spread across the nation like a prairie fire. It once more aroused the interest of the general public leading them to think more seriously of fitness. This renewed interest and concern provoked discussion in the House of Commons, resulting in the passage of Bill C-131 (Appendix A). This bill, unlike the National Fitness Act passed in 1943, was non-controversial and received the unanimous support of all parties. Great care was taken to eliminate many of the shortcomings of the previous act. The formation of an advisory council which was primarily a citizens' committee ensured a stronger and more authoritative organization to advise the government. The fruits of this act will not be known for some time, but its impact has already been felt across Canada.

CANADIAN LEGION INVOLVEMENT

The Royal Canadian Legion, which has always been interested in fitness of Canadian youth, made several attempts to inaugurate some type of program. One of these was the track and field clinic held at the Canadian National Exhibition annually. In August 1958, a team of specialists employed by the Royal Canadian Air Force, under the direction of Dr. Doris Plewes and Dr. W. A. R. Orban, conducted the Canadian Physical Efficiency tests on the athletes at this clinic in Toronto. Stimulated by the results of the athletes' fitness profiles which demonstrated general and specific weaknesses, the Legion undertook to develop a program for youth across Canada.

However, the Legion did not meet with success either in the field clinics which were held annually or in their attempt to develop physical fitness programs. The reason for failure in the clinics was probably the lack of follow-up of the individuals who participated in the clinics. The athletes, once they had completed the instructional phase at the clinic, were permitted to return to their homes without any further guidance. On the other hand, the physical fitness program was ineffective simply because it lacked co-ordination in top-level planning and the continuity which such a program requires.

Although the Canadian Physical Efficiency tests were not accepted because of the many limitations in administration, particularly in rural situations, they had played their role in stimulating interest in physical fitness. They stimulated the interest of the Royal Canadian Legion who saw the need for some type of tests in running a fitness program. Thus they became interested in a test battery developed by Spicer of New

Brunswick. These tests were relatively simple, and gave rural schools the impetus of simplified tests. They required little equipment, and could be administered by relatively inexperienced instructors. Supplementing this testing program with an exercise program gave birth to the "Starshooter program."

It quickly spread across Canada through the regional commands. However, it too failed to win complete public acceptance. One reason for its failure was finances. At the time when the Legion should have been vigorously promoting this program, it was necessary to curtail its efforts and to lend support to the track and field program.

Although there was some interest in adult fitness during this development, it was Dr. Thomas Cureton, an exercise specialist from the United States, who made the greatest contribution in this area. He did much to spread the interest of adult fitness in Canada beginning in 1958. He accomplished this by conducting clinics at Y.M.C.A.'s at different cities across Canada. Although a controversial figure, he had an impact on all those who flocked to take part in his physical fitness clinics. Although he may be criticized for aiming at too high a level of physical fitness for most middle-aged people, he did stimulate their interest and desire to become more physically fit.

RECOGNITION BY THE MEDICAL AND TEACHING PROFESSIONS

If the speech of the Duke of Edinburgh in 1959 started a wave of interest in physical fitness in the general population and government legislatures, it rocked the Canadian Medical Association. In the face of the challenge made to the doctors, the Medical Association took action. In June 1961, its committee on public health decided to determine if the charges made by the Duke concerning the state of Canadians' health were true. They consulted with physiologists, physical educators, deputy ministers of health and education, officers of the Department of Health and Welfare, individual physicians, and citizens interested in sports and fitness. Their report contained a compendium of comments, communications, statements, and references which were widely discussed with these people. The medical profession accepted the idea that they did indeed have a responsibility to help individually and as an association the cause of physical fitness.

The committee recommended that the executive committee of the Canadian Medical Association take positive measures to champion the cause of physical fitness; it responded by approving the recommendation by the public health committee to request a conference with the Canadian Association for Health, Physical Education and Recreation.

This meeting was, in fact, held less than a year after the submission of the report; it was another milestone in the continuing interest concerning physical fitness of Canadians. For the first time medical people sat down with physical educators to explore and discuss the various phases of physical fitness from the pre-school child up to and beyond the middle-aged. This meeting demonstrated the necessity for interdependence of the two professions if physical fitness programs were to be successful. As a result of this meeting, the need for a closer liaison between these two professions was recommended to the respective parent bodies.

Subsequently the Canadian Medical Association formed a committee on physical education and recreation which became a sub-committee of the public health committee. The Canadian Association of Physical Education and Recreation also formed a committee and charged it with the responsibilities of discussing mutual problems of physical fitness and acting as liaison between the two parent bodies.

The two committees had a series of meetings to determine areas of responsibilities and methods of approach related to the problems of fitness. Although the impact of the efforts of this co-operation between C.A.H.P.E.R. and C.M.A. is yet to be felt there are signs that the discussion phase is coming to a close and action is about to begin. This is reflected by the tone of the discussions which took place at a meeting in Toronto in March of 1963. Sincere efforts were made by each side to exchange ideas and to become more informed about the other profession's attitude and knowledge.

Another indication that the momentum is still increasing is the fact that in 1962 the Canadian Conference on Education requested the President of C.A.H.P.E.R. to convene a panel of physical educators and medical doctors on fitness. This was a significant advance in the cause of fitness, because the Canadian Conference on Education, composed of nineteen national associations in 1958, increased to seventy by 1962. However, the real significance of this meeting was not the large number of people who attended the conference, but rather the fact that these national organizations represented a true cross section of life in Canada.

The event that accelerated an already rapidly increasing interest and concern in fitness was the passing of Bill C-131. The National Advisory Council formed in January of 1962 has taken a firm hold of its responsibility. The council's action at the time of this writing produced a high level of optimism in the continuing interest in and development of physical fitness. Known as the "thinking thirty," this group has formulated policies related to the implementation of the aims and objectives of the Fitness and Amateur Sport Council. Thus far they have given every indication that they are determined to avoid the errors which plagued the National Fitness Council of 1943. The council demonstrated its seriousness of purpose by implementing the act in April of the same year—only three months after its appointment.

After the first full year of operation, April 1962 to March 31, 1963, the cornerstones of a constructive and imaginative program had been laid. The council has emphasized its interest in and concern about fitness by making large sums of money available for leadership training, research, and promotion of sports.

Just as this act received wholehearted support from all the parties at the time of its enactment, so it has received the same support from the provinces, general public, sports—governing bodies, and universities. Never has fitness received so much attention and emphasis in Canada as at the present time. Never have people been more conscious of physical fitness than today. The key to the continuance of this movement is the professional physical educators and the support which they receive from the Fitness and Amateur Sports Council.

BIBLIOGRAPHY

1. Brief submitted by the Canadian Advisory Council Concerning the Problems Arising from Physical Fitness Deficiencies in Canada, March, 1957.
2. Canadian Medical Association, *A Report of the Committee on Public Health* (June, 1960).
3. "Council Presents Brief to Federal Government"; Ottawa *Citizen*, March 28, 1957.
4. Hansard (Official Report of the House of Commons Debates), December 21, 1957, pp. 249-51.
5. ———, (Official Report of the House of Commons Debates), February 16, 1959, pp. 1037-76.
6. ———, (Official Report of the House of Commons Debates), September 25, 1961, pp. 8832-65.
7. ———, (Official Report of the Senate Debates), February 10, 1960, pp. 131-38.
8. ———, (Official Report of the Senate Debates), September 26, 1961, pp. 1177-84.
9. The Duke of Edinburgh's Presidential Address to the Canadian Medical Association, June 30, 1959.
10. The House of Commons of Canada, Bill C-131, An Act to Encourage Fitness and Amateur Sport.
11. The National Fitness Act, May 23-24, 1944.

Maxwell L. Howell

Professor, Faculty of Physical Education
University of Alberta, Edmonton

DEVELOPMENT OF RESEARCH ON THE NORTH AMERICAN CONTINENT

There has been a considerable growth of interest in physical education research on the North American continent in the last ten years. To symbolize, perhaps, the development in the profession, in the United States, for example, there have been two editions of *Research Methods,* a book by the American Association for Health, Physical Education and Recreation; annual volumes of *Completed Research in Health, Physical Education and Recreation*: the growth in status and quality of the *Research Quarterly* in the United States; and the development of the Research Council of A.A.H.P.E.R.

Whereas the scientific spirit of progression on this continent was exemplified in the past by a few such as A. H. Steinhaus, P. V. Karpovich, C. H. McCloy, T. K. Cureton, many more distinguished names may now be added to the list—F. M. Henry, A. T. Slater-Hammel, H. Harrison Clarke, L. A. Larson, M. Broer, W. R. Pierson, W. Johnson, A. Espenschade, A. W. Hubbard, K. W. Bookwalter, M. Gladys Scott, B. H. Massey, P. Hunsicker, D. K. Mathews, P. Sigerseth, J. Lawther, L. Morehouse, D. K. Brace, F. Hellebrandt, G. L. Rarick. The research departments in the physical education schools have increased from a few—at Springfield College, George Williams College, Iowa and a few others—to over 100 accredited institutions in the United States giving master's degrees, and over thirty-five giving doctor's degrees, with consequent growth of research facilities and practices.

DEVELOPMENT OF RESEARCH IN CANADA

Canada has been slow to awaken to the need for research in its university physical education departments. Until the last few years, the concentration has been on undergraduate teaching, coaching, the development of facilities, and the development of the gradual acceptance of the profession within the universities.

However, the question of research has come increasingly to the fore, and in the last few years there has been a remarkable change, of which many may not be aware. Owing to recent national developments following the passage of Bill C-131, there has been an increased number of graduate students, an increased awareness of the need for graduate studies in Canadian universities, national grants for research, and three Fitness Research Institutes formed, at the Universities of Alberta, Montreal, and Toronto. Research information concerning physical education is often out-of-date before it is published, because of the frequency of discoveries. It will be no exaggeration to say that in the next five years there will be more developments in research in physical education in Canada than in all the years previous to the development of undergraduate schools of physical education.

Publications of a scholarly nature are still few in number, but there are people doing research, with research laboratories, however limited, at the Universities of Alberta at Edmonton, British Columbia, Montreal, Ottawa, Saskatchewan, Western Ontario, and Toronto.

Up to and including 1962, only two universities in Canada offered graduate degrees. The University of British Columbia offered an M. P. E. degree, the University of Alberta an M. Sc. and an M. A. degree. Two additional universities, the Universities of Western Ontario and the University of Saskatchewan, now provide graduate work, and at least two others are considering this expanison.

The recent development of research in Canada is understandable in light of the rapid increase of doctoral degrees awarded to Canadian professors presently teaching in Canada. Until 1950, there were only four physical educators in all of Canada with doctoral degrees. By 1958, there were twelve, and by 1964, more than fifty.

RESEARCH COMMITTEE OF C.A.H.P.E.R.

A research committee has been formed within the Canadian professional association. The first meeting of this Committee was held at the Biennial Convention of C.A.H.P.E.R. at McMaster University in June

1961. This historic meeting was chaired by Dr. W. A. R. Orban. The members of the committee for 1961-63 were Dr. W. A. R. Orban, (Chairman), M. L. Howell, M. Yuhasz, J. Alexander, F. Hayden, D. Bailey. The following papers were presented: Kirk Wipper "The Comparison of Different Types of Physical Fitness Programs of University Men"; H. Armstrong. J. H. Ebbs, R. J. Slater, "Studies in the Mechanism of Exercise Proteinuria"; W. A. R. Orban, Norm Sklov, "Fat Distribution, Step Test Results of Champion Male Athletes"; John F. Alexander, Robert S. Fraser, Caesar Cavero, "An Evaluation of the 5BX Program of Exercises by a Treadmill Performance Test"; Michael S. Yuhasz, "Weight Prediction from Body Measurements of College Men and Women"; Frank J. Hayden, "The Validity and Reliability of Indoor and Outdoor 300 Yard Run Times and 300 Yard Drop-Offs, as Measures of Running Endurance"; Maxwell Howell, John Moncrieff, W. R. Morford, "Learning Rate of Beginning Swimmers; Age and Sex Difference, Distributed Versus Massed Practice"; and Donald Bailey, "The Reaction Time and Speed of Movement of Canadian Sprinters." Dr. Orban was succeeded by Dr. F. J. Hayden, and the committee for 1963-65 was Dr. F. Hayden (Chairman), Dr. S. Brown, Dr. M. L. Howell, Dr. W. Orban, Dr. D. Bailey, Dr. M. Yuhasz, Dr. G. Metivier, Prof. F. Landry, Dr. E. Doroschuk.

The Research Committee of 1963-65 made a significant advance in physical education. Over the years, various individuals throughout Canada have suggested tests to measure various abilities, leading to the establishment of local norms and tests. The Research Committee agreed on a C.A.H.P.E.R. Fitness Performance Test, and a national sampling and testing program was undertaken, assisted by a federal government grant of up to $25,000. The principal investigators were Dr. F. Hawden and Dr. M. Yuhasz; the other members of the Research Committee were responsible for the work in their individual provinces. Norms are now available for Canadian boys and girls, seven to seventeen years of age, on the following physical performance items: bent arm hang, 300-yard run, 50-yard dash, shuttle run, standing broad jump, and speed sit-ups.

It was planned that these co-operative endeavors, by rotating members of the committee as principal investigators, would expand in the future to include both tests of a physiological nature and tests for adults. Few if any, countries, can point to such attempts at national solutions of research problems.

The Fitness and Amateur Sport Directorate, Department of National Health and Welfare, is empowered to grant moneys to institutions and individuals for research under the terms of Bill C-131. A Research Review Committee was formed in 1962 to screen research proposals and make recommendations concerning them. The first chairman, Dr. J.

Harry Ebbs of the University of Toronto, was succeeded in 1964 by Dr. John Merriman of the University of Saskatchewan.

Research is being undertaken by many physical educators in universities in Canada. Each university doing research was asked to contribute a section and only those that replied are included. The individual contributions of each university, reproduced in their entirety where possible, should afford an over-view of developments from 1958 to 1964. These developments, so significant over such a short period of time, foretell a still greater surge of interest in research endeavors.

The present chapter is concerned solely with the contributions of physical educators to research in Canada. Others representing various disciplines have made significant contributions: Dr. Hans Selye of University of Montreal, for his work on stress; Dr. K. Key, a research chemist, for taking part in the Harvard Fatigue Studies; Dr. W. J. Josenhans of Dalhousie University, for his investigations on oxygen debt and income in relation to the contraction tension during sustained contractions of large muscle groups and the metabolic cost of isometric contractions; Dr. P. M. Rautahargu of Dalhousie, for his work on the role of physical activity on the prevalence and incidence of coronary heart disease and the theoretical and technical aspects of cardiac function tests; Dr. Albert Cox of the Department of Medicine, University of British Columbia, for the utilization of treadmill techniques to assess functional capacity of cardiac patients before and following open heart surgical procedures; Dr. E. Cumming of Winnipeg, for his studies using a bicycle ergometer in order to assess work capacity; Dr. R. S. Sproule of the University of Alberta, for his definitive work on the estimation of maximal oxygen intake; Dr. R. S. Fraser of the University of Alberta, for his studies on effect of exercise programs on fitness; Dr. John Merriman of the University of Saskatchewan, for his varied studies in the area of fitness research; Dr. J. V. Basmajian of Queen's University, for his work on electromyography and kinesiology as well as motor unit training and learning; Dr. John Firstbrook of the University of Toronto, for his telemetric studies of pulse rate changes in pulmonary diffusing capacity; Dr. John Brown of the University of Toronto, for his studies on fitness. These are but a few of the outstanding Canadians in other disciplines who have made significant contributions pertinent to physical education.

UNIVERSITY RESEARCH IN CANADA

UNIVERSITY OF WESTERN ONTARIO* The first four-year honors Bachelor of Arts degrees in physical, health and recreation were granted to

---

* Information on the University of Western Ontario supplied by Dr. M. S. Yuhasz.

three students in 1950. In 1963, a Master of Arts degree in physical education was introduced.

Growth in the Laboratory The physical Education measurement laboratory, directed since 1954 by M. S. Yuhasz, was used predominantly for the senior course in Tests and Measurements. The laboratory was the centre for the development of sports skill tests and the Western Motor Fitness and the Western Motor Ability Tests. With the introduction of the graduate program a second laboratory came into being.

Research at the University of Western Ontario The early research projects at the university were in the motor fitness area. M.S. Yuhasz developed the Western Motor Fitness Test and fostered the development of a variety of sports skill tests. Collaboration with John Faulkner resulted in the development of the Western Motor Ability Test, and the London Physical Efficiency Test. Subsequently, work was initiated in the anthropometrical symmetry analyses for college women. In collaboration with R.B. Eynon, weight control classes were conducted as a part of an investigation to determine changes in the overly fat college male. The measurement of body fat by caliper and the determination of total body fat through body density has continued to be a major interest of his laboratory.

Normative tables for adult men were developed in 1960 and the effect of programs of exercise activity upon their body fat, muscular strength, muscular endurance, and cardio-vascular endurance have been studied. In 1964, a special exercise program was initiated with a group of post-cardiacs to study the effects of a graduated exercise program upon these men. Drs. P.A. Rechnitzer and H.A. Pickard collaborated in this study. At the same time, a pilot study was initiated with the aid of Dr. A. Pavio of the Department of Psychology, who devised a semantic differential test to ascertain the effect of a program of exercise upon the feelings and mood of adult men. Both of these studies are continuing on a longitudinal basis with adult men.

Two major research grants were awarded the University of Western Ontario in 1964. A $25,000 grant was received by the University of Western Ontario to conduct a study resulting in the C.A.H.P.E.R. Fitness-Performance Test. This test was devised by the Research Committee of C.A.H.P.E.R., who appointed two of its members, Drs. F. J. Hayden and M.S. Yuhasz, as its principal investigators. The second grant was for a study of interval training with swimmers by means of radio telemetry, undertaken by M.S. Yuhasz, R.B. Eynon, and Dr. P. Hauch.

With the collaboration of W. Selter, Yuhasz has undertaken a longitudinal growth and physical performance study with high school boys and girls in the city of London.

Undergraduate Student Research Projects Since 1954, it has been the practice for undergraduate students to submit a research project in their senior year. At first these projects were usually attempts to construct sports skill tests or cross-sectional surveys of the motor fitness of high school and college students. The more recent projects show greater diversity and depth of study. But several students worked with the Department of Physiology, studying cardiac and metabolic cost of step tests and muscular endurance type tests. Others have worked in the Pulmonary Physiology laboratory at Victoria Hospital studying the phenomenon of second wind. The studies in the department of Physical Health and Recreation Education have dealt with the effects of various athletic training programs, skills analysis by cinematography, interrelationship studies in the area of motor fitness and motor ability, and the effects of various activities on body fat.

Research Equipment:

Motor Fitness: Basic sports equipment, watches, timers, etc; strength dynamometers, and cable tensiometer; reaction timer; flexometers.
Anthropometric: Calipers fat, breadth and depth; tapes, constant tension; body density tank and other apparatus.
Physiologic and Metabolic: Motor-driven treadmill adjustable for speed and grade; electrocardiograph; radio telemetric equipment; direct writer polygraph; gas analyzer.
Other: Calculator; 16 mm. movie camera.

Research Interest and Projects of Staff Members Professor R. B. Eynon's major research interest is sports training, specifically, interval training in swimming. He is presently involved in a study of the telemetered heart rate during interval training in swimming.

Frank J. Hayden has a particular interest in the psychology of exercise, particularly as regards the motivational, emotional, and personality aspects of sports and exercise. For several years he has been involved in the development of physical activities to meet the needs of children with severe mental deficiency.

He worked extensively in the motor fitness area while at the University of Illinois and during an appointment with the R.C.A.F. The C.A.H.P.E.R. project which developed national norms of physical performance for boys and girls seven to seventeen years of age under the direction of Hayden and Yuhasz.

Dr. Hayden's more basic research has been in the cardio-pulmonary area and includes work at the University of Illinois and the University of Toronto. These studies, which involve assessment of the effects of various training regimens on cardiac function and pulmonary diffusion capacity, were carried out mainly with adults as subjects.

Michael S. Yuhasz's major research interest is in the anthropometric area. He has been particularly occupied with the measurement of body fat and the prediction of body weight with young men and women, as well as with adult men. He has studied the effects of various training programs upon changes in body density and subcutaneous body fat with overly fat college men, college athletes, college women, and adult men.

His work with adult men was begun at the University of Illinios and continued at the University of Western Ontario where he published "Physical Fitness Appraisal Booklet for Adult Men." His interest in the fitness of adult men led to the institution of a program of exercise for post-cardiac adult men and to the investigation of the effects of exercise upon these men.

Dr. Yuhasz's early interests in motor fitness and motor ability brought about the Western Motor Fitness and Western Motor Ability Tests. Dr. J.A. Faulkner co-operated in the latter project as well as in the London Physical Efficiency Test. M.S. Yuhasz devised the five-minute Muscular Endurance Test. Yuhasz and Hayden were named the principal investigators for the C.A.H.P.E.R. Fitness Performance National Study.

RESEARCH REPORTS AND PUBLICATIONS

Eynon, R. B., "Somatotype and Motor Fitness in Young Boys." Unpublished Master's Thesis, University of Illinois, 1958.

Faulkner, J. A., and M. S. Yuhasz, "The London Public Schools' Physical Efficiency Study," *Journal of C. A. H. P. E. R.*, XXVI, 2 (1960), pp. 5-10; XXVI, 3 (Feb.-March 1960), pp. 26-31; XXVI, 5 (June-July 1960), pp. 32-37.

Hayden, F. J., "The Effects of Exercises on Personality States," *Journal of C. A. H. P. E. R.*, XXVI (1960), pp. 18-19.

———, "The Effects of Physical Training on the Strength and Endurance of Severely Mentally Retarded Children (I. Q. < 50)." Paper presented to the Research Section of C. A. H. P. E. R., Saskatoon, June 1963. Abstract published in the Proceedings.

———, "The Influence of Exercise and Sport Programs on Children with Severe Mental Deficiency." Paper presented at the First International Congress of Psychology of Sport, Rome, Italy, April 1965. Published in the Proceedings.

———, "A P-Technique Factor Analysis of Cardiovascular Variables." Paper presented at the Annual Meeting of the American College of Sports Medicine, Mineapolis, May 1963.

———, "A P-Technique Factor Analysis of Cardiovascular Variables." Unpublished Ph.D Thesis, University of Illinois, 1962.

———, *Physical Fitness for the Mentally Retarded.* Metropolitan Toronto Association for Retarded Children, Toronto, 1964.

——, "Physical Fitness Status of Children with Severe Mental Deficiency." Paper presented in the Research Section of the Fifth National Conference on Mental Retardation, Halifax, N.S., September 18-21, 1962. Published in the Proceedings.

——, "Research on Exercise Programs for the Mentally Retarded." Paper presented at the 96th Annual Meeting of the Canadian Medical Association, Toronto, June 1963.

——, "The Validity and Reliability of Indoor and Outdoor 300-Yard Drop-Offs, as Measures of Running Endurance." Paper presented to the Research Section of C. A. H. P. E. R., Hamilton, June 1961. Abstract published in *Journal of C. A. H. P. E. R.*, XXVIII, (June 1962), p. 22.

——, P. Levitt, and J. B. Firstbrook, "Effect of Physical Training on Pulmonary Diffusing Capacity." (In Publication)

Wearring, George, "An Investigation of the Status of Boys' Physical and Health Education in the Secondary Schools of the Province of Ontario." Unpublished Master's Thesis, University of Southern California, 1956.

Yuhasz, M. S., "Adult Physical Fitness Program." Paper presented at the 96th Canadian Medical Association Convention, Toronto, June 1963.

——, "The Five-Minute Muscular Endurance Test," *Journal of C. A. H. P. E. R.*, XXIX, 5 (June-July 1963), pp. 13-14.

——, "The Effect of Sports Training on Body Fat in Man and Predictions of Optimal Body Weight." Ph.D Thesis, University of Illinois, 1962.

——, "The Effects of Physical Education Activities upon Human Physique," *Proceedings College Physical Education Association*, December 1955.

——, "Improving the Physical Fitness of an Adult Male Through Swimming and Exercise," Journal of C. A. H. P. E. R., XX, 6 (February 1955), p. 4.

——, "A Metabolic Analysis of Treadmill Jogging by Adult Men." Master's Thesis, University of Illinois, 1951.

——, "Weight Prediction from Body Measurements of College Men and Women." Paper presented at the Biennial Convention of C. A. H. P. E. R., Hamilton, Ontario, 1961. Abstract published in *Journal of C. A. H. P. E. R.*, XXVIII, 3 (1962), pp. 21, 39.

——, "Why Research?" Editorial, *Journal of C. A. H. P. E. R.*, XX, 6 (Feb. 1955).

——, and R. B. Eynon, "An Experiment in Weight Control." Paper presented at the C. A. H. P. E. R. Convention, Hamilton, Ontario, June 19-23, 1961.

——, and J. A. Faulkner. "The Western Motor Ability Test," *Journal of C. A. H. P. E. R.*, XXIV, 3 (1958), pp. 18-22.

——, and P. T. Thomas, "A Report on the Physical Fitness Field Testing of All-Weather (Fighter) Air Crew, R.C.A.F." January 1957.

UNIVERSITY OF NEW BRUNSWICK* Since its inception in 1957, the Division of Physical Education at the university of New Brunswick has concentrated entirely on the development of its undergraduate program.

_____

* Information on the University of New Brunswick supplied by Prof. G. Barry Thompson.

Any research has been restricted to such undergraduate surveys as could be conducted without the need for a physical education laboratory.

Research Studies and Papers Completed by Members of the University of New Brunswick Staff.

Chazan, Alfred E., Gordon M. Gibson, and G. Barry Thompson, "A Re-Study of the Effectiveness of Five Instruments for Recording Muscle Strength," *Research Quarterly*, December 1954.

Meagher, John W., "A Projected Plan for the Re-Organization of Physical Education Teacher-Training Programs in Canada," Ph.D. Thesis, Pennsylvania University, 1958.

———, "The Status of Degree Graduates of Four Canadian Schools of Physical Education." Master's Thesis, Pennsylvania State University, 1958.

Research Completed by Others Within the Province Stanley Spicer, in conjunction with Dr. Mary Southern-Holt of the Department of Health, conducted a pilot project involving mental and dental examinations, Canadian Physical Efficiency testing, and a nutritional survey in two sections of New Brunswick. These were carried out in 1958.

Growth of a Laboratory A physical education laboratory for research did not exist in 1964.

Present Projects of Members of Staff First is a survey, by A. B. Martin of the New Brunswick Teachers' College and G. Barry Thompson of the University of New Brunswick staff, of current physical education testing and grading practices and attitudes in Canadian schools. The second is part of a major study by the Technical Assistance and Research Group for Physical Rehabilitation of the application of electromyography in the rehabilitation of paraplegics.

The first phase of the latter project is to determine the feasibility of amplifying the electrical impulse created by the contraction of certain muscles of the shoulder and upper arms to operate a mechanical feeding device for quadriplegics.

Studies of the effectiveness of various types of electrodes and of the ability of an individual to isolate and control the contraction of several major muscles in order to operate such a device have been under way since September 1962. This research is being conducted jointly by R. N. Scott, Department of Electrical Engineering at U.N.B., G. B. Thompson, Department of Physical Education and Dr. Josephine Sommerville and Dr. Lynn Bashaw of the Rehabilitation Centre staff.

MCMASTER UNIVERSITY* The main emphasis at McMaster University

---

* Information on McMaster University supplied by Prof. A. J. Smith.

has been on the undergraduate program, and consequently the purchase of equipment has been mainly for demonstration and undergraduate use.

The present equipment includes: a back and leg dynamometer, grip dynamometers, spirometer, goniometer, sphygmomanometer, stethoscopes, flarimeter, pocket spirometer, balances, Harpenden skinfold caliper and Harpenden anthropometric caliper.

UNIVERSITY OF OTTAWA*

Research Work, Studies and Papers of Members of Staff The staff members of the Institute of Physical Education of the University of Ottawa have all been involved in research during their graduate training. Eight staff members completed Master's, and one a Ph. D. thesis. The titles of their unpublished theses are listed hereunder:

Beauchesne, J. M., "Recommended Provincial Legislation for the Regulation of Public Bathing Areas and Facilities in Quebec, Canada." M.S. thesis, Recreation, University of Illinois, 1961.

Hupe, A. S., "The Effects of Training and Supplementary Diet on the Cardiovascular Condition of Young Boys." M.S. thesis in Physical Education, University of Illinois, 1958.

Landry, J. F., "The Effects of the University of Illinois Sports Fitness Summer Day-School on the Motor Fitness of Young Boys." M.S. thesis in Physical Education, University of Illinois, 1955.

Marcotte, G. E., "The Effects of Two Different Training Programs in Ice Skating on the Physical Fitness of Two Adult Men." M.S. thesis in Physical Education, University of Illinois, 1960.

Metivier, J. G., "An Evaluation of Physical Education Programs in High Schools for Boys of Ottawa and Eastview, Ontario, Canada." M.S. thesis in Physical Education, University of Illinois, 1959.

Metivier, J. G., "The Effects of Five Different Programs of Physical Exercises on Blood Serum Cholesterol in Adult Women." Ph.D. dissertation, University of Illinois, 1959.

Pelletier, R., "A Summary of Physical Education and Athletic Administration in Canadian Universities and Colleges." M.S. thesis in Physical Education, Springfield College, 1958.

Sheedy, A., "Relationship of Health Knowledge and Emotional Stability with Health Practices of Senior High School, College Freshmen, Sophomore and Graduate Students of the University of Ottawa, Ontario, Canada." M.S. thesis, Health Education, University of Illinois, 1955.

Saint-Denis, C., "The Fastest Method of Starting from a Stationary Position in Ice Hockey," M.S. thesis, Physical Education, Springfield College, 1956.

In 1958 and 1959, the Institute of Physical Education offered its collaboration for the administration in the Province of Quebec of the Cana-

---

* Information on University of Ottawa supplied by Dr. Guy Metivier.

dian Physical Efficiency Test Battery developed jointly by the Department of National Health and Welfare and the Fitness and Recreation Branch of the R.C.A.F.

Fernand Landry, Director of Physical Education, conducted large-scale fitness testing projects at Le Seminaire de Valleyfield with the aim of assisting the fitness levels of the students. Local fitness and performance standards were developed from the data.

In 1957, Professors Fernand Landry and Arthur Sheedy were two of Dr. Orban's assistants in the background research to the R.C.A.F. 5BX plan. In 1958, Mr. Landry again assisted Dr. Orban in the British Empire and Commonwealth Games Physical Fitness Testing Project.

Growth of the Laboratory   Dr. Guy Metivier was given the responsibility of developing the Laboratory of the Institute of Physical Education. In 1960, with the co-operation of the Departments of Preventive Medicine and Physiology of the Faculty of Medicine, he was successful in obtaining a grant of $10,000 from the Atkinson Charitable Foundation of Toronto. The grant was used to equip a Physical Fitness Laboratory with the equipment necessary for the investigation of the effects of participation in ice hockey on the total blood serum cholesterol level of adult males.

Further developments occurred after Dr. Guy Metivier was given a research grant of $12,732.00 (August 1962) by the federal government under Bill C-131. Part of the grant was used to complete the laboratory equipment to allow and facilitate a wide variety of physique, organic, and muscular efficiency tests.

Facilities and Equipment   Rooms and general furnishings: Large 25' x 25' laboratory with hot and cold water, sink, heavy wiring, tables, chairs, benches, cabinets, and hospital beds.

Office, and one other general utility room adjacent to laboratory.

Research Equipment:
Anthropometric:
Scales, tapes, flexometers, fat calipers, conformateur, depth calipers, wall charts.
Organic Efficiency:
Collins wet spirometer, portable and stationary shpygmomanometers, B. and D. stethoscopes, standard and maximum ventilation mouth valves, Douglas bags, precision wet gas meter, Parkinson high speed gas meter (dry), Scholander gas analyzers, Collins motor driven treadmill (hydraulic adjustable speed and inclination), electrocardiograph.
Hand dynamometers, back and leg dynamometer, visual and auditory reaction timer.
Biochemical:
Precision scale, Bechman ultra-micro analytical system, (spectro-colorimeter,

microfuge, micromixer) for determination of blood bilirubin, phosphorus, total protein, uric acid, glucose, cholesterol and other values.

Miscellaneous:

Stop watches, clocks, 8 mm. still camera, 35 mm. still camera, 8 mm., 16 mm., and 35 mm. projection cameras, Underwood-Olivetti calculator, electric typewriter.

Present Projects of Members of Staff

Metivier, Guy: "The Effects of One Season of Ice Hockey on the Total Blood Serum Cholesterol Level of Adult Men." (Part II completed in 1963).

———, *et al*: "The Effects of Participation in Vigorous Winter Sports on Cardio-Respiratory and Motor Indices." (Started late 1962).

Graduate Degree The Institute of Physical Education of the University of Ottawa has the intention of offering a French language degree in physical education, as soon as its staff members have attained the necessary qualifications and experience.

UNIVERSITY OF SASKATCHEWAN (SASKATOON) * *Completed Research Studies and Papers by Members of the University of Saskatchewan Staff.*

Bailey, D. A., "A Comparative Study of the Reliability and Validity of Selected Health Knowledge Tests." Unpublished M.S. in Education thesis, Bowling Green State University, Bowling Green, Ohio, 1956.

———, "The Effect of Foreperiod Variation upon Expectancy as Measured by Simple Reaction Time." Unpublished doctoral dissertation, Indiana University, 1959. *Dissertation Abstracts*, XX, 1, 1960.

———, and W. Orban, "An Investigation of Second Wind by Means of Radio Telemetry." Paper presented at 11th Annual Meeting of the American College of Sports Medicine, Minneapolis, May, 1963.

———, and W. Orban, "Comparison of Cardio-Pulmonary Responses to Maximal Isometric Exercises and a Maximal Treadmill Run." Paper presented at 15th Biennial Convention of C.A.H.P.E.R., Saskatoon, June 1963.

———, and W. Orban, "Speed of Movement and Simple Reaction Time," *Journal of C.A.H.P.E.R.*, XXX, 5 (June 1964), p. 14.

———, W. Orban, and B. Holmlund, "Monitoring All Out Work by Radio Telemetry." Paper presented at the 1964 National Telemetering Conference, Los Angeles, California, June 1964.

———, W. Orban, and J. Merriman, "A Comparison of Oxygen Requirement with Extent of Training in Treadmill Running." Paper presented at 10th Annual Meeting of the American College of Sports Medicine, Minneapolis, May, 1963.

———, W. Orban, and J. Merriman, "The Reliability of Selected Cardio-Pulmonary Responses During Resting, Exercise and Recovery Periods of a Treadmill Run." *Proceedings of 15th Biennial Convention of C.A.H.P.E.R.*, Saskatoon, June 1963.

---

* Information on University of Saskatchewan supplied by Dr. D. A. Bailey and Dr. W. A. R. Orban.

Bailey, D. A., W. Orban, J. Merriman, and B. Holmlund, "Heart Rate Response to Interval Running Using Radio-Telemetry." Paper presented to 10th Annual Meeting of American College of Sports Medicine, Minneapolis, May 1963.

———, Orban, W., J. E. Merriman, and D. Orchard, "Comparison of Cardio-Pulmonary Responses between a Highly Trained and an Untrained Group of Boys." Paper presented at the 9th Annual Meeting of American College of Sports Medicine, Oklahoma City, May 1962.

———, Orban, W., J. E. Merriman, and D. Orchard, "The Effects of Training on the Cardio-Pulmonary Function of Boys." Proceedings of the Canadian Federation of Biological Societies, 1962, V, p. 58.

———, W. Orban, and H. Nixon, "The Reaction Time and Speed of Movement of Canadian Sprinters." Presented to Research Section of C.A.H.P.E.R., Hamilton, July 21, 1961. Abstract published in Journal of C.A.H.P.E.R., XXVIII, 5 (June 1962), p. 23.

Cureton, T. K., W. Orban, A. J. Barry, E. E. Phillips, E. L. Herden, and A. S. Carhart, "Improvement in Fitness Associated with the U.S. Navy Training in Underwater Swimming and Dietary Supplements." Unpublished report submitted to United States Navy Department, 1957.

Merriman, J. E., and W. Orban, "Heart Rate Response to Exercise." Paper presented at the Royal College of Physicians and Surgeons of Canada, Western Regional Meeting, Regina, November 23, 1961.

———, W. Orban, and D. A. Bailey, "A Comparison of Oxygen Requirement with Extent of Training in Treadmill Running." Presented at 10th Annual Meeting of American College of Sports Medicine, Minneapolis, May 1963.

———, W. Orban, and D. A. Bailey, "The Reliability of Selected Cardio-Pulmonary Responses During Resting, Exercise and Recovery Periods of a Treadmill Run," Proceedings of 15th Biennial Convention of C.A.H.P.E.R., Saskatoon, June 1963.

———, W. Orban, D. Bailey, and B. Holmlund, "Heart Rate Response to Interval Running Using Radio-Telemetry." Paper presented to the 10th Annual Meeting of the American College of Sports Medicine, Minneapolis, May 1963.

———, W. Orban, D. A. Bailey, and D. Orchard, "Comparison of Cardio-Pulmonary Responses between a Highly Trained and an Untrained Group of Boys." Paper presented at the 9th Annual Meeting of the American College of Sports Medicine, Oklahoma City, May 1962.

———, W. Orban, D. A. Bailey, and D. Orchard, "The Effects of Training on the Cardio-Pulmonary Function of Boys." Proceedings of the Canadian Federation of Biological Societies, V, 1962.

Nixon, H. R., "A Score Card for Evaluating Canadian High School Health and Physical Education Programs." Doctoral dissertation, Indiana University, 1959. Dissertation Abstracts, XX, 8, 1960.

———, W. Orban, and D. A. Bailey, "The Reaction Time and Speed of Movement of Canadian Sprinters." Presented to Research Section of C.A.H.P.E.R., Hamilton, July 21, 1961. Abstract published in Journal of C.A.H.P.E.R., XXVIII, 5 (June 1962), p. 23.

Orban, W. A. R., "An Analysis of Measurements of Organic Efficiency of Boys." Unpublished Ph.D. thesis, University of Illinois, 1956, p. 199.

Orban, W., "Dynamometer Strength Tests and Performance of Weight Lifters in International Competition." Paper presented to the American College of Sports Medicine, Atlantic City, March 16, 1961. Published in *The Journal of Sports Medicine and Physical Fitness*, II (March 1962), p. 12.

————, "Item Analysis of Personality and Temperament Traits of Young Boys." M.S. thesis, University of Illinois, 1954. Microcard Publications (Psychology #100). University of Oregon.

————, and D. Bailey, "An Investigation of Second Wind by Means of Radio Telemetry." Paper presented at 11th Annual Meeting of the American College of Sports Medicine, Hollywood, California, March 1964.

————, and D. Bailey, "Comparison of Cardio-Pulmonary Responses to Maximal Isometric Exercises and a Maximal Treadmill Run." Paper presented at 15th Biennial Convention of C.A.H.P.E.R., Saskatoon, June 1963.

————, and D. Bailey, "Speed of Movement and Simple Reaction Time," C.A.H.P.E.R., XXX, (June 1964), p. 14.

————, D. Bailey, and B. Holmlund, "Monitoring All Out Work by Radio Telemetry." Paper presented at the 1964 National Telemetering Conference, Los Angeles, California, June 1964.

————, D. Bailey, and J. Merriman, "A Comparison of Oxygen Requirement with Extent of Training in Treadmill Running." Presented at 10th Annual Meeting of the American College of Sports Medicine, Minneapolis, May 1963.

————, D. Bailey, and J. Merriman, "The Reliability of Selected Cardio-Pulmonary Responses During Resting, Exercise and Recovery Periods of a Treadmill Run," *Proceedings of the 15th Biennial Convention of C.A.H.P.E.R.*, Saskatoon, June 1963.

————, D. Bailey, J. Merriman, and B. Holmlund, "Heart Rate Response to Interval Running Using Radio-Telemetry." Paper presented to 10th Annual Meeting of American College of Sports Medicine, Minneapolis, May 1963.

————, D. Bailey, and H. Nixon, "The Reaction Time and Speed of Movement of Canadian Sprinters," Presented to Research Section of C.A.H.P.E.R., Hamilton, July 21, 1961. Abstract published in Journal of C.A.H.P.E.R.., XXVIII, 5 (June 1962), p. 23.

————, T. K. Cureton, A. J. Barry, E. E. Phillips, E. L. Herden, and A. S. Carhart, "Improvement in Fitness Associated with the U.S. Navy Training in Underwater Swimming and Dietary Supplements." Unpublished report submitted to United States Navy Department 1957.

————, J. E. Merriman, "Heart Rate Response to Exercise." Paper presented at the Royal College of Physicians and Surgeons of Canada, Western Regional Meeting, Regina, November 23, 1961.

————, J. E. Meriman, D. A. Bailey, and D. Orchard, "Comparison of Cardio-Pulmonary Responses between a Highly Trained and an Untrained Group of Boys." Paper presented at the 9th Annual Meeting of American College of Sports Medicine, Oklahoma City, May 1962.

————, J. E. Merriman, D. A. Bailey, and D. Orchard. "The Effects of Training on the Cardio-Pulmonary Function of Boys." *Proceedings of the Canadian Federation of Biological Societies*, V, 1962, p. 58.

————, and N. Sklov, "Superficial Fat Distribution, Muscular and Organic Test Results of Champion Male Athletes." Paper presented to Research Section of C.A.H.P.E.R., Hamilton, June 21, 1961. Abstract published in Journal of C.A.H.P.E.R., XXVIII, 2 (January 1962), p. 24.

Laboratory   The school of Physical Education has built up an extensive laboratory. The following facilities and equipment are provided.

Facilities

Metabolic room with treadmill, two bicycle ergometers, complete gas analysis equipment, recorder, etc.

Reaction time room with chronoscopes, interval timers, cycle timers, etc.

Somatotype room with complete photographic equipment.

Strength room with Elgin strength table, dynamometers, tensiometers, strain gauge, isometric rack, weights, etc.

General laboratory room with work bench and various miscellaneous anthropometric, strength and metabolic equipment.

Calculator room with three calculators.

Equipment:

Anthropometric: Scales, tapes, Harpenden fat caliper, depth calipers, sliding calipers, goniometers, flexometer, stadiometers, somatotyping equipment.

Metabolic: Collins wet spirometers, sphygomomanometers, stethoscopes, Douglas bags, Beckman continuous oxygen analyzer, CO_2 analyzer (Godart), treadmill, electrocardiograph, 8-channel recorder, high speed gas meter, standard mouth valves, bicycle ergometers, basal metabolic apparatus, gasometers (large), heartometer, 8-channel direct writer, 4-channel radio telemetry transmitter, large Tissot tank, Haldane gas analysis.

Strength and Fitness Testing: Elgin strength table, hand dynamometers, manuometers, tensiometers with cable tension attachments, back and leg dynamometers with benches, isometric rack, Harvard step test benches.

Psychological: Reaction-movement timer, chronoscopes, interval timers, repeat cycle timers, photoelectric cell assembly.

Miscellaneous: Stop watches, Monroe calculators, 16 mm. analyst projector, 35 mm. high speed camera.

Present Projects of Members of Staff   Dr. W. A. R. Orban and Dr. D. A. Bailey of the school of Physical Education and Dr. R. E. Du Wors of the Department of Sociology of the University of Saskatchewan were recipients of a $13,000 research grant in 1963 and $19,000 in 1964 from the Department of National Health and Welfare to initiate a fifteen-year longitudinal study on the growth and development of young children as applied particularly to fitness and athletic performance. Two hundred and forty boys, age six, comprised the initial sample tested in 1964. By 1978 complete data over 15 years on many metabolic, anthropometric, strength and motor learning variables on approximately 100 subjects will have been obtained.

In 1961, a biomedical-engineering research group was formed on the University of Saskatchewan campus. Through this group the discipline of physical education has co-operated with the engineering and medical disciplines. Of particular importance has been the work of this group in the area of radio telemetry. Radio telemetry studies have been carried out investigating second wind and the effects of all out performance on the track upon heart rate, respiratory rate, and temperature.

In 1964 Dr. Bailey and Professor Holmlund of the Division of Biomedical Engineering received $14,000 from the Department of National Health and Welfare to work on the problem of monitoring ventilation volume by means of radio telemetry. In 1964 the work of this group attracted the attention of the American Institute of Aeronautics and Astronautics and Dr. Bailey was asked to present a summary of the work carried on in the area of exercise physiology, and track and field to the National Telemetering Conference.

In addition to these projects, work is continuing in the metabolic area concerned primarily with oxygen debt and deficit and in the psychological area of reaction time and movement time.

Graduate Work A master's program in physical education was initiated in 1963. Students will follow one of two areas of specialization: physiology of exercise and sports or psychology of exercise and sports.

UNIVERSITY OF TORONTO* Research conducted at the University of Toronto has been directed primarily to the needs and activities of university students.

The following objectives have been given emphasis in studies conducted to date (1962).

1. Experimentation with a wide variety of tests selected for measuring the physical fitness of university men. The tests applied have been of the pulmonary, cardio-vascular, and performance type.
2. Exploration of methods for evaluating strength, power, agility, endurance, flexibility, and balance in university students. In these consideration was given to testing time, interest of students in the tests, activity value inherent in the tests, and such secondary factors as rest, living and study habits, nutrition, and so forth.
3. Development of norms for university men for physical fitness and, related to this, a study of the intensity and frequency of activity to maintain reasonable standards of fitness.
4. Since many students are exempted from physical activities by the Health Service, owing to health defects as well as marked deviation from the normal range of physical build and nutrition, studies were undertaken to devise suitable programs for such individuals to determine degree of improvement in physical fitness.

To date the following studies have been conducted by the University of Toronto School of Physical and Health Education:

1. Wipper, K.A.W., "A Study of the Influence of Two Types of Physical Education Programmes on the Physical Fitness of Participants." Unpublished M.A. thesis, University of Toronto.

---

* Information supplied by Prof. K. Wipper of the University of Toronto.

2. A study of three groups of men engaged in the University of Toronto Service Programme to determine physical fitness benefits derived from participation in selected individual activities as opposed to team games.

3. A study of physical fitness of men enrolled in the School of Physical Education at the University of Toronto. Of this group a very large number were active athletes.

4. A study of physical fitness changes in men over forty-five years in which a modest program of regular activity was introduced and maintained over a four-month period.

Related studies by staff, graduates and associates of the school of Physical and Health Education (primarily growth, development and nutrition facts) under the direction of Dr. J. H. Ebbs.

1. A survey of health knowledge of upper high school and junior university students.

2. A study of the effects of severe physical exercise upon excretion of protein and blood products in the urine.

3. An extension of the height-weight and age studies of school children in the Toronto area.

Anticipated Research   Until the new mens' Building for Athletics and Physical Education is erected with suitable facilities for research on a more advanced level, studies will be conducted in problems which may be classified as applied physical education. Simultaneously, co-operative studies will be conducted in problem areas where mutual advantage might be gained in a combined study. One example is the School of Hygiene and Preventive Medicine which presently has the following equipment in a Cardiovascular-Pulmonary Laboratory: treadmill, Beckman oxygen analyzer, Beckman CO_2 analyzer, Haldane apparatus, two spirometers, telemetric devices.

General Comments   Very recently the University of Toronto altered the Physical and Health Education Program to four years. It is obvious that some experience with this new plan will be advantageous before launching into graduate work. In the interim, students will be introduced to research methods, tests, and measurements and to the practical administration of tests. Some students will apply the introductory research courses to the final assignments (profession papers) required of each student in the senior year.

McGILL UNIVERSITY *Institute of Education**   In the past, McGill has concentrated its energies upon the development of a strong undergraduate program and the resultant production of well-qualified teachers. Consequently, graduate research of an experimental nature has been somewhat limited. However, steps are now being taken and, with the

---

* Information on McGill University supplied by Professor James Widdop.

full co-operation of McGill's famed Medical School, new courses are now being offered which include a wide range of research projects in the fields of physiology and kinesiology. A new fourth year course offers: "Physiological and Kinesiological Investigations of Exercise. Physiological principles involved in body adaption to physical activity with special emphasis on their practical application to exercise and training programs; factors and principles underlying human motor performance; application of kinesiological principles in teaching motor skills." This course will be given full academic rating rather than being "professional."

The blending of university facilities and interests will, in the near future, include the Physics Department—with an emphasis on ballistics, and the effects of gravity; and the Electrical Engineering Department where advice and assistance will be obtained in examining both conventional and new electronic devices.

Grants have been used to expand the present excellent equipment possessed by the Medical and Physiology Departments, rather than attempt to duplicate existing facilities. This wholehearted co-operation of all faculties has resulted in a projected planning far beyond previous hopes. For example, it will now be possible to measure cardiac output during exercise, and also the metabolic cost of exercise, i.e., by direct measurement. E.C.G. and heart sounds will also be studied.

It is doubtful whether comparable facilities can be offered elsewhere in Canada, and the future of research work at McGill is unlimited. "Research for the sake of research" is not the aim, but research with the purpose of producing teachers with a more thorough knowledge and a better understanding of their subject. (See Appendix F.)

Other Research Being Carried Out   George Andrew has studied the relationship of fitness to the factors limiting physical performance. Robert Wilkinson has researched the various aspects of motivation. The Protestant School Board of Greater Montreal has carried out research in the schools in the areas of eye-hand co-ordination, balance, and laterality. Miss Eileen Reid, Primary Physical Education Supervisor, and Dr. S. Rabinovitch were the advisors in these projects.

University of Montreal*   In the fall of 1960, Dr. Eugene Doroschuk was engaged by the School of Hygiene, Department of Physical Education to develop a Physical Fitness Laboratory with a program of research, teaching, and service. Assisted by a National Health Grant for a three-year study of the physiological capabilities of industrial workers, and by a Fitness and Amateur Sport Research Grant for a three-year study of sport-

---

* Information on University of Montreal supplied by Dr. Eugene Doroschuk.

fitness of adolescent boys, the laboratory has been well established with equipment in space as follows:

Anthropometric Room: Anthropometer set (3 piece), stadiometer, chest depth caliper, standard medical scale, shoulder breath caliper, pedograph, Harpenden fat caliper, somatotype 5 x 7 Rembrandt portrait camera, vital capacity spirometers (2).

Motor Fitness Room: Back and leg strength dynamometer, Stœlting hand dynamometer, Jamar adjustable dynamometer, cable tensiometer, Dekan reaction timer, flexometer, wall chin bar, wall dip bar, standing broad jump mat, Sargent jump board, Cureton balance beam, stop watches (3).

Medical Examination Room: Medical table, electrocardiograph, sphygmomanometers (3), blood pressure cuffs, stethoscopes (6).

Biochemical Analysis Room: Microscholanders (2), Haldane analyzer, balance, timers, Hamilton gas chromatograph, Fisher 1 millivolt recorder, glassware, chemicals, tools, etc.

Work Capacity Room: A R Young 0-15 MPH, 0-30° treadmill, Collins portable 0-5 MPH treadmill, Holmgren bicycle ergometer, Doeblen bicycle ergometer-portable, step benches 16″ (2), step bench progressive 12-20″, step bench progressive 2-10″, automatic blood pressure recorder, Douglas bags, Kofrani gas meters (2), Parkinson dry gas meters (3), radioelectrocardiograph, Collins respirometer.

Office Space: Secretarial: Filing-library, Statistical: Friden calculator.

In addition to the research projects the fitness laboratory was involved in fitness measurement of: (a) 1,000 school boys aged 12-23; (b) adult men and women in various occupations and different training programs; (c) champion athletes—hockey, football, track, canoeing, tennis, swimming; (d) sports teams at the university; (e) entering physical education students. In the past four years all students applying to physical education were obliged to take a physical fitness exam which formed part of the screening process.

Current Work. Several papers have dealt with the theoretical and practical aspects of the research work. The factor analysis work tests the hypothesis of configurational invariance of the basic structure of fitness on successive age levels. The adolescent training project describes results of methods of endurance training and effects of various systems of training on adolescent boys. The adult research project is an investigation of various methods of testing fitness, maximal oxygen intake, and especially work capacity. Practical application of this research work should be obvious.

Another paper completed describes a short and effective hockey test. This test will enable hockey coaches to screen large numbers of players in initial try-outs with a high degree of accuracy. Work presently under way is an attempt to develop a short and equally effective test for gymnastics.

Preliminary work in conjunction with the neurology department of the Montreal Children's Hospital has proved encouraging in this respect.

Development of norms and standards for all ages is a continuing program of the fitness laboratory. These norms are used to compare results of people of all ages and occupations who express the desire to know how fit they are. Champion athletes have also been tested in the research laboratory. These include Bruce Kidd, Bill Crothers, Jean Lacoursier, Francois Godbout, as well as members of the Canoe Team to the World Championships in 1962.

The program of the Fitness Research Laboratory is now well under way—*research* in basic and applied aspects of physical education, *teaching* of methods of research, and *service* to the community in the form of information and direction where possible.

Research, Studies and Papers Completed by Members of Staff

Doroshuk, Eugene V., "A Comparison of Seven Separate Factor Analyses of Fitness Test Results on Young Men Aged 12-23." C.A.H.P.E.R. Proceedings and Research Papers, Saskatoon, 1963, p. 150.

——, "Modern Medical Opinions on the Benefits of Exercise." Report of the Fitness Research Review Committee, Saskatoon, 1963, p. 66.

——, and T. K. Cureton, "Diet in Athletics, Conditioning and Training," Wychowanie Fizyczne i Sport, IV (1960), pp. 274-76.

——, and T. K. Cureton, "Physical Fitness Tests as Predictors of Endurance Performance." American College of Sports Medicine Meeting, Minneapolis, May 1963.

——, and T. K. Cureton, "The Relationship of Oxygen Intake to All-Out Running Performance." Midwest A.A.H.P.E.R. Research Section, Indianapolis, 1960.

MEMORIAL UNIVERSITY OF NEWFOUNDLAND* The following studies have been done in Newfoundland:

Snow, Graham, "A Curriculum Guide in Physical Education for Newfoundland Schools." Unpublished Master's thesis, Springfield College, 1960.

Foster, Matthew J., "A Suggested Methodology in Functional Movement Training for Boys' Gymnastics in Elementary School." Unpublished Master's thesis, Springfield College, 1962.

Gerstman, Thelma, "An Appraisal of the Nutritional Status of Newfoundland College Women, Based on the Pryor Width-Weight Tables." Unpublished Master's thesis, Montana State University, 1961.

UNIVERSITY OF BRITISH COLUMBIA† In 1958 the University of British Columbia inaugurated the first Master of Physical Education degree in Canada. At this time beginnings were made on the development of scien-

---

* Information on Memorial University supplied by Thelma Gerstman.
† Information on University of British Columbia supplied by Prof. Robert F. Osborne.

tific research in physical education, particularly under the direction of Dr. M. L. Howell. Subsequently, under the guidance of Dr. S. R. Brown, Chairman of the Research Committee of the School, the research program has grown to the point where studies have been conducted in direct co-operation with the Faculties of Medicine, Education, Rehabilitation Medicine, and certain other departments. The major topics of recent research have been cardio-vascular fitness, strength analysis, curriculum, recreation, psychological implications, and evaluative techniques.

Information concerning studies which have been completed at the University of British Columbia may be obtained by referring to Appendix G.

A Research Laboratory is in existence and is used in connection with the graduate program and for basic research.

UNIVERSITY OF ALBERTA AT EDMONTON

Research, Studies and Papers Completed by Members of theUniversity of Alberta Staff

Alexander, J. F., *et al.*, "An Evaluation of the 5BX Program by Treadmill Performance Test," *Journal of C.A.H.P.E.R.*, XXVIII, 3 (Feb. 1962), p. 21.

Anderson, Ruby O., "A Study of the Leisure Time Interests and Activities of First Year Women at the University of Alberta," *The Alberta Journal of Educational Research*, VII, 2 (June 1961), pp. 65-73.

Drake, C. J., *et al.*, "Effect of Strength Development on Speed of Shooting of Ice Hockey Players." Research Paper given at Research Section of C.A.H.P.E.R., Saskatoon (June 1963); published in *Research Quarterly*, XXXV, 2 (May 1964), pp. 101-7.

Eriksson, A. W. E., Smoking Practices of First year Education Students at the University of Alberta, Edmonton, Alberta, Canada. *Journal of C.A.H.P.E.R.*, XXX, 1 (Oct.-Nov. 1963), pp. 2-23.

Howell, M. L., "Use of Force—Time Graphs for Performance Analysis in Facilitating Motor Learning," *Research Quarterly*, XXVII (March 1956), 12-22.

———, "Influence of Emotional Tension on Speed of Reaction and Movement," *Research Quarterly*, XXIV, 1 (March 1953), pp. 23-32.

———, "The Development of Strength and Muscular Endurance by Isometric Contractions." Paper given at British Commonwealth Physical Education Conference, Perth, Australia (Nov. 1962).

———, and K. Coupe, "Effect of Blood Loss Upon Performance in the Balke-Ware Treadmill Test," *Research Quarterly*, XXXV, 2 (May 1964), pp. 156-65.

———, and K. Coupe, "Phlebotomy and Its Effects on the Balke-Ware Treadmill Test." Research Paper given at Research Section of C.A.H.P.E.R., Saskatoon (June 1963).

———, J. D. Dennison, and W. R. Morford, "Effect of Isometric and Isotonic Exercise Programs Upon Muscular Endurance," *Research Quarterly*, XXXII, 3 (Oct. 1961), pp. 348-52.

Howell, M. L., James Hodgson, J. F. Alexander, and Dale Bjornson, "Effects of Circuit Training on Strength and Muscular Endurance," *Australian Journal of Physical Education* (Nov 1962).

———, James Hodgson, and J. Thomas Sorenson, "The Effect of Circuit Training on the Modified Harvard Step Test," *Research Quarterly* XXXIV, 2 (May 1963), pp. 154-57.

———, R. Kimoto, and W. R. Morford, "Effect of Isometric and Isotonic Exercise Programs upon Muscular Endurance," *Research Quarterly*, (Feb. 1963).

———, John Moncrieff, and W. R. Morford, "Learning Rate of Beginning Swimmers: Age and Sex Differences, Distributed Versus Massed Practice," *Journal of C.A.H.P.E.R.* XXVIII, 5 (June-July 1962), pp. 22-23.

———, J. Moncreiff, and W. R. Morford, "Relationship Between Human Buoyancy Measures, Specific Gravity and Estimated Body Fat in Adult Males," *Research Quarterly*, XXXIII, 3 (Oct. 1962), pp. 400-405.

———, J. Moncrieff, and W. R. Morford, "Acquisition of Elementary Swimming Skills," *Research Quarterly*, XXXIII, 3 (Oct. 1962), pp. 405-10.

———, B. J. Sproule, R. S. Fraser, and J. F. Alexander, "Effects of 5BX on Hockey and Treadmill Performance." Research Paper presented at American College of Sports Medicine, (May 1963).

Macnab, R. B. J., H. J. Montoye, and E. P. Reineke, "Effect of High Fat or High Carbohydrate Diet on Inclination to Exercise in Mice." Research Paper presented at American College of Sports Medicine, Kansas City (March 1958).

———, and H. J. Montoye, "Exercise Equipment for Research with Small Animals." Research Paper presented at American Association of Health, Physical Education and Recreation, Kansas City (April 1958).

———, H. J. Montoye, R. Nelson, and P. Johnson, "Effects of Exercise on Swimming Endurance and Organ Weights in Rats." Research Paper presented at American Association of Health, Physical Education and Recreation, Portland (March, 1959); published in *Research Quarterly*, XXXI (Oct. 1960, pp. 434-39.

Mendryk, Stephen, "Recreation Time, Movement Time, Task Specificity Relationship at Ages 12, 22 and 48 years," *Research Quarterly*.

Research Completed By Others Within the Province

Wilberg, Robert, "Hand-Eye Co-ordination Determined by the Variability in Visual and Motor Errors." Unpublished M.S. Thesis, University of Oregon, 1960.

Hetherington, M. R., "A Survey of the Programming and Management of the Public Swimming Pools in Alberta, Canada." Unpublished M.S. Thesis, University of Oregon, 1962.

Growth of a Laboratory   Extensive research facilities are at present available in the Faculty of Physical Education. The following equipment is available:

Rooms and General Furnishings

Two large laboratories with hot and cold water, sinks, heavy wiring, work benches, finished tables and cabinets, two treadmills and a bicycle ergometer in one lab, one large semi-automatic treadmill and a bicycle ergometer in the other lab.

Smaller laboratory for strength, anthropometric, and basal metabolic tests.

Microcard Room. All the University of Oregon microcards are available, plus a viewer.

Research Reading Rooms. Research books and journals are available for students.

Calculator Room. A calculator and microfilm room is to be constructed.

Motor Learning Room. Research equipment pertaining to psychological-type research (reaction and movement time, kinesthesis, force-time, starting blocks in swimming and track and field, balance and so on).

Animal laboratory.

Research Equipment: Scales; tapes (German) (4), maintain constant tension; Harpenden fat caliper; depth calipers; sliding calipers; goniometers; flexometer.

Organic Efficiency: Collins wet spirometers (2); sphygomomanometers (4); stethoscopes (4); Douglas bags (2 complete sets with portable trolleys); Beckman continuous Oxygen analyzer (3); Animal treadmill and oxygen consumption apparatus; CO_2 Analyzer—Godart capnograph (2); treadmills (3)—adjustable speed and grade; electrocardiograph (two small portable units, one large; portable Douglas bag framework (2); bicycle ergometer (3—one Collins, 2 Astrand Monark bicycles); basal metabolic apparatus; telemetering equipment; gasometers (large); heartometer.

Strength and Motor Fitness Testing: P.F.I. apparatus; tomometer; coordination test equipment; hand dynamometers; manuometers (4); tensiometers (4) with cable tension attachments; cable tension table for Clarke's 38 strength tests; back and leg dynamometers with benches (3); quadriceps table with strain gauge and potentiometer for measurement for quadriceps strength and endurance (built with cooperation of Electrical Engineering, Electronics, Buildings and Grounds); isometric power rack; tensiometer with grip attachment; Harvard step test benches—16″, 18″ and 20″—one with a photo-electric beam to ensure stepping the required height.

Reaction and Movement Time and Psychological-Type Apparatus: Apparatus has been specially constructed in conjunction with electronics and measures reaction time to visual and auditory stimulus. A portable control panel with five chronoscopes to measure movement time has been built as well, with variable delays of 1 to 5 seconds. There are two units for hand and leg reaction and movement. Apparatus to measure speed and velocity and accuracy of hockey shots (constructed by Electrical Engineering). Electrical Starting Blocks for sprint start in track and field—adjustable for variations in foot distance—measures reaction and movement time on each foot and amount of force exerted by each foot and how that force was exerted. Timing stations at 5 yard intervals record electrically as well (built by Electronics and Works Department). Electrical Starting Blocks for Start in swimming—adjustable for height and angle—measures reaction time and amount of force exerted. Timing stations included (built by Electronics and Works Department). Apparatus for measuring weight on the hand and reaction and movement time in the football charge and pull (conducted by Electronics and Works). Kinesthesis apparatus, Bechman ladder, stabilometer, psychogalvanometer, Apparatus for measuring reaction and movement time in ice skating. Tromometer.

Miscellaneous: Stop watches, Monroe calculators (3), typewriter, 16 mm. and 45 mm. projector, work bench, densitometry equipment for underwater weighing, ditto machine for graduate students.

Projects of Members of Staff Dr. J. F. Alexander and Dr. M. L. Howell, of the Faculty of Physical Education, and Dr. Fraser and Dr. B. Sproule, of the Cardio-pulmonary Laboratory of the University of Alberta Hospital, were recipients of a $17,750 research grant in 1962 and a $13,000 grant in 1963 from the Department of National Health and Welfare. The pilot project for which the grant was given was to study the effects of training in various sports on the Balke Treadmill Performance Test. Similar research was carried out by Drs. Alexander, Fraser, and Sproule on the effects of the 5BX program on a treadmill performance. Dr. J. F. Alexander is now at the University of Minnesota.

Dr. J. F. Alexander, in conjunction with Dr. Haddow of Electrical Engineering, P. Reichenbach, G. Schultz, and C. Drake of the Faculty of Physical Education have studied the speed and accuracy of ice hockey shots and the effects of strength training on such shots.

Stephen Mendryk is studying the effect of strength training on reaction and movement time in specific movements.

Dr. Howell is carrying out investigations into the effect of single and multiple isometric contractions on the development of strength and also under study are the effects of circuit training on components of fitness; the effect of a program of isometric contractions for athletes on speed, flexibility; anthropometric measures; strength, muscular endurance, and the physical fitness index; and the effect of blood donation on treadmill performance.

Dr. W. D. Smith, P. Reichenbach, Professor H. J. McLachlin and Dr. M. L. Howell and Miss R. O. Anderson have studied the performance of University of Alberta students on the A.A.H.P.E.R. Youth Fitness Tests.

Miss R. O. Anderson, in conjunction with Dr. M. L. Howell and Dr. M. Gulutsan of the Faculty of Education, is studying the relationship between personality variables and motor ability.

Dr. R. J. Macnab, who is in charge of the physiology of exercise and animal laboratories, is working on the energy cost of physical activities and the problem of maximal oxygen intake.

Professor H. J. McLachlin, in conjunction with Dr. M. Carpendale of the University of Alberta Hospital, is doing work on electromyography.

Dr. W. R. Morford, who is in charge of the motor learning laboratory, is doing research on kinesthesis and motor learning.

One major development for graduate research is the University approval of a research building for physical education graduate students.

Graduate Work In 1961, the University of Alberta at Edmonton accepted a student, Wayne Lalor, to study for the M. S. degree, thus becoming the second university in Canada to offer graduate work. This was followed by three students in 1962 and twenty-seven students in 1963.

University of Alberta at Calgary* The University of Alberta at Calgary instituted an undergraduate degree in physical education in 1963, modelled on that of Edmonton. Research has been limited but is planned for the future.

Research, Studies, and Papers of Members of Staff

Bratton, R. D., *et al.*, "Changes in Serum Enzyme Levels After Exercise in Trained and Untrained Subjects," *Journal of Applied Physiology*, XVII, 6 (November 1962), pp 943-46.

———, *et al.*, "Effect of Exercise on Serum Enzyme Levels on Untrained Males," *Research Quarterly*, XXXIII, 2 (May 1962).

Reichenbach, P. J., *et al.* "Effect of Strength Development on Speed of Shooting of Varsity Ice Hockey Players," *Research Quarterly*, XXXV,2 (May 1964), pp. 101-7.

———, *et al.*, "Effect of Strength Development on Speed of Shooting of Ice Hockey Players." Research paper given at Research Section of C.A.H.P.E.R., Saskatoon, June, 1963.

Proposed Research The following studies are being investigated by members of staff:

A study of instantaneous acceleration and velocity curves of selected limb movements and their relationship with individual differences and subsequent changes in static strength.

Research Laboratory A temporary 30' x 30' room has been equipped for research. The following equipment is presently in use:

Sliding calipers, scales, curved chest caliper, tapes, stadiometer, Gulick tape, steps, metronome, flarimeter, sphygomomanometer, stethoscope, vertical jump board, flexometer, wet spirometer, manometer, back and leg dynamometer, calibrated tensiometers and conversion tables, accelerometers, oscilloscope.

University of Manitoba† There has been little research at the University of Manitoba, owing partly to the fact that a degree course only began in September 1964. However, there have been a number of studies done by Manitobans (see Appendix F).

In addition, there has been considerable research in other program fields of physical education and recreation; for example, the Greater

---

* Information supplied by Professor Robert Bratton of the University of Alberta at Calgary.

† Information on University of Manitoba supplied by Dr. Frank Kennedy.

Winnipeg Parks and Recreation survey of Physical Education and Recreation in Manitoba, the Manitoba conference on Physical Education and Recreation. Some of these are continuing kinds of studies which do result in changing emphasis on administration. For example, in at least one area, considerable progress has been made in meeting the challenge of community-school co-operation and action involving the relationships of these two groups in the province as a whole will be forthcoming.

GRADUATE RESEARCH BY CANADIANS The profession is indebted to Professor Arthur Eriksson of the University of Alberta for compiling lists of graduate research. This list (See Appendix F) taken from articles by Professor Eriksson and others in the *Journal of C.A.H.P.E.R.* (I-XIII) is supplemented by material from various research journals and reported thesis topics. This list is undoubtedly incomplete, but it is, nevertheless the best available.

SUMMARY

This analysis of research by physical educators in Canada makes clear certain fundamental points:

1. There was very little research in university physical education departments prior to 1958.
2. Research specialists are now in the majority of Canadian universities that offer degrees in physical education.
3. Outstanding laboratories for research have been developed in a few years in certain Canadian universities and are mostly superior to those in the United States.
4. Approximately 200 Canadians, up to 1964, have completed post-graduate degrees in physical education and recreation.
5. Graduate schools have gradually developed in Canadian universities. The first graduate degree offered was the M.P.E. by the University of British Columbia in 1958, followed by the University of Alberta at Edmonton offering the M.A. and M.S. degrees, and then the University of Western Ontario and the University of Saskatchewan. An increasing number of students are availing themselves of a graduate education in a Canadian university.
6. Graduate theses in Canadian universities are providing increasing information of a research variety.
7. The availability of research grants through the Fitness and Amateur Sport Directorate, Department of National Health and Welfare, has assisted materially the growth of research pertaining to fitness.
8. The granting of $50,000 a year for five years for the formation of Fitness Research Institutes at the University of Montreal, University of Toronto, and University of Alberta at Edmonton should result in significant contributions to fitness-type research.

9. The availability of scholarships through the Fitness and Amateur Sport Directorate, Department of National Health and Welfare, has encouraged many young Canadians to continue graduate studies and obtain research training.

10. The professional association, C.A.H.P.E.R., has been instrumental in promoting research through its Research Committee, founded in 1961. Its first national undertaking was the C.A.H.P.E.R. Fitness Performance Tests, which developed national norms for boys and girls seven to seventeen years of age on six physical performance tests. The national sample totaled 11,000 and was drawn up by the Dominion Bureau of Statistics. The research specialists in each university co-operated in this national study, the principal investigators being Dr. M. S. Yuhasz and Dr. F. Hayden of the University of Western Ontario. Future national studies are planned.

These developments are significant indeed. Physical educators have been slow to awake to the need for research, but since 1960 quite remarkable changes have taken place. Canadians can be very proud of these achievements and it is hoped that more and more Canadians will avail themselves of the opportunities available in graduate study in Canadian universities. Such a chapter as this is out of date as soon as it is written owing to the phenomenal changes that are occurring, but a cursory analysis will show that as of 1964 the achievements are considerable and the future possibilities are unlimited. Each passing year the research should grow in quality and magnitude.

BIBLIOGRAPHY

1. Eriksson, Arthur, "Graduate Research by Albertans," *Journal of C.A.H.P.E.R.*, XXV, No. 2 (1958), 31-32.

2. ———, "Graduate Research by Canadians," *Journal of C.A.H.P.E.R.*, XXV, No. 6 (1959), 27-28; XXVI, No. 3 (1960), 9-10; XXVII, No. 1 (1960), 24-25, 33-34; XXIX, No. 5 (1963), 26-28; XXX, No. 3 (1963), 8-10, 36.

3. Howell, Maxwell L., "Physical Education Research at the University of British Columbia," *Journal of C.A.H.P.E.R.*, November 1956; December 1956; January 1957; February 1957.

4. ———, "Research at the University of Alberta," *Health and Physical Education Council Bulletin of the Alberta Teachers' Association*, II No. 2 (1963), 10-13.

5. ———, "Research at the University of Alberta," *Health and Physical Education Newsletter of the Alberta Teachers' Association*, XX, No. 21 (1963).

6. ———, and Robert Morford, "Research Report from the University of British Columbia," *Journal of C.A.H.P.E.R.*, XXVII, No. 1 (1960), 20-23.

C. R. Blackstock

Executive Director
C.A.H.P.E.R., Toronto

Only a fool will build in defiance of the past. What is new and significant must be grafted to old roots, the truly vital roots that are chosen with great care from the ones that merely survive. And what a slow and delicate process it is to distinguish radical vitality from the wastes of mere survival, but that is the only way to achieve progress instead of disaster.

Bartok[1]

THE BEGINNING

This Association, at its beginnings in 1933, was grafted to vital, ancient tap-roots stretching back into a very long past. The grafting was initiated by able, distinguished leaders.

In Canada, the "climate," both geographic and social, has been con-ducive—it might be said compulsive—to vigorous work and play. By the early twenties there were people spotted across the country who recognized the benefits of proper human growth and development to be derived from planned physical training, sports, and outdoor recreations. In many provinces some form of physical training and hygiene instruction was a part of the curricula for elementary and secondary schools. Colleges and universities required undergraduates to take two years of physical training. The Y.M.C.A. and Y.W.C.A. had physical education programs. Playgrounds made sports and games a major program emphasis.

The Quebec Physical Education Association was founded in 1923,

---

[1] Quoted in Basil Spence, "Pheonix at Coventry," 1962, p. xvii.

through the leadership and efforts of Miss Ethel Mary Cartwright and Dr. A. S. Lamb, both of the staff at McGill University. It was from this group that the seeds came for the establishment of a national association.

In 1931, Dr. A. S. Lamb and Miss Jessie Herriott, through the Quebec Association, initiated correspondence with leaders in every province, proposing the formation of a Canadian Association. The response was favorable, with the result that Dr. Lamb made the following proposition to the Quebec Association in May, 1931: "Initial steps have been taken towards the formation of a Canadian Association, and I would respectfully suggest that the Quebec Branch express itself in favour of the formation of such an Association, if it thinks [it] wise. McGill University will undertake the cost of launching and supporting this new Association for at least a year, if the Quebec Branch concurs with this suggestion."[1]

Some 196 replies were received from the 464 letters sent out to people in all parts of the country, inviting them to be charter members of a national Association; 163 replies were from Ontario and Quebec.

A CONSTITUTION

Miss Herriott, working with a group in Toronto headed by F. L. Bartlett and Miss Mary Hamilton, set up the founding meeting in Toronto, in April 1933. She organized interim committees, chief of which was a Constitution Committee chaired by F. M. VanWagner of McGill, which prepared a draft for presentation at the first meeting. It called for the Association to be governed by a Legislative Council and an Executive Committee consisting of the officers and the presidents of provincial associations. (Appendix G)

The Canadian Physical Education Association was well rooted. It did not spring grown, girded, and skilled to assist in the improvement of growth and development; nor was it immediately prepared to undertake the training of leaders and teachers; nor to initiate a full-blown public education program. Yet the eventual achievement of all these goals was its main purpose, recognizing that it would indeed take time and effort from many to accomplish.

Under the terms of the first constitution, membership was open to individuals and provincial associations. An individual could also belong through a provincial association. The real problem during the first years

---

[1] Clerkson, "History," p. 2.

of the National Association was that there were only two or three provincial associations.

During the twenties, within provincial education associations, physical education sections had been established. These Associations had annual meetings and sometimes regional meetings, which seemed to meet the needs of teachers. In one or two cases, efforts made to have such physical education sections affiliated as branches of the Canadian Physical Education Association failed after a year or so of trial.

The Y.M.C.A. and the Y.W.C.A. had their own societies which met regionally and from time to time nationally. The rising Playgrounds and Parks group did much the same.

For the new national Association, distances and a Depression were addititional handicaps to developing a large membership and provincial branches. These circumstances led to a revision of the first constitution in 1934. It remained the basic structure of the Association until 1942. The conditions of membership were expanded.

The first decade of the Association was a very eventful one in the world and particularly in Canada. The Depression affected everyone and all levels of education and recreation. The build-up of political tensions in Europe with the rise of totalitarian governments sharpened the focus on fitness and corrective health measures. The trend to more urbanized living and shorter work hours gave point to increased emphasis on physical education and recreation in school and community programs.

Studies and surveys of children and young people revealed that the new knowledge of nutrition had effected an improvement in well-being and growth and development. More and better-trained personnel entered the field, bringing a reasoned philosophy of physical education, comprehensive programs, proven methods of evaluation, and a contemporary attitude toward play and recreation. Educators began to recognize health education, physical education and recreation education as legitimate parts of the total curriculum. Specialist teachers in these areas were acknowledged as belonging in the ranks of educators.

It was against this background that the Canadian Physical Education Association was launched. The total membership in the national Association was never large during the first ten years. Those who were members brought their influence to bear on their associates locally, and on the community in which they lived.

A review of the record, in the pages of the *Bulletin*, the Association's official publication, reveals the variety of concerns, interests, and activities of the Association and many of its members. Also evident were the benefits and influence on C.P.E.A. of the early affiliation of the Quebec Association with the American Association.

Three presidents, Dr. A. S. Lamb of McGill University, Miss Florence

Somers of the Margaret Eaton School, and Mr. J. G. Lang of the Montreal Protestant School Board, directed the affairs of the Association through the first ten-year period. A small membership and an untried constitution required them to use a great deal of ingenuity to meet the situations which arose within the Association and in the country.

The physical educator was gradually recognized. Many Canadians went to the United States for undergraduate work. On their return, they were quickly placed in the schools, universities, and the Y.M.C.A. and Y.W.C.A., effecting major improvements in programs.

C.P.E.A. spoke out for the establishment of schools of physical and health education at Canadian universities. And they did come in the early forties at the University of Toronto, McGill University, and the University of British Columbia.

For many years, the basic text for physical training in Canadian schools had been the British Army "Manual of Physical Training." The controversy over formal and informal instruction was joined in many places, especially on platforms. Probably the Y.M.C.A., through such leaders as J. H. Crocker, Ed Otter, and W. R. Cook, led the way to an inclusion of more of the "play" and recreational activities in physical education programs. Formal calisthenics and gymnastics remained, the former frequently executed to music.

A 1931 cross-country tour by a Niels Buhk Folk High School group, from Olerup, Denmark, had a very marked influence on gymnastic class programs. The rhythmic calisthenics, group apparatus activities and folk dance were accepted into physical education programs all over the country. This emphasis continued throughout the decade. The suitability and place that Danish gymnastics should have in the programs was a hot topic of argument and debate at most meetings during this period.

Dr. Lamb led a crusade to expose the deplorable lack of fitness among the young people of the country. This subject was a topic at all meetings. C.P.E.A. forced the matter to the attention of the federal government. Robert Jarman, the Director of Physical Education for Winnipeg and Manitoba, Gordon Brandreth and Ian Eisenhart of British Columbia, Merl Harding, the National Secretary of the Y.M.C.A., J. G. Lang of Montreal, and many others joined in the effort which resulted in a resolution sent from the 1942 Convention in Montreal, to the Hon. Ian Mackenzie, Minister, Department of Pensions and National Health, and his Deputy Minister, Dr. J. J. Heagarty.

C.P.E.A. had offered to assist the government in any way possible. The President and other officers of the Association were called to Ottawa for frequent consultations during the ensuing year. The result was that in March 1943, a Bill was presented to the House of Commons Social Security Committee. This Bill became Canada's first National Physical Fitness

Act, proclaimed October 1, 1943. A National Council on Fitness was formed with each province having representation. It is fair to say the C.P.E.A. was the organization chiefly responsible for this development. It was not without its flaws, but to the extent that provincial governments were willing to participate in the scheme it brought great, if limited, benefit to many people. Certainly it did much to encourage young men and women to enter the leadership ranks and to take either undergraduate or graduate specialist training in recreation and physical education.

CONVENTIONS

The conventions of the Association have become the forums at which the members come to grips with the problems confronting an emerging specialist group of educators. Those of 1935 in Montreal, and 1937 in Toronto were primarily concerned with details of the functions and operations of the Association itself. Membership was to be small. The benefits of belonging to a national Association were not obvious. A clear-cut, single "cause" was not identified. Individuals struggled with larger issues at the local levels. The central executive and the Council were without Association funds needed to hold regular, fully attended meetings. The greatest economy had to be practiced in putting out the *Bulletin*, which reached few people or organizations other than the members. The accomplishments of the Association were the result of volunteer effort done at the expense of the individual or the institutions with which these people were associated.

The original constitution was modified immediately it was adopted, the revision being accepted by the Legislative Assembly at the 1935 Convention. The membership was opened to "individuals, members, Provincial Associations, National Organizations and kindred interests."[2]

The Executive Committee was increased to include five vice-presidents, each representing a region of the country.

Committees were established with concern for health, physical education, and recreation. The Women's Committee undertook to suggest and recommend philosophy and programs adapted to girls and women.

The chief burden of all Conventions up to that of 1942 was to establish identity and recognition of physical education and the specialist teacher or director, the physical educator. Other educators, school boards, departments of education resisted vigorously, looking upon the areas, and the people in them, as unnecessary in a program or curriculum of formal education.

---

[2] Canadian Youth Commission, *Youth and Health*, p. 2.

At the 1937 Convention, leaders in other disciplines were invited to present their views, to indicate the relationships already existing and in need of being established. For instance, Mr. Hugh Plaxton, M. P., reported his support in the House of Commons, of the suggestion that a Ministry of Sport be established. E. D. Mitchell, University of Michigan, the renowned proponent of the expanded intramural program, presented the need for opportunities for all to participate, not just the highly skilled few who were chosen to the representative teams. Dr. John T. Phair, of the Ontario Department of Health, reported the growing need for health instruction courses which, more and more, were being offered in the schools by physical education teachers. Joseph McCulley, Headmaster of Pickering College, acknowledged the increasing importance of well-directed, well-taught programs of physical and recreation education not only in our schools but also in every community. From the general educator's point of view the sooner there were more well-educated leaders in the country, the better it would be for all. Dr. Harold Storms, a physiotherapist of considerable note, doubted the need or value of required physical education; with the exception of compulsory correction of posture defects. Dr. Duncan McArthur, Deputy Minister of Education, Ontario, brought the Administrator's point of view to the fore. He was especially concerned with the attitudes physical education and its teachers created in the minds of the students, since these would affect behavior long after school was over.

The 1939 Convention in Vancouver took on a somewhat different character. In British Columbia, the provincial government recreation program was well established under the direction of Ian Eisenhart. It was intended to reach the out-of-school people of all ages.

Under the terms of the C.P.E.A. Constitution, the Legislative Council was made up of representatives of branches according to a formula; each branch with at least ten active national members was entitled to one representative; with twenty active national members, two representatives; and for thirty or more active national members, three representatives. Three was the maximum fixed for any branch.

The British Columbia Provincial Branch had recruited many more than thirty national members, especially from among the leaders employed in the "Pro-Rec" program. With the Convention in Vancouver, it was easy to have a large number of B. C. Branch members, who were also national members, on hand, and they were there to argue the case at the Executive Committee and Legislative Council for an increase in the number of representatives from large branches. The reasons—chief of which was that the Association had been and was run by Easterners—were probably sound. Their argument led to a careful examination of the constitution with respect to membership, classifications, and the structure of provincial Associations. The existing structure was confirmed by the Legislative Council.

The Second World War followed close on the Vancouver Convention, at which Miss Florence Somers, Director of the Margaret Eaton School, Toronto, was elected President. It was not possible to arrange another Convention until 1942, when it was held in Montreal in April.

The general topics considered related to the war effort; fitness as a part of preperation prior to entry into the armed forces; fatigue as a factor in industry and the forces; the benefits from recreation in industry, the civilian population, and forces on the development and maintenance of morale.

While it had not been possible to hold a Convention in 1941, the biennial election of officers was maintained. J. G. Lang, Supervisor of Physical Education, Montreal Protestant School Board, took office and organized and directed the effort of the Association to get the federal government to establish a Physical Fitness Council. This was accomplished when the first National Physical Fitness Act was proclaimed on October 1, 1943.

The new president was elected in 1943, Robert Jarman, Supervisor of Physical Education, Winnipeg School Board. He remained in office until 1946.

The sixth Convention was set for November 1944, in Winnipeg. The program was an indication that physical education had finally been accepted. It was acknowledged that activities such as the ballet, remedial and rehabilitation activities and mental health, and general and specific fitness were helped by good programs of basic physical education.

The proceedings of this Convention, entitled the "Winnipeg Papers," were printed in both English and French by the King's Printer, through the good offices of the National Fitness Council. The "Winnipeg Papers" is an important historical document because in it has been reported the Canadian War effort in the area of fitness. As well, suggestions for the future were recorded.

Two prominent United States leaders in the fitness field made major contributions to the program. A. H. Steinhaus, George Williams College, Chicago, brought a real note of authority on the main topic, "Fitness," from his internationally recognized physiology laboratory. Miss Dorothy LaSalle, then a senior member of the United States Federal Committee on Physical Fitness, emphasized the need for fitness for women.

This Convention can be thought of as bringing to a close the "growing years" of the Association. A depression and a massive war had served to sharpen the focus not only on the need for instruction programs in recreation and physical education for everyone, but also on the fact that such programs were not to be had without well-trained leadership.

RELATED DEVELOPMENTS

During this first decade the number of strong voices speaking for the Association's purposes slowly increased. They were listened to more often in the higher councils of the educational world. Community Playground Commissions began speeding up in-service training courses, recognizing that their programs would be no better than the leadership provided. Health education leaders argued that there would be little health benefit to the citizen as long as the curriculum was based on the information and facts available in the twenties.

The Association progressed into its second decade bolstered by a new self-confidence, a more general acceptance of its role, sure that it could contribute significantly to the general well-being of all. Added to these developments was the newly created National Fitness Council, and at least one university offering a degree course in physical education.

The major factors and conditions existing at the beginning of the Association's second decade gave the future a brightening cast. The pioneer leaders had indoctrinated many able younger "seconds" who came to the fore to assume the task of developing a truly national professional association.

The Second World War had revealed the need to get at the hidden enemies of health and the handicappers of development, and to develop organized programs that met the physical and recreational requirements of people if they were to be "fit," for life. The "Winnipeg Papers" summarized the thinking and the programs that could evolve from it.

The Dominion-Provincial Youth Training Scheme, set up in the late thirties, had brought into sharp focus the needs of the out-of-school youth. This resulted in provincial schemes such as the British Columbia Pro-Rec, and later the Saskatchewan Recreation Movement.

The Canada and Newfoundland Education Association published the report, in 1944, of its "Survey of Educational Developments" which revealed the need for curriculum change, improved training and status for teachers, and greater support to education generally.

The Canadian Youth Commission, a private and independent body, was established in 1943, with Sidney E. Smith its Chairman, and R. E. G. Davis its Director. Its objectives were to study the main problems of young people from fifteen to twenty-four years of age; to draft reports and recommendations based on these studies; to promote acceptance of these recommendations by governments and private agencies having responsibilities in this field. Two reports (5) of this Commission provided background and support for the work of C.P.E.A.

In March 1947, the Canadian Education Association and the Canadian Public Health Association, published "A Health Survey of Canadian

Schools." A chapter was included on "Physical Education Teaching in the Schools," covering each province.

During the thirties every province developed a group or groups especially interested in improving health education and physical education. These were usually sections of the provincial Education Association. The older institutions, such as the Y.M.C.A. and the Y.W.C.A., maintained their existing specialist societies but began to join with other organizations through C.P.E.A. at its conventions and in joint projects. Provincial governments established in their Departments of Education, physical education branches, and in the early forties, recreation branches, sometimes called Community Programmes branches.

The armed forces had developed trade specialists in physical training and recreation to meet the needs for a cadre of leaders in these two areas. Following the war, many of these people sought and found employment in communities which were setting up Recreation Commissions and programs. Many of these young men and women entered the new degree courses at universities.

The establishment of the first Physical Fitness Act and the accompanying Council in 1943 was looked upon as a real boon, not only because it drew public attention to the great needs in the three areas of interest and concern for C.P.E.A., but because it was considered the instrument with which to assist in developing the leadership needed to carry on the nationwide program.

The constitutional changes made in 1942 were designed to open the membership in the C.P.E.A. The provincial or local Association membership was retained. Individual membership was broadened to Active, Associate, Student, and Sustaining. An individual in any of these categories could apply directly to the National Secretary without necessarily belonging to a local branch, which in most provinces either did not exist or found it difficult to get provincial members to extend their interests and support to include the national Association.

The membership always rose in a Convention year, but this did not mean much in the way of financial help to C.P.E.A., since the fee for an individual remained at one dollar per year.

The revised constitution empowered the President to appoint members-at-large to the Legislative Council in those provinces where there was no active branch. This made it possible to have every province represented.

The Quebec Physical Education Association had been accepted, during the twenties, as an affiliate of the American Physical Education Association; this affiliation was tranferred to the newly-founded C.P.E.A. During the thirties many Canadians were made welcome at District and National C.P.E.A. meetings. The war and the frequent exchanges, especially through the armed forces, between the United States and Canada, gave the C.P.E.A. a background against which to change and grow. The return from the armed forces to civilian life of the many teachers, directors, and supervisors was another factor which gave added impetus to the extension of physical and recreation education programs in schools and communities.

C.P.E.A. had at least established itself on the Canadian scene. It had made its influence felt in high and low places. Internally C.P.E.A. had worked out a method of operation; it was growing in numbers slowly, but what was more important, its members were in positions of authority and often in the forefront wherever discussions of education occurred.

The presidents of the first half of the second decade, J. G. Lang, Montreal, Robert Jarman, Winnipeg, and M. M. Bruker, Montreal, provided aggressive leadership for the Association. They laid the plans for the projects which marked the first real achievements of C.P.E.A.

The years 1948 to 1955 were the coming of age period of C.P.E.A. A. S. Bird of Edmonton, Miss Iveagh Munro of Montreal, and Hart Devenney of Winnipeg guided the Association through some rough times as it endeavored to match its efforts with a suitable constitution and operating codes, and then to find the funds needed to implement the planned growth and development. It was during this time that the Association and the officers had the benefit of the tireless help of Dr. Doris Plewes, Assistant Director of the Physical Fitness Act, and later Consultant on Physical Fitness, Department of National Health and Welfare.

The National Physical Fitness Act was the first major event around which President J. G. Lang (1941-43) rallied the members of C.P.E.A. The implementation of the act depended upon each province's entering into a fund-matching agreement with the federal government. The two big provinces, Ontario and Quebec, did not take up their shares of the annual grant. The provincial physical education association—where there was one—and individual members co-operated with the governments to get the benefits under the act to communities. The National Physical Fitness Council, with Mr. Ian Eisenhart as Chairman of the Council and Director of the Act, met and organized for action.

Joint meetings of the Council and C.P.E.A. Legislative Council helped to get action on some matters, such as the publishing of the "Winnipeg Papers," the survey studies of recreation and physical education facilities, and the production of aquatic standards.

It was under the Council that study grants were made available which enabled graduates of Canadian schools to go abroad to take advanced degrees in health, physical, and recreation education. Many of these men and women returned to take leading roles in many organizations and are presently the leaders in C.A.H.P.E.R.

The first National Physical Fitness Act failed to come to full bloom, chiefly through lack of government interest and support. It was rescinded in the mid-fifties.

C.P.E.A. did little more than hold biennial conventions during the first two decades. The conventions did a great deal to establish identity of the physical educators and their programs, and they provided a regular time for face-to-face communication and exchange of ideas and concerns. Conventions were occasions when resolutions were prepared and dispatched to the appropriate bodies.

The executive Committee and the Legislative Council created a few standing and special committees, early in the thirties. After the War these committees were revitalized and others added.

A committee on girls' and women's athletics was one of the first set up with Miss Ethel Mary Cartwright the general convenor. This has become one of the most active and productive of the Associations committees.

At the request of the National Council on Physical Fitness in 1945, C.P.E.A. established research committees to develop a program of tests and measurements; to make recommendations with respect to leadership training; to prepare national standards for teaching and testing swimming and life-saving; to report the findings of the Youth Commission's Survey of Recreation. Miss Florence Somers chaired a committee that made a survey of physical education in Canada. A. M. Harding of the Y.M.C.A. chaired the committee working with the Canadian Adult Education on the Dominion-Provincial Youth Training Plans.

The Depression had focused attention on the great need for recreation in all its many facets. The B. C. Pro-Rec (1934) programs were developed by provincial and local government agencies. Other provinces studied this scheme. By 1947, most of them had well established programs functioning.

By late 1946, a President's Policy Committee, chaired by M. L. Van Vliet, reported. Its first recommendation: That the present name be changed to read "The Canadian Association for Health, Physical Education and Recreation." This was followed by six other "general" recommendations, and by others for the "Dominion Association," the "District Associations," and "Local Branches."

It was following this report that President M. M. Bruker put the question of changing the name of the Association to a mail vote which approved the change.

The report was notice, too, of the urgent need for increased and expanded Association activity and effort. If this was to take place, the whole constitution would have to be revamped and the Association incorporated. Following the 1948 Convention, the necessary work was begun. Through the efforts of Presidents Stuart Bird and Miss Iveagh Munro, and past President J. G. Lang, the revised constitution and necessary documents were submitted to the Secretary of State of the federal government. The Association is indebted to the very great assistance which Dr. Doris Plewes provided in guiding the application through the proper channels and checking the documents prior to presentation.

The Association received its Federal Charter of Incorporation in January, 1951. A photostat of this official document appears in the present printed Constitution and By-Laws.

RECENT DEVELOPMENTS

The forerunner of the third decade was the incorporation of the Association. The 1950 Convention in Vancouver decided to develop codes of operation patterned after the recently published United States Codes. Each office, division and committee was given terms of reference and modes of operation, through the codes.

This decision came at a low point in the affairs of the Association. Membership had fallen off. The financial resources were very small, so small that the Council decided to suspend publication of the *Bulletin* for at least a year.

The small national membership made it difficult to man divisions and committees without having the same member serving on more than one of them. Communication and travel were not easy, so that by the time a chairman had appointed a committee, the next convention was upon them, with little or nothing to report.

While the first Fitness Act had helped in many ways, including assistance to students to proceed with graduate work, the federal government lost interest in the project. Ernest Lee succeeded Ian Eisenhart for a short time as Director. Following Mr. Lee's resignation, the government made no effort to find a replacement, appointing Dr. Doris Plewes as Acting Director.

During Dr. Plewes's administration, the Council set up the first university course at the University of British Columbia, for the preparation of recreation educators. Mr. Barry Lowes headed up this course for a year. Then in the mid-fifties the act was rescinded in spite of wide demand for it, or a drastically revised replacement.

In 1952, Earle F. Zeigler, then at the University of Western Ontario, took over as Chairman of the Publications Committee. He and other volunteer members of his staff replaced the newsletter that had been issued from the fall of 1951 when the original *Bulletin* had been suspended, with a journal.

Like every editor who attempts to publish a regular journal, the usual difficulties of soliciting articles, getting them written and edited plagued

Dr. Zeigler. Volunteer secretarial assistance was another difficulty. Preparation of the materials, the assembling and the mailing of each issue of the mimeographed journal was taken over by J. G. Lang and J. B. Kirkpatrick of the Greater Montreal Branch. These two made each issue a "bee" for a group of members, providing a real service to the Association in a time of great need.

Through Hart Devenney's term as president the Association began to slowly stir and flex its muscles. Lorne Brown, the next president, began a vigorous assault on the lethargy of past years that had slowed progress to a crawl. By correspondence and visits to branches and finally a cross-country trip with stop-overs, leading to the Halifax Convention in 1957, he managed to fan enthusiasm and effort into the visible flame.

M. L. Van Vliet became president in 1957. The big decision to publish a printed journal was taken and became a fact, under the lead of W. Donald Smith, as Chairman of the Publications Committee, and its members. A. F. Affleck, the editor, played a big part in this effort by broadening the coverage of the *Journal* to include many more subjects and authors.

Quite a number of projects were launched at the 1948 Convention in Montreal. Research was set up under a committee, headed by J. B. Kirkpatrick. Its efforts were modest, undertaking to review and report on current and completed studies which might have implications and applications for Canadian situations.

Thirteen years later, the Research Committee, through the efforts of Presidents G. A. Wright and M. L. Howell, finally was given some terms of reference and with W. A. R. Orban's help became a strong committee to which were assigned some specific tasks. By 1964 it had really taken hold, being well advanced in the work of producing The C.A.H.P.E.R. Fitness-Performance Test,which will establish national norms of physical performance for the ages seven to seventeen years.

The Professional Register was set up within a Standing Committee of the Representative Council, which endeavored to equate several kinds of training with that of the degree courses offered by universities. The intention was to give those people in recreation an improved status, by having the Association acknowledge their training, by a membership category. As was expected, this Committee had a very difficult task. A number of people tried their hand at it following M. M. Bruker's start. Succeeding Boards and Councils of the Association asked for revisions and modifications. At one time, the Registry had some one hundred and twenty names on it.

The need for the Professional Register changed. Persons seeking degrees in recreation had more opportunities to get undergraduate courses in Canada. Except for those in the government services, fewer requests for this category of membership were made. Two dates were set by the Representative Council to close it, and the Professional Register was finally discontinued at the Council meeting in Saskatoon, in 1963.

Another project was started in 1941, the Golden Jubilee year for basketball. Miss Dorothy Jackson, University of Toronto, School of Physical Education, and Merl Harding, National Secretary for Physical Education of the Y.M.C.A., headed up this effort. Remnants of the effort survived into the fifties, though the Association did little more than publicize them.

The 75th Anniversary of R. Tait McKenzie was suggested as a project in the early forties. As a result, the Association established the R. Tait McKenzie Honour Award (See Appendix E) in 1948, which is used to recognize the distinguished contributions of its members.

At the 1952 Convention, the R. Tait McKenzie Memorial Lecture was established, to be on a scholarly subject related to the fields of Health, Physical Education and Recreation, at the biennial convention. This has been a most worthwhile project.

In the early fifties, following Mrs. McKenzie's death, a small group made an effort to raise the necessary funds to purchase the Mill of Kintail. Major J. F. Leys, also concerned with preserving the mill, became its owner in the mid-fifties. The Association offered him its meagre help and co-operation. It is from these beginnings that the members have enjoyed a most happy association with the Major and Mrs. Leys. Major Leys has made a very great contribution to this Association, and several others, through his herculean work to reveal R. Tait McKenzie as the great physician, artist, and physical educator that he was. Physical and recreation education will be forever indebted to this scholarly, modest, and devoted man, Major James F. Leys.

The resurgence of life in the Association corresponds to the impact of the people from the increasing number of physical and recreation education graduates in the three fields. The real punch has come from the return to Canada of those who had proceeded through graduate work chiefly in the United States and to a lesser extent in Great Britain and Europe.

Another group which abetted this revitalization was the immigrants to Canada with excellent training backgrounds in Europe. Acknowledgement of them as expert specialized educators could not be denied. They entered the fields at all levels—communities, government, departments, universities—providing a "yeast" that, combined with the products of Canada's own professional preparation centers, has produced the improved programs and services Canadian society needs.

The first Fitness Act was no sooner rescinded than the Association mounted a drive to get a new one established. Presidents M. L. Van Vliet and G. A. Wright led this effort. The officers and Board were consulted frequently by the government, during the drafting of the act which was enacted in late 1961 as Bill C-131, An Act to Encourage Fitness and Amateur Sport.

This act, supported unanimously by all parties in the Houses of Parliament, has been a great help in assisting with the improvement of existing leadership and the development of new leadership. It has benefited amateur sport by increasing the opportunities for more people to participate at all levels—community, provincial, national, and international.

The act is administered under the Minister of National Health and Welfare, the Honourable J. Waldo Monteith being the first.

After incorporation in 1951, the dream of a national office was thought to be nearer to realization. The low ebb of the financial position of the Association in the early fifties clouded the vision. Dr. Doris Plewes served ably as the Executive Secretary for several years. Others have assumed the office on an honorary basis.

In, 1959 the Association was able to have the part-time services of C. R. Blackstock as Executive Secretary. A year later office space was taken with an office secretary to handle the details of membership and correspondence. At the time of writing, this national office is well established, expanding and extending the services offered to members. Through the sale of publications, those produced by the Association and those produced by A.A.H.P.E.R. and others, the income of the Association is nearing the point where it supports, at least, the basic services.

The Association has received assistance under the Fitness and Amateur Sport Act for important large-scale projects. The 1964 Board and Representative Council, meeting in Winnipeg in June, decided to employ, full-time, an Executive Director.

Thirty years later, the dream of the pioneers gathered around Miss Ethel Mary Cartwright and Dr. A. S. Lamb in 1931-1933 was realized. The association has come a long and troubled way. It has far to go in the future if it is to achieve the goals its present members and officers have set for it.

BIBLIOGRAPHY

1. Bray, Maureen Clifton, "The History of the Canadian Association for Health, Physical Education and Recreation, Incorporated." Unpublished Master's thesis, University of Oregon, 1957.
2. Canadian Physical Education Association, *Bulletin*, IX, No. 4., April 1942.
3. Canadian Youth Commission, *Youth and Health*. Toronto: Ryerson Press, 1946.
4. ———, *Youth and Recreation*. Toronto: Ryerson Press, 1946.
5. Clerkson, Maida, "History of the Quebec Physical Education Association," Canadian Physical Education Association *Bulletin*, VIII, No. 1 (1940).
6. Constitution, Article 111: Membership, a-d, Canadian Physical Education Association *Bulletin*, II, No. 4 (1934).
7. National Committee for School Health Research, "A Health Survey of Canadian Schools 1945-1946." Toronto, 1947.

THE FITNESS AND AMATEUR SPORT ACT

A

BILL C-131

An Act to Encourage Fitness and Amateur Sport

(Assented to 29th September, 1961.)

Her Majesty, by and with the advice and consent of the Senate and House of Commons of Canada, enacts as follows:

SHORT TITLE

1. This Act may be cited as the Fitness and Amateur Sport Act.

INTERPRETATION

2. In this Act,
    (a) "agreement" means an agreement entered into under this Act;
    (b) "Council" means the National Advisory Council on Fitness and Amateur Sport established by this Act;
    (c) "member" means a member of the Council; and
    (d) "Minister" means the Minister of National Health and Welfare.

OBJECTS AND POWERS

3. The objects of this Act are to encourage, promote and develop fitness and amateur sport in Canada, and, without limiting the generality of the foregoing, the Minister may, in furtherance of such objects,
    (a) provide assistance for the promotion and development of Canadian participation in national and international amateur sport;
    (b) provide for the training of coaches and such other personnel as may be required for the purposes of this Act;

293

(c) provide bursaries or fellowships to assist in the training of necessary personnel;

(d) undertake or assist in research or surveys in respect of fitness and amateur sport;

(e) arrange for national and regional conferences designed to promote and further the objects of this Act;

(f) provide for the recognition of achievement in respect of fitness and amateur sport by the grant or issue of certificates, citations or awards of merit;

(g) prepare and distribute information relating to fitness and amateur sport;

(h) assist, co-operate with and enlist the aid of any group interested in furthering the objects of this Act;

(i) co-ordinate federal activities related to the encouragement, promotion and development of fitness and amateur sport, in co-operation with any other departments or agencies of the Government of Canada carrying on such activities; and

(j) undertake such other projects or programmes, including the provision of services and facilities or the provision of assistance therefor, in respect of fitness and amateur sport as are designated to promote and further the objects of this Act.

4. The Minister, in furtherance of the objects of this Act, may with the approval of the Governor in Council make grants to any agency, organization or institution that is carrying on activities in the field of fitness or amateur sport.

AGREEMENTS AUTHORIZED

5. (1) The Minister may, with the approval of the Governor in Council, enter into an agreement with any province, for a period not exceeding six years, to provide for the payment by Canada to the province of contributions in respect of costs incurred by the province in undertaking programmes designed to encourage, promote and develop fitness and amateur sport.

(2) In this section, "costs" incurred by a province means the costs incurred by the province determined as prescribed in the agreement made under this section between the Minister and the province.

(3) In this section the expression "programmes designed to encourage, promote and develop fitness and amateur sport" in respect of a province, means programmes, as defined in the agreement made under this section between the Minister and the province, that are designed to further the objects of this Act.

6. Any agreement made under this Act may be amended

(a) with respect to the provisions of the agreement in respect of which a method of amendment is set out in the agreement, by that method; or

(b) with respect to any other provision of the agreement, by the mutual consent of the parties thereto with the approval of the Governor in Council.

COUNCIL ESTABLISHED

7. (1) There shall be a Council to be called the National Advisory Council on

Fitness and Amateur Sport, consisting of not more than thirty members to be appointed by the Governor in Council.

(2) Each of the members of the Council shall be appointed to hold office for a term not exceeding three years.

(3) The Governor in Council shall designate one of the members to be chairman.

(4) Of the members of the Council, at least one shall be appointed from each province.

(5) A majority of the members constitute a quorum of the Council, and a vacancy in the membership of the Council does not impair the right of the remaining members to act.

(6) In the event of the absence or temporary incapacity of any member, the Governor in Council may appoint a person to act in his stead during such absence or incapacity.

(7) The Council may make rules for regulating its proceedings and the performance of its functions and may provide therein for the delegation of any of its duties to any special or standing committee of its members.

8. (1) The Chairman of the Council shall be paid such remuneration for his services as may be fixed by the Governor in Council.

(2) The members other than the chairman shall serve without remuneration, but each member is entitled to be paid reasonable travelling and other expenses incurred by him in the performance of his duties.

9. (1) The Minister may refer to the Council for its consideration and advice such questions relating to the operation of this Act as he thinks fit.

(2) The Council shall give consideration to and advise the Minister on

(a) all matters referred to it pursuant to subsection (1); and

(b) such matters relating to the operation of this Act as the Council sees fit.

10. The Minister of Finance shall, upon the certificate of the Minister, pay out of the Consolidated Revenue Fund such amounts not exceeding in the aggregate five million dollars in any one fiscal year as may be required for the purposes of this Act.

11. Such officers, clerks and other employees as are necessary for the administration of this Act shall be appointed under the provisions of the Civil Service Act.

12. The Governor in Council may make regulations

(a) defining for the purposes of this Act the expressions "fitness" and "amateur sport";

(b) respecting the provision of facilities in respect of fitness and amateur sport; and

(c) generally, for carrying into effect the purposes and provisions of this Act.

13. The Minister shall, within three months after the termination of each fiscal

year, prepare an annual report on the work done, moneys expended and obligations contracted under this Act and cause a report to be laid before Parliament if Parliament is then sitting or, if Parliament is not then sitting, on any of the first fifteen days next thereafter that Parliament is sitting.

14. This Act shall come into force on a day to be fixed by proclamation of the Governor in Council.

EARLY LEADERS IN THE PROFESSION OF PHYSICAL EDUCATION B

The work of four pioneers in physical education in Canada should be definitely recorded.

Dr. R. Tait McKenzie—*Physical educator, Medical doctor, sculptor, author*

A Canadian by birth, Dr. McKenzie set an extremely high standard
A Canadian by birth, Dr. McKenzie set an extremely high standard and gave dignity to the physical education profession. He was Director of Physical Education for Men at McGill University from 1890 to 1903, and at the University of Pennslyvania from 1903 until his death in 1938. He is best remembered for his work during and following World War I in rehabilitation of disabled army personnel through physical therapy. In addition his name will live on through the many outstanding pieces of sculpture that he carved, e.g. The Joy of Effort, The Sprinter, Brothers of the Wind, Column of Youth, as well as many war memorials.

Because of his great contribution to the fields of medicine and physical education, the Canadian Medical Association and the Canadian Association for Health, Physical Education and Recreation have combined to persuade the Canadian Government to preserve the Mill of Kintail, his home and studio in Almonte, Ontario, as a national shrine to his memory.

Dr. A. S. Lamb—*Physical educator and medical doctor*

An Australian by birth, Dr. Lamb came to Canada as a very young man; he devoted his energies untiringly for the welfare of the citizens, especially the youth. From 1912 until 1949 (except for two years during

World War I, when he served in France and Belgium as a Captain with the Canadian Army Medical Corps, he was Director of Physical Education at McGill.

Dr. Lamb has on many occasions been referred to as the Dean of Physical Education in Canada, a title warranted because of the many worth-while services and organizations that he initiated. At McGill he organized the first Student Health Service in Canada and was responsible for introducing a regulation which required all students to have an annual chest X ray. He organized the Quebec Physical Education Association in 1923 and the Canadian Physical Education Association in 1933 (President, 1933-38); he was Canadian representative to the Legislative Council of the American Association for Health, Physical Education and Recreation from 1925 to 1950 and was elected a member of the American Academy of Physical Education in 1931. He served his term as President of the Amateur Athletic Union of Canada. Dr. Lamb was Canadian representative to International Congress on Athletics and Physical Education in 1924, 1925, 1928, and 1932, and was Secretary and Manager of Canadian Olympic Teams in 1924 in Paris and 1928 in Amsterdam. "Dad" Lamb is remembered by many Canadians as their teacher, in his role as Director of the McGill School of Physical Education.

Miss Ethel Mary Cartwright

Miss Cartwright was born in England and educated at Chelsea College of Physical Education. She came to Canada a few years after the turn of the century and she served Canada and her chosen field for more than fifty years. Her first post at the Halifax Ladies' College, after which she came to McGill University as Director of Physical Education for Women, where she remained from 1906 to 1927.

Realizing the need for trained personnel in physical education, Miss Cartwright initiated a teaching program in 1912 which led to the formation of the McGill School of Physical Education.

In 1927 she gave up the teaching of physical education, but only for a short period. The appeal was too great, and in 1929 she joined the staff of the University of Saskatchewan. There she founded her second School of Physical Education and remained as a professor until her retirement in 1943.

Although Miss Cartwright endeared herself to all women students at these universities and made a deep and lasting impression on them, her influence upon those who came under her professional training was especially strong. Through them her high standards and influence have lived on.

Miss Mary Hamilton

A Canadian from Fergus, Ontario, Mary Hamilton was appointed in 1910 to head up the work in physical education at the Margaret Eaton School of Literature and Expression. In 1926 there was a reorganization and Miss Hamilton became Director of the Margaret Eaton School of Physical Education, a position which she held until 1934.

Many students who graduated from this school look back with joy to their experience at Camp Tanamakoon, a private camp for girls owned and directed by Miss Hamilton, at which students learned first hand the skills of camp counselling. From 1925 until 1948, Camp Tanamakoon provided important experiences for professional training.

Space does not permit the inclusion of biographical sketches of the many others who have given so much in the past, nor of those who are still actively engaged in furthering the work of this profession, whose personalities, ideals and teachings will have left a deep impression and have greatly influenced the future of Canada and her citizens.

NATIONAL WINNERS OF THE VELMA SPRINGSTEAD MEMORIAL TROPHY AWARDED BY THE WOMEN'S ATHLETIC ASSOCIATION FEDERATION

1934	Phyllis Dewar	Swimmer	Vancouver
1935	Aileen Meagher	Sprinter	Halifax
1936	Betty Taylor	Hurdler	Hamilton
1937	Robina Higgins	Javelin	Winnipeg
1938	Noel MacDonald	Basketball	Edmonton
1939	Jeannette Dolson	Sprinter	Toronto
1940	Dorothy Walton	Badminton	Toronto
1941	Rose Mary Thacker	Figure Skater	Winnipeg
1942	Joan Langdon	Swimmer	Vancouver
1943	Joan Langdon	Swimmer	Vancouver
1944	Rhoda and Rhona Wurtele	Skiers	Montreal
1945	Barbara Ann Scott	Figure Skater	Ottawa
1946	Irene Strong	Swimmer	Vancouver
1947	Barbara Ann Scott	Figure Skater	Ottawa
1948	Viola Meyers	Sprinter	Toronto
1949	Eleanor McKenzie	Sprinter	Vancouver
1950	Rosella Thorne	Sprinter	Montreal
1951	Betty Hamilton	Fencer	Montreal
1952	Luella Law	Sprinter	Vancouver
1953	Ernestine Russell	Gymnast	Windsor
1954	Ernestine Russell	Gymnast	Windsor
1955	Ernestine Russell	Gymnast	Windsor
1956	Marlene Stewart	Golfer	Fonthill
1957	Irene Macdonald	Diver	Hamilton
1958	Lucille Wheeler	Skier	St. Jovite
1959	Anne Heggveit	Skier	Ottawa
1960	Anne Heggveit	Skier	Ottawa
1961	Mary Stewart	Swimmer	Vancouver
1962	Mary Stewart	Swimmer	Vancouver

300

(a) *Active Members*

Amateur Athletic Union of Canada
  Boxing
  Fencing
  Gymnastics
  Handball
  Track and Field
  Weightlifting
  Wrestling
British Empire and Commonwealth Games Association of Canada
Canadian Amateur Basketball Association
Canadian Amateur Hockey Association
Canadian Amateur Ski Association
Canadian Amateur Speed Skating Association
Canadian Amateur Swimming Association
Canadian Association of Amateur Oarsmen
Canadian Badminton Association
Canadian Canoe Association
Canadian Civilian Association of Marksmen
Canadian Cricket Association
Canadian Figure Skating Association
Canadian Lawn Bowling Council
Canadian Lawn Tennis Association
Canadian Olympic Association
Canadian Snowshoe Union
Canadian Table Tennis Asociation
Canadian Wheelman's Association
Canadian Yachting Association
Dominion Curling Association
Parachute Club of Canada
Royal Canadian Golf Association

(b) *Associate Members*

Canadian Intercollegiate Athletic Union
Canadian Motorcycle Association
Canadian National Exhibition
National Council of Y.M.C.A.
Ontario Federation of School Athletic Associations
Royal Canadian Legion

(c) *Observers*

Canadian Amateur Bob-Sledding and Tobogganing Association
Canadian Association for Health, Physical Education and Recreation
Canadian Association of Amateur Oarsmen
Canadian Badminton Association
Canadian Canoe Association
Canadian Amateur Ski Association
Canadian Field Hockey Association
Canadian Horseshoe Pitchers' Association
Canadian Lacrosse Association
Canadian Olympic Association
Canadian Red Cross Society
Canadian Soccer Football Association
Canadian Table Tennis Association
Canadian Volleyball Association
Canadian Water Polo Association

R. TAIT McKENZIE HONOUR AWARD RECIPIENTS
IN THE C.A.H.P.E.R.

E

1948—In Montreal	Dr. A. S. Lamb, Montreal
	Dr. Doris Plewes, Ottawa
	Mr. C. R. Blackstock, Newmarket
	Mr. H. H. Crocker, London
	Miss Ethel Mary Cartwright, Magog
1950—In Vancouver	Silas Armstrong, Toronto, Recreation
	M. M. Bruker, Montreal
	E. W. Griffiths, Saskatoon
	Robert Jarman, Winnipeg, Physical Education
	J. G. Lang, Montreal, Physical Education
	Joseph H. Ross, Alberta
	Miss Florence Somers, Toronto
1952—In Toronto	Oscar Pearson, Toronto, Recreation
	Dr. Jules Gilbert, Montreal, Health
	Wray Youmans, Winnipeg, Physical Education
1955—In Winnipeg	Miss Mary Barker, Toronto, Physical Education
	A. J. Dulude, Ottawa, Recreation
	Miss Iveagh Munro, Montreal, Physical Education
1957—In Halifax	Capt. William Bowie, Montreal, Recreation
	Miss Cecile Grenier, Montreal, Physical Education
	Miss Alberta Hastie, Edmonton, Health Education

1959—In Edmonton   Rev. Father M. Montpetit, O.M.I., Quebec,
                              Physical Education
                          N. R. Speirs, Toronto, Health Education

1961—In Hamilton   Lorne Brown, Vancouver
                          Miss Helen Bryans, Toronto
                          Stanley T. Spicer, Fredericton
                          F. S. Urquhart, Montreal

1963—In Saskatoon   M. L. Van Vliet, Edmonton
                          Miss E. M. McFarland, Edmonton
                          G. A. Wright, Ottawa
                          H. A. Noble, Halifax
                          W. Hutton, Calgary (Posthumously awarded)

1965—In Fredericton   J. Wesley McVicar, Toronto
                          Miss M. Gladys Bean, Montreal
                          Dr. W. Donald Smith, Edmonton
                          Arthur W. E. Eriksson, Edmonton
                          Jack H. Passmore, Toronto
                          Feu Lucien Plante, Montreal, (Posthumusly
                              awarded)

1933	Dr. A. S. Lamb
1935	Dr. A. S. Lamb
1937	Dr. A. S. Lamb
1939	Miss Florence A. Somers
1942	J. G. Lang
1944	Robert Jarman
1946	M. M. Bruker
1948	Stuart A. Bird
1950	Miss Iveagh Munro
1952	H. M. Devenney
1955	Lorne Brown
1957	Dr. M. L. Van Vliet
1959	G. A. Wright
1961	G. A. Wright
	Dr. M. L. Howell
1963	Dr. M. L. Howell

1. Alderman, Richard B., "A Comparative Study of the Effectiveness of Two Grips in Teaching Beginning Golf." M.P.E. thesis, University of British Columbia, 1960.

2. ———, "The Influence of Local Fatigue on Speed and Accuracy in Motor Learning." Ed. D. thesis, University of California at Berkeley, 1964.

3. Alexander, John F., "An Evaluation of Thirteen Brands of Football Helmets by Certain Impact Measures." Ph.D. thesis, Michigan State University, 1960.

4. Anderson, Dave, "A History of Physical Education in Winnipeg Schools." Unpublished Master's thesis, University of California at Los Angeles.

5. Anderson, Ruby O., "Leisure Time Interests and Activities of First Year Women at the University of Alberta." M.Ed. thesis, University of Alberta, 1959.

6. Andrew, G. McG., "Effects of Training on Cardiovascular Dynamics." M. Sc. thesis, McGill University, 1963.

7. Armstrong, Janet Jackson, "The Effects of Isometric Exercise on Certain Anthropometric Measurements, Muscular Endurance and Muscular Strength of College Women." M.A. thesis, University of Alberta, April 1963.

8. Arnett, Michael Richard, "A Study of Skiing Accidents Occurring at Selected Areas in Western Washington and Western British Columbia." M.S. thesis, University of Washington, 1958.

9. Bailey, Donald A., "A Comparative Study of the Reliability and Validity of Selected Health Knowledge Tests." M. Sc. thesis, Bowling Green State University, 1956.

10. ———, "The Effect of a Forehand Variation Upon Expectancy as Measured by Simple Reaction Time." P.E.D. thesis, Indiana University, 1959.

11. Bakogeorge, Andrew Peter, "The Relationship of Selected Anthropometrical and Physiological Variables to the Balke Treadmill Test and a Terminal Step Test and Test Interrelationship." M.Sc. thesis, University of Alberta, July 1964.

12. Banister, Eric W., "The Relative Effectiveness of Interval Circuit Training Compared with the Three Other Methods of Fitness in the School of Physical Education Program." M.P.E. thesis, University of British Columbia, 1962.

13. Baycroft, Gerald H., "An Evaluation of the Modified Astrand-Rhyming Nomogram as an Estimator of Maximal Oxygen Consumption." M.Sc. thesis, University of Alberta, August 1964.

14. Beauchesne, J. M., "Recommended Provincial Legislation for the Regulation of Public Bathing Areas and Facilities in Quebec, Canada." M.S. thesis, University of Illinois, 1961.

15. Biek, Elizabeth Hydman, "A Study of the Health Knowledge of Grade XII Students in the Province of Saskatchewan, Canada." M.S. thesis, University of Washington, 1939.

16. Bird, Evelyn ,"Conditions and Attitudes Influencing Extra-Curricular Sports Participation of Eastglen Composite High School Girls." M.Sc. thesis, University of Washington, 1961.

17. Boswell, M. David, "A Study of the Scoring Merits of the Sweep Shot, Slap Shot, and Snap Shot as used in Ice Hockey." M.Sc. thesis, Springfield College, 1958.

18. Boyko, Steve, "Current Practices in Extra-curricular Activities in Alberta Centralized Schools." M. Ed. thesis, University of Alberta, 1959.

19. Bratton, Robert Dickson, "The Effect of Intensity of Exercise on Multiple Blood Serum Enzyme Levels." M. S. thesis, University of California at Los Angeles, 1961.

20. Bray, Maureen, "The History of the Canadian Association for Health, Physical Education and Recreation." M. A. thesis, University of Oregon, 1957.

21. Brown, Annie May, "The Effect of Circuit Training on the Physical Fitness of Grade I Girls." M.P.E. thesis, University of British Columbia, 1961.

22. Brown, Stanley R., "The Effects of the Health-Walker and Ro-Trim Exercise Machine on Cardio-Vascular Fitness." M.S. thesis, University of Illinois, 1957.

23. ———, "Factors Influencing Improvement in the Oxygen Intake of Young Boys." Ph.D. thesis, University of Illinois, 1960.

24. Cameron, Peter John, "A Survey of the Physical Education Curriculum, Facilities and Administrative Organizations in the City High Schools in the Province of Saskatchewan during the 1958-59 School Term." M. S. thesis, University of Washington, 1959.

25. Cooper, Leonard A., "A Comparison of the Effects of Short Intensive and Prolonged Intensive Exercise Programmes on Treadmill Performance and Certain Cardio-Respiratory Functions." M.Sc. thesis, University of Alberta, 1963.

26. Coyne, Lawrence Lee, "The Relationship of Maximal Oxygen Intake to Body Composition and Total Body Weight in Active Males." M.A. thesis, University of Alberta, 1963.

27. Cunningham, David A., "The Effect of Breathing High Concentrations of Oxygen on Treadmill Performance and Selected Physiological Variables." M.Sc. thesis, University of Alberta, 1963.

28. Davidson, Stewart A., "A History of Sports and Games in Eastern Canada Prior to World War I." Ed. D. thesis, Columbia University, 1951.

29. Dempsey, Jerry A., "Anthropometrical and Physiological Observations on Obese and Non-Obese Young Men Undergoing a Program of Vigorous Physical Exercise." M. Sc. thesis, University of Alberta, 1963.

30. Dennison, John D., "Phlebotomy and Its Effect on the Work Output of Athletes." M.P.E. thesis, University of British Columbia, 1960.

31. Dewar, John, "A Physical Education Curriculum Guide for the Calgary Separate Schools." M.A. thesis, Ohio State University, 1959.

32. Doroschuk, Eugene Vale, "The Prediction of All-Out Treadmill Running of Young Boys from Oxygen Utilization Measures." M.S. thesis, University of Illinois, 1959.

33. ———, "The Relationship of Metabolic Cardiovascular and Motor Fitness Tests with Endurance Running of Young Boys." Ph.D. thesis, University of Illinois, 1962.

34. Downie, Dave, "A History of Physical Education in the Public Schools of Manitoba." M. A. thesis, University of Manitoba.

35. Duncan, Ruth, "The Significance of Movement in Education." Thesis for Award of Associateship, University of London, England, 1957.

36. ———, "The Relationship of Perceptual Motor Ability and Reading Achievement at the Grade I Level." M.A. thesis, University of Minnesota, 1964.

37. Eckert, Helen Margret, "The Development of Organizaed Recreation and Physical Education in Alberta." M. Ed. thesis, University of Alberta, 1953.

38. ———, "Linear Relationships of Isometric Strength to Propulsive Force, Angular Velocity, and Angular Acceleration in the Standing Broad Jump." Ph. D. thesis, University of Wisconsin, 1961.

39. Eriksson, Arthur, "A Survey of Physical Education and Health in Representative One Room Schools of Alberta." M.S. thesis, University of Washington, 1943.

40. Errington, Joseph, "An Evaluation of Undergraduate Professional Preparation in Physical Education for Men in Canada." D.P.E. thesis, Indiana University, 1957.

41. Field, Arthur E. J., "A Reliability Analysis of the American Association for Health, Physical Education and Recreation Youth Fitness Test Items." M.P.E. thesis, University of British Columbia, 1964.

42. Foster, Matthew J., "A Suggested Methodology in Functional Movement Training for Boy's Gymnastics in Elementary Schools." Master's thesis, Springfield College, 1962.

43. Fournier, Lionel J., "A Survey of Recreation Components in Selected Areas of Alberta." M. A. thesis, University of Alberta, 1964.

44. Fraser, A. J., "The Effect of Heavy Resistance on Vertical Jumps." Master's thesis, University of Manitoba, 1962.

45. Gerstman, Thelma, "An Appraisal of the Nutritional Status of Newfoundland College Women, Based on the Pryor Width-Weight Tables." Master's thesis, Montana State University, 1960.

46. Gish, Harold Bruce, "A Survey of School Health Services in Alberta. 1950-1951." M. Ed. thesis, University of Alberta, 1952.

47. Glassford, Robert Gerald, "A Comparison of Maximal Oxygen Consumption Values as Determined by Predicted and Actual Techniques." M.Sc. thesis, University of Alberta, August 1964.

48. Goodwin, L., "An Evaluation of Teacher Education in the Physical Education Degree Program at the University of Alberta." Ed. D. thesis, University of Washington, 1962.

49. Grant, Al, "The Status of Physical Education in the Public Schools of the Municipality of Burnaby, School District No. 41, British Columbia, Canada for the School Year 1953-54." M. S. thesis, University of Washington, 1954.

50. Grant, George, "A Survey of Physical Education, Curriculum and Administration Organization in the Elementary Schools of Greater Victoria, B.C." M.S. thesis, University of Washington, 1953.

51. Grierson, Kenneth Miller, "An Evaluation of the Physical Education Facilities and Programs in Secondary Schools of Alberta." M. Ed. thesis, University of Alberta, 1955.

52. Hayden, Frank, "The Physique and Motor Fitness Effects of Machine Exercise." M.S. thesis, University of Illinois, 1958.

53. Hetherington, M. R., "A Survey of the Programming and Management of the Public Swimming Pools in Alberta, Canada." M. Sc. thesis, University of Oregon, 1962.

54. Hindmarch, Robert G., "The Relationship Between Various Anthropometric and Physical Performance Tests and Selected Trunk Flexibility Criteria." M.S. thesis, University of Oregon, 1959.

55. ———, "Significance of Physique, Maturational, Body Size, Strength, Motor Ability and Reaction Time Characteristics of Eight Year Old Boys." Ed. D. thesis, University of Oregon, 1962.

56. Hodgson, James Lee, "The Effect of Circuit Training and Isometric Exercises on Treadmill Performance." M. Sc. thesis, University of Alberta, 1963.

57. Hohol, Harry James, "An Evaluation of Performance in a Physical Ability Test Administered to Selected Male Students at Victoria Composite High School in Edmonton, Alberta, 1961-62." M.S. thesis, in Physical Education, University of Washington, 1962.

58. Howden, J. R., "Difference Between and Within Individuals on Seven Physiological Responses at Rest and During Exercise." Master's thesis, University of Illinois, 1964.

59. Howell, Maxwell L., "Speed of Movement and Reaction Related to Emotional Tension." Master's thesis, University of California at Berkeley, 1952.

60. ———, "Facilitation of Motor Learning by Knowledge of Performance Analysis Results." Ed. D. thesis, University of California at Berkeley, 1954.

61. Hughes, Richard, "A Survey of Physical Education Programs in the Secondary Schools of Greater Victoria, British Columbia Area." M. Sc. thesis, University of Washington, 1946.

62. Hunt, Edmund Arthur, "An Electrocardiographic Study of Twenty Champion Swimmers Before and After 100 Metre Swimming Competition." M.P.E. thesis, University of British Columbia, 1960.

63. Hupe, A. S., "The Effects of Training and Supplementary Diet on the Cardiovascular Condition of Young Boys." M.S. thesis, University of Illinois, 1959.

64. Johnson, Joseph R., "The Development and Investigation of a Single Item Test to Measure Soccer Ability." Master's thesis, University of British Columbia, 1963.

65. Jonason, Jonas Christian, "A Survey of School Grounds, School Plant and Teacherage Conditions in 80 Schools Situated in Central and Northern Alberta." M.A. thesis, University of Alberta, 1940.

66. Kaplan, Jack, "A Survey and Evaluation of the Physical Education Facilities in the Secondary Schools of Greater Winnipeg." Master's thesis, University of Minnesota.

67. Kelsey, Ian Bruce, "An Experimental Study of the Effects of Mental and Physical Practice Upon Muscular Endurance." M.P.E. thesis, University of British Columbia, 1959.

68. Kennedy, Frank T., "A Comparison of the Tensiometer to the Dynamometer in Back and Leg Lifts for College Men." M.Sc. thesis, University of Oregon, 1956.

69. Kennedy, Kathleen, "A Teaching Guide for the Development of Creative Rhythmic Movement in Children of Grades 1, 2, 3." Master's thesis, University of Minnesota.

70. Kennedy, W. F. R., "Health, Physical Education and Recreation in Canada." Ed. D., project report, Teacher's College, Columbia University, 1955.

71. Kenyon, Gerald S., "Comparison of Verbal Communicative Ability Among Students Certified to Several Professional Schools at Indiana University." M.S. thesis, Indiana University, 1957.

72. ———, "The Effects of Exercise and Physical Training Upon Circulating Eosinophilic Granulocytes." Ph. D. thesis, New York University, 1960.

73. Kerr, Barry A., "The Effect of Strength Training Upon Speed of Movement and Reaction Time in a Knee Extension Movement." M.A. thesis, University of Alberta, April 1964.

74. Kimball, Edwin R., "Current Practices in the Control of Intercollegiate Athletics." Ed. D. thesis, (microcarded), University of Oregon, 1955.

75. King, Alan John, "The Effect of Student Rating on Teacher Behavior." M.S. thesis, University of California at Los Angeles, 1959.

76. Kirchner, Glenn, "The Construction of a Battery of Tests Designed to Measure Strength, Endurance, Power and Speed Among Elementary School-age Boys." Ed. D. dissertation, University of Oregon, 1959.

77. ———, and Don Glines, "Survey of Eugene, Oregon, Elementary School Children with the Kraus-Weber Test of Minimum Muscular Fitness." M.Sc. thesis, University of Oregon, 1956.

78. Kirkpatrick, J. B., and E. W. Griffiths, *Physical Fitness*. Toronto: Copp Clark Publishing Co., 1943. (Doctoral project of J. B. Kirkpatrick, Teachers' College, Columbia University, 1944).

79. Labonowich, Stanley, "A Study of Recreation Patterns and Attitudes Towards Recreation Among Selected Jewish Families in Skokie, Lincolnwood and Marton Grove, Illinois." M.S. thesis, University of Illinois.

80. Landry, J. F., "The Effects of the University of Illinois Sports Fitness Summer Day-School of the Motor Fitness of Young Boys." M.S. thesis, University of Illinois, 1955.

81. Lawson, Patricia A., "An Analysis of A Group of Motor Fitness Tests which Purport to Measure Agility as They Apply to Elementary School Girls." M.S. thesis, University of Oregon, 1959.

82. Lowenberger, Arnold George, "The Relationship Between Participation in Intramural Athletics and Scholastic Achievement of Male Students at the University of Saskatchewan During the 1959 University Year." M.S. thesis, University of Washington, 1959.

83. McAllister, J. W., "The Rural School as a Community Centre; A Discussion Dealing with the Assimilation of New Canadians in Western Canada." M.Sc. thesis, University of Alberta, 1925.

84. McDairmid, John, "A History and Analysis of the Influence of Strathcona Trust on Physical Education in the Public Schools of Manitoba." Master's thesis, University of Minnesota, 1957.

85. McFarland, Elsie M., "The Effects on the Skill of Low Level Beginning Bowlers of an Exercise to Increase Strength—Especially Gripping Strength." M.S. thesis, University of Wisconsin, 1951.

86. MacGregor, A. J., "A Study of the Sources and Effectiveness of Health Education in a Group of Pre-School Children." Doctoral thesis, Faculty of Medicine, University of British Columbia, 1963.

87. Macintosh, Donald, "The Effect of Regular Exercise Program on the Physical Efficiency of Grade X Male Students at Crescent Heights High School in Calgary, Alberta. 1959." M.S. thesis, University of Washington, 1960.

88. ———, "The Relationship of Individual Differences and Subsequent Changes in Static Strength with Speed of Forearm Flexion Movement." Ph.D. thesis, University of Oregon, 1964.

89. McKenna, K. E. J., "Testing of Somatotyping and Motor Skills to Determine a Gymnastic Proficiency Level." Master's thesis, State University of Iowa, 1952.

90. McLachlin, Herbert J., "A Survey of the Physical Education Curriculums, Facilities and Administrative Organizations in the Senior High Schools in the Cities of the Province of Alberta, Canada." M.Sc. thesis, University of Washington, 1952.

91. McLean, William Douglas, "The Relationship of the Degree of Athletic Participation to Social and Personal Adjustment in Selected Twelfth Grade Male Students, Edmonton, Alberta." M.S. thesis, University of Washington, 1960.

92. Macnab, R. B. J., "The Effect of High Fat and High Carbohydrate Diets on Spontaneous Activity in Albino Mice." M.A. thesis, Michigan State University, 1959.

93. ———, "Computer Analysis of Stomach Content, Length-Weight Relationship and Growth of Fish Population." Ph.D. thesis, Michigan State University, 1958.

94. Marcote, Gaston, "The Effects of Two Different Programs of Ice Skating on the Physical Fitness of Two Adult Men." M.S. thesis, University of Illinois, 1960.

95. Martens, Fred, "A Testing and Grading Program Based on Achievement in Physical Ability Tests for Selected British Columbia High Schools." M.S. thesis, University of Washington, 1954.

96. Meagher, John W., "The Status of Degree Graduates of Four Canadian Schools of Physical Education." Master's thesis, Penn. State University, 1958.

97. ———, "A Projected Plan for the Re-organization of Physical Education Teacher-Training Programs in Canada." Ph.D. thesis, Pennsylvania State University, 1958.

98. Metivier, J. G., "An Evaluation of Physical Education Program in High School for Boys of Ottawa and Eastview, Ontario, Canada." M.S. thesis, University of Illinois, 1957.

99. ———, "The Effects of Five Different Programs of Physical Exercises on Blood Serum Cholesterol in Adult Women." Ph.D. thesis, University of Illinois, 1959.

100. Mitchell, J. Reid, "The Modification of the Macdonald Soccer Skill Test for Upper Elementary School Boys." Master's thesis, University of Oregon, 1963.

101. Moncrieff, John, "Variations in the Effects of Two Training Methods Upon Work Output." M.P.E. thesis, University of British Columbia, 1963.

102. Morford, Walter R., "The Effect of Weight Training on Certain Measures of Agility." M.P.E. thesis, University of British Columbia, 1959.

103. ———, "The Value of Supplementary Visual Information During Practice on Dynamic Kinesthetic Learning." Ed. D. thesis, University of California, Berkeley, 1964.

104. Mullins, Peter M., "An Experimental Study of the Value of Kinesthesis in Learning the Basketball Free Throw." M.S. thesis, Washington State University, 1954.

105. ———, "Measurement of the Extent to which Certain College Physical Education Activities Contribute to Certain Strength and Endurance Objectives." Ed. D. thesis, Washington State University, 1961.

106. Neil, G. I., "A History of Physical Education in the Protestant Schools of Quebec." M.A. thesis, McGill University, 1963.

107. Nix, Margaret Elizabeth, "Teachers' Concepts of a School Health Program." Ph.D. thesis, University of Michigan, 1953.

108. Nixon, Howard R., "A Score Card for Evaluating Canadian High School Health and Physical Education Programs." P.E.D. thesis, Indiana University, 1959.

109. Noble, Hugh A., "Report on Physical Education in England and Wales and Its Application to Nova Scotia, Canada." A.I.E. thesis, University of London, 1956.

110. Olsen, Mildred Isabelle, "The Development of Play Schools and Kindergartens and an Analysis of a Sampling of These Institutions in Alberta." M.Ed. thesis, University of Alberta, 1955.

111. Orban, W. A. R., "An Item Analysis of Personality and Temperament Traits of Young Boys." M.Sc. thesis, University of Illinois, 1954.

112. ———, "An Analysis of Measurements of Organic Efficiency of Boys." Ph.D. thesis, University of Illinois, 1956.

113. Panton, James, "A Survey of Men's Intramural Programs in Universities and Secondary Schools in Manitoba, Saskatchewan, Alberta, and British Columbia and a Suggested Plan for Organization in Secondary Schools." M.S. thesis, University of Washington, 1948.

114. Paplauskas-Ramunas, Antoine, L'Education physique dans l'humanisme integral, Ottawa: Les Editions de l'Université d'Ottawa, 1960.

115. Parsons, David R., "Personality Traits of Canadian Champion Swimmers." M.P.E. thesis, University of British Columbia, 1963.

116. Pastuck, Russ, "History of Interscholastics in Manitoba and an Item Rating Questionnaire in High School Athletic Associations." Master's thesis, University of Minnesota, 1955.

117. Pelletier, R., "A Summary of Physical Education and Athletic Administration in Canadian Universities and Colleges." M.S. thesis, Springfield College, 1958.

118. Pennington, Garfield, "A Survey and Evaluation of the Physical Education Curriculum, Facilities and Administrative Organization in the Public Schools of New Westminister, British Columbia, Canada, in the School Year, 1959-60." M.S. thesis, University of Washington, 1960.

119. Perry, Jack, "A Proposed Program of Physical Education for Boys in Alberta Junior High Schools." M.Ed. thesis, University of Alberta, 1953.

120. Pomfret, Jack, "An Experiment to Determine the Relative Effectiveness for Improved Swimming Time When Using the Free Style Tumble Turn in Comparison to the Free Style Throw-Away Turn." M.Sc. thesis, University of Washington, 1962.

121. Popowich, William, "Determination of Conditions for Optimum Work Output in Single-Bout Shoulder Flexion Ergography under Conditions of Exhaustion Testing." M.S. thesis, University of Oregon, 1958.

122. Ramsay, Richard L., "A Proposed Guide for the Recreation Programme for Mentally Ill Patients in the Mental Health Services of British Columbia, Canada." Ed. D. thesis, Columbia University, 1963.

123. Read, Edwin Albert, "A Comparative Study of Sex Education in the Schools of Great Britain and the United States." M. Ed. thesis, University of Alberta, 1949.

124. Richardson, John R., "The Effect of Brief Isometric and Isotonic Exercise Programmes on the Development of Strength and Muscular Endurance." M.Sc. thesis, University of Alberta, 1963.

125. Ross, William D., "Relationship of Selected Measures to Performance of the Hanging in Arm-Flexed Position Test for Girls." M.S. thesis, University of Oregon, 1954.

126. Routledge, Robert, "A Study to Establish Norms, for Edmonton Public Secondary Boys, of the Youth Fitness Tests of the American Association for Health, Physical Education and Recreation." M. Ed. thesis, University of Alberta, 1961.

127. Sawchuk, Theodore Jacob, "A Proposed Program of Physical Education for Boys in Victoria High School, Edmonton, Alberta, Canada." M.A. thesis, State College of Washington, 1949.

128. Schrodt, Phyllis Barbara, "Objectivity and Validity of a Motor Fitness Test Battery for Girls in Senior High School." M.S. thesis, University of Oregon, 1958.

129. Scott, Harvey Alexander, "The Effect of Physical Conditioning on the Motor Fitness and Cardiovascular Condition of College Freshmen." M.P.E. thesis, University of British Columbia, 1964.

130. Scott, T. Stewart, "A Muscular Endurance Study of Toronto High School Boys." Master's thesis, University of Illinois, 1952.

131. Selder, Dennis J., "Anthropometric Cardio-Vascular and Motor Performance Characteristics of University Hockey Players." M.P.E. thesis, University of British Columbia, 1964.

132. Sexton, Ella, "An Outline of the Aims of Physical Education in the United States from 1880 to 1948." M.Sc. thesis, University of Wisconsin, 1950.

133. Sheedy, A., "Relationship of Health Knowledge and Emotional Stability with Health Practice of Senior High School, College Freshmen, Sophomore and Graduate Students of the University of Ottawa, Ontario, Canada." M.S. thesis, University of Illinois, 1955.

134. Smith, Leon E., "Relationship Between Learn-to-Swim Achievement and General Motor Capacity." M. Ed. thesis, University of British Columbia, Vancouver, 1958. Published in *Australia Physical Education Journal*, No. 16 (June-July 1959).

135. Smith, William Donald, "A Study of the Development of the Physical Education Branch, Department of Education, Province of Ontario, Canada." Ed. D. thesis, University of Buffalo, 1957.

136. Snow, Graham, "A Curriculum Guide in Physical Education for Newfoundland Schools." Master's thesis, Springfield College, 1960.

137. Sorochan, Walter D., "An Electromyographic Study of Selected Superficial Muscles Involved in the Movement of the Femorascetabular Joints." M.S. thesis, University of Oregon, 1956.

138. Spicer, Stanley Thompson, "A Graduated Programme in Physical Education for Junior High Schools in Nova Scotia." M.P.E. thesis, Springfield College, 1947.

139. Stangroom, Robert W., "A Study of Selected Swimming Pools in the Province of British Columbia with Reference to Established Standards." M.Sc. thesis, University of Washington, 1956.

140. St. Denis, C., "The Fastest Method of Starting from a Stationary Position in Ice Hockey." M.S. thesis, Springfield College, 1956.

141. Storey, Edward H., "A Survey of the Recreation Resources for Dependent Youth Living in Married Quarters Communities of the Royal Canadian Air Force." M.S. in Recreation, University of Illinois, 1958.

142. Stratton, Stephen T., "Methods of Grouping Boys Nine Years of Age According to their Level of Aspiration as Interpreted from a Maximum Grip Strength Effort." M.S. thesis, University of Oregon, 1960.

143. Street, Richard H., "Measurement of Achievement in Skiing." Unpublished M.S. thesis, University of Utah, 1951. (Microcarded 1960 at the University of Oregon.)

144. Taylor, Albert W., "A Study of the Fitness Effects of Varsity Wrestling and Required Wrestling Training Programmes." M.P.E. thesis, University of British Columbia, 1964.

145. Taylor, Bryce M., "The Effect of Certain Fitness Programs Upon the Cardiovascular and Muscular Status of Business Men." M.P.E. thesis, University of British Columbia, 1962.

146. Thomas, Paul, "Economy of Learning at Beginning Levels of Gross Motor Performance." Ph.D. thesis, University of Southern California, 1961.

147. Tobacco, Charles Terrence, A Historical Study of Track and Field at the University of Washington Prior to 1960." M.S. thesis, University of Washington, 1960.

148. Turek, Henry A., "An Investigation of School District Special Tax Legislation for Public Recreation Programmes in Six Selected States." M.S. in Recreation, University of Illinois, 1962.

149. Turkington, Harold David, "A Comparative Study of an Interval and a Traditional Method of Training for Competitive Swimming." M.S. thesis, University of Washington State, 1959.

150. Turner, Ann, "An Analysis of Staff-Volunteer Relationships in the Young Women's Christian Association of Canada." Master's thesis, University of Illinois.

151. Tyler, Earl John, "A Method of Measuring Character in Physical Education." Ph.D dissertation, University of Utah, 1954.

152. Urquhart, F., "Reaction Time in Track Starts." M.P.E. thesis, Springfield College, 1935.

153. Van Vliet, Maurice Lewis, "A Guide to Administrative Policies for Physical Education in Canadian Public Schools, Grades One through Nine." Ed. D. thesis, University of California in Los Angeles, 1949.

154. Vidruk, Kas, "The Current Status of Scholastic Eligibility Regulations in Winnipeg High Schools." Master's thesis, University of Minnesota, 1956.

155. Walker, Margaret C., "A Guide for Counsellors in Training Program in Girls' Private Camps." Master's thesis, State University of Iowa, 1958.

156. Watkin, J., "Extra-curricular Activities in Alberta High Schools." M.A. thesis, University of Alberta, 1938.

157. Watson, Ronald C., "Cardio-respiratory Effects of Ice Hockey Upon Treadmill Performance." M. Sc. thesis, University of Alberta, 1964.

158. Watt, Norman Scott, "The Comparison of Two Methods of Physical Fitness Training in Low-Fitness Males at the University of Oregon." M.Sc. thesis, University of Oregon, 1960.

159. ———, "Maturity, Structural Strength and Motor Convergence Growth Analysis of Boys Seven Through Seventeen Years of Age." Ed. D. thesis, University of Oregon, 1963.

160. Whittle, H. Douglas, "Effects of Elementary School Physical Education Upon Same Aspects of Physical, Motor and Personality Development of Boys Twelve Years of Age." Ph.D. thesis, University of Oregon, 1956.

161. Widdop, J. H., "On Testing and Measurement in Physical Education with Particular Reference to Motor Ability." M.A. thesis, McGill University, 1962.

162. Williamson, Kenneth Ray, "Quantitative Strength Changes Resulting from Varied Isometric Contractions." M. Sc. thesis, University of Alberta, 1963.

163. Winslade, Donald K., "The Effect of the 8 mm. Slow Motion Colour Film on the Learning of Specific Motor Skills." M.P.E. thesis, University of British Columbia, 1964.

164. Wipper, K. A. W., "Fitness of First Year Students at the University of Toronto Between November and March, 1956-57." M.A. thesis, University of Toronto, 1959.

165. ———, "A Study of the Influence of Two Types of Physical Education Programmes on the Physical Fitness of Participants." M.Ed. thesis, University of Toronto, 1963.

166. Wilberg, Robert B., "Hand-Eye Coordination Determined by the Variability in Visual and Motor Errors." M.Sc. thesis, University of Oregon, 1960.

167. Yard, William E., "A Study of Three Specific Areas in the Administration of Canadian YMCA Childrens Camps." M.S. thesis, George Williams College, 1959.

168. Yarr, Alan D., "The Relationship of Brachial Pulse Wave Measurements to the Performance of Cross Country Runners." M.P.E. thesis, University of British Columbia, 1963.

169. Yuhasz, M. S., "The Effect of Sports Training on Body Fat in Man and Predictions of Optimal Body Weight." Ph.D. thesis, University of Illinois, 1962.

170. ———, "A Metabolic Analysis of Treadmill Jogging by Adult Men." M.S. thesis, University of Illinois, 1951.

171. Zukaluk, Bernard, "The Organization of a Secondary Schools Athletic Association for the Province of Manitoba." Master's thesis, University of North Dakota.

THE FIRST OFFICERS AND LEGISLATIVE COUNCIL MEMBERS
OF THE CANADIAN ASSOCIATION FOR PHYSICAL EDUCATION

Executive Officers

President: A. S. Lamb, B.P.E., M.D., Director of Physical Education, McGill University.
Vice-Presidents: R. Jarman, Director Physical Education, Province of Manitoba, School Board Offices, Winnipeg.
                       Mary Hamilton, Principal, Margaret Eaton School of Physical Education, Toronto.
                       Ethel M. Cartwright, Physical Director for Women, University of Saskatchewan, Saskatoon.
Secretary-Treasurer: Fred Bartlett, B.A., Supervisor Physical Education Public Schools, Toronto.
Editor of *Bulletin*: Jessie S. Herriott, B. Sc., M.A., Physical Director for Women, McGill University, Montreal.

Additional Members of Legislative Council

Leila Werthy, Physical Director, Y.W.C.A., Saint John, N.B. (The Maritimes).
J. G. Lang, B.P.E., Supervisor Physical Education, Protestant Board, Montreal.
K. H. Murray, B. Sc., Physical Director, Westmount High School, Westmount, P.Q.
A. A. Burridge, B.A., Physical Director, McMaster University, Hamilton, Ontario.
George M. Allan, Physical Director, Westdale Collegiate Institute, Hamilton, Ontario.
Mrs. Roberts, St. Vital, Winnipeg, Manitoba.
A. V. Pigott, B.A., Physical Director, Isaac Newton High School, Winnipeg, Manitoba.
Joe Griffiths, Physical Director for Men, University of Saskatchewan, Saskatoon, Saskatchewan.
W. A. Wellband, Physical Director, Y.M.C.A., Regina Saskatchewan.
W. G. Brandreth, M.I.H., B.P.E., Supervisor of Physical Education and Cadet Corps, Vancouver, B.C.
Flora Musgrave, B.A., Physical Education Instructress, King Edward High School, Vancouver, B.C.